THE SCANDINAVIANS
IN HISTORY

by

S. M. TOYNE

With a Foreword by

G. M. TREVELYAN, o.m.

BARNES
&NOBLE
BOOKS
NEW YORK

THIS BOOK IS DEDICATED TO THE COMPANION OF MY
FIRST AND FIFTIETH CROSSING OF THE NORTH SEA

MY WIFE

TO WHOSE CONSTRUCTIVE CRITICISM AND
ENCOURAGEMENT I OWE SO MUCH

Originally published in 1948.

This edition published by Barnes & Noble, Inc.

1996 Barnes & Noble Books

ISBN 0-76070-082-6

Printed and bound in the United States of America

M 9 8 7 6 5 4 3 2

FG

FOREWORD

Mr. Toyne's history of the Scandinavian countries should be welcome to Englishmen. We are all aware of our kinship to them, our debt to them in the remote past, and our likeness to them in the present. We are indeed blood of their blood and bone of their bone. The Danes and Norsemen, who settled in such numbers in Britain long ago, planted in this island the commercial and sea-going habits which the earlier Anglo-Saxons had forgotten.

And perhaps we also owe to them in large measure our love of individual liberty and our respect for law and " lawmen ".

At any rate to-day we recognise in the Scandinavian peoples the same attitude to life and to politics as our own. How like the work of the House of Vasa was to the work of the House of Tudor! It seems to illustrate the fundamental similarity of political development in Scandinavia and England.

The interest of this book is that it tells a long story, going down the ages, of people very like ourselves but living under different geographic conditions. It is at once so like to and so different from British history.

The Empire of Canute, a union of freemen, disappeared, but its shade still seems to linger. At any rate we and the Scandinavians once belonged to it—and not to the Empire of Charlemagne.

G. M. TREVELYAN

FLO

PREFACE

My aim in writing this short history of the Scandinavian countries is to give English-speaking readers some clearer conception of these great peoples than can be formed from the very meagre and disconnected references in our histories. With the passing of Canute it would almost appear that the Scandinavians had returned to a far-away island home, from which at rare intervals some great leader emerged to wake up the rest of Europe to a realisation of their existence. The brilliant military exploits of Gustavus Adolphus have received due notice, but the background which made such victories possible, is almost entirely ignored. The tragedy of Charles XII is so poignant, that the underlying purposes of his campaigns have been overlooked. The story of the peoples is almost unknown, and yet ties of kinship and democratic ideals should have been sufficient to have aroused a sympathetic interest and ensured a larger space in our histories.

Greatly daring, I have treated of some modern questions such as the South Slesvig case, which appeared to me to have their roots implanted in the past and yet are of vital importance to the present generation. Space would not allow detailed descriptions of many events of historic interest, and small happenings have been recorded only when they shed light on some major problem or illustrate the opinions and feelings of the less famous men.

I have been greatly honoured by the kindness of Dr. G. M. Trevelyan, who has written a foreword to this modest work. To his master hand I have left the task of stressing the importance of increasing our knowledge of Scandinavian history.

I am deeply indebted to many helpers in the various sections of this book.

For the chapters on modern Danish history, I should like to record my sincere thanks to Mr. Tyge Lassen of Aalborg and Lektor Stegman, R.D., and other Danes. Without their assistance and knowledge, I could never have reached any degree of accuracy on the complicated history of the Slesvig Holstein question. Not only did they supply books and statistical papers quite unobtainable in England, but they kindly offered valuable suggestions in the finished manuscript, which they carefully scrutinised. I should also like to express my appreciation of the Danish Embassy in sending me copies of the Danish " Hansard " and other documents, from which to form an opinion on the attitude of the Danish Government. For the Swedish chapters, I have to thank Fröken Kerstin Widén for her kindness in the careful reading of the manuscript at a particularly inconvenient time. Her valuable suggestions and criticisms were most useful. For the references to Göteborg, I should like to acknowledge the help of Professor Jonasson, who allowed me to make use of his valuable books on its history past and present, besides answering several queries. Doctor Greta Hedin suffered me to submit a lengthy questionnaire on educational matters for inclusion in Chapter XIV, and during the course of her hospitality was able to clear up many small points on Swedish literature; I must, however, make it quite clear that I am entirely responsible for the opinions expressed. This applies also to the section on Finland in Chapter XV, for which I am greatly indebted to Mr. Hampden Jackson's book, which changed several preconceived personal views. The Honorary Secretary of the Historical Association, Mr. J. W. Herbert, was kind enough to read through the typescript of the first twelve chapters. For the short excursion into military history anent Gustavus Adolphus, I am deeply grateful to that most careful of all research workers and cartographers, the late Major A. F. Becke. I should like to record my appreciation of the careful work of Mrs. Ian P. Hunter in typing unfamiliar names and assisting me in achieving a uniform method of spelling words appearing in different forms in the Danish and Swedish languages. Spelling has presented a real problem. To have been consistent would have meant confusion. Therefore where names have become Anglicised, e.g. Copenhagen, Canute, Gustavus Adolphus, etc., English forms have been used. When a name appears only in the Danish or Swedish section, the spelling of the country has been used. When they appear in both, the spelling most commonly used in England has been adopted, e.g. Skagerak, Öresund. When place names have been altered, e.g. Christiania to Oslo, Abo to Turku, one is given in brackets unless the meaning is quite clear.

Perhaps most of all, I must be grateful to my publishers for their suggestion that this book should be written. They have made it possible for me to fulfil a desire, growing stronger with each visit to Scandinavia—a desire to record my interest in and admiration for the country and the people.

S. M. T.

CONTENTS

LIST OF ILLUSTRATIONS

MAPS

PART I: MEDIEVAL SCANDINAVIA

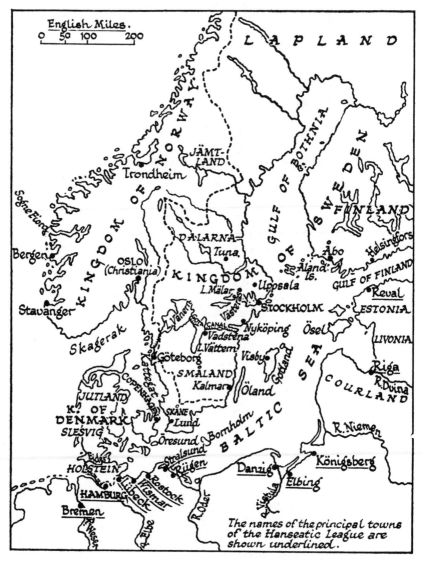

MAP I. SCANDINAVIA

This general map will aid the reader in the interpretation of the text, especially those parts of it not covered by the more detailed maps which appear subsequently.

CHAPTER I

GEOGRAPHICAL FACTORS. ORIGINS

THE word Scandinavia is a geographical term and it is almost as misleading to apply it to any form of racial unity, as was the German attempt to create a Nordic myth.

It is derived from the name of the southern province of modern Sweden, Skåne or Scania, and the old Gothic word *awi* meaning "coast" or "island". It is significant that this comparatively small tract of land has given its name to the group of countries now known as Denmark, Sweden and Norway and is not infrequently applied to Iceland and Finland as well. It has played an immensely important part in shaping their histories, from Roman times to the cutting of the Kiel Canal and the invasion of Denmark in 1940. Its importance rests on its position as commanding the Öresund, the narrow waterway between the Baltic and the North Sea. When Germany saw that the other great powers would frustrate her absorption of Denmark, she cut the Kiel Canal to ensure a private passage between those two seas. Originally, however, the Skåne problem was of more local interest and forms one of the many geographical influences of the Scandinavian countries. When the sea was a highway and not a barrier Skåne was closer to Denmark than to Sweden proper, which lay to the north, for the natural boundary of Jutland was the belt of country lying south of the great Vättern Lake. A traveller going north from Malmö or Helsingborg to Jönköping, the seat of the great Swedish match industry, cannot fail to notice the belt of lake and forest, which cuts Sweden in half. South of the belt the more fertile and undulating country running to the coast was a valuable prize for any owner, Dane, Goth or Swede. The intervening "no-man's-land" was a convenient *point d'appui* for the Danes to attack the Swedes, or the Swedes to attack the Danes. Its possession was the prime cause in preventing peace between the two countries and the insistence of the Danes in making it Danish was one of the chief reasons, though by no means the only reason, why the great union failed so grievously.

Geographical factors, more than racial have shaped the different developments of the three countries of Scandinavia and in fact have had no little influence in determining the racial distribution. In the case of Sweden, the marked contrast between the north and south and between the east coast and the west has had a curious effect from the earliest days of known history. North of a line, roughly corresponding with the present Göta Canal from Göteborg to Stockholm, the land is adapted to the formation of communities; the communications are sufficiently easy to give some sort of unity, but not sufficiently easy to ensure strong centralised government. Thus, although Uppsala became the centre of the government and the great Temple was the centre of the pagan worship of Thor and Odin, a democracy was not long in taking root; and the critical Icelandic historian Snorri has left a true and authentic account of the relative powers of king and the popular assemblies in the early years of the eleventh century. The spirit lived on to the days of the democratic statesman, Engelbrekt of Dalarna. Here, too, Gustavus Vasa found his peasant army.

The difference between the east and west coasts is equally marked. The west from Göta River to the creek at Angelholm, some five miles north of the entrance to Öresund, is studded with small inlets and with the possible exception of Varberg unsuitable as points of assembly for offensive purposes. Göteborg was of comparatively modern growth and artificially but successfully developed after being planted with Walloons. The east coast on the other hand has deep indentations, on which naval and mercantile stations and towns could be built and protected, the most notable example being Stockholm itself, built originally as a protection against Teutonic marauders. The result was that in the Viking age, the Swedes went east and are often described as the Eastern Vikings. They raided and traded with the eastern and south-eastern Baltic and finally penetrated to the Black Sea. In later days, the Swedes were "Baltic-minded", as a general rule, until almost the eighteenth century, when Sweden was shorn of its "Dominium Balticum". There were exceptions to this general rule and in one of the biggest Viking expeditions to the North Sea a Swedish admiral-king shared the command. It was, indeed, the Swede, Olaf Trygvasson, before he was King of Norway, who led the successful attack in 991, which began the series of English defeats culminating in the conquest by Canute.

In Norway the configuration of their barren land turned the inhabitants into sea rovers (not as popularly supposed sea pirates only), sea fishermen and individualists socially. The deep indentations of the fiords were ideal for offence and defence. From Trondheim to Stavanger it would appear that nature had designed the country for that purpose. The Sogne fiord, the Bergen fiord and many others afforded ample protection and very little inducement for agricultural pursuits. From this coast started the plunder raids to the North of Scotland, Dublin, Greenland and later the settlement raids. From the Oslo fiord, the Vikings more often combined with their Jutland cousins, and, in later times, this was the district which came rather more under the Danish influence. However, the lack of communication prevented any real conquest of Norway, the small farmsteads were then, as now, miles apart; the feudal lords had a very nominal sway and it was only rarely that an overlord held real sovereignty over East and West Norway. Before 1939, this lack of union, hardly antagonism, between east and west was clearly evident. It is perhaps not always remembered that the railway between Oslo and Bergen was not completed till 1917, and the only east–west road, as apart from ski track in winter and cart track in summer, was finished in 1929—skirting the south of the Hardanger Glacier. Thus we find a sturdy individualism in the earliest days, a national spirit in face of a real foreigner, but not national unity. Strangely enough it was after the unpopular union with Sweden, forced on her in 1815, that Norway developed a democratic form of government. Still more strange is it, that its vocal and constructive powers were in no small measure due to the foundation of Oslo University by the last Danish Viceroy, afterwards Christian VIII, and yet Denmark itself was still in hands of the reactionary forces of absolute monarchy.

The impact of Denmark's chief geographical features on her history affords a striking contrast. North Jutland and South Jutland (the modern Slesvig) were the homes of the Cimbrians (as marked on Ptolemy's map), Jutai, and the Danes, and although the name by which the inhabitants were known was changed, the centre of their kingdom was not shifted to Copenhagen for many centuries. The peninsula was eminently suitable for townships and agriculture and the growth of population was sufficiently great to encourage expansion. When the Jutes or Danes had acquired the Eastern Islands—now Fünen and Sjaelland—as well as Skåne and the important islands of Bornholm and Ven, the guardians of the narrow straits, the strategic position for defence was extremely powerful. There were, however, some grave disadvantages. To maintain this position, a strong fleet was a necessity, especially during the long centuries when dues were extracted from ships passing through the Sound. Denmark became in turn the envy, the friend and the enemy of every maritime power aiming at trade or naval ascendancy. Sweden, the Hanseatic League, Holland, Spain, England, France, Russia, Prussia and Germany form an imposing list of foes and it was only by adroitly playing one against the other that Denmark has survived the periods of weakness. On the other hand her enemies were prepared to offer vital parts of Denmark as a bribe for assistance. Charles X of Sweden offered North Jutland to Cromwell and North Slesvig and Fünen to the Duke of Gottorp, if they would assist him in blotting out the Danes. However, the greatest cause of trouble has been and is the thick neck of the peninsula on the southern boundary. After the absorption of "the islands" there were two courses for expansion open: one to the west either by sea or south across the Eider and then west across the Elbe to the Weser, the other east towards the Oder and Vistula.

Temporarily blocked by Henry the Fowler and also by a treaty or arrangement with Charlemagne in A.D. 811 the raids of the Vikings resulted. It was not long before land and amphibious expeditions to the South Baltic brought the Danes far beyond the Oder.

The possession of Holstein, the island of Rügen and their subsequent connexion with Schwerin-Mecklenburg, Mecklenburg and other fiefdoms recognising the ruler of the Holy Roman Empire have coloured the whole of Danish history. Most of the calamities and disasters which hindered the country's development and made it the pawn of foreign dukes can be ascribed to this fateful neck of land. If only nature had created a barrier like the Alps or Carpathians south of the Eider, how different and how much happier would Danish history have been. The nobles modelled themselves on their selfish Teutonic neighbours and except when some outstanding personality enforced the supremacy of an absolute monarchy, personal interests came before the country's good. In these circumstances how could a democracy be born? Rarely did the people get the opportunity of showing their true character. Overshadowed by German influence, it was not till the nineteenth century that the Danish language supplanted German as the court language, and the tragedy of the two provinces Slesvig and Holstein has not yet reached its final act.

The real marvel is that this seafaring people have been able to maintain the skill, enterprise and daring of their ancestors.

The position of Finland squeezed between Russia and Sweden and its dangerous consequences speak for themselves and need no comment here. Iceland, the outpost of Norway, stood also as a half-way house for the voyagers to Greenland. It passed automatically as part of Norway to Denmark in 1389, remained nominally Danish in 1815, and was not affected by the Union of Norway and Sweden nor by their separation in 1905. It preserves a strongly independent spirit and claims to have the longest continuous record of popular government of any country in Europe. Its position in the twentieth century and its future importance will be discussed in the last chapter. Does its hope lie in neutrality or a Scandinavian Confederacy or a close alliance with the United States?

Before leaving the geographical influences on the three main countries, it is essential to emphasise the effect of distance on the possible success of a Scandinavian Union. The importance of the " distance factor ", as it is sometimes termed, on the relations of the leading northern countries may well be compared with those of England and her American colonies in the eighteenth century. In both instances, the would-be dominating power failed to realise the impracticability of efficient central control. Unless one has visited and travelled in Sweden and Norway frequently, it is difficult to realise what the distances really mean. At the airport at Malmö in Southern Sweden, a striking map brings home very vividly the astonishing fact that Turkey in Europe is nearer, as the crow flies, than is the North Cape and the north of Finmark. True, it is only a matter of a few miles, but this serves to show the problem that faced Denmark. The land communications from east to west are extraordinarily difficult also and the easiest way was by sea. Yet the journey by sea from Malmö to the most northern point is almost precisely the same length as from Calais to Gibraltar. This " distance factor " alone would have been sufficient in the past to thwart union and to promote independence.

The geographical conditions also invited invasion by other peoples, if not races. The Goths found infiltration easy. Their incursions and infiltrations over a long period of years left their marks, and the name of the island Gottland and the province Gotland are still evidences of the success which they attained. These " Goutoi " had established a kingdom south of the Suiones, whose strongholds lay along Mälar Lake. Here they apparently had remained, driving out a remarkable tribe called Heruls, which separated them from the Danes in Skåne. Some migrated to the South Baltic coast, but when finally defeated by the Suiones either at a bloody battle, Bravalla, or in a long series of battles, the king or overlord was killed or retired to the island Gottland. Those who remained owed allegiance to the King of the Suiones—the Ynglings —and for centuries they seemed to have retained their own customs and laws. Much of their finely wrought work in gold and other metals remains, and it is probable that they taught their craftsmanship to their conquerors. Curiously enough, after driving out the Heruls, these Goths seemed to have had friendly relations with their new neighbours—the Danes. The remaining Goths were slowly absorbed by the Swedes, whose leading tribe at Uppsala had achieved the hegemony over the others, but as late as the thirteenth century Magnus Barnlocks was crowned " King of the Swedes and Goths ", thus apparently laying stress on the fact that Swede could still be distinguished from Goth.

Who were the original inhabitants and where they came from are matters of considerable doubt, and it is unlikely that any evidence which may be discovered in the future will be sufficiently conclusive to persuade experts to arrive at an agreed opinion.

The controversy, which has been thrown into some prominence lately by the wild inventions of the Germans about the Aryan and Nordic myths—they can hardly be called scientific theories—is not modern. Rudbek of Uppsala proved to the satisfaction of the Swedes that Dalarna was the Garden of Eden and that Adam and Eve were the direct ancestors of the Swedes. Lyscander, biographer of Christian IV, proved with even greater show of conviction, that Noah's Ark made its landfall on Jutland near Fredericia. As the waters subsided, the Little Belt and the Great Belt were left to surround Fünen. Thus the Danes were clearly the original inhabitants after the Flood. Some may like to link this delightful story with racial memory of the Ice Age. By and large, it does not seem of much moment to the present generation and may be left to the speculation of anthropologists. When the mists of the early ages of stone, bronze and iron are lifted, we find kindred race stocks in Jutland, Sweden and Norway, with a preponderance of "broad skulls" of Alpine origin in the south and a preponderance of "long skulls" in the north. The long skulls show undoubted kinship with the Mediterranean peoples commonly known as the Iberians, because they migrated up the western fringe of Europe. A considerable amount of evidence is forthcoming to show that the Highlanders and the inhabitants of Northern Norway and Sweden were closely related. The inhabitants of Finland were for many centuries considered to be Mongols, but now it is usually admitted that this is incorrect and they are known as Ugro-Finns, a distinct race of uncertain origin. The earliest inhabitants of Finland were probably the nomadic Lapps, gradually pushed northwards by more incoming Ugro-Finns.

Too much importance should not be laid on the purity of "race", and those who wish to consider the question further will find a witty account in Julian Huxley's brochure *Race* (Oxford Pamphlets).

After and during the Folk Wanderings, some more definite boundaries emerge, and the shape of the historical Scandinavia is clearly discernible when the Viking Age is reached in about 800 A.D. The Danes were in possession of North and South Jutland, the islands of Fünen, Sjaelland, Bornholm and the adjacent groups of small islands, but they were also firmly established in Skåne and the important coastal provinces on either side of it, Blekinge on the east, and Halland which stretched right up the west of Sweden to the Göta River. These three possessions on Swedish soil ensured Danish control over the Öresund and Kattegat. The northern boundary of Skåne was ill-defined but the Gothic wedge had disappeared and the Swedish king from Uppsala held sway over the remaining Goths, the island of Gottland being their only remaining stronghold. The north-west boundary between Norway and Sweden —the modern Jämtland—was also ill-defined and, as in many parts of medieval Europe, allegiance of landowners was personal rather than national. In Norway, the overlords' authority was shadowy, but three main seats of power existed, one, the most powerful, in the Oslo Fiord, another at Trondheim and the third round about Bergen. When one king was acknowledged by all three, it would not be incorrect to speak of Norway, but the rulers' hold was not secure and their powers as ill-defined as the boundaries.

Having briefly examined the disintegrating forces of Scandinavia, we must redress the balance by giving a brief summary of what led to the common bonds—the bonds which made Christian Europe tremble and narrators of history give to the inhabitants the common name of Norsemen, Normanner or Vikings. Till the death of Canute kinship undoubtedly was a bond, but historians, I should like to contend, have been too ready to accept this easy theory. All the evidence seems to point to the fact that the bond of kinship was easily forgotten and the internecine feuds, wars and murders outweigh the temporary alliance, contracted for some specific purpose.

However, granted that, for the purpose of a raid or defence against a common danger, kinship played its part and that a Viking fleet on occasions did contain Swede, Dane and Norwegian, two other factors were in the early times far more potent—language and religion. There was a common basic tongue—Norsk, more often called " Old Icelandic " because in the Icelandic literature of the twelfth and thirteenth centuries it is still preserved. The evidence of its common usage is in the runic stones of all the countries. Sweden is particularly rich in these, as in cliff drawings depicting scenes of agricultural, hunting and mercantile pursuits. The famous Jellinge Stone in Denmark is in the same old Norsk as the Swedish Stones. Taken by the Norwegians to Iceland, old Norsk there became the language of a rich literature reaching its peak in the sagas and the critical history of Snorri Sturluson. He was a true historian, not a mere narrator like his contemporaries elsewhere, and from him much of our evidence is taken. The other countries engaged in continual warfare are painfully dumb for some two hundred years and give isolated and disconnected scraps. As the Swedish and Danish forms of the original Norsk drifted apart, the Dansk being more influenced by German than the Svensk, so did the bonds of union become loosened. It is said that in the thirteenth century a Jutlander could hardly understand a man from Dalarna. There is some interesting evidence that this separatist tendency had become perceptible and was fraught with danger. The saintly S. Birgitta founded a monastery at Vadstena for monks and nuns, and here she tried to promote a common Scandinavian language. At the time of its foundation (1370), Norway and Sweden were nominally united and her idea was to assist in extending this unity and so make the work of the Church more efficient. The pillars supporting the union were to be Christianity and a common language. Unfortunately she became involved in political attacks on her king and patron. Consequently her scheme met with little success in Sweden and in 1389 it was overshadowed by the Pan-Scandinavian Empire of Margaret.

It is, perhaps, hard to decide whether the development of the different languages was the cause or effect of the separation of the countries, but it is incontestable that each helped to aggravate the other. The strongest bond of all was undoubtedly the pagan religion, if religion it can be called. There were undoubtedly many local deities with local temples, but three outstanding deities were common to all—Thor, Odin, and the particularly unpleasant god of fertility, Frey, Frö or Fricco. The idealised picture of the gods, portrayed in the Icelandic saga *Edda* and immortalised by Wagner, must not be taken as a true account of this pagan cult as followed by the Scandinavians. Some Christian virtues were assigned to these gods, a band of supermen living in the grandeur of an Olympic society. The great virtue, which was extolled, was bravery—the unthinking courage and fury of battle known by them as *berserk* or *berserkgangr*. In spite of the utterly barbarous practices, such as the human sacrifices and the sexual orgies in honour of Frey, the gatherings of the peoples, the great festival every nine years at the temple at Uppsala, attended by people from every part, must have acted as a common bond. The gods were feared, if not reverenced. The various kings had certain priestly duties; some like the Ynglings claimed divine descent. The arm of Thor was the battle-axe, borne as a badge by the warriors in the same way as the Cross was carried by the Crusaders. The battle-axe was the terror of the Christians, but it was the rallying symbol of the Vikings calling on Thor to give them " berserk " courage. The victory of Christianity not only ended the Viking age of aggression and peaceful emigration, but it did much to break up the bond of Scandinavian power.

Christianity approached Scandinavia with a sword in its hand, or so it seemed to the inhabitants. Had it approached all the countries at the same time, it might have promoted unity; but this was not the case. The nominal conversion of the Danish king, largely for political reasons, came first. Harald wisely received baptism in 826 to prevent further attacks from the Emperor, a zealous, but militant, Christian. The arrangement to allow missionaries into Denmark, and at the same time to fix a southern boundary, suited both parties admirably. Ansgar, the Apostle of the North, accompanied the royal party down the Rhine after their baptism near Mainz and started the conversion of Jutland. In less than a year he was expelled. Nothing daunted, Ansgar journeyed to Birca, the chief port of Sweden, where he baptised a chieftain and built a church. This attempt met with little success, and his missionaries were soon compelled to flee the country. The Emperor then created him Archbishop of Hamburg, his diocese being Scandinavia. In 845, however, Horik, King of Denmark, sacked Hamburg, destroyed Ansgar's church, monastery and the school which he had established for young Danes. His second attempt in Sweden met with only temporary success and it was left to two English missionaries and a Swede to gain a permanent hold at the beginning of the twelfth century. For some thirty years previously (*circa* 1066–1100) pagan Swedes had fought with converts who had been in contact with Christian Europe. The converted pagans even then were prone to regard Christ as a new deity to be added to their list, but they had seen the success of Christian peoples and were persuaded to be baptised. The real conversion of Sweden was due to Cistercians, sent by S. Bernard, who founded the monasteries of Alvastra, Nydala and Varnhem. The Englishman, Nicholas Breakspeare, was nominated to organise the Scandinavian Church. After founding an archbishopric at Trondheim, he proceeded to Sweden. Here again Christianity failed to bring peace owing to the rivalry of Uppsala and the Danish archbishopric at Lund in Skåne. Thus it will be seen that Sweden remained pagan for nearly two centuries after Denmark. After the death of Ansgar in 853 the history of Denmark is confused for some ninety years. It is known, however, that the Danevirke or powerful earthwork to guard the boundary of the River Eider was completed. Secure against invasion from the south, the numerous princelings (no less than fifty kings are named in this period) were forced to own the sovereignty of one King Harold Bluetooth, who reigned forty-six years. He was the first Christian King of all Denmark. On the Jellinge Stone we read, " King Harald . . . conquered all Denmark and Norway and made the Danes Christians." Haakon of Norway refused to become a convert and Harold had tried to introduce Christianity by his Danish battle-axe without success. Before the end of the century Olaf Trygvasson, King of Norway, now freed from Denmark, was baptised by the Archbishop of Canterbury and enforced conversion on his subjects. Possibly this conversion was partially political also. Neither Dane nor Norwegian appear to have been influenced by spiritual convictions for some time after their conversions, nor felt profound regard for the foreign prelates. A Viking's axe severed the head and shoulders of the very archbishop who baptised King Olaf. The hold of the old paganism was undoubtedly shallow and the conversion of Iceland affords an illuminating glimpse into the mind of the people—Olaf Trygvasson having ordained Christianity for Norway, sent his orders to the head Lawman of Iceland to proclaim Christianity in the island. It is said that he pondered on the orders for three days and nights before bringing them before the Althing. This body, not the king, made and altered laws. It was agreed that the people should be baptised and become Christian, but there were two provisos: (1) They must be baptised in the hot water of the springs; (2) the pagan rites could be continued in the houses of the people.

In Norway, we may conclude that conversion did not go very deep for another hundred years. In Sweden it was later still. In Denmark, however, Canute brought a more real type of Christianity back from England, which spread from Ribe and Roskilde to Lund and it was on his foundations that the saintly Canute II built. Gregory VII took the opportunity of utilising this spiritual Danish king to strengthen the papal hold over the Danish clergy. The archbishopric of Lund was founded. S. Canute himself is reputed to have designed the Stone Church where rest his remains at Odense, the city of Odin. It is a lasting memorial to the triumph of Christ over paganism and marks the passing of an age. Odense was destined to mark, through her citizen Hans Andersen, yet another, though shorter, epoch in Danish history, the Golden Age of Literature.

How far the spread of Christianity was responsible for the cessation of the Viking raids is a matter of conjecture, but the difference of so many years in its establishment in the three countries undoubtedly led to division and wars. The old pagan bonds disappeared. Denmark fought Norway, and Sweden, the last of the pagans, turned her face resolutely to the East. However great the blessings of civilisation and culture bestowed on Scandinavia by Christianity, and great they were, it is incontestable that for some two hundred years the strength of the Northmen for good and evil was sapped. The twilight of their own gods descended on them with the passing of the Viking Age.

What, then, is meant by the glories of this Age? What did it mean to Europe? Can we assess the benefits which it bestowed and weigh them against the horrors of war, of pillage and sacrilege which it brought in its train?

CHAPTER II

THE VIKING AGE TO THE DEATH OF CANUTE, 1035

THE term " Viking Age " is commonly applied to the two and a half centuries which followed the Folk Wanderings of Germanic tribes on the disintegration of the Roman Empire. These wanderings lasted for some four hundred years and helped to build up new states in the Roman Ruins. The state which is our chief concern was founded by the Angles, Saxons and Jutes in England. There is considerable difficulty in fixing with any accuracy the dates and manner of these incursions and settlements. They occurred in the period aptly described by Trevelyan as " History's Blank Page ". It is not firmly established whether such well-known names as Hengist and Horsa denote actual people, but it can be asserted that they or people with similar characteristics did invade England and that the kingdoms of Wessex, Sussex, Kent, Mercia and East Anglia gradually emerged. It is, however, of great importance to bear in mind that the Jutes were first cousins and the Saxons second cousins of the Danes, who first founded the Danelaw in England and finally under Canute formed part of the great though shortlived Scandinavian Kingdom. This helped to ease his problem of establishing union in England. The home of the Angles is a point of more than historic interest to the Danish people, who maintain that they came from Angel in Slesvig and that the Eider has been from time immemorial the natural outlet of their people. On the other hand, the Jutes had migrated to the Elbe and undoubtedly joined with the Saxons, starting from round about the Frisian Islands in their raids on Southern England. Probably the invaders started from many points at once, as did the Vikings in later days for their initial attacks. After some successful raids, the Jutes, who had ceased to " wander" into Saxonia, established settlements from the Thames to the Isle of Wight, but the South Saxons had a settlement in Sussex, as well as in Dorset and Hampshire. These Anglo-Saxons were more like the Germanic tribes described by Tacitus, and their attributes cannot be ascribed to the Viking invaders some centuries later. The Vikings had points of similarity, but, when they burst upon a recovering Western Europe, they had developed characteristics of their own. In England, they must have been astonished that their cousins had lost all sense of the sea and at the civilisation, which had followed the adoption of Christianity. Not only had these farmers lost their sense of the sea, but they had lost the art of building boats and Alfred hired Frisians to build his fleet in Poole Harbour.

The word "Viking" is derived from the Old Icelandic *Vikingr* and means "sea-rover", or one who has been on a *Vikinge* or "voyage". It was merely popular usage and mispronunciation— Vi–Kings—which gave it a false connotation. It is possible that *vik* (a bay, creek or inlet) has some derivative connexion and the rovers undoubtedly issued from the many creeks and fiords of the Scandinavian countries; sea-rovers they were, not creekmen, who invaded Great Britain and Normandy. The purpose and causes of these raids are manifold and the same reasons cannot be applied to all the raids. Their characteristics underwent an obvious change. Swedish historians lay stress on overpopulation as the main cause, and trading enterprise as a strong but on the whole a secondary motive.   Sweden and Skåne undoubtedly suffered severely from overpopulation in the eighth century. Large landowners—the old families—had gained possession of most of the available arable land and the most enterprising preferred to try a life of adventure abroad instead of trying to drain marshland or clear forest. This was the incentive which spurred the hardy Swedes to emigrate to America in later times. Some from Skåne crossed over to the islands of Denmark after Jutes and possibly Angles had gone with the Anglo-Saxon invaders of England. The same cause may have started the Norsemen from Norway, where the patches of arable land were few and isolated and even the most fertile parts round Oslo and Stavanger would not support a growing population.

The second reason—trade—undoubtedly led to the voyages of the Eastern Vikings, who founded Novgorod and Kiev and finally reached the Black Sea by way of the Dnieper. The stories of the wealth of the West were slowly spread through the land, merchants had traded with the cities on the northern coast of the Continent. Doubtless, the thirty Danish boys whom Willibord brought away from Denmark to convert and educate in Western Europe would tell on their return tales of wealthy monasteries and cities. Plunder and greed played their parts.

There is also some evidence to show that the herring were followed from their habitual feeding grounds across the North Sea to Scotland, so food may have been a further incentive to the fisherfolk. Romantic writers would like us to believe that " wanderlust ", the spirit of adventure and love for exploration or—to use a modern phrase—a desire to see the world, were the inspirations of the Vikings. They played their part, no doubt, but the earliest voyages had more prosaic, if less creditable, motive forces. When the earlier voyagers discovered the lands were without any maritime protection —the Seine, the Rhine, the Thames, the Ouse and the Liffey were all equally inviting to the marauder—it became almost part of the young Scandinavian's upbringing to make his *vikinge*. Adventure, profit and maritime training, this a proper branch of education for a seafaring people, could all be obtained in the kind of raid which was popular for the first fifty years of the Golden Age of the Viking period and had been practised, though not regularly, for a century earlier. Towards the middle of the ninth century, the character of the raids underwent a change. After the spearhead of the expedition had secured its *point d'appui*, other ships brought more of these warriors, who were soldiers and sailors—a regular marine corps. Then followed women and children and the *point d'appui* became a settlement. The ideal *point d'appui* was an island, such as Walcheren, which by a piece of incredible lack of judgment on the part of Louis the Pious had been given in fief to a king of Denmark on condition he became a Christian. From Walcheren started the marauding parties for France and Burgundy. These parties paved the way for the settlers on the Lower Seine, who in their turn opened the doors to Rollo, the conqueror of Normandy.

Similarly, the Isle of Wight facing the inlets from the Stour and Avon to the Hamble provided the *point d'appui* for Southern England. The Isle of Thanet was also used on occasions but does not appear to have been such a permanent base. By similar means, settlements were made in East Anglia, especially at the mouths of the rivers. It did not, however, mean that the purely plunder raids ceased. Far from it, they were intensified and their widespread character threatened to encircle the whole coast line of the Continent and overthrow the Europe just emerging from the Dark Ages. The pincers nearly closed—the Eastern Vikings reached the Black Sea, the Western embraced Scotland and Ireland, and the Middle Western passed through the Straits of Gibraltar and raided Luna near Pisa on the Gulf of Genoa, and one Viking ship is said to have penetrated the Levant. It is beyond the scope of this book to describe in detail the multifarious routes of the Vikings, but it is essential to estimate the lasting effect of the migratory raids from which new states developed, states blended from inhabitants and invaders.

These Vikings may not have been Christians, but they were not savages, nor were they undisciplined hordes. It was not surprising, however, that they got an evil reputation. Imagine a country with river mouths and no ships—a few inshore fishing boats perhaps in England and North France, a few coracles in Ireland. The defenceless inhabitants gaze on a fleet of ships with square sails and oars approaching their land. As the ships get closer, their wonder turns to fear. The sails are lowered, some of the oars are shipped, the shields from the bulwarks are unhooked and from the ships, as they touch the shore, spring fierce warriors waving their terrifying battle-axes. They sweep over the neighbouring country, then retire, sail away, leaving a trail of pillage, murder and utter desolation. Small wonder that their reputation was not of the best. Centuries were to pass before a more dispassionate view could be taken of these marauders. Though Snorri may tell us of Rolf Krake, "most renowned for his manners, generosity and loyalty", or of Dan, "so strong that he squeezed a bear to death", or of Fridlev, "so cunning that when he failed to capture Dublin by assault he tied flaming straw to the tails of sparrows so that the town was burned to the ground", yet the reputation for ferocity and ruthless cruelty remained as true and beyond dispute.

Their ships, carrying some forty to sixty men, bore resemblance to a Roman galley, a Maori war canoe and a whaler. They combined the virtues of all three and were eminently suited to brave the dangers of the " short " high waves of the North Sea, and with prow and stern sharp-pointed to penetrate creeks and rivers and make a speedy " get-away " if attacked from the land. The shields of the warriors on the outside of the bulwarks afforded extra protection against the short but high waves. It is probable that the Viking losses incurred on their raids on Spain were not wholly due to the ferocity of Moors and Basques. As far as the Loire they could avoid, to some extent, the full force of the Atlantic rollers. Nantes

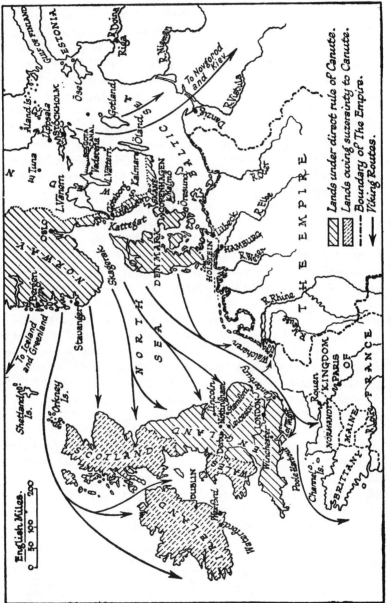

MAP II. THE VIKING ROUTES AND THE EMPIRE OF CANUTE

Lands under direct rule of Canute.
Lands owing suzerainty to Canute.
Boundary of The Empire.
Viking Routes.

was an easy prey. Toulouse was pillaged with equal success, but from that point they suffered severely in men and ships, and their type of ship may have been the more prosaic but truer cause of defeat than the overwhelming odds which they faced. The reputed speed of these boats is almost incredible in spite of the fact that the combined use of oar and sail allowed them to sail very close to the wind. The time taken to reach Greenland from Oslo is given on good authority as six days[1] and the course was not direct, but up the Norwegian coast and thence via the Faroes or Iceland. Two of these boats are in very good preservation on the west coast of the Oslo Fiord and the skilled and tough construction gives a lie to the picturesque epithets of " frail " or " flimsy " so often applied to these craft. They embellish the story, but do not make history.

The actual numbers of these ships which sailed together in the various raids is not often given. Vague terms—" a huge host ", " a small fleet followed by a mighty fleet "—may mean anything, but there are indications that some expeditions consisted of only six to ten boats, while ninety-three were reported in the Thames at the end of the tenth century, and no less than fourteen hundred were mustered by Canute against Norway in 1028 A.D., and " more than six hundred " were employed by him against England in 1015. The mere size of these armadas demanded powers of organisation and a strict code of laws; some writers contend that the naval discipline of the Crusaders was copied from the Scandinavian code, but there seems to be no direct evidence of this attractive theory. A certain proportion of special rules must be common to every amphibious expedition, but the evidence of the early respect of the Danes for law must be found elsewhere. A settlement of Jömborg, which lay on the Baltic coast, near the Oder, affords evidence of a very ancient code of Viking laws to govern their internal relations. This code is considered to be the same as that imposed by Rollo in Normandy.[2] There were traditional rules for the conduct of the expeditions, mostly concerned with loyalty and the punishments for treachery and cowardice, and the division of loot.[3]

[1] The recorded speeds of Vikings sailing from Bergen to Cape Farewell in Greenland in six days and from Jutland to England in three, were regarded with suspicion until 1892. In that year twelve Norwegians sailed in an exact replica of the Gokstad Viking ship to America for the Exhibition at Chicago. Its average speed was nine knots, and at times it exceeded eleven. This substantiates the truth of the medieval records.

[2] Skeenstrup *Normannerne.*

[3] *The Laws of the Wise King*—a mythical hero.

The reverence and respect for law are preserved in the very name —Danelaw, and at the close of the Viking period, this respect for law was extended to the code of the lands in which they made permanent homes. It was not Danish Law, but the code of King Edgar, which Canute enforced in England. However, many centuries were to elapse before district laws were supplanted by a common law of the land. Even in these modern and highly organised days, it is worth remembering that the sentences imposed by magistrates in different districts vary in their severity for precisely the same offences. The historic example of Danish legal administration is provided by the foundation of the " Five Boroughs ", Lincoln, Stamford, Nottingham, Derby and Leicester. Their original object was military; not unnaturally they became the centres of trade. " Trade followed the flag ", and though the original purpose was never obliterated, a large community clustered round and within the walled towns. Old Roman cities, especially those on navigable rivers, were modelled on similar lines. York affords an excellent instance, where the Roman walls and the Danish superstructure or repair work can be clearly distinguished. Each borough had its special " lawmen " and the market its special regulations. Some of the garrison were granted lands on a " burgh " tenure in return for their military duties while stationed there. In many cases, there was probably a tendency for these rights to become permanent and hereditary, but they must not be confused, however, with the hereditary land tenures of feudalism, carrying with them military duties to a particular overlord. Danes undoubtedly bought land with their rewards for services rendered. The famous housecarls of Canute were a paid military guild and did not receive land gifts, as did the Norman supporters of William the Conqueror. It would be truer to say that the two great Scandinavian invasion periods of the ninth, tenth and eleventh centuries promoted forms of feudalism among their opponents. There was a growth of the practice of " commendatio ", that is to say, lesser men bound themselves to greater men to ensure protection against the Danes of the Danelaw. The Norsemen, who had settled in Normandy, had adopted the form of Continental feudalism and superimposed that system on England after the Conquest. William, however, saw the weakness of the royal power which might and did result from both forms, and so, by the retention of the fyrd and the Oath of Salisbury, he was successful in getting the best out of both by binding all the

nobles to the central power. The flexibility of the Danish organisation was mainly due to two things: the independence of their
character, which previously has been attributed in part to their
geographical environment in their Scandinavian homes, and also
to the very nature of the expeditions. The leaders were elected
ad hoc—the kings of the homeland were not the leaders, though
as the expeditions grew in scope and intention the kings had
directive power. Canute himself was not King of Denmark when
he made his first conquest. Thorkel was a usurper, though he paved
the way for Sweyn. Thus on one of their successful and more lasting
incursions into France, the hardpressed Franks had difficulty in
finding with whom to make terms. " We have no King " was the
answer they received. This freedom from control of home government was contributory to the willingness with which they settled
down. Iceland and Greenland were under some loose form of
control, but the settlements in Ireland, England, Scotland and
France were from their very inception independent. It was to
Canute's credit and genius that the new idea of a united empire
owed its origin.

These settlements could not have been a success had it not been
for the outstanding adaptability of their people. This trait of
character has been conspicuous in the Britisher since the Age of
Exploration began once more in the day of the Tudors, but our less
honourable, though at times useful, gifts for compromise and
improvisation are not obviously of Scandinavian origin.

This adaptability has expressed itself in a great variety of
forms. One of the most remarkable is the attitude of the Vikings
towards Christianity. Few could have pillaged church and
monastery with greater thoroughness than the pagan warriors.
Yet when a treaty had been made and a settlement guaranteed, the
baptised pagan became an enthusiastic benefactor of the Church.
Rollo endowed, built and rebuilt churches in Normandy. Olaf
Trygvasson forced conversion on Norway, and the Danes, when
once in London, did much to promote the building of churches.
In a sort of reverse order, the Danes in Denmark adapted themselves to English forms and the teaching of Christianity was
exported in Canute's time to Denmark.

Another striking case of adaptability, or in the first case possibly improvisation, is afforded by their quick appreciation of the
value of the horse. They were not by nature horsemen, but in

the first century of the golden age of the Vikings, they would commandeer farm horses and use them to scour the neighbour- hood and return to their ships. After their settlement in Normandy they quickly adapted themselves to the " horse " and evolved a cavalry arm, which set up a model for the knights of Europe. The " Normanner " took to land warfare surprisingly quickly and, owing to the shameful clause of 912 which gave Rollo a right to ravage Brittany, they came face to face with sturdy Bretons, who had not forgotten seafaring ways and had no little intercourse by sea with the Channel Islands and a coastal trade with Spain. The Rance was a river of battles and remained a dividing line between the Breton sailorfolk and the Norman landsmen.

The Normans appear to have borrowed more from the Latin- ised inhabitants and also from their neighbours in the south than did the Danes in England, especially is this the case in language, as witnessed by the use of different names for the days of the week. It must, however, be remembered that one set of Vikings were meeting Franks and the others Anglo-Saxons. The way in which some of the sailors learned to farm but some remained traders and sailors in England is common knowledge. These Scandinavians were not Swedes, who were ahead of the other two Scandinavian countries in the arts of agriculture for many cen- turies, for although Swedes joined in many of the plunder raids, they did not settle in England or Normandy. In the seventeenth century and after, many Swedes went as farmers to America and one way in which they showed their skill was by going to the less fertile land, as in Minnesota, to the great advantage of the Americans already there, and making it as prosperous as the rest. It may be urged with some truth that their lasting character- istic of adaptability combined with their independent spirit has been one of the reasons why the Scandinavian peoples have not founded colonies which have remained as part of the motherland. They went everywhere on the globe, they traded everywhere, they founded trading ports, but with the exception of the short-lived New Sweden, these settlements were within the compass of the land in which they were situated. New Sweden did not make a very serious attempt to maintain her connexion with Sweden. Denmark sold her few West Indian Islands to America in 1917. It is not enough to say that Denmark and Sweden were " Baltic-minded " and Norway looked to Iceland and Greenland. With the immense mercantile marine, and the large emigration from their own countries—there are no fewer than 700,000 Swedes in America—it would appear that colonies were inevitable under these conditions. The explanation lies very largely in the inherent power to adapt themselves to their new land and indeed to forget their paternal, but to remember their commercial home of origin. This has affected in many ways the commercial and foreign aspects of their policy and Englishmen find them hard to understand. For Englishmen have been faced with very similar problems in very similar circumstances and yet the development of the British Empire is dissimilar. It is a contradiction of the misleading cliché " History repeats itself " and helps to confirm the truer statement that history is not an exact science.

Of other characteristics possessed by these early invaders, it is easy to pick out such virtues as courage and generosity to a vanquished foe from reading the sagas, and following the enticing leadership of William Morris. Indeed, it is easy to prove that their savage cruelty can be matched by equal cruelty in more senseless forms by their Christian opponents. After all, what could be more cruel or stupid than the massacre of Danes on S. Brice's Day in 1002? But in a general survey, such as this book is attempting to give, abstractions may lead the reader a long way off the path and the impact of Scandinavia on Europe at different epochs may be lost in a maze of delightful myths.

This does not in any way disparage the value of the sagas. Without them it would be difficult to get a true picture of the past and through them it is possible to interpret much of what would otherwise be unintelligible. They are, however, written some centuries later and possibly owe not a little to the Celtic culture, which the Vikings did so much to destroy in Ireland. It has been said that they showed that these early heroes lived near to the realities of life. They showed a fighting race, fighting against the hardship of nature and revelling in a struggle with the rest of mankind. The Vikings were out to conquer any foe, human or natural, and this gave them the robust vigour which they infused into the people of Normandy and England. This infusion on both sides of the Channel made the Conquest of England a union rather than a conquest, for in 1066 Normandy was more like England than France.

The exact doses of new blood brought into England by Danes

and by Normans will never be known with any accuracy. Who can prove the numbers of Celts left in any district of England? Doubtless they were pushed westwards, but some were surely left in the hidden places.

Similarly, it is not easy to estimate the actual numbers of Danes and Norsemen because the incursions were extended over many years. Moreover, it is not known with any accuracy how far the Danelaw was fed from Denmark after Alfred had made the Treaty of Wedmore in A.D. 878 and the boundary had been fixed—" Up the Lea to Watling Street and thence to Chester ". Whatever the proportion of the population, there can be no doubt that by 1035, on the death of Canute, the Danish influence was very great. It was rendered all the greater because Canute used and trusted the Anglo-Saxons as administrators—Earl Godwin was his chief minister—and except for his royal guards, his army was not Danish. The Danish merchants, on the other hand, became the chief men in the trading centres. Even in London, the bulwark of resistance, they soon became firmly established.

Through them a lasting trade with the Baltic and Norway was established. This trade did not pass away and was never wholly extinct in the worst days of Danish history. Underlying the surface there has been a sense of kinship which has shown its face quite suddenly in the most unexpected times and ways. (A Swedish S.O.S. for English aid against Baltic pirates in the fourteenth century. An English S.O.S. for Norwegian timber after the Fire of London.)

The commercial trade sense of the English can be placed among the gifts of Scandinavia and there have been relatively few trade disputes with England. Disputes about fishing rights have been surprisingly few considering the nature of the trade and the wayward caprices of the herring, which have caused most of the trouble. The increase of trade provided the incentive for building boats. By the end of the eleventh century, it would not be an exaggeration to call Great Britain a seafaring country; in the ninth century Alfred had to import men to build his ships.

The Scandinavian influence on our shipbuilding continued until the Tudor period, when new styles began to be necessary for the Atlantic. Boats built for the Baltic trade, however, still preserved the lines of the Scandinavian builders and in Cook's day, the Whitby type—such as the *Endeavour*—could be seen in the

Skagerak and Öresund and it is said that Danish seamen could not tell, until they got very close, to which nationality they belonged.

Such then are some of the legacies, for good or evil, which were left in England and in Englishmen, but Canute left one for Northern Europe. This, the conception of a united Northern Kingdom of Scandinavians, cannot be dismissed as merely a dream. It faded away on his death, because the kingdoms were not united except in his person. Neither Harald, the son of Alfifa (Elgiva), his first wife, nor Hardicanute, his son by Emma, widow of Ethelred II, was a big enough man to carry on their father's work when he died at the early age of forty. By marrying Emma of Normandy, he had hoped to secure his southern boundary, so open to invasion, as he knew, and at the same time to unite his English people. In these two objects he succeeded, but he left two rival sons and even his missionary work in Denmark had not drawn the ties of Denmark and England close enough to stand the strain. Norway also was not ready. It was a dream, but dreams recur, and it was realised by Margaret of Denmark in a different form, Sweden taking the place of England. A revival in the form of a Confederacy was discussed and took shape as an alliance of mutual defence in 1914, but as Jon Stefannson wrote in 1916, "the dream can only come true if the Scandinavian countries should enter a Federated British Empire for their own safety and security".

Perhaps it is better that we cannot see too far into the future, but in 1940 many Scandinavians may have wished that Canute's dream had been realised.

TABLES TO SHOW THE DISSOLUTION OF CANUTE'S KINGDOM

Harald Bluetooth,
First Christian King of all Denmark,
940–985

Sven Fork Beard,
985–1014

Harald, 1014–1018	Alfifa (Elgiva) = Canute, King of Denmark, 1018–1035; King of Norway, 1028–1035	= Emma of Normandy, widow of Ethelred II	Estrith = Earl Ulf Canute's Viceroy of Denmark 1025–1035
Sweyn, Viceroy of Norway to 1035. Supplanted by Magnus the Good, King of Norway, 1035–1047; King of Denmark, 1042–1047	Harald I, King of England, 1035–1040	Hardicanute, King of England, 1040–1042; King of Denmark; 1035–1042	Sweyn Erithson, 1047–1076

N.B. 1035 Magnus King of Norway, Harald of England, Hardicanute of Denmark.

CONTEMPORARY KINGS OF SWEDEN

Sven Fork Beard = Sigrid = Eric the Victorious,
(vide above)   King of Sweden, died 993 (994?)

Olaf Sköt-Konung, 999–1022

Anun Jacob, 1022–1050

CHAPTER III

SWEDEN IN MEDIEVAL TIMES

THOUGH many individual Swedish leaders with their bands of followers joined in the Viking incursions on the West, the settlers were predominantly from Denmark and Norway. The number of Anglo-Saxon coins found in Sweden is fairly conclusive evidence that the Swedes did manage to annex a goodly share of the Danegeld. The runic stones tell their tale of Swedish prowess, and one is in memory of a Swedish soldier, who was a member of Canute's famous bodyguard. Thus the assertion that the Swedes went South and East, and the Danes and Norsemen West, is a generalisation which demands some qualification. It is, however, true that the main results on European history follow the activities of those countries in those directions. The chief qualification, perhaps, is that the Danes made some progress beyond their Viking settlement at Jömborg along the south Baltic coast, but, on the whole, it was the Swedish naval power which dominated the Baltic until the rise of the Hanseatic League.

The story of the Swedish or Eastern Vikings affords a striking contrast almost from the very beginning. Before the so-called Viking Age, in fact in the early part of the fourth century, the virile tribe of Heruls had made a daring raid on the Roman Empire. When they were squeezed out by the Danes in Skåne and the Goths to the north of them, they set off on a mass "folk wandering" through the Balts, probably down the Dvina into the modern Ukraine, and finally succeeded in driving a wedge westwards into Hungary.[1] The remnants left in Sweden were known later as the Virdars. The Heruls set up their Scandinavian Kingdom between the Southern Slavs in the Balkans and the Slavs of Poland. It is a fascinating speculation to probe into what the history of this disturbed battleground of Europe might have been had not this wedge been driven

---

[1] Some contend that they went through Southern Finland and that Ugro-Finnish tribes joined the wandering in sufficient numbers to justify the theory that the majority, though not the leaders, were Ugro-Finns.

firmly in between Slav and Slav. The Pan-Slav movement might have taken shape centuries ago with its centre in Poland or Jugo-Slavia. But the wedge not only held firm, it widened the gap and the Heruls drove still further westwards. When the original dynasty failed in the sixth century, they sent to Sweden for another king. The chosen warrior arrived in Hungary with a bodyguard of only two hundred Scandinavian warriors. These Heruls became the ruling class and were known as Magyars, and in early medieval times Hungary was sometimes called the land of the Magyars. In A.D. 899 the Hungarians, led by the Magyars, drove on to the plains of Lombardy and continued to be a menace to the south-east of the Empire for more than a century. The Emperors had to take them very seriously and many lives were lost before they were forced back to Hungary. They were never conquered. They could always retire to the mountains and were still a dangerous foe and an uncertain ally in the Thirty Years War of the seventeenth century. They had lost their territory, but not their fighting qualities. Hungary was never really subjugated by Austria. Maria Theresa realised this and wisely granted them the status which remained until the revolt of 1848. Their history ceased to be of great concern to Scandinavia, though it was many centuries before they lost complete touch with the land of their origin, and this enclave from South Sweden has been and is a European problem.

In the ninth century, the Eastern Vikings made numerous raids on the lands of the Eastern Baltic. They penetrated Finland, Courland, and Estonia and tried to extort tribute from the various tribes. These countries were poor and devoid of any central organising authority. The tributes were hard to collect and any small settlements were constantly open to attack: booty and treasure, such as rewarded so richly the marauders on the West, were hardly worth the losses incurred.

These considerations seem to have turned the Eastern Vikings into traders, and their commercial enterprises led to their expeditions into Russia and down to the Byzantine Empire. The Mohammedan grip on the trade routes of the Mediterranean had partially closed the trade in silks, spices and other Eastern products, much in demand in Europe. Pirates captured nearly as much merchandise as got through safely; some of the booty was passed on to middlemen, and was obtainable in Europe only through the prototype of the modern Black Market at enhanced prices. With the

Moors in Spain, and the capture of Sardinia in 711, of Crete in 825, and of Syracuse in 877 after attempts covering fifty years, the "throttle-hold" was tighter still. In these circumstances the Viking trade route grew at each stage of the advance of Islam. As the Mediterranean door closed tighter, the Dnieper door opened wider to the Black Sea. The pointed Viking ships sailed up the rivers, and were hauled across land to waterways leading south. Goods were generally brought to Birca on Lake Mälar and to the harbours of Gotland, thence to be transhipped to the town of Slesvig or bought by merchants themselves coming to Sweden. Visits of even Frisian merchants are recorded and many from the towns of North Germany. These traders were purchasers of furs from Finland and Russia as well as of Eastern goods. Some idea of the extent of the trade can be gathered from the mere fact that as many as forty thousand Byzantine coins have been found in Sweden. Even after Olaf Skött-Konung had begun minting Swedish coins, they were ordinary currency among merchants and in the coast towns, but hardly any money was used by the people living in the country before they were forced to pay taxes in the fifteenth century. It soon became evident that the trade routes needed permanent guard-posts, but the earlier attempts of the Varangians, as the Vikings were called, were not very successful. The term Varangian was adopted from the Swedish *Vaeringjar*—followers of a "wayfaring" or Viking chief, and when these men in later years took service as the household guards of the Emperor at Constantinople, they were known as *Vaerings*. There is no reason to doubt the veracity of the Old Russian Nestor Chronicle, which gives a simple account of how the settlements became permanent, the chain of *gard, gorod*, or walled towns came into existence, and how the Russians received their name and founded a central Slav Kingdom under a Swedish dynasty which lasted till 1598[1] Having driven out the Varangians, who were trying to impose dues, the tribes, Finnish and Russian, found themselves the losers and their lands in chaos. They finally invited the Swedes to send them rulers. Thus spake the Chronicler: "The peoples then began to govern themselves, but it went badly; clan rose against clan and there was internal strife among them. Then they said to each other: 'Let us seek a prince, who can reign over us and judge what is right.'

[1] For full accounts of early Slavonic migrations and Russian history and its relation to Sweden and Finland vide Pares' *History of Russia*.

And they went over the sea to the Varangians, to the Russ, for so were these Varangians called, and said to them: 'Our land is large and fertile, but there is no order in it: come ye, therefore, and reign and rule over us.'" (Translation from Hallendorf and Shück, where the Nestor Chronicle is quoted and discussed.)

In answer to the appeal, three brothers set out to the three main centres—Rurik the Russ, Oskold and Dir. On the death of the latter two, Rurik, who had gone to Holmgard (Novgorod), combined the whole into one united Russian state. The chain of walled cities, Novgorod on the Neva, Polovsk on the Dvina, Smolensk and Kiev on the Dnieper, guarded the whole trade route to the Black Sea. Kiev was soon the most important of this chain and became the seat of government. This state was independent of, but friendly with, Sweden. Rurik the Russ had his Scandinavian household guards, and fresh emigrants from Sweden continued to flow into the cities and trade was almost entirely in their hands. As time went on, this led to a cleavage between town and country dwellers. A more serious cleavage came later, when occurred the inevitable clash of Russian and Swedish interests. The Muscovite dynasty lasted till the death of Feodor, son of Ivan the Cruel, in 1598, but the rift between Slav and Swede had begun four centuries earlier, when a fierce pitched battle was fought at Novgorod in 1164. Peaceful trade and an invitation led to the foundation of a Russian Kingdom under the guidance of the Swedes, but soon the child grew up and the wonder is that it remained so long under the guidance, but never domination, of the parental dynasty. The explanation is that the Czars were able to point out the importance of the Swedish commercial bond, that the steady stream of Swedish immigrants helped to influence the opinion in the towns, where it found a focal point, and lastly the removal of the government to Kiev turned the eyes of restless warriors towards the richer Byzantine Empire. They made no less than six raids on Constantinople, and Russians penetrated to Thrace and the Adriatic in A.D. 907. It was not till the eleventh century that peaceful relations were established, and still longer before the Greek Orthodox Church began to influence the Slavs with their Swedish rulers. They had become land warriors and had lost what little of the seafaring spirit had been instilled into them by contact with the Varangians. Strangely enough, the ancestry and profession of their self-imposed rulers are commemorated in their name. *Russ* was their own name for the *Ruotsi* and *Roddsmen,* who had come from Roden, the Roslagen of the Uppland coast of to-day, a district bound by law to furnish ships and rowers in time of war.

Thus before the Western Vikings had become finally established in England, the Eastern Vikings had been instrumental in founding two new dynasties in Eastern Europe. The motives and manner had been different. They did not preserve direct governmental connexion with the homeland nor was there any attempt to found a vast Scandinavian Empire, but their impress on the formation of the Eastern Europe of the future was equally permanent, if less conscious than in the West.

It must not be inferred, however, that Swedes and Danes had any understanding about " spheres of influence ", as they might be termed in the twentieth century. Individual Swedes and Norwegians might join in Danish expeditions, but fierce rivalry between the rulers existed before and after Canute's death. Eric the Victorious received his title from his victory near Uppsala over an army of Danes and Jomsborg Vikings led by his own nephew Styrbjörn. Eric carried the war into Denmark and managed to seize the whole country when Sven (Sweyn) was busy ravaging Finland. War seemed a regular pastime and, like boxers, these kinsmen shook hands and were friends till the next contest. Eric's son, Olaf Skött-Konung, made peace with Sven, who married his mother. Olaf and Sven joined up for a united attack on Olaf Trygvasson, King of Norway, whom they defeated and killed at Svold, as has been described above. Canute did not try to persuade Olaf Skött-Konung to join in his invasion of England, but he secured his approval to prevent any attack, on Skåne and Jutland in his absence. How close this alliance might have grown had Canute not died at the age of forty can only be surmised. He had a statesman's outlook, not that of a politician, who deals " with phenomena as they may arise ". There were some small indications which point to infiltration—moneyers from Lincoln at the Danish mint at Lund, moneyers from Lincoln at the Swedish mint at Sigtuna. Swedes were with Canute's expedition and cannot fail to have noticed the contrast between the power of the two Scandinavian Kings over their peoples. Sweden was in the throes of a struggle between Christianity and Paganism. Olaf had been baptised and even called his son Jacob, but the heathen temple was not destroyed till a hundred and fifty years had elapsed and some bloody civil wars had taken place. Sweden was still a free land, governed by the assemblies of *bonder* (freemen) and their lawman, and on Olaf's death Jacob had to change his name back to the Norse, bowing to the will of the Assembly at Uppsala. Canute, after his easy conquest of Norway, might well have extended his Empire northwards to Lake Vättern and the Union would have been complete, and perhaps have continued as a purely Scandinavian Empire, even if England had not remained as part. His premature death put an end to this possibility for over three centuries. On the other hand, Sweden had developed on different lines from Denmark. Apart from the fact that Christianity had but few converts north of Lake Mälar, the influence of the Continental system —perhaps more rightly termed " caste " than feudal—had not been felt to any great extent. Snorri Sturluson has left a perfect picture of the king and his people—the limitations on his powers, the rights of the assemblies of the *bonder* and the local lawman. The right of freedom of speech, and of maintaining local laws and customs, was the breeding-ground of the democratic spirit, which begat the resistance to Danish oppression and the early form of rule through the Riksdag in the days of Engelbrekt. It forms a picturesque description of a free people, but it meant weakness against a determined and organised foe. Democracies are notoriously slow movers, but good stayers. Sweden, owing to her geographical position and the internecine wars of Denmark and Norway, was not put severely to the test for nearly three centuries after Olaf's death. The democratic form of government remained much as Snorri described it until Magnus Barnlocks began to centralise the governments, give a law common to all the land and, owing to the acquisition of Skåne, create a new tax-free nobility to provide the necessary cavalry.

Here is the picture of King Olaf, who was bent on war with Norway, seated in the centre of the Assembly at Uppsala surrounded by his *hird* or bodyguard and courtiers. The *bonder* (freemen) and their Lawman stood in a circle round the royal party.[1] It was midwinter 1018, but the deliberations were in the open, like the Althing in Iceland. A deputation had arrived unexpectedly from Norway craving the hand of the Princess Ingigerd, Olaf's daughter, for the King of Norway. Earl Ragnvald of

---

[1] Snorri's *The Kings of Norway and the Round World* has been translated into English by William Morris.

Gotland tried to speak in favour of the suit, but was roundly abused as a traitor by Olaf, who forbade the Norwegian ambassador to say more. Then up spoke the old Lawman to the King: "The Kings of Sweden are minded otherwise than they were of yore. They were friendly and easy for the freemen to approach, but the King who now reigns wishes to hear only that which pleases him and is bent on ruling Norway, which no Swedish King has ere now coveted. We freemen will stand this no longer. We demand you make peace with Norway's King and give him your daughter in marriage. If you will not do as we say, we shall slay you, as our forefathers did with self-willed kings." This was greeted with loud cheers and the king bowed to their will in his foreign policy and betrothed Ingigerd to the King of Norway, afterwards St. Olaf. The marriage, however, did not turn out as planned, because Earl Ragnvald substituted Astrid her half-sister and she was married before either king had realised the deceit. Such was the limitation of royal power and the strength of the Assembly of Uppsala, which was only one of the many assemblies, as each province possessed its own. They were not as powerful as that at Uppsala, but still had many powers including a voice in the election of the king. The practice of electing the king was jealously guarded and even Margaret of Denmark after her election as "Lady Mistress of Sweden" could not persuade the nobles to accept Eric as hereditary monarch. The nobles had supported the assemblies' cherished right and the succession was declared hereditary in the House of Vasa, with the important provision that the king took a sacred oath to obey the law of the land. He remains within the law and not outside it to this day. The king was chosen from members of the royal family by acclamation and usually the eldest son of the late king was selected by the three Things of Uppland. He then had to visit the Thing of each province and swear to obey the particular laws of that province, whose freemen then took an oath of allegiance. The king had no power to levy taxes and had to live on the revenues received from his own personal estates. The provincial Things had a head "lawman" who was responsible for knowing not only the laws, but also previous verdicts. Each province was divided into small districts—either on a basis of population or acreage, and each had its own local Thing and lawman.

Self-government and local government were the keynotes of the system and the first attempts at centralisation met with violent opposition.

The king had absolute power in war and had discretion over the only general tax, which was not unlike our Ship Money. *Roddare*, the crew, and in the case of larger districts, ship's equipment and even a ship, had to be furnished. The contribution required from each district seems to have been assessed originally by the king at Uppsala, but the incidence on individuals was arranged first by the provincial Thing and finally by each small district. The king was the admiral and conducted the "manoeuvres" annually. As these manoeuvres were in fact profitable raids, there was competition to be a *roddare* and there was an excess of volunteers. The contribution for equipment was a gamble and profits had to be shared. The ship was the possession of a wealthy *jarl* or more usually belonged to the royal navy. The ownership of ships differed at different periods. The crews, in the case of both Denmark and Sweden, were trained as soldiers and sailors, but all the rowers were freemen. The slaves sold by the Varangians were probably prisoners of war.

Though powerful as admiral-king, during times of war and training for raids, the royal person had one permanent function which placed him ahead of all the others—he only could perform certain religious rites—he was the High Priest and so in a class by himself. The original line, Ynglings, were proud of their alleged divine descent. Eric the Victorious dedicated himself to Odin in 983 for ten years and in 993 Odin "took him to himself from off the earth".

The religious aspect of kingship, deriving respect and veneration from the office of priest, gave more stability to the throne than the seasonal aspect which drew respect and loyalty according to the efficiency of the king as an admiral. The great temple, which drew huge crowds every year and still huger crowds every nine years, was the most powerful, if not the only, point of unity between the loosely federated provinces. There all the people of Sweden and delegates saw the king—their king—the symbolical figure of unity—in the flesh. Bagehot many years ago laid stress in his book, *The English Constitution*, that the Sovereign was a necessity for the British Empire, whether she (or he) had any real executive power or not. There must be a central point on which the loyalty of every part of the Empire could concentrate.

It is almost an exact analogy with the position of this priest-king in this simple and loose federation of self-governed little entities. Stated thus, it might appear to be an idyllic state born from the imagination of the author of *News from Nowhere*, who has done so much to make a study of early Scandinavian history possible. There is, however, another side. Provided everyone was content to live the simple life and nature provided plenty, and the winters of the north did not exist and humanity had no ambitions, things might have remained idyllic ever afterwards. But first of all, the religious ceremonies were horrific as well as beautiful in their simplicity. Frey, Thor and Odin, who were the three chief gods after whom our days of the week are named, demanded human sacrifices. Frey, the god of fertility was carried in honour round the fields to ensure good harvests. To make doubly sure, the blood of animals and human beings was spilled first on the altars and then sprinkled on the fields. Orgies of sexual rites formed an integral part of the great nine-year festival. Contact with the West brought more antagonism to this paganism, it is said, than did the efforts of the early missionaries. At once a difficulty arose. Christianity meant the loss of power to the king and his court, a bishop meant at once an "imperium in imperio".

Secondly, in the face of aggression, the isolated units could not be knitted together in time to meet the invader, nor very efficiently in any case. It was one thing to fit out a raiding expedition and attack some spot unprotected by any ships, it was another to meet an organised expedition by land or sea, where the leader could choose his time and place of attack. Lastly, as commerce increased, some unified system of government was an absolute necessity. If this were not established, either trade ceased or the "peace and laws of the market" would fall into the hands of aliens. This last view must have forced itself on the Swedes, because they themselves had profited by the chaos of tribal disunity in Russia and themselves been the aliens who had brought cosmos out of chaos. Pirenne in his brilliant history of Europe rather unfairly maintains that the Swedes "exploited" this inefficiency.

The changes did not come suddenly, and unfortunately the eleventh and early twelfth century is one of the most barren periods of Swedish history. One fact of great importance stands out prominently. The first attempt to Christianise Sweden failed signally and Jacob was forced to change his name to Anund by the assembly of the heathen Uppsala. On the death of Anund's brother, the old line of Uppsala ceased to exist and Stenkil of West Gotland was elected king. For the first time, power began to move southwards and the southern provinces had already begun to lean towards Christianity. Stenkil showed his zeal by allowing a bishopric to be established at Skara. Encouraged by this success, Christian nobles regarding God as the new god of victory, tried to burn the Temple of Uppsala. Stenkil saved the temple for the heathen, believing that Christianity should not be forced upon his people by fire and sword, or, as others relate, he saw the possibility of a violent war of Odin and Christ. The temple was saved, but nevertheless civil war broke out.

The heathens elected their own king at Uppsala, but Stenkil's son, Inge, a zealous proselytising Christian, burnt the heathen king and his priests in the royal house. He then destroyed the temple, and by the beginning of the twelfth century Christianity was established in the land, but not in the hearts of the people. A new god of victory had displaced Thor and Odin, but the many local gods, who had been venerated from time immemorial, were not altogether forgotten. As time went on, saints took their places and pagan attributes were transferred to them. Perhaps the most startling transference of all occurred when King Eric, a burning zealot who led the crusade against Finland, was canonised and took the place of Frey as god of fertility. His effigy was carried round the fields and the most binding of all oaths became " By God and S. Eric ". As in Denmark, the spiritual conversion followed the formal and enforced baptism, when S. Bernard sent his party of Cistercians to found the monasteries at Alvastra, Varnhem and Nydala.

The civil wars and the introduction of Christianity had not only caused desperate miseries and clan enmities, but they had shaken the ascendancy of Uppsala as the religious and civil centre of power. The choice of a king outside the Uppsala circle had been the beginning of the trouble, but it had made subsequent kings realise that the easy-going local self-government needed some reform. By the middle of the twelfth century the country was rent still further by the deposition of King Sverker, Earl of East Gotland, and the election of Eric IX. For six years till his death in 1156 Sverker ruled in Gotland and stirred up the old Gothic feelings against Eric, now King of Sweden. Eric adopted the plan, with which we are now familiar, of diverting the people's attention from their own troubles and firing them with some ideology. He revived the old familiar Viking raids under the guise of crusades. With Henry, his English Bishop of Uppsala, the counterblast to Sverker's Bishop of Lund, he carried out a successful mission in Finland, where Henry remained with the first Swedish settlers. He was, however; assassinated after a few years, was canonised, and became the patron saint of Finland. Eric was also assassinated when the Danish army had penetrated as far north as Uppsala. Eric was surrounded in a church at prayer and was slain, but his dead body performed so many marvellous feats against the Danes that he too was canonised, and a Mass was annually said on May 18th. His bones repose in Uppsala Cathedral. Out of a wearisome recital of wars emerge two recognisable changes:

(*a*) Sweden is Christian by A.D. 1200, except in very remote districts, and an archbishopric has been established at Uppsala.

(*b*) Sweden has begun to look east once more, and her settlements in Finland show signs of becoming a permanent foothold.

Both these facts have a direct bearing on her relations with the Slavs. Many Swedish historians trace the age-long feuds between Russia and their country to the first meeting of the Greek and Roman Churches at the most unfortunate of all moments, when the very independent state of Novgorod saw its interests threatened by Swedes in Finland. These various factors, coupled with some spasmodic attacks by Danes, lead to a stiffening of Swedish rule in order both to ward off aggression and to raise national pride by aggression.

The miserable period of civil war had led to the decline of Sweden's naval power and the East Baltic had become infested with pirates. So in 1187 Stockholm was built to guard the entrance to Lake Mälar and soon it takes the place of the less convenient and rather discredited Uppsala as the seat of government. The separation of the seats of religious and civil government has proved of benefit to both cities, especially as Uppsala became the seat of the first university. The position of Lund in Danish Skåne was now offset by Uppsala and to this day a rivalry exists, but a friendly rivalry, comparable but not so clear-cut as that between Oxford and Cambridge or Harvard and Yale. A less happy effect of the wars was a decline in the prosperity of the peasants; they had suffered more than any other class. Of the landowners, some had been killed or outlawed, but the survivors had increased their estates and power at the expense of the vanquished.

CHAPTER IV

PRELUDE TO THE UNION OF A.D. 1389

THE thirteenth century was to witness many changes both in the relations of Sweden towards other countries and at home. In a period of continual struggle and wars, internal and external, some features can be clearly distinguished against the confused background:

(*a*) A renewed desire for expansion and power which is directed towards Finland, and also southwards on the mainland towards the Danish Skåne.

(*b*) The influence of the establishment of Christianity brings Sweden into closer contact with Rome and Western Europe. This expresses itself in two ways—a desire for more culture, and a zeal for missionary crusades in Finland. This zeal justified the dual nature of the settlements round Åbo.

(*c*) During the civil wars, the German naval and mercantile league with its headquarters at Lübeck had become the dominating naval power in the Baltic. Not only had it challenged the Swedish supremacy in the East Baltic, but it had stretched its tentacles as far as Bergen and firmly established its *Hansa* in that port. Norway was almost bound to acquiesce owing to its dependence on Baltic corn. Denmark's naval power was also in danger, as were her rich fisheries and carrying trade. However, Sweden was at this period the chief sufferer, because of the virtual capture of the important island of Gottland and the establishment there of the fortified Hanseatic town of Visby. This commanded the Russian trade route and threatened the very existence of Sweden as a naval power.

(*d*) Internally the king seeks to increase the royal power and as a ruler of his people to regain rather more than he had lost by ceasing to be the High Priest.

(*e*) The nobles in the general confusion had greatly increased their power at the expense of the peasants and in some districts at the expense of the *husabyar* or royal bailiffs, not to be confused with the *rättsbetjänt*, the land bailiffs or agents of the great land-owners themselves. A form of feudalism was imperceptibly introduced.

(*f*) The peasants in their distress will turn to the king, who may hope to find in them a means of centralising and consolidating his kingdom.

Sweden found herself able to produce some statesmen of vision who succeeded in guiding her in this formative period of her history. The struggle, however, left her divided internally and uncertain of her loyalties, and so may be regarded as paving the way for the experiment of union.

It was, however, an educative period—an empiric education painfully borne and endured. Two men were able to interpret the experiments of the enlightened Earl Birger, the Regent (1250–1266), Magnus Barnlocks (1275–1290), Torgils the Regent (1290–1298) and Magnus Erikson, who became King of both Sweden and Norway in 1319. Those two men were Engelbrekt Engelbrektson (Regent 1435) and Gustavus Vasa (1521). They profited by the mistakes, successes and failures of the past and it is in the light of the future history of Sweden that the thirteenth and fourteenth centuries may be regarded as something more than a stormy period of the struggle for existence or wearisome warfare between self-interested nobles and the crown. These years, if they weakened Sweden sufficiently to encourage the attempt for union under Danish rule, at the same time produced a sturdy undergrowth which in the end gave her the solid power and produced a national democracy under her great kings.

Three factors were chiefly responsible for the disastrous wars which raged almost continuously from 1130 to 1250. First of all, the throne was elective and so long as " the Wealth of Uppsala " was the most powerful in the land, the succession was assured to their nominee. When, as has been related, the more southern provinces began to contest this hegemony divisions arose. The climax came when Sverker from Östergötland became king about 1130. An ardent supporter of the Church and especially of the monastic Order of the Cistercians, he attempted to extend the royal power, much to the anger of many of the nobles. On his death Eric, also connected with the Stenkil dynasty, seized the throne. His election was provincial.

Secondly, the provinces already giving evidence of a desire for separation saw in this usurpation an opportunity to gain their own ends. Rival dynasties of Sverker and Eric struggled for possession of the throne and the royal demesnes. A " War of the Roses " began and continued until the descendants of both branches died without male issue.

Thirdly, in spite of these wars at home, it was apparently recognised that in view of the dangers abroad, some unity had to be maintained in order to prevent annihilation from outside. This was probably the unconscious motive which underlay the immense authority which was gradually vested in the power of the " Earl ", who assumed many of the powers of the king-admiral of earlier days. It was almost a necessity for self-preservation and can hardly be ascribed to national patriotism when rivals had no qualms in enlisting the help of Danish armies to gain their own ends.

The result was manifest. The earl became more powerful than the ruler and in the general chaos shared with the Church the only institutional power which was universally respected.

At the beginning of the thirteenth century, the position of Jarl had been almost appropriated by members of the Folkung family. It is hardly an exaggeration to say that a Birger of the Folkung's followed a Birger. They had further strengthened their position by securing bishoprics for their own family and even intermarrying with one or other, or both, of the rival royal families. The earl had to depend for support on the nobles, who in their turn became more powerful as local rulers. The power and prosperity of the peasants had sharply declined, many offering themselves as serfs till forbidden by law. The nobles had usurped many of the rights of the provincial assemblies, though new laws had still to be passed by them. To ensure their easy passage, the lawmen of the provinces were not infrequently connected with the Folkungs, and the local lawmen were related to or nominated by the lesser nobles. The earl himself was Admiral of the Fleet, received the " Ship Money " from the *roden* and even was supplied with some of the royal revenue for defence purposes.

Such was the position in 1250 when the last of Eric's sons died, leaving no male heir and no rival descendant of Sverker. The great earl, Birger Magnusson, had been the actual ruler for some years, and, very astutely, he did not aspire to the throne himself, but secured the election of his young son Valdemar, first of the Folkung Kings.

Earl Birger lost no time in consolidating the power of the crown. He summoned an assembly of nobles—the germ of the first estate in the future Riksdag. They gave assent to his new regulations and undertook to engineer their passage through the various Things.

By this means the new laws, largely security measures to enforce peace in the land and provide measures for defence against force, became statute laws, and for the first time the statute laws became common to all the various provinces. This ingenious method of gaining unity was adopted by the Things, which did not realise that their authority was slipping away. Magnus Barnlocks hoped to go yet further and unify the whole legal code of Sweden. A beginning was made by preparing the "Uppland Code", sanctioned during the Regency of Torgils, which applied to the three original divisions of Uppland. It was not until 1347 that Magnus Erikson instituted a code common to all Sweden. There was opposition to this measure, but it was overcome by an even more ingenious device. He posed before the peasants as their protector and forbade the billeting of nobles' retinues on the tenant farmers. Hence his nickname "locker of barns"; but at the same time ordered the appointment of one host to supply travellers in each village. But the travellers had to pay "mine host", who was the forerunner of the "innkeeper". At the same time, the provincial Things could propose legislation and the proposals could be forwarded through their lawman to the king and his council or Råd. This Råd was a new institution and chosen from the civil and religious aristocracies. The clergy could deliberate separately before the main discussions of the Råd on purely church matters. Although the Råd did not meet the assemblies, we find that the king was recognising the voice of three estates—peasants, nobles and clergy. Their functions were not clearly defined and were dependent no doubt on the king's pleasure. The fourth estate, which appeared in the first Riksdag of Engelbrekt in 1435, can be said to have been recognised for the first time in this reign. Not only were charters issued to the cities, but there was a council of burghers, who were responsible for law and order in the town. Commercial rules proposed by them could be converted into statute laws if it was deemed advisable to make them universally applicable. It was from these urban councils that the representatives were sent to the Riksdag.

Here then can be seen the seeds of the Four Estates, which played so important a part in later history and retained separate representatives till the middle of the nineteenth century.

It was fortunate for the future of Sweden that the importance of the peasant and townsman was recognised from the very start. It gave a balance which has been, and still is, very marked in her economy. The towns were engaged in foreign trade, but some of their export was dependent on a rapidly growing mining industry. The connexion of miner and peasant is a notable feature of Swedish history, as will be seen later, and there has been no Town and Country feud or an attempt to win privileges for one to the exclusion of the other.

As Magnus amplified the legislative policy of his father, Earl Birger, so was he largely influenced by his economic and foreign policies also. It should be explained that the Earl, wise though his general rule had been, had committed one fatal error. Although Earl Birger was the ruler until his death in 1266, Valdemar had been nominal king since 1250. Influenced by the fear of there not being a powerful Folkung to succeed Valdemar and that civil wars might again devastate his country, he decreed that, on his death, the second son Magnus should be created Duke of Sweden, and the third, Bengt, Duke of Finland. Possibly he had already realised that Valdemar was a vicious young man, though not without talents, who needed the advice of a powerful " Earl ". The arrangements duly came into force, and Magnus became Duke of Sweden with the powers of his father, Earl Birger. The shocking conduct of Valdemar, intolerable even in those robust days, led to more civil wars between the brothers, and finally when all hope of agreement had disappeared, Magnus and the nobles compelled Valdemar to abdicate. Thus there was a gap of nine years before Magnus could continue the work of the Great Earl in 1275.

The economic problem of the greatest urgency, which faced Earl Birger and his son Magnus, was the status of the German merchant and worker in Sweden itself. Following closely on that came the question of the policy to be adopted towards Lübeck and the Hanseatic League. Thus foreign policy and economic became inseparably linked up. The problem set by German merchants, craftsmen and miners was complicated, and no easy solution offered itself. The German cities were well organised and wealthy, and it was to the advantage of Sweden that their merchants and craftsmen should settle there. Earl Birger encouraged them, but they presented a case very similar to that of the foreign merchant in China six hundred years later. These merchants were willing to come and sink their capital, but they expected extra-territorial rights. In cases of dispute they would readily appeal to their home towns in Germany, and sometimes their stay in Sweden ended after their business was established; but they managed from Lübeck, or even Hamburg, to keep control over their Swedish branches. With the miners, the position was somewhat different. They came to make their homes round the rich copper mines in Dalarna, some of which were developed by German capital. So successful were they, that in the reign of Magnus the system was extended to open up new iron mines which were to form the base of Swedish industrial prosperity. Here, the danger lay in foreign colonies or settlements, such as the Varangians themselves had founded in Russia and the Danes in England and France. Birger was quite firm in his insistence that these miners should be subject to Swedish law and custom, and naturalised they became. In the case of the merchants, he did not stand on such firm ground. Similar action would inevitably mean a clash with the Hanseatic League and its powerful navy. Swedish trade was slowly recovering, and notable expansion was taking place in the Russian trade with Novgorod. The Slav Russian state was completely free from Swedish influence by this time, but trade as between one state and another was increasing and likely to increase more, to the mutual advantage of both. The Swedish settlements on the western side of Finland were proving a profitable investment, and commercial dividends were now forthcoming from the missionary crusades of the past. Any rupture leading to a naval war might ruin this peaceful and progressive economic expansion. Birger's policy was essentially one of peace abroad, and Magnus followed his example in maintaining a friendly attitude to Denmark and Norway. During the fateful nine years following Birger's death, the Germans had not only gained complete commercial ascendancy over the strategically important island of Gottland, but had converted Visby into a strong naval base. The island bears evidence of their occupation to this day in its architectural features, and it must not be forgotten that the Goths had never vacated it. Magnus made his policy quite clear from the outset. There was to be no " imperium in imperio", and he was crowned "King of the Swedes and Goths". He proceeded to make his suzerainty over Gotland more than nominal. Visby was closely invested after a costly battle in the open country and finally surrendered. He was King over Sweden, and the new trade routes were secured and all foreigners in Sweden were obliged to submit to Swedish law. Magnus had triumphed, but he had earned the enmity of the Hanseatic League, although it had not openly declared war. It realised that the time had not arrived for revenge. The right policy for the League was obviously further to increase its commercial and naval power, and then wait for the clash between Denmark and Sweden. The League would hold the balance and reap the profits.

We have mentioned that both Birger and Magnus encouraged friendly relations with Denmark, but Magnus was keenly alive to the Danish threat, which would be bound to be there as long as Skåne remained in Danish hands. He also realised that Sweden was sadly deficient in cavalry and that if ever war broke out, the superiority of the Danes in this arm would seriously impair any chance of a decisive victory. He therefore determined to encourage the nobility, and even those who did not rank as noble, to form a new class of knight. These cavalrymen should be exempt from the universal system of taxation which had superseded the antiquated provincial methods through the Things. The new system of taxation was fair, and inevitable in an organised state, but it was extremely unpopular. It strengthened the central power of the state, but as the collection was based on the new firmly established feudal system, the nobles considered that it might still further increase their power. When this new offer from the king was promulgated, they saw an opportunity of evading the taxes themselves and yet keeping the feudal dues which they received. As a temporary measure of defence, the plan was a success, but it created a new social class outside the law, and the cleavage between this "mounted noble" and the ordinary small landowner soon presented a grave danger to the stability of the state. For the first time in Swedish history is found "a privileged class", and when this order is established it is not easy to destroy nor to enforce equality before the law. However, in the reign of Magnus and Torgils, the evils of the measure did not make themselves felt, nor did the feud between the old and new nobility break out openly. The rulers were strong men and gave peace and prosperity to the land, and the only open opposition came from the ecclesiastical party who, in the following reigns, demanded the same exemption from taxation as that enjoyed by the knights. The Church was strengthening its hold and saw its growing powers threatened. Torgils was not the actual king, but as Marshal had presided over the Council, and had been particularly active and successful in the pursuit of the Finnish expansionist policy. He was too vigorous in some ways, because, after building the fortress at Viborg, he got involved in war with the Russians, and there is reason to believe that he advocated the seizure of land on the South Baltic—Carelia and Estonia—to ensure for Sweden what in later times was called the Dominion of the Baltic.

Sweden was not yet strong enough to carry out such a policy, but it is worth recording that it was even contemplated, as it is evidence of the immense progress attained by the Folkungs since 1250. Torgils continued the policy of the great Birger and Magnus, and was strong to oppose the demands for exemption of Church lands from taxation, and wise enough, it is said, to have the unified code of laws written, so that it could be known which of the provincial laws had fallen into desuetude or been modified. He continued to act as regent for Magnus' young son Birger even after the latter had come of age and, as regent, he made the same error as did Earl Birger before him. Birger's younger brothers Eric and Valdemar were created Duke of Sweden and Duke of Finland respectively. An even more savage and barbaric war broke out between the brothers within four years. Eric sought the aid of the Norwegians and eventually married Ingeborg, the eldest daughter of King Haakon. Birger and Torgils relied on Danish support. The more powerful nobles backed the two dukes against the king. Pretending to wish for a peaceful settlement, the dukes invited their brother king Birger to Hatuna, but after a royal banquet, they threw him into prison. Finally in 1310 a treaty for a partition of Sweden into three parts was arranged by the King of Denmark at Helsingborg, the port of Skåne facing Denmark. Sweden was once more torn by factions, and what made the situation worse, the factions were legalised by the treaty. In 1317 Birger staged his revenge for what he termed "Eric's surprise joke at Hatuna". After a peace banquet in honour of his two brothers in his castle at Nyköping, he hurled them into a dungeon and threw the keys into the river so that his brothers died of starvation. The nobles rose once more, captured his young son, whom they beheaded, and drove the almost demented Birger into exile in Denmark, where he died in 1321. Power thus fell into the hands of the nobles, where it remained except for short periods, until the break up of the union two hundred years later.

In 1319 Magnus, Eric's only son, was elected king at the age of three, and as his grandfather, King Haakon, also died in the same year, he became King of Norway as the heir by direct hereditary succession. The union of Norway and Sweden (1319–1371) was purely nominal, as the governments, such as they were, remained in a separate caucus of nobles for each country. A league of nobles managed to deprive the Queen Mother Ingeborg of all power, and even forced her to dismiss her Danish adviser. In this miserable state of affairs, it was only the greater discord and misery which existed in Denmark that saved Sweden.

Denmark was on the verge of complete dissolution. Torn with religious and civil wars, dismembered by foreign princes, the country had fallen to the lowest point in its history. When the Scanians rebelled, Gerard III, Count of Holstein (not the nominal king) sold the provinces of Skåne and Blekinge to Sweden. The Scanians, fearing the rule of some German prince, had appealed to Magnus for aid and had little cause for opposing this wholesale purchase. Eight years later (1340) Halland was also sold for the immense sum of Kronor 15,000,000—the equivalent of nearly two millions in our money to-day. Thus in one of the blackest moments of Swedish history, she had succeeded in bringing the whole of modern Sweden under one rule. The price, however, was ruinous. The Norwegians, who gained nothing, objected strongly and their State Council sitting in a joint session with the Swedish Council decided on the election to the throne of Norway, of Magnus' younger son Haakon, as soon as he became of age in 1355. Eric, the elder son, would be King of Sweden and thus separation would be attained. Until then, Magnus would remain as regent, but the Norwegian Council of Nobles would retain all power. This was the first repercussion to what seemed a good purchase to secure unity in the country. The treasury, however, was empty before the purchase, and now became utterly bankrupt. In desperation, Magnus borrowed from the Church and his own nobles. Even then he could not pay his way. Early in his reign the Russian

Wars had been ended by the first Slav-Swedish treaty in history at Nöteborg. The Swedes were not able to profit much by the Torgils' adventure—the chief beneficiaries had unintentionally been the Teutonic Knights, who had become possessed of Livonia and Estonia. In his extremity Magnus started a second Russian War, hoping to pay off some of his mortgages and debts out of the spoils. For twelve years he fought, and the only results were new debts. He had mortgaged his castles and sold his demesnes from which the royal revenues were derived. His only remaining source of income lay in the herring fisheries and the market dues which accrued from the German traders to Falsterbo and other Scanian trade centres. It is only fair to Magnus' reputation to say that he considered that from the profits of the Scanian herring fisheries he would be able to pay off the mortgages. A contemporary account gives some idea of their worth. No fewer than forty thousand boats containing three hundred thousand fishermen frequented the Straits for two months. "As God commandeth the herring pass, yet only for two months, in such multitudes that it is a great miracle, so many in the Sound (Öresund and the south of the Skagerak) that one may cut them with a sword.[1] The second miracle is that forty thousand boats with crews of six to ten men from all Germany and Prussia gather solely to fish herring. Five hundred large ships (later called "busses") do nothing but salt them in barrels. . . . Three hundred thousand men do nothing else. . . . I wrote this so that God's grace to Christendom manifested in the abundance of herring for Lent might be recognised." The income from this source alone exceeded all other sources of revenue to the Danish crown. Magnus was surely justified in thinking that this would be his. Unhappily for Sweden, Valdemar, nick-named *Atterdag*, from his famous Low-German expression (perhaps the nearest equivalent is the Yorkshire "Bah Gum"),[2] succeeded in welding Denmark together again. He defeated the Duke of Holstein, and, through the crafty mediation of the Duke of Mecklenburg, a quarrel was picked with Sweden. Skåne was retaken and the king's finances were irretrievably wrecked. To crown all, the

---

[1] This is no exaggeration. When serving on a herring drifter in the North Sea, I have seen a piece of net the size of the top of a grand piano, so choked with herring that four men could hardly haul it up.

[2] Literally, *Atterdag* means "There is a to-morrow". It denoted dogged determination and avoidance of precipitate action.

Black Death swept the country—towns and villages alike—the population was reduced by a third.

The land was ripe for a revolution. It only needed a spark and a gentle breeze to fan the flames. The saintly S. Birgitta (Bridget) was a Folkung, and was the first Swede to have any European influence. She was married to Ulf, a State Counsellor, and was appointed Mistress of the Robes. She was exactly forty years of age when her husband died in 1343. She "took as her second consort Christ Himself" having received revelations as to her mission. Saint though Birgitta became, she still remained a politician. Like a female Isaiah, she roundly abused her patron the king, and her mistress Blanche of Namur. She condemned the deal with Valdemar Atterdag, and warned the king that he was "a flatterer who piped to snare his bird", while the smooth-tongued Duke of Mecklenburg was "a snake in the grass". She proved right, but her outspoken criticisms were not palatable. She desired to found a monastery for monks and nuns. The objects were to purify the life of the people, including the nobles and court, and to promote Christianity in a purer form, laying stress on acts of piety and good conduct rather than theology, and to form an educational centre with a common Scandinavian language. The king very magnanimously granted her his estate at Vadstena with its round and rather grim squat tower, though she did not cease to flay him and castigate the sins of his queen. However, she had to visit Rome to receive permission to found her new "co-educational" order. The Pope was reluctant to grant it, but after some long delay, the new order of "Bridgittines" was permitted, but it was subject to the rule of S. Augustine. It became highly popular on the Continent, but did not achieve the same success in Vadstena, where it had become so involved in politics. Finally, in 1363, the nobles were so hard driven by the state of the country that, incited by her denunciations, they declared against the king and so began the final schism which ended by one party of nobles inviting Margaret of Denmark to act as Lady of Sweden in 1389. Probably the schism would have come at a later date even if the fiery Birgitta had not ascribed all the evils that beset her country to the weakness and sinfulness of Magnus. These were not her only politico-religious achievements. On good authority it is stated that on one of her visits to the Pope at Avignon, she saw "her visions" and heard "the voices". On seeing the Pope next day, she raged at His Holiness for his pusillanimity in remaining at Avignon. So convincing and threatening was this vital saint of some seventy winters, that Gregory XI had no peace of mind till he followed her advice three years later, and returned to Rome. Full of honours, she died in Rome on her way back from a pilgrimage in 1373, and was canonised in 1391. Her work did not perish with her. Bridgittine convents were founded all over Europe. One, in Middlesex, was richly endowed by Henry V, and never ceased to keep in close contact with Vadstena. Though suppressed during the Reformation, it was refounded in the reign of Queen Mary, removed to Portugal during the repressive period following the Armada, and did not return to England till the more tolerant days of the twentieth century. It still survives in Devonshire to bear witness to the universality of the founder's ideals. It was perhaps a happy thing for her that she did not reach Sweden; she would have seen her country lying prostrate, waiting only for some foreigner to enslave her, or to shame her into action to free herself from the selfish domination of the nobles and regain her pride of place among the northern nations. The final act of the drama, telling of the follies of the king imported from Mecklenburg, and the repressions of his chancellor, Bo Jonsson, must be left to the next chapter.

TABLE OF KINGS DURING THE UNION
(1389–1523)

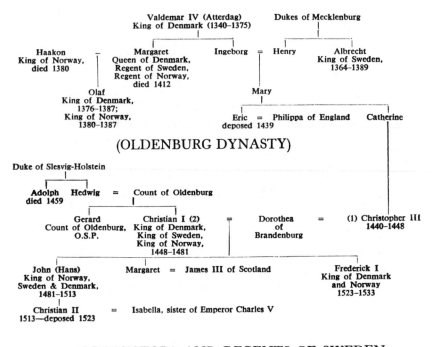

(OLDENBURG DYNASTY)

PROTECTORS AND REGENTS OF SWEDEN DURING THE UNION

Engelbrekt, 1435–1436
Karl Knutson, 1436–1440, *elected* King of Sweden and Norway, 1448–1457,
         deposed by Christian I in 1457, returned 1467–1470.
Sten Sture the Elder, 1470–1503
    (John Hans, 1497–1501).
Svante Sture, 1503–1512.
Sten Sture the Younger, 1512–1520.

CHAPTER V

DENMARK AND THE UNION

THE history of Denmark in the centuries preceding the Union presents a picture of almost continual gloom but, when a bright period relieves the gloom, the inherent strength and powers of resistance displayed by the Danes are almost unique in European history. When the whole country seems dismembered and over-run by a greedy horde of foreign princes, a Danish leader arises, throws back the invaders, and soon becomes a conqueror of neighbouring lands.

This astonishing resilience, even after a hundred years of continuous civil war and bloodshed, when nine kings out of ten met violent deaths or imprisonment or both, needs some explanation. That a fleet of five hundred ships, and in one instance no less than a thousand, could be equipped and win outstanding naval victories and be effective on amphibious expeditions in the Baltic, was due to the seafaring coastal people who were not so affected as the agricultural population. Trade was never wholly at a standstill, and in a general way it is true to say that the marauding nobles were not seamen. Their interests lay on the land, their strength in their armies and their bridge into Denmark was through Holstein and Slesvig. Boats were necessary for passing from island to island, but land battles, not sea battles resulted, which allowed the Danish fishermen and seamen some immunity from the worst of the evils. The wars bore heavily on the peasant and small tenant farmer, but the nature of the armies left some potential reserve which could be called upon by energetic and capable kings such as the first three Valdemars (1157–1241) or Valdemar Atterdag a century later. The peasants strongly resented military service outside their own land and the Danish nobles and German princes had their own retinues of fighting men, similar indeed to the housecarls of Canute the Great. These could most easily be combined into a trained army such as fought in the Thirty Years' War to the detriment of the whole of Germany.

The nobles paid these men out of feudal dues and rents, and the peasants suffered to such a degree that at times the so-called freemen were reduced to serfdom. In theory the lawmen and local landthings were still responsible for local government and the landthing could propose a law to be presented to the king, but for the greater part of three centuries there was no central power to enforce it. Prominent men were called to *parlamenta* before Eric Klipping's Parlamentum in 1282, but the political theory of Denmark, if so it can be called, was that of a free and democratic peasantry under a patriarchal king. However, given a strong king who could quell the turbulent nobility, the peasantry did form a potential reserve of manpower. It must not be thought that the Dane had lost his prowess as a fighter. On the few occasions on which the peasants united, they fought magnificently. In Skåne they resisted the religious innovations with no little success in the twelfth century Two centuries later six thousand sturdy peasants of Ditmarsken defeated King Hans' trained army of fourteen thousand men, and not until 1559 could the dukes of Holstein curb their love of freedom. In 1534 Skipper Clement led a peasants' revolt in North Jutland and completely defeated an army composed of the nobles' bands. These three examples of military valour were performed by peasants in three provinces widely separated, and serve to show that the dogged spirit of the countryside was not confined to one district, and was kept alive through the most troublous times. It is, however, true that on none of these occasions was the finest branch of the Danish regular army employed against them—the cavalry arm. The Danes were the first to use cavalry as a cavalry arm and not as mounted nobles surrounded by attendant foot soldiers. This no doubt accounted for their superiority to anything in Sweden or North Germany till the fourteenth century, and for some of their recuperative powers after seeming impotence.

The foreign menace of German princes had its counterpart in ecclesiastical administration also. The English priests introduced by Canute had succeeded in achieving a peaceful conversion, and the Church became the centre of culture. Unfortunately however, the Archbishop of Hamburg was the spiritual head of the Scandinavian Church. That the Primate could not speak the language had always been a grievance, but when Jutland was divided into four bishoprics and Skåne possessed its Lund, the question of a Danish archbishopric became acute. This was opposed by Germans, who had gained some influence in the southern provinces so close to Hamburg and Bremen. German bishops had been proposed. Bishops were powerful nobles and some able soldiers. The most skilful Danish strategist before General Rantzau was Absalon (Axel), Archbishop of Lund, who planned the capture of Rügen. Thus, for the safety of Denmark, a Danish archbishop was a necessity. The king himself made the pilgrimage to Rome and was granted leave to found the desired see at Lund in 1103. Asser, the first to receive the crozier, received congratulations from Anselm, whom he resembled in some respects. Troubles began almost at once because, owing to the more direct contact with Rome, he tried to enforce a stricter discipline. The peasants protested against the titles and the celibacy of the clergy, rose in rebellion, and tried to prevent the building of the beautiful cathedral which was to supersede the old church. No sooner had this trouble been overcome by royal help, than the Concordat of Worms (1122), which was to place the Church outside the law, caused a rupture between the Pope and the king. This was never formally settled and the Danish kings refused to give up the right of appointment of archbishop and bishops. A compromise was reached and, though the chapters received *congé d'élire*, the name of the king's nominee was sent to them and they had to confirm his appointment. The result was that if the king were strong he controlled the Church, but the papal power was ever on the watch for the assertion of its rights. This trouble continued till the Reformation. On many occasions an interdict was imposed, and more than once the archbishop was temporarily suppressed and even suffered imprisonment.

Though heralded by disturbances, the new regime brought many advantages to the land, and its influence affected the lives of the people very deeply For some two hundred years there was a feverish outburst of church building—sometimes old wooden churches were rebuilt, sometimes entirely new churches were erected. Consequently the number of parish priests grew rapidly and so did their power. This activity extended from Skåne, with its three hundred and fifty churches and cathedral, to Jutland and Fünen. The many Danish churches, with their rounded arches dating from the thirteenth century, still remain to bear witness to these changes. It was almost a new religion which had arrived—

a colourful French influence which appealed to those Danes who had accepted Christianity as expounded by the English, but who still had a superstitious fear of their old gods. Following the arrival of Asser and the Benedictines, pious observances helped to counter their old fears. Church bells called to prayer morning and evening. Men and women knelt in the fields, they repeated their *Ave Marias* and *Paternosters*, they crossed themselves, and need no longer fear the wrath of their old deities. The priest's blessing was sought to bring success to harvest of land and sea. No new ship would be launched without the priest. The old feasts and pagan songs could not live side by side with the new religion, and the natural desires for emotional expression were satisfied by the growth of song and dance throughout the countryside. This fashion is said to have come from France also, and undoubtedly the taste for music was encouraged if not directed by the hymns and chants of the revived Catholic Church. The folk-dancing in the villages became immensely popular and the feasts of the Church were the occasions for these festivities.

With the establishment of the Danish Primate came the establishment of centres of culture. Even the warlike Absalon was not unmindful of the need for learning. Largely owing to him, were written the early histories by Saxo and others, and education began not to be a monopoly of those who could afford a foreign teacher. A Danish "College" was established in the University of Paris, though Copenhagen University was not founded till 1479.

Thus was gradually formed a rallying point for civilisation in the scattered parts of Denmark, which helped to save the country when ravaged and stricken by its endless wars. But there was no sense of national or even personal loyalty until the rise of Valdemar the Great, and his greatness was largely due to his great archbishop.

How far Denmark was from being one, and how nearly she became a part of the German Empire, can be gleaned from the manner in which the throne fell to Valdemar, posthumous son of Canute Lavard. At nineteen years of age, Canute Lavard had been appointed Jarl of South Jutland with the idea of stopping the incursions of the Wends.[1] So successful had he been that he was

---

[1] The term " Wends " was loosely applied by the Germans to various branches of the Slav race. It is here used in the more limited sense of Slavs inhabiting

called " Prince of the Wends ". Finally he was granted Holstein
by the German king, thus for the first time since the River Eider
was recognised as the southern boundary, a Dane was legally, in
his own right, Jarl of South Jutland (Slesvig) and ruler of Holstein
on the south of the Eider. He became so powerful and popular
that he excited the jealousy of the royal family and was murdered
by the king's son, Magnus, with the connivance of his father.
Eric Emune ("not-to-be-forgotten "), a half-brother of Canute
Lavard, raised a rebellion and after three years' civil war, slew
Magnus, five bishops, and sixty priests at the battle of Fötevik in
Skåne. The king was also massacred and Eric seized the crown
and managed to hold it for three years by murdering his brother
and nephew. On his assassination, four claimants appeared in the
field. Eric Lam was elected, but after feeble efforts to drive back
the Wends and other invaders, he retired to a monastery. Sweyn
III, a bastard son of Eric Emune, was the most powerful of the
other claimants, and temporarily secured the throne by introducing
German mercenaries. He finally accepted the proposal of the
Emperor Barbarossa that Denmark should become a fief of the
Empire. The Emperor saw that his power would be extended to
the Baltic and that by these means the unruly Wends, always a
disturbing Slav and pagan element, might be kept in some sort
of order or exterminated. Sweyn was in the hands of the
Emperor, being his guest at Merseburg, and considered that only
by his help could he crush his two rival claimants, Canute, son
of Magnus, and Valdemar, son of Lavard. However, for ten years
the triangular war continued, until the Bishop of Ribe mediated
between the combatants, and it was agreed that Denmark should
be divided into three parts. Sweyn was to have Skåne and
Bornholm, Valdemar Jutland (Holstein was his by right), and
Canute Fünen, Sjaelland and the islands. This page of history is
sufficient to prove the baneful influence of Denmark's German
neighbours and also that the rulers had no conception of a
national kingdom. Their idea consisted of royal possessions which
could be given away or divided at will. Each of the three took the
title of king.

   At the proposal of Sweyn, a mighty feast was prepared at

" Venden ", as the Scandinavians called the country stretching from near Lübeck
along the South Baltic coast to the Vistula, and just beyond. Its centre was the
Isle of Rügen.

Roskilde to celebrate this peaceful settlement and the end of internecine war. Towards the end of the banquet, Sweyn's guards rushed in and slew Canute, but Valdemar, a quick thinker, extinguished the lights and as all began to fight all, he cut his way through the guards. Sweyn never got out of Jutland, which was the staunch supporter of Valdemar, son of their beloved Jarl. He was surrounded by a hostile peasant force under Valdemar and finally stabbed by a peasant near Viborg.

Thus Valdemar found himself the sole survivor and king of a Denmark wasted by twenty-five years of civil war, with Wendish bands roaming over a third of the land.

The astonishing success of Valdemar in restoring the power and partial prosperity of Denmark was due to his wisdom, patience and firmness of purpose. Displaying no little statesmanship and insight, he realised the three main causes of trouble: the disputed succession, the Wendish incursions, and interference by Germans. The first was settled by eliminating his rivals and securing the coronation of his seven-year-old son, Canute, as his successor. On the same day as the coronation, the old Archbishop Eskild published a Papal Bull granting canonisation to the founder of the line—the murdered Canute Lavard at whose grave, according to the Bull and popular tradition, many miracles had been performed. At one stroke he had freed himself from rivals and secured the support of the Church. Valdemar then turned against the Wends. These expeditions were undertaken in the name of Christianity, and their success was in no small measure due to his faithful friend, the new Archbishop of Lund. This robust prelate had studied military strategy as well as theology. Surprise tactics led to the fall of Arcona in 1169. Cavalry was transported by sea, and the whole of Rügen fell into his hands. The heathen temple was destroyed and the great wooden effigy of the four-headed Svantevit was burned as firewood. This was followed up by a further expedition which led to the capture of the Wendish capital. The Wends were baptised and Rügen was annexed to the Bishopric of Roskilde. Henry the Lion was furious at the Danish victory, and demanded half of the tribute and spoils as overlord of the Wends. With admirable restraint, Valdemar acceded to this demand, as he felt that Denmark could not yet face the strength of Germany. When, however, Henry incited the Wends on the mainland to further incursions, he led another Danish army and captured Stettin. The far-seeing Absalon realised that a naval base was necessary to protect Sjaelland and the east end of the Sound from pirates and marauders, and so founded *Kaupmanna Havn* or the Merchants Haven. This new town was greatly favoured by the king, and grew into the Köbenhavn or Copenhagen, the present capital. On the site of Absalon's Castrum de Havn stands the palace of Christiansborg of to-day. The foundation of this city had no little bearing on Danish history. It gave Denmark a potential grip over the Baltic, and also brought her closer to the province of Skåne across the Öresund. When Valdemar, "Primus Sclavorum expugnator et dominator, pacis conservator", died in 1282 at the early age of forty-seven, it allowed his son to carry on his policy of Danish expansion to the east with less risk of the extended communications being cut. Before his death, no German king could challenge the Danish power. Canute VI, again with Absalon's help, conquered Pomerania and Mecklenburg and, as ruler of the Wendish lands from the Elbe to the Vistula, assumed the title of Rex Sclavorum, a title still held by the kings of Denmark, though the late King Christian X was crowned "King of Denmark and Iceland". Valdemar II the Victorious carried the Danish arms as far as the Gulf of Finland. After a bitter battle against the pagan Estonians near Reval, in which the Danish flag (*Dannebrog*) was miraculously dropped from heaven, the city fell to him. Here again the Church and State went hand in hand. A bishopric was established, a fortress built, and the Danish flag incorporated in the city's arms. Before his accession as Duke of Slesvig he had conquered the territories south of the Eider, and after his coronation, Frederick II, the Hohenstaufen Emperor, recognised him as Lord of Norldalbingia, a territory including Hamburg and Lübeck.

In 1220 Valdemar held sway over the greatest empire since Canute the Great. From the Elbe to Estonia, he was supreme. Nor was his dominion confined to the coastal strip which made the Baltic a Danish lake. Besides Mecklenburg, parts of Prussia bowed to his rule, and the Pope Honorius III gladly authorised the Danish rule over all the lands which might be conquered.

Great though this empire appeared with its overwhelming maritime power which could assemble fourteen hundred ships to invade Estonia, it had feet of clay. It was in some ways like that of Canute, based on a great personality. Its weakness lay not so much in its long coast line, for that was, in a sense, a source of strength as long as Denmark maintained her unchallenged supremacy at sea, but the conquests had not only excited the jealousy of German princes, they had also been carried out in too close association with the militant Church. The reign of Valdemar I had ended in Skåne peasant revolts against Absalon's stricter ecclesiastical regime. Nobles resented the appointment of his relations to high offices. The acquisition of Hamburg produced an acute crisis leading to an ecclesiastical war led by the treacherous archbishop Valdemar illegally elected to the rival see of Bremen. Round him centred the malcontents of Germany who wanted to see the overthrow of Valdemar the Victorious. The climax came when Henry, Count of Schwerin, arrived back from a crusade to find part of his fief transferred to the king. He went to get compensation from the king, who was hunting on a small island off Fünen. The king entertained him royally after a day's sport but, so the story runs, was himself overcome with wine. The count seized him and his son, the heir, and carried them off to his castle in Dannenburg. There lay Valdemar in prison for two and a half years and no one raised his voice in protest against this treachery except Honorius III. The threat of excommunication left Count Henry quite unmoved, as he was strongly supported by the Emperor Frederick II, now jealous of Valdemar's power. Denmark was thrown into chaos, with no ruler and no prince as heir. Finally Valdemar was allowed to return, but to a kingdom shorn of its power and its newly-won lands. The River Eider once more became the boundary, cutting Slesvig from Holstein, and only two monuments remained to mark the great rule of the Valdemars—the island of Rügen and the fortress city of Copenhagen. The monastic annals of the day succinctly put it thus: "The crown fell off the head of the Danes. From that time forth they became a laughing-stock to their neighbours through their civil wars and destruction of each other, and the lands which they had won with honour were not only lost, but caused great disasters to their own kingdom."

That sums up what resulted from the dramatic kidnapping of the king. In one night the empire collapsed like a pack of cards, and for a hundred years, 1241–1340, war after war brought Denmark back to the state from which it had been rescued.

The only stable institution was the Church. It is, however, true to say that the status of the Thing had recovered from the ignominious position in which the Valdemars had found it. When Eric Emune had been asked by the peasants at Ribe to preside at their Thing and hear their grievances against a landowner named Plog, the latter attended also, showed his contempt for the jurisdiction of the assembly and the king's acceptance of its request to attend, by stabbing the king with his spear. Unmolested he then returned to his own estates. By the end of the Valdemar's reign, the laws for all the three main divisions of Denmark, Skåne, Jutland and Sjaelland had been written down, and even if they were not strictly kept during the long succession of following civil wars, they were there and stood for justice and a rallying point for the " lawmen ". The civil frame assumed a more legal aspect by the compilation of a code of laws (*Pov samling*) and of a Danish Census corresponding in some respects to our Domesday Book,[1] and after Valdemar's release and final failure to recover Holstein in 1227, he devoted the last fourteen years of his reign to improving the internal administration. Without his reforms, it is doubtful whether Denmark could have stood the strain of another century of war. She had no friends save the Church, which had realised the benefit she had conferred on Northern Europe by driving out the pagans. Two further results of her conquests left their imprint on history: they had drawn a rough line running north and south between Roman and Greek Church, and a similar, though shorter and less regular, line between Slavs and Western Europe.

In the gloomy period preceding the reign of Valdemar IV (Atterdag), the harmony between Church and State was broken and added to the confusion and misery. One pious and venerable

---

[1] Valdemar's *Jordeborg*, or more specifically the Danish book of land taxation, consists of registrative notes from the thirteenth century. The notes were for practical use in the Royal Chancery. The first half of the manuscript is continuous and is usually called the Main Part. There is no methodical plan and the subdivisions for the *Herreds* (small counties) contain a heterogeneous collection of information on Royal income and Royal land property. There are numerous empty spaces apparently for additions and alterations. " Possibly the Main Part is the beginning of a book of reference on which work was begun in the Chancery in A.D. 1231 . . . any generally acknowledged result does not exist ". " Despite difficulties of interpretation (the Danish word *Fortolkning* applies to problems of meaning—not to linguistic difficulties) it is one of the most important sources of information during the Middle Ages " as regards social conditions and place names. Owing to translations into Latin, it is sometimes called *Liber census Daniae*, but it is somewhat misleading to call it the Danish Domesday Book. Vide *Den lille Salmonsen* Redigeret (Marke and Raunkjaer) Vol. VII, page 93.

archbishop fighting for the same principles as Thomas à Becket was chained up in a dungeon with foxes' tails tied to his hair. The king died suddenly three months later. A monk was said, probably incorrectly, to have administered poison. Another archbishop, after a year's degrading imprisonment, escaped to Rome, and the king was forced to pay a heavy fine to be rid of one of the many interdicts imposed. Thus the one civilising and stabilising force suffered oppression and unfortunately many of the monasteries and bishoprics lost their sense of discipline and love of culture in the struggle for existence.

In this period of spiritual darkness the people clung to their parish priests, but their isolation—almost separation—from a central authority, had the effect, not unnaturally, of promoting a disregard for authority which paved the way for the Lutherans in later years. In certain districts the peasant class was less affected than in others, but any power they had possessed slipped from them. On rare occasions, however, the people raised their voice and, just after a violent dispute between Church and State, Eric Klipping promulgated a charter which was to found a " Parlamentum " to make new laws and enforce the old. In theory the king had been the patriarchal guardian of a democratic peasantry. Some clauses resemble those of the Magna Carta, but its origin, objects, and results, are so different that to call it the Magna Carta of Denmark is grossly misleading. Prominent men had been called " ad Parlamenta " on special occasions, and it was at one of these meetings at Vordingborg in 1282 that " the best men, lay and learned," discussed and then published the written constitution. This constitution was often ignored, especially the clause to call an annual " Parlamentum ", but, like the legal codes of Valdemar, it did remain on record and was the foundation of the Danehof of the fourteenth century and the father of the present Constitution.

With these few exceptions the state of Denmark in 1340 was even worse than two hundred years before. There was no question of her power stretching south of the Eider. Gerard, Duke of Holstein, had become guardian of the so-called king from 1326–1330. On the king's coming of age, the kingdom was divided up among foreign princes, and the lion's share went to the duke, who consolidated his position in Jutland on the king's death in 1332. He sold Skåne to Sweden to raise money for his own ends, but he could only just retain his power against the other robbers. Fighting continued incessantly and Gerard, in Jutland, reduced "peasant and landowner alike to serfdom". Finally one, Nils Ebbesön, murdered him while praying with his chaplain, guarded safely as he thought by German troops. There was a national clamour for the Valdemar then living, and the dead duke's sons came to terms with him. Though elected king, Valdemar found an empty treasury, and Sjaelland, Fünen and South Jutland were in the hands of others. Even part of the north of Jutland was mortgaged and this he redeemed out of the dowry of his wife Hedvig, sister of Duke Valdemar, ruler of South Jutland and part of Fünen.

Many glamorous tales are told of this able young king, and it is hard to estimate his true character, but his ability must be appreciated by comparing the torn and tattered Denmark of 1340 with the Denmark of 1375 which brought about the Scandinavian Union. In nine years, he had recovered all Denmark except a portion of Slesvig. His empty treasury was replenished by selling his shadowy rights in Estonia to the Teutonic Knights, and by forfeiting the estates of landowners who had tried to rise against him after the Black Death. Some of the means by which he managed to oust the landowners and divert their dues to the royal purse do not bear too close a scrutiny. This restless and adventurous financier approached John, King of France, with an offer to invade England with twelve thousand men in return for a large sum of money. Having defeated Edward III, Valdemar would then raise his claim to be King of England (as a descendant of Canute) and the Franco-Danish alliance would dominate Europe, including their common enemies in Germany. This sounded plausible, but the battle of Poitiers in 1356 rather spoilt the plan.

Foiled in this scheme, he turned his attention to Sweden who, by the Duke of Holstein's iniquitous bargain, held Skåne and the other coastal provinces, thus depriving the Danish Crown of its most certain and most lucrative source of income.

Through crafty designs and the unscrupulous and dishonest mediation of the Duke of Mecklenburg, he found himself in possession of the old provinces by 1360. Not only that, but he was master of a full treasury and, with its usual gift for recovery, the Danish naval power had only one rival in the Baltic—the Hanseatic League. What were the ultimate aims of Valdemar at this point, it is impossible to say. He may have envisaged the Scandinavian Union or, on the other hand, he may have sought an alliance with

Norway, and a stranglehold on Sweden sufficiently tight to cripple her for ever. His move was against the island of Gottland with its powerful Hanseatic town of Visby, nominally under the suzerainty of Sweden. Without even bothering to advance any pretext, the Danish fleet swooped down and captured Visby and with it the whole island. Valdemar assumed the title of "King of the Goths" and thought that he could now dominate both the Hanseatic League and Sweden in its hopeless state of anarchy. In 1363, his daughter Margaret was married at the tender age of ten to Haakon, King of Norway. The Hanseatic League, enraged at the interference with their commerce, equipped their fleet to open the narrow straits, but it was decisively defeated off Helsingborg. However, that double-faced mediator, the Duke of Mecklenburg, secured the election of his nephew to the Swedish throne, and no longer was prepared to countenance the growing power of Denmark. In 1368, in alliance with the League, Mecklenburg stopped any further development of the Danish power. Valdemar saw the castle of Copenhagen and Falsterbo fall into their hands. He appealed to the Danish Council and the Danes were able to negotiate a peace at Stralsund. Its terms were humiliating, as the Hansa got free trading rights in the Sound, and the right of free passage to their Bergen station. Denmark, however, was not utterly beaten and Valdemar, before his death, recovered South Jutland.

When he died, Margaret immediately secured the election of her son Olaf, aged five, to be King of Denmark under her regency, to the exclusion of the Mecklenburg claimant. Thus she became Regent in 1376 when Queen of Norway, and her son Olaf was not only nominal King of Denmark but heir to the throne of Norway as well. Four years later she became Regent of Norway also, as the king, her husband, died and Olaf was only nine years of age. Things moved in her favour, because Albrecht of Mecklenburg, the King of Sweden, had become completely overshadowed by his greedy Viceroy, Bo Jonsson. In 1387 Olaf died and so did Bo Jonsson. Two years previously Margaret had conciliated the counts of Holstein by offering them Slesvig, which they had already seized, provided they recognised her as suzerain, and recognised Olaf as "the true heir to Sweden". This direct challenge and insult to Albrecht roused his indignation, but stirred him to no direct action during the life of Bo Jonsson. Albrecht owed his position in Sweden to his uncle, also named Albrecht, and had he lived in the twentieth century, he would have been written off as suffering from an inferiority complex. In his youth he had been the pawn of his uncle, and then he was completely overshadowed by one of his Swedish subjects, and finally this girl-queen flouted him. This poor alien king, endowed with a third-rate brain, thought that he saw his opportunity to assert his manhood when both Bo Jonsson and Olaf died in the same year. He at once tried to seize the vast estates of his ministers by right of escheat, and at the same time assert his authority as an autocratic king. He did not know Sweden or the Swedish nobility. The latter, remembering Margaret's claim, invited her to be "Lady Mistress of Sweden, protector of the Realm". She accepted with alacrity and no little tact. The king put up some show of resistance, but was utterly defeated at the battle of Falköping in 1389. The dream had come true—Sweden, Norway, Denmark with Finland and Iceland were united under one Regent Queen and all that was required to perpetuate the union was the consent of all three countries to one and the same hereditary heir.

The young queen propitiated the Swedes by enrolling as a Swedish Bridgittine. The nobles of "both countries were stricken with fear and wonder at the wisdom and strength of this royal lady". The Norwegians knew her well before this time, for she had become their queen in 1363, as a child of ten; she had been educated there by the daughter of the Swedish S. Bridget who had received canonisation, a distinction rare and almost unique for a married woman. They knew that she possessed a cool, calculating mind and almost masculine courage. She has been compared with Queen Elizabeth to her advantage on the score that although Elizabeth had two religious factions to placate, she had exceptionally competent advisers and loyal citizens who placed their country before religion, whereas Margaret had to rely on her own judgement to control three separate peoples hitherto disunited among themselves. Neither queen had a son to succeed nor a kinsman who stood out as the obvious successor to her subjects.

With her clear political insight, Margaret saw that the Union would have little chance of becoming permanent unless all three countries agreed to adopt the principle of hereditary succession, and vest their right in the person of one man, and that must be Eric, her great nephew, already accepted by Norway and Denmark.

Try as she would she failed to persuade the Swedish nobility, who cherished their right of election. At the Union of Kalmar in 1397, all three countries agreed to Eric, but the Swedes reserved the right of election, which she realised jeopardised the whole of the Scandinavian Empire. However, she hoped that time would prove a healing force and that Eric's son would follow in due course. Paradoxical as it may appear, it was this very Union under a Danish king which not only started the separatist movement in Sweden but created a democratic government which ultimately forced the nobles to share their power with the peasants in the New Sweden of Modern Times.

CHAPTER VI

THE TRANSITION TO MODERN TIMES—THE UNION (1389–1521)

IN England there has been an age-long custom to consider that Modern Times began with a jerk at the accession of Henry VII. It was convenient in many ways to split English History into two watertight compartments, with a solid wall between them, composed of the end of the Wars of the Roses and the beginning of the Tudors. Having fixed on this theory, historians then found many specious reasons to bolster up this contention. Pollard, in his *Factors of Modern History,* made a brave attack, showing how far back lay the deep roots of the outstanding movements of the New Age. "Natura nihil facit per saltum" was true of the passing of the Middle Ages. The new outlook meant that the old perpendicular lines of world estates, ecclesiastical and lay, and a feudal structure of class society were deeply scored across by horizontal lines of national governments. In other words, definite national boundaries were being more clearly defined, and within those boundaries the power of the nation would not brook outside interference. A duke or a count could no longer hold lands in two countries, he must belong to a certain nation. This process took time and did not achieve completion in all lands at the same time, nor were the old claims likely to be abandoned without a struggle. The last country to achieve a sense of nationality which could obliterate the class loyalties of nobility was Germany. The proximity of Denmark to this land, so slow in developing its new political sense, had a profound effect on the Union. The outlook of Sweden was more akin to the England of that time as regards political development. In no small degree, this difference of outlook is the fundamental reason of the failure of the Scandinavian Union. Minor causes, immediate causes resting on political errors, can be found in legion in its history during the fifteenth century, but the basic cause was the difference of national development of the two countries. A community of interests was strong enough to overcome the difference under the astute guidance of a gifted woman like Margaret, but on her death in 1412, it was only a matter of time before the ultimate separation would come. Nominally the Union lasted till 1521, but on each occasion that the Danish king attempted to make it real, his success was short-lived. This failure cannot be attributed to the character of the kings, but rather to the character of the Union. On the other two attempts to form a union, firstly in the middle of the nineteenth century and secondly in 1914, it was common fear of a common danger which led to the renewal of the Union movement. The outbreak of the Crimean War removed one danger, the defeat of Germany removed the other, and the movement died a natural death. Paradoxically as it may appear, the Union, which under Margaret gave such a show of promise, hastened the Separatist movement, intensi- fied the divergence of outlook and led to periodic wars for many centuries. The scars were not healed till after the Congress of Vienna in 1815.

Sweden emerged as a democratic country with great national leaders and took a leading place in Europe. Denmark sank into a dismal period of impotence known in her history as the Age of the Nobility.

The kingdom under Margaret's control in 1400 was the largest in Europe. England and France, in deadly combat, sought her aid. Henry V's sister married Eric, her heir. Although Henry and the other kings of Europe had slowly realised the rise of this powerful new state, they were never able to use its power. It was left to Gustavus Adolphus and Sweden to show Europe that Scandinavia had not lost the fighting qualities of the past. Sweden became a leading military force; Denmark was relegated to the position of a naval power whose help might be sought as a useful addition to the navy of a major state at war.

The Union forms the prelude to Modern Times in Scandinavia. At its dissolution two nations had arisen, though some of the boundaries had not been finally settled. The Sweden of which Gustavus Vasa became king differed slightly from the Sweden of to-day.

Skåne, Halland and Blekinge still remained Danish through the mediation of the Hansa towns. Norway, Iceland, the Faroes and Greenland remained attached to Denmark, though by previous agreement, Scotland remained in possession of the Orkneys and the Shetland Islands which had been part of the dowry of Margaret, daughter of Christian I, on her marriage to King James III.

The Universities of Uppsala (1477) and Copenhagen (1479) had been founded. The introduction of printing and the Renaissance spirit sponsored by Hemming Gadh, the tutor of Gustavus Vasa before his struggle for freedom and the popular resistance movement, had made Sweden a nation conscious of herself and of her independence. It is rare that we find contemporaries who can realise such subtle changes, for usually they cannot see the wood for the trees. But Gustavus Vasa was, as Svanström aptly puts it, a "crowned revolutionary. He bridled forces still lingering on from the anarchical conditions of the later Middle Ages. Nothing perhaps is more characteristic of him than his undisguised contempt for all that his opponents called ancient and time-honoured. To Gustav the present existed exclusively for the future." He ends his brilliant characterisation by Gustavus' own written words: "It seems to us that the conditions of this age are unlike those of the old, and that the world is ever changing." The Middle Ages for Sweden had passed for ever.

To trace the varied details of the Union would be tedious and unprofitable, but the story of the events which led to enduring changes throws much light on the history of the future as well as of the present.

Although Albrecht's insensate greed had so incensed the Swedes that Margaret had been called in to assist them, the throne was not won without a struggle. Albrecht brought in a German army from Mecklenburg to oppose her forces composed of Danes, Norwegians and Swedes. At Falköping, Albrecht was utterly defeated and taken prisoner. Even then Stockholm was not hers. It was strongly held by Germans supported by German burgesses, who proceeded to rob and murder Swedish citizens. German pirates, the Victuallers as they were called, proceeded to take advantage of the war and overran the Eastern Baltic. Nominally they were supporting the Germans in Stockholm; actually they preyed on shipping, raided the east coast of Sweden and captured Gotland. One of the chief sufferers was the Hanseatic League—a non-combatant, whose trade was severely dislocated. With the assistance of the Hanseatic fleet, a conclusion was put to hostilities in 1395, on terms greatly to the advantage of the Hansa. Albrecht was released on condition of paying a ransom of sixty thousand silver marks in three years' time or of surrendering Stockholm to Margaret. Meanwhile Stockholm was to be held in trust by the Hanseatic League. In 1398 Margaret secured the capital as Albrecht had failed to pay. Meanwhile the Teutonic Knights had captured Gottland and the Hansa was established in the chief town, Visby. The result of these first stormy years was the vastly increased prestige of the League, which was enabled to resume its trade on very advantageous terms, not merely in the Baltic itself, but at Bergen, which had been ravaged by the pirates.

Margaret began to set her house in order by securing the consent of the three countries to the succession of Eric, but, as previously stated, the Swedes stoutly maintained the elective principle of succession and from that position they would not budge. Margaret had to be content with this result of the Kalmar Conference. Her next move to secure a more efficient administration was to appoint bailiffs in Sweden, and to a lesser extent in Norway. This office has no exact parallel in history—it was not quite that of the English Sheriff or the Norman *Bailli*. It combined the duties and powers of a sheriff, seneschal, a Roman provincial governor and Cromwell's major-generals. The bailiff was responsible for law and order, for the extortion of taxes and, as a military governor, he had a military force at his disposal, and also could call for levies to serve in the army. The bailiffs' powers seemed to have increased considerably after their original appointment by Margaret. Her intention was probably to create officers not unlike the *bailli* in the States of Jersey—they degenerated into the worst type of gauleiter. In the twentieth century, they would have been termed " little Hitlers ", so wide were their powers. Doubtless, some form of royal officer directly dependent on the crown was a necessity, until order and trade had been restored, and anarchy and faction suppressed. How far the system was designed as a temporary measure cannot be judged with certainty, because certain features aroused almost immediate hostility. These bailiffs were nearly all Danish. They were given the estates of the Swedish aristocracy, who had been supporters of Albrecht or took the place of the old *husabyar* on the royal domains. After the dispute between Albrecht and Bo Jonsson, a wide intepretation of the term " royal demesne " could be employed with some show of legality. The majority of nobles felt their possessions in danger, while the Riksråd or Council saw its power being undermined. It seemed of little moment what legislation was passed, if the bailiffs had unlimited executive powers. The local Things still existed, but the people had no say in the matter of taxation, and no adequate method of appeal against injustice. However, had prosperity reigned or had the people felt that the hardships which they endured were in the interest of Sweden, the discontent might not have come to a head. Unfortunately, Margaret was engaged in a continuous series of wars on her southern boundaries. She was determined to have her defences secure by land and sea. Already, since 1408, Gotland had been restored by the Teutonic Knights to Sweden, but the Holstein question was Denmark's " running sore ". With admirable firmness, combined with tact, she managed to prevent any open rupture in Sweden, and appealed to the sentiment and good sense of the Swedes. Margaret enrolled as a Bridgittine at the Swedish foundation, a gesture in no way hampering her actions and at the same time informed the Riksråd that the Holstein affair was nearing a successful conclusion. Her success there would mean less taxes and a large increase in trade with Hamburg, Bremen and the Rhine ports. This was undoubtedly true, and an armistice had just been declared to settle the Holstein question to the satisfaction of all parties for all time.

In October 1412 Margaret herself went to review and give her personal thanks to members of the Danish fleet at Flensborg. She died suddenly during the night on board the flagship. Eric was recognised as king of her great Empire, which dominated the Baltic and the North. At her death, there seemed no foe capable of challenging her power. The Teutonic Knights, who had been a dangerous force, had suffered a crushing defeat at Tannenburg. The Hanseatic League had undergone a violent change from a patrician to a democratic government. This undoubtedly lowered its effectiveness as a naval power, though its mercantile interests were broadened. The only discernible weaknesses lay in Sweden and in Holstein, where the proposed armistice did not become translated into a peace. Eric immediately went to Sweden to soothe the rising discontent and at the same time show his power. He renewed promises of redress and implemented some of them before leaving Stockholm. The seizure of lands was stopped and some of the Crown Lands were restored, which would allow the revenues to be used for the benefit of Sweden and relief of taxation. His queen, the English Philippa, who inspired some affection and achieved some popularity, followed Margaret's example and became a Bridgittine at Vadstena, where she was ultimately buried.

Eric returned and found that the war had broken out again. He granted concessions to the Hanseatic League at Lübeck to gain their support, but he was unable to take the Holstein stronghold Gottorp. After his initial successes, Eric proved quite unable to cope with the difficulties which faced him. He had not the statesmanship of Margaret, and began by making two fatal errors. Firstly he appointed a most dissolute Dane as Archbishop of Uppsala, thus undoing all the benefits of his early visit of conciliation. Swedish susceptibilities were aroused and the situation seemed so threatening that he had to yield to pressure. The Archbishop was removed and made Bishop of Iceland. The Icelanders showed their disapproval and independence, however, by putting his head in a sack and throwing him into the sea. Eric's second blunder was in making promises of relief from taxation and from oppression by Danish bailiffs. It was perhaps Eric's misfortune, rather than his fault, which made the relief from taxation impossible. The wars could not be maintained without money which would be current in the Continent. Therefore the taxes on the peasants and miners were altered from payment in kind to payment in cash. There were not enough coins in circulation, so that an inflated currency was rapidly ordered, resulting in a sudden rise in prices. An economic crisis was the immediate result and the peasants and miners were the first victims. Eric alienated the Swedes by forsaking the example of Margaret of making frequent visits to Sweden and hearing grievances, even if she did not remedy them. It is true Philippa went in his stead, but Eric paid no heed to her entreaties on behalf of the peasants who were being driven to starvation and desperation. Instead, he added to his previous blunder of the appointment of the dissolute Dane as archbishop by sending a Jute, notorious for his cruelty, as his representative in the North. He robbed the peasants, harnessed the women in carts, let loose his soldiers to pillage whole villages, and finally, when some peasants resisted he had five hung up over a fire till they were smoked to death. That was the climax. It began the movement which led to the final separation, because at the first sign of revolt the miners and peasants found a leader.

The resistance movement was strongest in the Dalarna area, where feudalism had least hold over the mixed mining and agricultural population. There the Danish oppression became the most unbearable and there happened to lie the home of Engelbrekt Engelbrektson. He was a mine-owner, and was a representative of the Crown, ranking as a lesser noble. He was above the burgesses in status, his position carried with it many of the privileges and duties of the higher aristocracy. He himself was exempt from taxation, but responsible for the payment of the taxes in the neighbourhood. His sympathy with the sufferings of the people, and his attempts to secure for them some alleviation, soon brought him into conflict with the ruthless Danish officer. He quickly realised that no court of appeal existed in Sweden. Under Margaret's administration, the royal ministers were controlled by the queen. Her visits to Sweden ensured justice, for although the hardships were great, the higher authority was alive to the discontent, and local cruelties were suppressed. The centralised system did work, but it depended on the ruler. Under Eric, the system broke down. He ignored the acts of his local bailiffs.

The Swedish Riksråd was never summoned, and the two highest offices of the Swedish administration—the Lord High Constable and Chancellor—were left vacant. No one sat in judgment at the Thing, in fact the whole work of the state collapsed. Eric demanded so much in revenue from the bailiffs, who squeezed the people, paid the king the required quota, and kept the balance. In these circumstances, Engelbrekt went in person to Copenhagen to lay the grievances of Dalarna before the king. In spite of the efforts of Philippa, who perhaps was mindful of the Peasants' Revolt in England, Eric failed to grasp the significance of the dangerous situation. Unable to see further than the power of the Danish noble, the Danish bailiff and the Danish army and navy, he turned a deaf ear to Engelbrekt, and thus alienated one of the ablest statesmen of Europe. Engelbrekt returned to Dalarna convinced that the salvation of Sweden could lie only in complete separation from Denmark. He became the implacable enemy of Eric and everything Danish, but at the same time he realised that he could not rely on the Swedish nobility to share his views. The nobles had supported the Union and it was doubtful how far he could convert them to his new policy. He made his first appeal to the people—not merely to the miners, but to all. In no country, do industry and agriculture work more closely together than in Sweden. Engelbrekt with his clear insight was the first to draw the bonds together. Messengers were despatched throughout the whole of Dalarna to let everyone know the failure of the mission to Copenhagen and to summon a mass meeting. Engelbrekt was endowed with a magnetic power over men, and in 1434 the magnet drew nearly every able-bodied man in the province to form his resistance forces. Instantaneous success attended this ill-armed, ill-disciplined, but zealous army, which swept down into Central Sweden. Stronghold after stronghold fell before it, the hated Danish bailiffs were killed or fled south. The nobles were amazed at the success and alarmed lest they too should be swept aside by this popular tornado. When Engelbrekt marched still farther south, and Eric seemed unable to extricate himself from the Holstein troubles, the aristocracy began to join the movement. In fact, the noble, Eric Puke, commanded the Northern Campaign, and the Bishop of Strängnäs brought over many of the higher clergy, himself writing the *Song of Freedom*—a literary Swedish *Marseillaise*. The country had been liberated in under three months, except for some of Halland, isolated castles, and Stockholm. Engelbrekt himself commanded the army which cleared Halland, and then prepared to invade Denmark itself. Two factors caused him to halt. Eric had arranged one of the periodical armistices in Holstein, and mustered a force to recover the lost provinces and Sweden. Instead of landing in Skåne and thence attacking Engelbrekt, he sailed direct to Stockholm and sought to split his enemies by fair promises and by using his natural personal charms, which had so impressed the court at Vienna in his early days and had not yet deserted him.

Many of the nobles had been coerced into supporting Engelbrekt, when he had burst into the Council Chamber at Vadstena, leaving his peasant army in the courtyard shouting approval of their beloved leader. Now the questions forced themselves on others as well as the nobles, " What did this movement mean? Was its aim separation from Denmark? If so, what was to be the form of government? If not, was its aim merely to redress the evils wrought on Sweden by the rule of the Danish bailiffs? " Engelbrekt's answer would have been clearcut and unequivocal. A democratic monarchy was his ideal. The focal point of national unity was to be the people, whose chief representative—first citizen, as he would have been called later—was the king. Most of the nobles, however, feared this democratic leader, and were well aware that the very elective principle for which they had stood out at the Union of Kalmar would undoubtedly have meant the election of the very man they distrusted. So in November 1434 they came to an agreement with Eric: that a tribunal of Swedes, Danes, and possibly Norwegians (their inclusion is implied but not specifically stated), should arbitrate between the king and his people and decide how redress of evils could be attained if illegalities were proved. To prevent civil war, Engelbrekt agreed to this arrangement, but as soon as it became apparent that the policy of the nobles meant a restoration of the Union and that redress of evils meant merely the substitution of nobles for bailiffs, he sought means to destroy the scheme before it became operative. He was determined that the will of the people should be able to find expression, and that the nation should nominate an assembly with full legislative authority. The executive would be appointed by the assembly, and its functions would include the election of the king.

Barely two months after Eric had come to terms with the Council, and six months after Engelbrekt's dramatic burst into the Chamber at Vadstena, he summoned an assembly of nobles, clergy, burghers and peasants at Arboga in January 1435. This meeting proved to be the foundation of the Riksdag ("nation's day"), the Swedish Parliament. It was, in a sense, revolutionary, because the four estates swore jointly to observe and carry through whatever decisions were determined by the majority. The existence of four estates was recognised, and there was no attempt to alter that feature of the Constitution till the middle of the nineteenth century. The peasants included the miners, and all who were not embraced by the three other orders. All four estates had equal rights, and this principle was never questioned, even in the great struggle of " The Hats " and " The Caps ", when individual parties attempted to control the executive to the exclusion of the king. Engelbrekt's Riksdag is often compared with Simon de Montfort's Parliament. Some of its features bear a superficial resemblance, but the Riksdag was the work of a statesman aiming at the expulsion of the foreigner and the foundation of a national democratic government. Simon's Parliament was the work of a politician who saw no further than his own day.

The Riksdag decided on a separation of the governments of

Denmark and Sweden, but on the question of who should be titular king, opinion was divided. Finally at another Riksdag, an ultimatum was sent to Eric asking for his consent to the new popular administration of Sweden with an elected Protector. Eric did not reply, so the Swedes proceeded to elect the new officer without his permission. Engelbrekt had no desire to assume this office, rather he preferred to remain as leader of the democratic party, and as the nobles in the Riksråd (the Council, not the Riksdag) were still suspicious of him, Karl Knutsson was nominated the first Protector. The peasant party and most of the burgesses were furious at this manoeuvre, and finally Engelbrekt and Karl Knutsson were declared joint regents. The regency, the outcome of the great democratic and national movement, was brought to a sudden and tragic close by the foul murder of Engelbrekt by a jealous noble on a small island in Central Sweden. The peasants brought his revered body to Örebro Church, where he was honoured as a saint, and for some time rivalled in their estimation the national king and hero S. Eric, whose picture Engelbrekt had made familiar in his struggles, by having it on banners and the seal of the realm. Of the two, Engelbrekt has the stronger claims to canonisation and hero-worship. He was a selfless man, who at the end of his career showed the same high-minded purpose as at the beginning. As the old German chronicler wrote, " he began . . . with no arrogance of spirit, no lust for power, but from sympathy for those trodden underfoot ".

He was a great leader of men and, though his military genius is ignored as completely as the political genius of Gustavus Adolphus, he was no mean soldier. In three years he had broken Denmark's grip on Sweden. He had made the peasant party a lasting political entity, he had laid the foundation of modern Sweden, and he had established a representative Parliament. A truly great man.

His death left Karl Knutsson as sole Regent, but it was not till 1438 that Eric acknowledged his election or even the existence of such an office.

Eric was in dire distress in Denmark. He had been forced to surrender Slesvig to the Count of Holstein in 1436, and the nobles of Denmark and Norway revolted against him, and though by 1438 he had gained the upper hand, he was dethroned in 1439. Eric seemed sick and tired of his troublesome regal duties and left the country and settled in Gottland as a pirate king. For ten years he was the scourge of East Baltic trade. He seemed to thrive on wild orgies, debauchery and a hard life. His nephew, Christopher of Bavaria, succeeded to the Danish throne after a year's interregnum, but in spite of the entreaties of the trading classes, he did not feel inclined to cross swords with this courtier turned freebooter. "My uncle must live," he remarked. In 1499 Eric was closely besieged by a Swedish fleet, but managed to escape and offer the surrender of Visby to a Danish commander, provided he was conveyed to his old home in Rügenwalde Castle in Pomerania. There he spent another ten years, and as the means for piracy were denied him, he devoted them solely to debauchery.

The unsettled state of Denmark had its repercussions on Sweden after the death of Engelbrekt. Karl Knutsson is something of an enigma, though some of his inconsistencies were due to the fact that he had come into power as the nominee of the nobles, the majority of whom would have preferred a Union under a Danish King rather than a democratic government under a Protector. It was also clear that the leading state in the Union must be Denmark, as Sweden was still divided and Norway had fallen into that political apathy in which she was destined to remain for many centuries. For Denmark to fill that role it was necessary that the king should be an able man such as Valdemar Atterdag, who at that time was considered to have inspired the policy which Margaret carried through so successfully. The verdict of later ages is, however, not unanimous on that point.

Two distinct parties arose: the Unionists, who revived the policy of 1434, a titular king with no administrative power in Sweden, which was to be in the hands of the nobles; and the Separatists, who adhered to the Engelbrekt tradition of a national democracy. These parties were evenly balanced in power, but the Separatists or Swedish nationalists had the solid backing of the people, and latterly some of the ablest of the nobility to counteract Danish armed help.

For sixty years the tide ebbed and flowed, its times and seasons being dependent on the personalities of the Danish king and Swedish leaders. It was not unlike the Liberal and Conservative cricket match of English nineteenth-century politics. Each side had its innings, though usually the batting side suffered some severe injuries before retiring.

Karl Knutsson did not suit either side as a captain, but by adroitly offering his services to the side which seemed the stronger for that season, he managed to have no fewer than three innings. He might have had no break between his second and third innings, 1448–1457 and 1467–1470, had he been content with the title of Regent and not been crowned king. He made the further blunder of accepting the Norwegian crown at Trondheim in 1449, an act most unacceptable to the Unionists, who perceived that Denmark would be further alienated by this hostile act. Knutsson felt opposition growing and suspected treachery when Gotland fell into Danish hands after the successful blockade by the Swedish fleet. His suspicions were intensified by the Treaty of Bergen in 1450, which not only deprived him of all Norway, but sealed a pact of everlasting union of that country and Denmark. This pact was indeed unbroken until Norway was unwillingly attached to Sweden in 1814.

This uneasy state of affairs could not last for ever. It was unsatisfactory for both Denmark and Sweden. The end must come in one of two ways—either the National Separatists must find a succession of able kings, or the Danes must produce a statesmanlike king who had the political vision to frame a union on lines acceptable to both the parties in Sweden. With the advent of the powerful Sture family, who succeeded the temporising Karl Knutsson, it seemed quite probable that the Separatists would win the day. But after thirteen years of steady, but not colourful rule by Sten Sture the Elder, beginning in 1470, the Danish King Hans (John II of Sweden) offered the Swedish aristocracy a constitution after their own heart. The Danish kings did not renounce their claims to the Swedish throne after the sanguinary defeat of Christian I at Brunkeburg in 1471, but the success of Sten Sture's regime was making the royal claim more shadowy and the royal authority non-existent. Sten Sture, however, by continually summoning the Riksdag, over which he had complete domination, succeeded in preventing the realisation of Hans' policy, though the opposition of some of the Unionist aristocracy grew stronger. The final clash and appeal to arms came with the advent of Russia, as a country expanding westwards. It had been consolidated under the progressive policy of Ivan III. Though there had been minor wars in the past, they had been largely due to the expansionist policy of Sweden in

Finland. For the first but by no means the last time, Sweden was to face the Russian danger from the East. It is true that the Russians did not achieve any startling victories. They were ultimately repelled, but Sture found himself embroiled in a war on two fronts, for Hans, supported by Svante Nilsson Sture, leader of the Unionist party, landed an army near Stockholm. The naval authority of the Danes rendered the position of Stockholm precarious. Only the peasant body from Dalarna could be relied upon as Central and Southern Sweden were cut off and could not send help, even if they desired to do so. Hans entered Stockholm in 1497, and was formally elected king. At first, he adopted a conciliatory attitude towards both parties, even bestowing fiefs on Sten Sture, while Svante was made marshal. He proceeded to secure the election of his son as heir to the throne in spite of some opposition. Outwardly it appeared as if the union of Margaret was to endure or at least to be given a fresh lease of life. It was doomed to failure partly owing to the tactless and occasionally faithless actions of Hans, partly to the dissatisfaction of Svante at the paucity of the royal favours extended to him, but chiefly to the exertions of the remarkable Hemming Gadh, who became Bishop of Linköping. He had been appointed to Rome representing Sture's Nationalist Party. Here he had been profoundly impressed by the results of the Italian Renaissance, especially its political creeds. He had found the Machiavellian doctrines of *The Prince* exactly suited to his own nature. The subordination of the individual to the state fitted into his own conceptions of national unity and self-determination, whilst the ideas of freedom of thought—the very breath of the middle-class renaissance movement—affected him more than the cultural advancement which was its corollary. How far Gadh was actually responsible for the Elder Sture's success before the crisis of 1497 it is not easy to gauge. This point is of the same academic interest as in the case of Sully and Henry IV of France a hundred years later. The importance of the alliance lay in the fact that after the foundation of Uppsala University in 1477, the doctrines of Gadh had an enthusiastic and ever-increasing band of young followers bent on the establishment of a national Sweden. Hemming Gadh was the leader of a public opinion so strong that it could not be ignored by the Unionists, and it was due to his efforts that in 1502 the parties united once again to drive out the

Danes and re-establish a Regency or Protectorate. The revolt had been carefully timed to coincide with an expedition, led by Hans himself and Duke Frederick, which was going to wipe out the troublesome peasants of the Ditmarsken in Holstein. Instead of gaining an easy victory, the whole Danish army was utterly annihilated, and the king himself escaped by a miracle. So he was quite unable to send sufficient troops to Sweden to quell the united National Party. Peace, however, was not signed until after Hemming Gadh had enlisted the help of the Hanseatic League at a personal visit to its headquarters at Lübeck. Owing to the superiority of the Danish fleet, the Swedes had to enlist the aid of the unreliable League, whose policy, as always, was to hold the balance between the contending powers and sell itself to the highest bidder. The peace contained the seeds of future discord because, although the Swedish Protectorate was acknowledged, the Danish king was to receive an annual tribute, unless he or his son were elected King of Sweden.

The beginning of the end came in 1517, when two remarkable personalities were both determined to make a permanent settlement—Sten Sture the Younger and Christian II. The latter was a man of considerable intellectual qualities, unbounded courage, and a statesman. He was sympathetic towards the wrongs of the lower classes in Denmark and realised that the weakness of the State was due to the power of the nobles. On the other hand, he was ruthless, cruel, suspicious, and devoid of moral instincts, in fact a typical Macchiavellian prince. He had displayed both sides of his nature when as Viceroy of Norway (1506–1512) he stamped out rebellion, curbed the power of the Hanseates at Bergen, imprisoned the bishop, and formed a liaison with a Dutch girl named Dyveke. This love affair ended by causing his own downfall after he became king in 1513. "It began at a dance and in that dance he danced away the three Kingdoms of Denmark, Sweden and Norway" was the pithy comment of the Chronicler.

Sten Sture, according to the flattering accounts of his admirers, was an idealist, a veritable child of the gods, who willingly sacrificed his life for his country. A more sober view of his career is that he adopted the creed of Hemming Gadh and was determined to subordinate all the disintegrating powers in Sweden to the authority of the State. No one could deny his unflinching courage and determination in trying to carry out his policy, which brought him into conflict with the Church, the city corporations, a section of the nobility, and lastly with Denmark. The die was cast in 1517, when a militant ecclesiastic, Gustav Trolle, was appointed Archbishop of Uppsala and was deposed by the Riksdag under Sture's authority. The Archbishop had been in correspondence with Christian II and round him centred all the discontented parties of Sweden. His own family, one of the most powerful in the country, sought the downfall of the Stures.

The deposition of an archbishop by a protector was a direct challenge to Papal authority. It cut a deep horizontal line of nationalism across the perpendicular line of the ecclesiastical world state. The last link with the Middle Ages had been severed in the same year as Luther nailed his theses on the church door at Wittenberg. Christian II at once saw that if he did not seize the opportunity of interfering in the name of the Holy Church, he might find Sweden forever united and outside Danish influence. It is easy now to see how the Papal authority being linked with Danish ambition paved the way for the national Reformation in Sweden. The great leader of the Swedish Lutherans, Olaus Petri (" Father Olof ") happened to be in Wittenberg in this fateful year.

The Protector won the first round and the Swedish people backed him strongly. After a heavy Danish defeat in 1519 outside Stockholm, it seemed more than probable that he would be elected king. Christian II decided to make one more effort. His fleet was sent round the east coast and an army of ten thousand men, pinning the Papal interdict on the doors of the churches, marched victoriously northwards till it met the peasant army of Sten Sture on the frozen Lake Asunden. Here Sten Sture was mortally wounded and the whole course of Swedish history was changed.

Without their leader, the army melted away and the only point of resistance was in Stockholm where his gallant widow Christina made the last heroic stand.

With the Danish army investing the city by land and sea, she was ultimately forced to seek an amnesty by which pardon was granted to all the Sture party, including those who had deposed the Archbishop Trolle. King Christian II entered the city. In October 1520 he was proclaimed at a Riksdag as the *hereditary* king and subsequently crowned by Archbishop Trolle, who had resumed his charge of the see. Magnificent festivities followed the coronation, and then all the chief noblemen and burgesses were summoned to the assembly hall of the royal castle. To the amazement of all present, Trolle read an indictment against eighteen named persons who had persecuted the Church. Christina gallantly protested, urging that an amnesty had been solemnly promised and that the whole Riksdag had been responsible for the Archbishop's deposition.

The king ordered the castle gates to be closed. Next day the eighteen were pronounced guilty and the infamous " Blood Bath " began. The king ordered ninety executions in the market place, " the heads of bishops, nobles and worthy burghers were rolling together in the dust ".

The King extended the massacres to the provinces and the Sture party's leaders were annihilated. Even Hemming Gadh, who had in 1518 apparently been attracted to the Renaissance side of Christian II and left the Nationalist party, was murdered in Finland.

Christian II's triumph was complete. Satisfied that Sweden was " pacified ", he left Stockholm under the rule of the Archbishop and two Danes, and started on a journey to the Netherlands, where he could proudly show himself to his uncle Charles V, as ruler of all Scandinavia. The crafty King had forgotten one former deed of treachery, when before the death of Sture, Swedish hostages had voluntarily gone on board his flagship as security when he went ashore to an agreed parley. He never went ashore, but made the Swedes prisoners. Among them was a connexion[1] of Sten Sture named Gustavus Vasa, who had been educated under Hemming Gadh. The young Gustavus was thrown into a prison in Jutland, but in September 1519 he managed to escape, and, disguised as a horse dealer, arrived in Lübeck. The people refused extradition, and in May 1520 he arrived in Kalmar. Vainly he tried to raise levies against the Danes. Finally in despair after hearing that all his relatives had been murdered, he wandered about Dalarna, a hunted man, enduring many hardships and experiencing many hairbreadth escapes.[2]

News came that Christian II was leading his army out of

---

[1] Gustavus's mother was half-sister of Sture's wife, Christina.
[2] There are endless legendary tales of this period of Gustavus's life.

Stockholm to punish the peasants of the province for harbouring him and the few remaining supporters of Christina. Sorrowfully, he started out for Norway and reached its very border. The news about Christian was false, he and his army were bound for Denmark. When the peasants learned the error, their swiftest skiers started in pursuit of the fugitive and just caught up with him before he left Sweden for ever. He was brought back and two hundred peasants elected him as their leader at Tuna, near the traditional Crowning Stone of the old kings at Mora. In January 1521, Gustavus Vasa, not yet twenty-five years of age, started the final War of Liberation as " Lord of the Dales and of Sweden ". The Danish Government in Stockholm sent a message to Christian II, who had not yet left Skåne, that some peasants had made a disturbance of no consequence, and he continued his journey to meet Charles V in the Netherlands. By April, the famous Danish cavalry were called out to sweep away the peasant bands. Gustavus steadied his men, armed with pikes, and not only utterly defeated the Danes, but captured their artillery. After this victory at Västerås, all Sweden gradually swore allegiance to this young hero. In August 1521 he was elected Regent by the Riksdag at Vadstena. Only Stockholm held out for Christian. Without a fleet, it was impossible to invest the city. The siege dragged on wearily till at last Gustavus enlisted the help of Lübeck, already hostile to Christian. Danzig joined in with their ships, and finally Duke Frederick invaded Denmark from Holstein and claimed the throne. Swedish troops occupied a Norwegian province and part of Skåne on behalf of Frederick. Everything was now turning out in the Nationalists' favour, but the Riksdag, prompted by a canon from Västerås, foresaw a complication which might rob them of the fruits of victory. If Frederick became King of Denmark, might he not claim the Swedish crown, and was it not possible that the Unionists might seize this opportunity of regaining their ascendancy? It was imperative to elect a king of Sweden immediately. Gustavus Vasa refused to be elected at first, but finally accepted the crown on June 10th, 1523. The situation was saved. Frederick laid seige to Copenhagen on June 6th, as king, and Christian II with his court had left Denmark for ever.

Stockholm fell on June 20th, and that date may be reckoned as the beginning of the New Sweden and the end of Margaret's dream of a great Scandinavian Empire.

PART II: MODERN TIMES

CHAPTER VII

THE SIXTEENTH CENTURY AND DENMARK

WITH the accession of Gustavus Vasa, the Swedish barometer, which was at its lowest, began to rise steadily; with the accession of Frederick I, the Danish barometer, which was at its highest in 1521, began to fall steadily, and the Norwegian barometer, already at its lowest, remained constant at "set low", *dåligt väder,* for three hundred years!

Finland and Iceland watched sometimes with satisfaction, sometimes with apprehension, the weather glasses of their more powerful neighbours.

The fateful years which led to the separation of Denmark and Sweden, the devastating wars, and even the "Blood Bath" of Stockholm, were almost unnoticed by the Europe of that day. Three years after the great victory of Francis I at Marignano, we read that "general peace reigned over Europe for four years", that is to say from 1518 to 1522, when the Scandinavian wars were raging at their fiercest pitch. Francis I had conquered Milan and Florence and cowed the Pope into acquiescence. Young Charles V had found himself king of a united Spain. A new alignment of great nations had made its appearance in Europe. Great happenings in Europe itself might have been sufficient in themselves to distract attention from the Far North, but the discovery of America and tales of its fabulous wealth had also excited the minds of the rulers of the maritime nations. New problems faced their countries, new possibilities of power and lands. Naval interest was shifting westwards, while the military appetites of France, Spain and Germany had been whetted by a taste of Italian plunder. The curtain is thus being rung up on two scenes of long and sanguinary warfare—Italy is to become the victim and sufferer in the French, Spanish and Imperial struggles for its possession, while the Atlantic is to provide a larger stage for Spanish, Portuguese, English, French and other maritime powers to carry on their struggle for supremacy.

In both these arenas the Pope played an important part, but in both he was a loser. The storm broke at the very time when the Papacy became conspicuous in a new role. The Pope's position had been definitely altered by the fall of Constantinople in 1453. Nicholas V, the last of the Medieval Popes, as he has been called, made no effort to raise a Crusade against the Turk. He preferred to found the Vatican Library. After him, the Western and Eastern Churches ceased to be rivals, they were to remain separate and apart until centuries later the conflict was renewed in Poland. There were no more General Church Councils and Nicholas was the last pope to crown the emperor. After his death, the Papacy became involved in the struggles of the Italian States. Innocent VIII went to the length of recognising his own children and marrying his son to the daughter of Lorenzo di Medici, thus linking himself to one of the most powerful Italian families. The additional influence gained from this policy in Italy itself was more than counterbalanced by the consequent irritation in the new nation states of Europe, when a pope tried to impose his authority in the politics of their countries. At the beginning of the sixteenth century, England, France and Spain could each be termed a sovereign state, and their monarchs were rulers even if the despotism was screened by some form of a democratic parliament. There could be no *imperium in imperio*. The head of the state was bound to be faced with the problem of either allowing the Pope to be a real political force, if Church and State were to remain in the close relationship of the past, or himself to become head of the Church. A compromise might be effected, as had happened before, but it would not solve the problem satisfactorily for all time. The clash would come when an ambitious pope came into conflict with an autocratic king. A monarch of the new type spent money more freely in pageantry and wanted more money for his more centralised state. He could not let money go out of the country to help the Pope either for political or architectural schemes. England, Sweden and Denmark all welcomed an excuse to make the break. An annulment of a royal marriage suited Henry VIII; a murderous archbishop, Gustav Trolle, suited Gustavus Vasa; Lutheranism suited Christian II and Frederick I equally well. Charles V wanted no good excuse, as Alexander VI had divided up the New World to the advantage of Spain, so he supported the Papacy as far as it was to his advantage. Perhaps it was the division of the New World which first brought home to England the political aspirations of the Borgian Pope.

The financial campaign to pay for S. Peter's at Rome began to stir up resentment throughout Europe. The attempts at reform by appeal to Church Councils had awakened men's minds to abuses, but the popes had managed to retain their power over the cardinals and disregard the Councils. Tetzel's campaign to sell Indulgences wholesale affected both the pocket and the conscience. Luther's protest at Wittenberg was enough to set the whole smouldering mass alight.

Different countries were affected in different ways, and the rulers and their peoples were not always affected in the same way. In Denmark, Christian II allowed the Indulgences to be collected; he went even as far as to approve their theological justification. When Indulgences were drawn from this bank of good works by penances, self-denial and more good works, such as joining a crusade, there was some basis for their existence. But when the penances were put on a cash nexus to pay for buildings and the luxurious life of the Vatican, the whole case for the contribution to the Papal chest was changed. Stories of the life in Rome itself, and of the doings of certain prelates were now rife. The Bishop of Coutances himself was punished for his denunciation of the Papal Court. It was against these abuses that Luther wrote his theses, and not against the office of pope. The Papal Nuncio, Archimboldus, was sent to carry out the money-raising campaign of Tetzel in Denmark and Sweden. People were almost forced to buy Indulgences and penances out of the " treasury of merit " built up by the good works of the faithful. Having raised a considerable sum in Denmark, he went on to Stockholm to sell his Indulgences, but in his absence, Christian II confiscated the whole of the Danish collection and used the proceeds for his army against Sweden. In Germany and in Scandinavia, Luther's protest was construed as an invitation to revolt against the whole power of the Pope—political and spiritual—not merely an attack on certain abuses. In Sweden, Gustav Trolle, the archbishop, was regarded as the symbol of Danish domination, and it was only natural that Papal power and the national movement became irreconcilable. The first step in the Reformation in both Sweden and Denmark was purely political.

Archimboldus deposed Trolle from the archbishopric and

appointed himself after election by the Chapter at Uppsala. Hoping by so doing to have won favour with the Swedes, he offered to mediate between Sture and Christian II. His inter- ference was resented and he had to flee for safety to Lübeck, where he found a Papal Bull placing Sweden under an interdict for the deposition of Trolle. He returned to Rome in disgrace without any money from either Denmark or Sweden, leaving behind him a trail of hatred in both countries. The Pope, by this time heavily involved in the German revolt against his authority and uncertain of the attitude of Charles V, elected Emperor in 1519, allowed Christian II to keep his Indulgence money provided he led a Papal campaign against Sweden. Christian II gladly assented as he was determined to impose his authority over the rebellious Swedes, though he, too, had been attracted to Lutheranism and was turn- ing from Rome. The Danes in the towns, who had suffered most from the Indulgence payments, also began to be shaken in their adherence to Rome. At the Diet of Worms in this same year, 1520, Charles V had heard Luther's arguments and decided against him. "This man could never make me a heretic," he said, and then declared him to be an outlaw. His decision was due in no small measure to his fear that Luther would hinder his efforts to bring unity and order to the Empire, which he was visiting for the first time after his successful election. He did not yet understand the Princes of Germany, nor the effect of the Renaissance on his new subjects. His action was doomed to stir up more trouble, and sowed the seed of the Thirty Years War a century later. The spirit of enquiry and intellectual activity, which were the funda- mental characteristics of the Renaissance, had been reflected in Germany in a manner quite different from anything Charles V had seen in Italy or Spain. The Renaissance had not by this time stirred them to explore pagan or classical philosophy. The slower but more earnest German mind had centred its enquiries on the field of religious thought. Hence the criticism of what was un- thinkingly held to be true turned on Christian beliefs and dogmas rather than literary and scientific speculations. Thus it is true to say that the Renaissance paved the way for the Reformation to a far greater extent among the Teutonic people than elsewhere. Luther's pamphlets found a ready and eager audience. After the Diet of Worms, he was drawn into a new position which could mean nothing but a complete break with Rome.

Christian II wavered between Luther and the Pope. Two bishops had been murdered in the Stockholm massacre. He tried to throw the blame on Didrik, his favourite minister, whom he had made Archbishop of Lund, and at the instance of a Papal Legate, he put him to torture and then burned him publicly at Copenhagen. Previously, however, he had attempted to reform the Danish Church from within, and in so doing had undermined much of the Papal authority. Christian II possessed a Renaissance mind, alert and ever ready to probe into the truth. He was cultured and despised the ignorance of the Danish clergy. He chafed at the power of the nobles, and his humanitarian ideas revolted from their oppression of the peasants. Cunning, cruel and treacherous, this many-sided man desired to be master and carry out reforms far ahead of his times. He first turned his attention to the Council and humiliated its members by ignoring its advice—usually advantageous to the aristocracy—and appointing a civil service of men of low birth who were able and energetic administrators. Ordinances to enforce morality and cleanliness were passed amidst a host of others on social subjects. Law courts were reformed, witches were merely whipped and not burned alive, lepers were segregated, and finally he aroused the enmity of the nobles by permitting ill-used peasants to leave the district. They were no longer "bound to the soil" for compulsory labour and sold as "Christian slaves". Unemployment was forbidden in harvest times and labour was compulsory, and no fetes could be held during that season. Christian II was shocked at the state of the schools and instituted a modern system of primary and secondary education. Priests were bidden to teach reading and writing in the Danish tongue. The catechism was to be repeated in Danish for all to understand. Having begun his work as an enlightened despot two hundred years before the period of Enlightened Despots in Europe, the king turned his energies to Church reform. In his attitude to the spiritual needs of his people, he presented the same paternal benevolence, enforced with unflinching severity. No detail escaped him. As he had passed a law insisting on housewives cleaning their tables and floors every Saturday after his officers had reported on the prevailing lack of hygienic habits, so did his officers' report on the monasteries lead him to order the lives of monks and nuns. The ignorant and often lazy and dissolute priests were to be dismissed and replaced by men who had passed through the University of Copenhagen. No one could be ordained in the future unless he held a degree. The professorial staff was enlarged and enriched by men of science and the arts. To ensure that his ecclesiastical reforms were carried out, he established a Supreme Tribunal composed of the laity and the higher and lower clergy. As President of this Tribunal from which there was no appeal to Rome, he had moved no little way towards becoming Head of Church and State. In theory the Danish kings had never lost the right to appoint the archbishops and bishops. He chose his prelates and their appointment was confirmed by the chapters. The remaining possible source of interference from outside lay in the monastic orders. These were placed under the rule of the bishops, and any disputes—and they were not few—had to be brought to the all-powerful Tribunal. His new regime had begun to purify the Danish Church before Luther's first protest. It was no longer possible for a bishop or a priest to draw a stipend and neglect his church services. Such a scandal could be reported by the laity, in fact, the easy approach was a reason for complaint by the clergy early in the reign of Frederick I.[1] These changes were by no means popular with all sections. Even the Bishop of Ribe, who in 1514 was discovered to have failed to consecrate a Mass for sixteen years, had his supporters. It was some two years after Luther's first protest that the Elector of Saxony was requested to send a Lutheran preacher from Wittenberg to Denmark. Christian was interested in the new cult, and wanted to have first-hand information, and study the Lutheran methods. The tour of Reinhard the preacher was not a success among the people, as they could not understand a word he said, and merely watched his antics and listened to his thunderous voice. Towards the end of his stay, people regarded him as a show and openly laughed. Two reasons stayed any further attempts to introduce the new ideas. Sweden required all Christian's attention, and his brother-in-law, Emperor Charles V, was to pronounce the verdict on Luther at the Diet of Worms. The interest of Christian himself appears to have been increased and not diminished by Reinhard's ill-success.

As stated previously, Christian had left Stockholm in 1521 after his treacherous massacre, to visit Charles V in the Netherlands. Here, this queer mixture of culture and pagan cruelty searched out Erasmus so that he might learn more of Luther and his

[1] In 1527 at Odense.

works. Though never again in a position to influence the Danes in their religion, he undoubtedly became a Lutheran for an unknown period of time, and translated Luther's Old Testament into Danish and had the New Testament similarly translated by two friends. During his long visit, he imbibed the spirit of the Renaissance as he found it in the Netherlands. He was impressed with the culture, atmosphere and life of the Dutch towns, and became an ardent admirer of Dutch art and architecture: Dürer not only painted his portrait, but became a personal friend. While thus satisfying his intellectual cravings, he received news of the triumphs of Gustavus Vasa. At first he was inclined to belittle their importance, but finally returned to Denmark, where he proceeded to carry out more sweeping reforms in the towns. Stockholm still held out against Gustavus, but Christian was in no position to send relief. The Emperor had recognised his suzerainty over Lübeck and had granted him the fiefdom of Holstein in perpetuity. This provided him with two titles, but two bitter enemies. The royal authority had been apparently increased by these gifts and also by his new democratic laws aimed against the aristocracy of the cities, for his reforms were based on the urban local government which had so impressed him during his recent visit to the Netherlands. He went still further in his zeal to build up agricultural prosperity, and introduced a hundred and eighty-four Dutch families to teach better methods of horticulture. The whole island of Amager was leased to them. None of his philanthropic efforts were popular. He had roused nobles, burghers, peasants and bishops against him, and Lübeck and the Hanseatic League were waiting for an opportunity to attack him. The Swedish war was going badly and new taxes were imposed to equip an army—mostly German mercenaries—which was to oppose Gustavus. It required a bold leader to unite the discontented elements. His uncle Frederick, Duke of Holstein, was only too ready to fill that part, for he chafed at having to own his nephew as his overlord. In 1522 a secret league of the nobles and bishops of Jutland drew up a document reciting the evils brought upon the kingdom by Christian II, and thus justified their renunciation of allegiance. The crown was offered to Frederick, who answered by overrunning the whole of Jutland. Christian held out promises of redress of all the evils which his humanitarian endeavours were alleged to have brought on the country. The Assembly in Copenhagen, which was firmly held by Christian, proceeded to examine the king's proposals, but to the consternation of his adherents, the king, accompanied by a few friends, sailed away to the Netherlands to seek the aid of Charles V. Copenhagen and Malmö were left under military governors to hold out against Frederick, whose army was already in possession of the middle island of Fünen. Christian found Charles V already engaged in a war against France and he never returned to his kingdom as a free man, although after eight years in exile, he made one effort to recapture his dominions. In 1531, he swore to Charles V that he would abjure Lutheranism and restore Catholicism in Norway and Denmark in return for ships, men and money. He sailed for Norway. After losing half his force in a gale, he laid seige to Akershus, but the fleets of Denmark and the Hanseatic League arrived at the fiord before he could take the fortress. It was then agreed that he should be given a safe conduct to Copenhagen, where his uncle and he could arrive at some peaceful settlement. However, before he arrived orders were received that he should be taken to the island of Als, and imprisoned in Sönderborg Castle. He remained a prisoner for twenty-seven years, often in close and solitary confinement, until his death in 1559 at the age of seventy-seven. Such was the tragic end of the most remarkable monarch who has ever reigned in Denmark. Few personalities have presented so many conundrums to the historian and psychologist. Cruel, treacherous and barbaric, he was at the same time a humanitarian reformer with ideals far in advance of his time. His actions were at times inexplicable. The most puzzling, which can never be solved, was his flight from Copenhagen in 1523. He had shown himself to be a man of great energy and power. He had an almost impregnable position and could have mustered a formidable army in a comparatively short time. Yet he appeared to have been quite suddenly sapped of all vitality, and crumpled under the strain. The usual explanation is that, in his opinion, only a personal appeal could move Charles V to send assistance. There is no ground for this supposition. He had not shown himself to be a Lutheran at that date, and there is no reason to believe that his brother-in-law had any more faith in the orthodoxy of Frederick. As emperor, Charles would have supported the overlord rather than the Duke of Holstein, and an army moving up across the Eider would have so seriously embarrassed Frederick that, without ships, he might have had to face annihilation or surrender. Possibly the truer explanation is that his character had softened during his stay in the Netherlands. The warlike side of his nature had given way to the philanthropic. Had he acted otherwise than he did, the future history of Denmark might have been far different and happier. He did leave a lasting impression on Denmark, though its miserable succession of wars obscured the benefits which he had bestowed.

His permanent work was to pave the way for the Reformation by his changes in ecclesiastical administration. Without him, it is doubtful whether it could have been achieved with so little bloodshed.

Secondly, his educational work was to alter the standard of culture throughout the whole country. His linking of the university to the needs of the people showed a genius ahead of his time. Christian IV built on his foundations further to broaden the basis of education. The taste for a higher civilisation was not lost entirely. His efforts to destroy the stranglehold of the nobles did not succeed, but there was some amelioration of the peasants' lot, and in spite of the harsh treatment meted out to them later, they never became bound to the soil and sold with the land, as in the days before his reforms.

On the triumph of Frederick I, Denmark entered on one of its most stormy and troublous periods. He had owed his victory to the Holsteiners and the superior military qualities of his general, Rantzau, but the throne was never secure against Christian II's followers as long as he was in the Netherlands. At any moment Charles V might decide to turn his victorious armies against Denmark, and try to incorporate the whole country in the empire. His triumph over Francis I at Pavia in 1525. and his acquisition of Burgundy in the following year, rendered the situation delicate, if not dangerous. In Frederick's opinion, it was not safe immediately to declare for the Reformers as this might incite the Romanist emperor. He was probably correct in his belief that the lukewarm attitude towards Christian was due to his Lutheran leanings, but Charles's preoccupations elsewhere were stronger reasons. In 1527 the sack of Rome by the German-Spanish army altered the situation in the eyes of the Danish king.

To a contemporary living on the outskirts of the empire, the policy of Charles V must have appeared baffling in the extreme during the years following the dethronement of Christian. The

Peasants' Revolt in Germany aimed at the abolition of serfdom and based the "Twelve Articles" of its programme on the scriptures. Luther had disowned it. Charles had approved of its ruthless suppression. Charles had defied the Pope by appointing a General Council to settle the religious difficulties in Germany. At the Diet of Spires in 1526, he had given consent to the first measure of toleration, and established the famous principle, "Cujus regio, ejus religio ". The Pope tried to regain his control, whereupon an imperial army of Spanish Catholics and German Protestants drove him from the Vatican and utterly sacked the Holy City. Small wonder that Frederick decided to support the Reformers and break with the Romanists, who seemed to be on the losing side. By an adroit move, he dissociated many of Christian's adherents by his support of Tausen, who converted the friends of the exiled king to the new faith. In 1527 he held a diet at Odense, and it was agreed that all bishops and prelates should be appointed by the Archbishop of Lund, and all revenues formerly sent to Rome should go to the king. The nobles were compensated by receiving some of the tithes. This, however, did not mean the establishment of the Reformation, as did the Recess of Västerås in Sweden during this same year. The king maintained his right to be protector of religious freedom for all. The Catholics were determined not to yield without a struggle. The towns, except Elsinore, embraced Luther's doctrines, but the countryside, for the most part, remained true to the old faith. The majority in the Council opposed the Reformation, and looked forward to a Catholic king on the death of Frederick because they had already determined to elect the younger son Hans, who was a Catholic, and not Christian, who was a fervent Lutheran. Frederick uncertain of Charles's attitude, allowed matters to take their course until, by his expedition to Norway the ex-king Christian showed his intentions. If he had not been delivered into Frederick's hands by treachery, a religious war in which politics would have played a considerable part was bound to have resulted.

In April 1533 Frederick died and the storm broke. The Catholic majority postponed the election till the summer of 1534, and used the intervening months to suppress liberty of conscience and restore the power of the Catholic nobles and clergy.

The situation, however, was complicated by the sudden appearance of Wallenweber, the burgomaster of Lübeck, who together with Bogbinder and Kich, burgomasters of Copenhagen and

Malmö, demanded the restoration of Christian II. The real purpose of the Lübeckese was to create anarchy, dismember Denmark and utterly destroy their naval rival in the Baltic. Jutland replied by electing the Lutheran Christian III as king. Count Christopher was given command of the armies of Christian II, who not only began the fierce Count's War in Denmark itself, but ordered a Lübeckese army to attack Holstein, and so pin Christian III in Jutland. The Count's agents then stirred the Catholic peasants under " Skipper " Clement to rise in Jutland itself.

The war had become social and political. Lutherans from Copenhagen allied with Catholics in Jutland, and Lutheran Lübeckese were aligned against the Lutheran Christian III, supported by German soldiers and Catholic nobles of Jutland, Holstein and Fünen.

Charles V, actuated by commercial motives, was an interested spectator, and awaited the expected defeat of Christian III. He could then actively interfere and gain commercial and maritime privileges for his Dutch subjects, and in all probability he could divide Denmark into three dukedoms inside the Holy Roman Empire.

The outcome of this " Count's War " after two years' fighting deceived the prophets. Gustavus Vasa saw his chance to destroy the supremacy of the Lübeck and Hanseatic naval forces. He joined Christian III's fleet and utterly destroyed the naval power of Lübeck. It lost in two months the hegemony which it had held for two centuries. Rantzau slaughtered Clement's peasant army. Two thousand were put to the sword, and Clement was executed. He proceeded to annihilate Count Christopher's army at the battle of Oxnebjaerg, where Gustav Trolle, the deposed Archbishop of Uppsala, was killed, and, with complete command of the sea, Christian III proceeded to lay seige to Copenhagen. There, Christopher held out for a year, awaiting help from Charles V—help which never came. By July 1539 Christian III was undisputed king of Denmark and Holstein. It was not, however, until 1546 that Christian II, still in miserable captivity, renounced the right to the throne for himself and his heirs. Two years previously, by the Treaty of Speier, Charles V had come to terms with Denmark and Norway. In return for recognition as king of those countries and Duke of Holstein (still in the Imperial circle), Christian III granted special rights to Dutch traders passing through the Sound, a more lenient captivity for the unfortunate Christian II, and a guarantee that he would not join the Schmalkalden League of Protestant Princes, or interfere in German matters.

This unhappy period saw the official separation of Denmark from the affairs of Germany, though the Holstein question was only temporarily settled. The kingdom of Norway, by the charter of 1536, was made "subject to the Crown of Denmark for all time, like our other provinces Jutland, Fünen, Sjaelland and Skane." Two other important changes were made also at the popular assembly of Copenhagen in 1537. The new State Church under superintendents abolished the bishops and acknowledged the king as head of the Church. These superintendents did not last long, and the name bishop was restored, but Lutheranism was so firmly established that the Counter Reformation could make no headway. The king did reform the Church, and not merely reconstruct the fabric.

The crown was made hereditary, but in return, the nobles, who were members of the Council, retained the exclusive right to hold fiefdoms from the crown. A popular assembly of twelve hundred members drawn from every class of society, nobles, clergy, peasants, and burgesses, was democratic only in name; it signed away its powers, and not many years elapsed before the nobility once more had gathered all the power into its hands. The peasants sank back into their depressed condition, and the king depended on the nobility for his power. Once again the resilience of the seafaring classes is most pronounced. In spite of the utter desolation of the land, made more complete by a further slaughter of the freedom-loving peasants of Ditsmarsken, the Danish naval power continued to demand respect. A notable instance well illustrates the far-flung activities of her ships. Dues were demanded from and paid by English ships passing round the north of Norway on the newly discovered route to Archangel. Owing to the difficulty of exacting these dues, a composite sum was paid annually to Denmark to the end of Queen Elizabeth's reign.[1] With the destruction of the Lübeckese fleets, their only rivals in the Baltic were the Swedes, and it was not until the end of the Seven Years War (1563 to 1570) that Sweden was the undoubted mistress of the Baltic Sea itself, but Denmark retained her command of the

[1] The actual sum was 1,000 Danish Marks, paid by the English Company of Merchant Adventurers.

Sound. This was acknowledged by the Treaty of Stettin (1570) which contained a clause guaranteeing that all foreign ships of war should dip their flags to the Danish, and merchant ships should pay dues as they passed Elsinore, protected by Kronborg Castle. The title of "Dominus maris Baltici" was still applied to Denmark, with the implied responsibility of keeping the sea free from pirates, but, as the Swedes could muster a fleet stronger than the combined fleets of Danes and Lübeckese for the last two years of the war, it was an empty title except in the Sound and Skagerak, where the shores on either side were in Danish hands.

Though Christian III and Gustavus Vasa had remained on friendly terms after their combined attack on the Lübeckese, and even gone so far as to renew the alliance in 1541, their relationship had become strained towards the end of their reigns. Their successors, Frederick II and Eric XIV, had not the patience of their fathers, and neither realised how necessary was peace to both countries. It is, however, only a half-truth for Danes to place the blame for the outbreak of the Seven Years War on the unbridled ambitions of Eric, or for Swedes to accuse Frederick II of attempting the encirclement of their country.

Circumstances over which neither party had any control were the fundamental causes of the struggle which left both countries exhausted, but Denmark in a worse state than her rival.

In the first place, the Order of the Teutonic Knights, a medieval anachronism dating from the Crusades, was in a state of dissolution. It had been the power which had governed the north-east corner of the continent, roughly covered by Estonia, Livonia and part of Prussia. Their territory formed a barrier between Poland and Finland, and also between Russia and the Baltic. As the disintegration grew more evident to the neighbouring countries, the greater became the mutual suspicions of those interested in securing the most valuable part of the prey. The first move came from Russia whose Czar, Ivan IV, launched a huge army numbering, it was said, no less than seventy thousand, against Narva and on towards Livonia. His object was to secure ports on the Baltic and cut off Poland whom he regarded as his most dangerous enemy. The island of Osel was still nominally Danish, and the bishop appealed to Frederick II for assistance. Somewhat reluctantly, the king sent his brother Magnus, an incompetent youth of nineteen, as governor of Osel and Livonia. He was induced to take this course because he was determined to retain the hegemony of the Baltic and ultimately to re-conquer Sweden.

Eric XIV was drawn into the struggle for three reasons. He wished for the Swedish hegemony of the Baltic and expansion of Sweden on the south coast of its shores, but he also feared that his brother, Duke John of Finland, was planning a Baltic-Finnish kingdom under the aegis of Poland. John had married Catherine Jagellon of Poland, whose king Sigismund had granted John several castles in Estonia as security for a considerable loan of money. Eric also wished to block the Russian path to the Baltic. His excuse came with the request of Reval for Swedish help, a request with which he was ready to comply. With the stage thus set, the mutual hatred of Eric and Frederick was sufficient to convert this eastern war into a Scandinavian death struggle. Frederick made an alliance with the Catholic Sigismund, and came to terms with Russia. Eric defeated John and carried him and his wife Catherine off to Sweden, and then entered into the most extraordinary personal negotiations with the semi-Oriental Ivan. He was placated by the offer of Catherine's person, who was to be separated from her husband, Duke John.

The stage, set for a five-corner struggle, was thus cleared of Russia, Poland and Finland, leaving Denmark and Sweden to fight it out between them. After the first two years it was a case of the elephant and the whale. The Danes under their brilliant commander, Daniel Rantzau, captured Alvsborg (Elfsberg), the only Swedish port on the North Sea, and penetrated the forests of Central Sweden. Rantzau reported that if some more German mercenaries could be sent to him, Stockholm itself would fall. Frederick was utterly impoverished and could send none. Rantzau extricated himself by one of the great retreats of military history, only to be killed by a stray bullet in 1569. The Swedish peasant army, trained in Gustavus Vasa's reign by Eric himself, was once more proving itself a great defensive force, though it had not been able to withstand Rantzau's Germans in pitched battles. Meanwhile the Swedish navy had been able to assert itself. It kept the coastline free to Stockholm, and could supply the Swedish army in Estonia, and cut off supplies to Danes in that quarter. In 1568 Eric went mad and civil war broke out in Sweden, but the weakness of Denmark was so pronounced that no advantage could be taken of the confusion reigning in the north. At last the weary combatants came to terms in 1570. Although Sweden had to pay Denmark 150,000 riksdalers for the return of Alvsborg, and leave the Sound and its dues in Danish hands, she gained Estonia, and thus began the Baltic policy to be developed by Gustavus Adolphus. The vexed question about the Danish claim to the three crowns was left to arbitration, but the retention of Skåne and Gotland by Denmark contained the seeds of future disputes. John was king in Sweden when the Emperor and the Elector of Saxony, at the Stettin Peace Conference in 1570, intervened to stop the war, but his position was too precarious to allow him to press for better terms. This war marks the beginning of the Russian policy in north-east Europe, and of the Polish-Swedish antagonism which was to prove so costly to both parties. It clearly demonstrated the hitherto imperceptible change in Sweden's strength since the dissolution of the Union. She was a separate nation, and her status as such was never challenged by Denmark in the many wars which occurred between them in after years. The war is a landmark in Danish history, and Frederick II was the first to recognise her military and naval limitations. Her aim in the future was to be protected against foreign domination in the Baltic. No longer could she hope to dominate it. Diplomacy, a mercantile marine, and a navy sufficient to be useful to any ally stronger than herself, were the means by which she could play her new and less glorious role. In the last eighteen years of his reign, Frederick was determined to keep the peace and his foreign policy was shaped to this end. His diplomacy was shrewdly directed, and in the war between Spain and England he held his trump card—the control of the Sound —as a bait or a bribe to both parties, and finally tried to mediate between them. Religion played no part in the foreign policy. He remained on the best of terms with the Catholic Emperor, Matthias, and at one time tried to effect a settlement between Henry of Navarre and the king of France. After the revolt in the Netherlands, he allowed Philip II to be informed unofficially, that to curtail Dutch shipping in the Baltic, he might close the Sound to them if Spain gave certain privileges to the Danes. On the other hand, Queen Elizabeth was informed that Danish ships might be available against the Spaniards, and these negotiations only failed because she also demanded the closure of certain Hanseatic towns to prevent the Spanish from obtaining war material from them. Active help was promised to the House of Orange in case of defeat. The diplomacy was tortuous, but in the grand manner of the great nations, and it left Denmark outside the European religious and semi-religious wars. In the year before the Armada, Danish emissaries visited Paris, London and Madrid, and made a genuine attempt to bring about peaceful settlement, and their failure was a matter of real sorrow to Frederick if we can believe a letter of his to Queen Elizabeth. On the day of his death, the Armada set sail.

After the Treaty of Stettin, he began to set his house in order. The Slesvig-Holstein question was tackled, but his scheme did not settle the thorny problem for all time. Slesvig was divided into four parts—Adolph of Holstein-Gottorp, who, by Danish law, was nearer the succession than Christian III's son Frederick II, received one half, and the king took the rest. No settlement could be permanent which left Holstein to a Danish monarch as duke owing allegiance to the Emperor. The position was fraught with danger, and its incongruity was emphasised when the State Council refused to declare war on Sweden in 1611 and Christian IV announced his intention of doing so, as Duke of Holstein. The situation was bound to become equally impossible if the same man became Duke of Slesvig and Holstein, but not King of Denmark. Frederick's solution was a compromise to bring about a peaceful settlement, and did not look far enough into the future.

The most notable feature of the last part of the reign was the encouragement given to the sciences and higher education. Besides further gifts to the university, he founded a school with free board and education at Copenhagen, and the old cloister schools were opened to all. The difficulty outside Copenhagen was to find suitable teachers as, on the dismissal of the old priests and monks, educated men were not forthcoming in sufficient number to take their places. The most renowned figure of the time was Tyge Brahe, the scientist and astronomer; a man of European fame. Richly endowed by his royal patron, he gathered round him a devoted band of scientists. They formed a circle of scientific research workers who applied their knowledge to such wide uses as medicine, agriculture, printing, machinery, paint manufacture, as well as dynamics and astronomy. The king himself was no mean mathematician and scientist, and in the eyes of the nobles his learned pursuits were derogatory to his rank. They regarded him as a middle-class king, who was letting down the whole nobility. His mind was not " middle-class " in their sense, although he had wished to marry a lady-in-waiting while his father was still alive. Thwarted in his desire, he had been finally persuaded to marry his cousin, Sophie of Mecklenburg, who proved to be a lady of determination and a diplomatist hardly second to her husband.

Frederick's chief fault was that he was neither middle-class nor above the nobility; he was merely a noble who happened to be king—*primus inter pares*. The nobles took advantage of his dependence on them. They enlarged their estates, re-introduced compulsory labour, and the status of the peasant fell lower than it had been at the beginning of Christian II's reign. The king made but feeble protest except where his revenues were affected by expropriation. The system of "large" holdings, though bringing suffering to the small owners who sank to the position of labourers and hired men, undoubtedly improved methods of agriculture, and during this reign there was a huge expansion of trade, the most outstanding being the export of cows and pigs. The Danish cattle began to have a great reputation, and in one year no fewer than fifty thousand cows and a hundred and fifty thousand pigs were exported from Jutland alone.

The king himself was interested in scientific breeding, and the royal estates set an example in the treatment of the labourers, not followed by the other nobles. His philanthropic endeavours won some popularity for him, and his early death was deplored by the more advanced men of education, but the nobles hoped to increase their powers still further as his son Christian IV was only ten years old. A regency of four to govern in the new king's name seemed to stand in their way, as it contained an able bourgeois administrator, Valkendorf, as well as the cautious chancellor, Nils Kaas. They had both served the king well in their respective spheres, and were determined to continue the policy of peace abroad and prosperity at home. Their first clash came with the queen dowager, Sophie, who declared that she had no intention of interfering in the affairs of state, but she demanded three things: (1) the right to choose husbands for her daughters, (2) the right to supervise her son's upbringing until he became of age in 1596, and (3) the surrender of the crown lands, which she claimed as her rightful jointure. .

After a bitter controversy, the Queen Mother gained all her points. Her second daughter, Anne, was married to James VI of

Scotland, former suitor of her elder sister, who had been married to the Duke of Brunswick owing to the dilatory behaviour of the Scottish emissaries. They had finally broken down over the question of dowry and the ownership of the Orkneys and Hebrides. James found Sophie more amenable to his wooing of Anne now that the elder sister was safely matched, and Augusta betrothed to John Adolph, duke of Gottorp-Holstein.

The marriage was, apparently, distasteful to some members of the State Council, who considered that no advantages would accrue to Denmark. The princess, however, started for Scotland, but the ship was driven back by violent storms raised by witches in the pay of the councillors. The more modern explanation of her unfortunate start would be that she met a depression from Iceland, and that the captain decided to shelter from the north-westerly gale in Oslo. The result, however, was the same whatever the cause, and the princess remained for a month ostensibly awaiting a calmer sea when, without warning, James suddenly appeared to claim his bride. Although somewhat shocked by the forward behaviour of the bridegroom, Anne was duly married at Oslo. James made a royal visit to Denmark where he was deeply impressed with the scientific developments initiated in the previous reign, and formed a lasting admiration for Denmark which strengthened into an alliance after his accession to the English throne. The alliance did not bring any benefit to the Danes, but merely encouraged Christian IV in his foolish decision to join in the Thirty Years War. Sophie was finally firmly told by the Regency to desist from any activities in the perennial Holstein controversy after her support of John Adolph and so she had to content herself with building up the royal fortunes on the crown lands at Falsted. In this she was so successful that her son was able to borrow large sums, and finally inherit a prosperous and well-administered fortune when he was in great need of money.

The long reign of Christian IV—sixty years including the twelve years of the Regency—was full of promise, and had it not been for his fatal policy in participating in the Thirty Years War, Denmark might have had a very different and happier history. He was a young man of robust health and indefatigable energy. In some ways he resembled Christian II, as being a son of the Renaissance. He was a builder of cities, a designer of ships, an explorer, a general, and a scientist, but at the same time he had a simple mind which seemed unable to grasp the true value of things and left him bemused with small details of no importance.

Two entries in the king's diary[1] throw some light on the royal mind: " The lamplighter's wife, who is twenty-two, has just had twins. He is eighty-eight. I must investigate the matter."

" An elephant arrived in town, which could dance, fight and kneel. Also two Dutch ambassadors, who can do nothing."

" Must see that the nurse I have dismissed does not scratch the face of the new one."

The same man who entered such trivialities in the royal diary built new cities and castles, the most striking, perhaps, being Rosenborg, though his own favourite was the great Fredericksborg. French architects built in the style of the late Renaissance, but the Dutch influence, tempered with some purely Scandinavian features, became more marked as his fever for building increased. He is regarded as the architect of modern Copenhagen. The king, who supervised the plans and work on his most important buildings, extended his activities to Norway. The old capital was rebuilt and renamed Christiania, and not till the twentieth century did it revert to the old name of Oslo. His greatest personal interest lay in the sea and everything connected with it. He sailed in the ships which he designed; he made a voyage to the White Sea to investigate possible trade expansion. Merchant adventurers were encouraged to look beyond the Baltic and the North Sea. Chartered companies were given trade monopolies and privileges. The most famous were the Danish East India Company and the West India Company—the former establishing itself at Tranquebar and in later years founding the West African colonies sold to Britain in the middle of the nineteenth century.

It is for his heroic action in the naval battle off Kiel in 1644 that the Danes remember him as their greatest and bravest king. His undaunted courage as sailor and soldier, and his personal exploits, mark him as a national hero as well as the founder of the mercantile marine and the builder of the cities. His misguided foreign policy was forgotten when the people heard of his death, and it was left for the historians of later years to point out what he might have done to establish a sound democratic government. Christian clearly saw the evils of a too powerful nobility. He cur-

[1] Quoted in *Denmark in History.*

tailed their power, he flouted the State Council, if they tried to thwart him. He could be ruthless and jealous. His harsh treatment of Tyge Brahe whom he banished from the kingdom is inexplicable, unless he feared his riches. No rivals were allowed to his State Church, foreigners had to subscribe to his articles of faith, no teachers at the university were appointed unless they were Lutherans and churchgoers. He himself was a regular attendant, but his private life was marked by excesses of every kind.

He continually deplored the disputes between his legitimate and illegitimate children, though the favours he showered on the twelve children of Kristine Munk, whom he married on the death of his wife, Anne of Brandenberg, were sufficient to cause discontent among the aristocracy. Where he failed in his home policy was in his disregard of the National Assembly and the people. He ended the Age of the Nobility and ushered in the Age of Absolutism.

He was driven into the position of an absolute monarch by his own acts and their consequences, and though by nature a benevolent despot, his own love of the bourgeois and the peasant might have gained them more share in the government—at any rate local government—after the powers of the nobility and State Council had been curtailed.

His first error was in beginning a war against Sweden in 1611, usually known as the Kalmar War owing to the siege of that fortress. His ostensible reason was that Charles IX had called himself King of the Lapps and granted fishing rights off northern Norway to the people of the new town of Göteborg. His real reasons were his jealousy of Sweden and fear of her expansionist policy in Estonia and Livonia.

His State Council only consented to declare war because Christian announced his intention of making the declaration as Duke of Holstein if they refused. Charles IX challenged Christian to a duel, but this challenge was not accepted. Young Gustavus Adolphus came to the throne in the middle of the war and at his coronation dropped the offending title and pronounced himself ready to make peace. Next year through the mediation of James I, brother-in-law of Christian, the Treaty of Knäred was signed in 1613, whereby the *status quo* was restored, but Sweden had once more to pay a heavy indemnity for the restoration of Alvsborg, the fortress guarding Göteborg. Christian had gained little by this war except the satisfaction of a victory over Sweden. It was the desire to gain the undisputed hegemony of the Baltic which drove him into his fatal mistake in 1625. His first move was to secure the North German bishoprics for his younger sons. This aroused the anger of the German princes. He tried to soothe their susceptibilities by offering aid to the Protestants now hardly pressed by the forces of the Empire and the Catholic League under the command of the redoubtable generals Tilly and Wallenstein.

Encouraged by promises from France and England he moved an army of Danes and German mercenaries into the Empire itself. Disaster overcame him at Lutter near Brunswick. Seeing the Danish king utterly defeated, his German allies deserted him, and Wallenstein marched through Holstein and Slesvig into Jutland. The land was laid utterly desolate. Christian was left with only Fünen and Sjaelland, and the nobles and State Council would render him no assistance in the struggle which they contended with justice had been his own doing. The Emperor now decided to stamp out Lutheranism in the whole of North Germany and Denmark. Mass was celebrated again in the churches of Jutland, which was to be handed over to Spain. Wallenstein was created Duke of Mecklenburg and, as " General of the Baltic ", was to wrest the " dominium Baltici maris " from the Scandinavian countries. His first objective was the powerful fortress of Stralsund— the key to the North German coastline east of Denmark.

In spite of vigorous assaults and as close a blockade as was possible, Wallenstein failed in his attempt. His failure was almost entirely due to the help sent by Gustavus Adolphus, who realised the danger to his own designs if the whole of the southern shores of the Baltic fell to the Imperial army. The differences between the Danes and the Swedes were temporarily sunk in the face of the common danger. Gustavus was too wary to declare war at that time, but Scots and Swedes under Leslie were thrown into the fortress from Swedish ships.

Wallenstein's army suffered huge losses and had to retire. At the ensuing peace of Lübeck, the lost provinces were restored to Denmark, but she was denied the right ever again to interfere in the affairs of the Empire, and the secularised bishoprics were renounced. Denmark had fallen to the lowest level of impotence. She had no friend because, foolishly, the Swedish ambassador had been excluded from the Lübeck Conference and the Swedes felt, not unnaturally, that they had the right to reap some reward for their services which had saved Denmark from partition, if not extinction. Their only satisfaction lay in the defeat of Wallenstein. The story of Gustavus's meteoric career in Germany did not concern Denmark directly, and must be left to the next chapter. The Thirty Years War was still dragging out its weary course when, in 1643, Christian IV made an offer to mediate between the Emperor and Sweden. He hoped to restore Danish credit and prevent its complete eclipse by Sweden in the Baltic. He also tried to exclude its newly-won provinces from exemption of dues in the Sound. Oxenstierna, the able statesman of the late Gustavus Adolphus, decided to strike hard at the ungrateful Danes. The general Torstensson led his army with lightning rapidity from Moravia, and in a few weeks overran the unfortunate province of Jutland for the second time in twenty years. A Dutch fleet was sent to convey the Swedish army to the islands of Fünen and Sjaelland. With immense energy and courage, the old king, now sixty-seven years of age, raised a fleet and defeated the Dutch, who retired to Holland. A Swedish fleet arrived in June. Again Christian in person led the Danish fleet with great gallantry. Wounded in thirteen places and with one eye shot out, he continued to cheer on his men until the Swedish fleet retired, defeated, to Kiel harbour, where it was blockaded. The Danish admiral, however, who had taken command, allowed it to escape. Nothing daunted, Christian had the admiral shot, and led the Danes once more against a large combined Swedo-Dutch fleet which destroyed or captured all but two of the Danish fleet. With no army and no fleet, Christian was forced to sign the humiliating Treaty of Brömsebro on August 13th, 1645. By this, the islands of Gottland and Osel, and the province of Jämtland, were ceded to Sweden outright, while Halland was given as security for the exemption of Sound dues. Denmark never recovered from this blow, and in 1658 Skåne, Halland and Blekinge were ceded to Sweden, and have remained in her possession to this day. The king was shattered by this humiliation, and so ended his career in a blaze of personal glory and national ignominy.

On the credit side, he must always be remembered for the beautification of the cities, and as the founder and father of the great Danish merchant service. As a political and military power, his country faded away, but he pointed the way to its true metier, and to this it has firmly adhered to the present day. As a peaceful trading and maritime power, it has remained in the forefront of nations, and, in the construction of ships of quality, its shipyards are still regarded as second to none.

CHAPTER VIII

THE HOUSE OF VASA

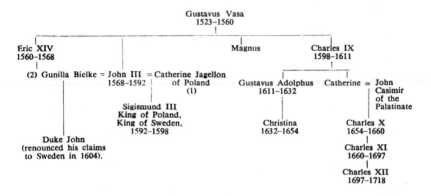

Gustavus Vasa
1523–1560

Eric XIV
1560–1568

(2) Gunilla Bielke = John III = Catherine Jagellon
1568–1592 | of Poland
(1)

Sigismund III
King of Poland,
King of Sweden,
1592–1598

Duke John
(renounced his claims
to Sweden in 1604).

Magnus

Charles IX
1598–1611

Gustavus Adolphus
1611–1632

Christina
1632–1654

Catherine = John
Casimir
of the
Palatinate

Charles X
1654–1660

Charles XI
1660–1697

Charles XII
1697–1718

THE triumphant campaign of Gustavus Vasa and his peasant army against the Danes was described in a previous chapter.[1] It was only by the aid of Lübeck and Danzig that Stockholm fell and the gallant Danish admiral, Norrby, was forced to take refuge in the island of Gottland. In 1523 a Riksdag was summoned to meet at Strängnäs. Owing to the massacre at Stockholm, new members were appointed to the Council who sat with representatives of the four estates—nobles, burgesses, clergy and peasants, which included the miners. Two representatives from Lübeck were also present, because it was asserted with justice that Hanseatic interests coincided with those of the nationalists. It was imperative that a king should be elected before Frederick, the new king of Denmark, could claim the throne of Sweden. The Lübeckese, besides opposing a Scandinavian Union, were determined to retain their hold on Swedish trade and exact their full pound of flesh for the services rendered by their fleet. There was one obvious choice, and the young conqueror, the " Lord of the Dales " and regent of Sweden, was unanimously elected. There is no reason to doubt the sincerity of Gustavus Vasa in alleging his reluctance to accept the offer of

[1] *Vide* Chapter VI.

the throne, and only bowing to the wishes of the people against his own will. Many times in the course of his reign, he reminded discontented subjects that it was their wish, not his, that he became ruler. On Midsummer's Eve, Gustavus Vasa entered his capital as king and founded a dynasty which held undisputed sway for three centuries.

The Sweden he found was in a sorry state. It was utterly spent by the supreme effort which had rid her of the Danish oppressor, and its resources were at their lowest pitch.

There was no army. Those who had flocked to his standards with one object returned to their homes now that their aim had been achieved.

There was no navy. He had borrowed foreign ships and sailors on onerous terms which drained the revenues and throttled Swedish trade. He saw the commercial wealth and undertakings pass into German hands.

By the defeat of Denmark and its stranglehold on Sweden, Lübeck had achieved a double victory for the Hanseatic League.

The treasury was drained. The only sources of revenue at his disposal came from the crown lands and his private estates. These were impoverished and straitened in extent. The nobility were divided. The higher nobility, jealous of the new king, were determined to recover their influence, and many still believed that the old union should be restored with restrictions on the royal power.

The peasants and miners, elated by their success and encouraged by the reliance and trust which Gustavus had displayed towards them, were ready to press home their grievances even by rebellion. They were eager to assert their power and formed a dangerous and inflammable element, easily incited to action by an opponent of the sovereign. The Church was in a state of turmoil and to the king and his contemporaries appeared to be the most urgent of all the problems of State. It proved to be the key to most of the other problems, and the king himself must have the credit for his quick recognition of its importance. The legal archbishop, Gustav Trolle, had left the country. He was regarded as the symbol of Danish domination and was held responsible for the murder of the two bishops in the " Blood Bath " The people were loyal Catholics except in Stockholm and a few cities where the teachings of Luther had already been spread by

Olaus Petri—known afterwards as "Master Olof". Brask, the good bishop of Linköping, was a staunch supporter of Rome, but a nationalist in politics. The vacant see, the mutterings of the Reformation, the popular belief that Danish domination and Papal rule were in league, all called for immediate action.

It is difficult to paint a blacker picture than that presented by Sweden on Gustavus's accession.

Before his death in 1560, he had solved the main problems, overcome most of the difficulties, and left a united Sweden.

His genius for administration and recognition of his country's needs showed itself in his system of forming a standing army, ready alike for defence against a Danish invasion, for foreign service and for the suppression of revolts by nobles or peasants. First of all, he instituted a modified feudal levy. Landowners were compelled to supply one or more soldiers who had to attend annual military exercises. These were not under the leadership of the landowner, unless he happened to be a regular officer. Then came a standing army consisting of battalions containing about five hundred men. They were stationed at various strategic points, usually at royal castles under the command of a trusted officer. An outstanding example of the "Vasa type" castle can be seen at Vadstena, at the north-east corner of Lake Vättern.[1] It is in perfect preservation and illustrates its double purpose of fortress and garrison depot—the grim round bastion faces the lake and the fortified living quarters behind are capable of housing the whole battalion—a curious contrast to the nearby church of the Nunnery of S. Birgitta. The training of these battalions was personally supervised by the king, and later by his son Eric, who was an able strategist. They formed the nucleus of the famous Swedish army of the great Gustavus Adolphus.

The building up of the army was a gradual process, but the construction of the navy was carried through with incredible speed. A larger type of warship was adopted and was not long in proving its worth. When Gustavus seized the opportunity of attacking the Lübeckese navy, during the Danish civil wars, these ships proved their superiority, and so shattered the enemies' fleet that the supremacy of the Hanseatic League could never challenge Sweden again for the naval supremacy in the Baltic. At the same time

---

[1] On visiting this castle, I was surprised to find it described as Renaissance. Except for minor interior decorations in the living quarters, it bears little resemblance to work usually termed Renaissance.

Gustavus threw off the Lübeckese yoke and Swedish trade came into its own.

The internal trade had already begun to improve. By somewhat despotic laws, Swedish merchants had been ordered to Stockholm so that the German monopoly of commerce could be broken. German merchants had either to become Swedish residents conforming with Swedish laws or leave the country. Extra-territorial rights and privileges were abolished. German miners, then the most advanced in Europe, were introduced to improve the iron and copper mines. The new methods soon put the industry on a sure footing. Fresh mines were started, the old brought up to date. Exports increased by leaps and bounds, and Swedish goods found their way to countries outside the Baltic. This necessitated a port on the west coast, for the fortress village of Alvsborg was primarily a military and not a commercial harbour. Shortly after the close of the century, the modern town of Göteborg (Gothenburg) was founded and the Danish threat of commanding the west coast from Halland to Norway had vanished. The expansion and protection of trade indirectly benefited the revenues of the crown, but Gustavus rightly considered that the royal coffers must have a more dependable source of supply. Not only must the king " live of his own " and be more wealthy than any of his subjects, but his many reforms cost money and the budget was not balanced. There must not be any mortgaging of the royal domains, which had proved so fatal in Denmark. By forfeiture and occasionally by compulsory purchase, he acquired some five thousand estates and farms under his private ownership and no fewer than eleven thousand for the crown lands.

A civil service, carefully supervised to prevent fraud, administered the public and private funds. Bailiffs were appointed to cultivate the estates in the most up-to-date and scientific manner. The royal farms were models which other agriculturalists were encouraged to imitate. A regulated proportion of arable to pasture was adopted where possible. Forests were cleared, marshes drained. Regular hunts were organised to kill off the wolves and bears which preyed on the stock. The furs were cured and those not required for home use were exported. Gustavus himself was a scientific farmer and delighted in journeying about his estates. He talked to the peasants and harangued, advised and admonished the farmer " as a good father would his children ".

Being a self-supporting country, the trade had been largely conducted by barter outside the cities and dues had been paid in kind.
Now money was required. To overcome this difficulty, centres
were established for the sale of the surplus after the needs of the
royal household and army had been satisfied. Goods unsold and
not exchanged for exportable merchandise were then taken to the
larger centres, whence they were used for foreign trade. In this
way they could be turned into cash or metals, from which the
currency could be enlarged to meet the increasing needs of the
country.

The greed and power of the nobles were curbed. The Riksdag
was used by the king to balance the power of the Council (råd),
which had tried to rule the country and flout the royal power.
Many nobles who resisted had to flee from the land and formed a
nucleus of discontented Swedish opposition—originally in the
Netherlands during Christian II's banishment and then in Poland.
These nobles were both political and religious opponents of the
new regime and proved a real danger on the accession of John.

The peasant problem did not offer an easy solution. Their
support was valuable, but insubordination was intolerable. When
warnings and chidings and appeals to their sense of gratitude
failed, the king struck heavily. The leaders were executed, but
there were never wholesale massacres of retribution. Usually five
or six of the ringleaders suffered death, and it was not long before
the others repented for their misdoings. "Old King Gösta"
regarded them as having been misled and he was probably right
in his judgment, and his easy and paternal talks soon restored
their affection for their deliverer from the oppressor.

The major problem was ecclesiastical. With his usual quick
appreciation of a situation he realised that in matters spiritual
the movement must be very slow. The people must not be coerced.
Changes deemed necessary must not be introduced before
preachers had explained their meaning. On two major principles
he was adamant: the superfluous wealth of the Church must be
for the benefit of the State, and Rome should not appoint prelates
who interfered with his State affairs. On these issues he was prepared to break with Rome. Many points of comparison are made
between the English and Swedish Reformation. The closest is
possibly the need of the State for money, but the fundamental
difference is that the very existence of a national and separate

Sweden was endangered by the Danish connexion with the hierarchy. England faced no invader with a Papal interdict in his pocket, when Henry VIII made his break with Rome.

The story of the Swedish Reformation is the story of the establishment of Swedish independence and that story does not end until after a long and costly war with Poland. It was due to the constructive work of Gustavus that his successors emerged in triumph.

Enough prominence has never been given to this remarkable founder of modern Sweden. What manner of man was he? Contemporary continental accounts give one picture, Swedish accounts another. Gustavus Adolphus paid him high tribute, Gustavus III listened to an opera in the heroic style extolling his virtues, but not till the nineteenth century was there any attempt to give a balanced account of this man, who combined the characteristics of new monarch, benevolent despot and democratic leader. As seen through the eyes of Danish and Catholic foes, he was a ruthless pillager of the Church, a murderer of peasants, an oppressor of those nobles who refused his bribes with the spoils of the monasteries and churches, and in his relations with foreign countries a breaker of treaties—a dominating tyrant, who knew no law save his own. This was the view which prevailed throughout Europe, except possibly in England and, towards the ends of his reign, in the Netherlands.

To the Swedes, he appeared as the saviour of his country, " the instrument of God, who brought prosperity to the fatherland ". severe but just, the enemy of abuses in Church and State, the father of his people, ready to hear complaints, but equally ready to punish the evildoer.

It is not surprising that he earned such contradictory reputations. It is true that he pillaged the churches, and his demand for one bell from every church roused the peasants of Dalarna, and their revolt was punished with great severity. He did rob the churches of much of their plate, and opposition was cruelly crushed; but it is also true that this wealth was used in the interests of the State and not squandered.

Monasteries and monastic lands were sequestered and some of the proceeds went to the nobles to secure their support, as well as to the State. Bishops, who had often been military leaders, were deprived of their castles, which, as in the case of Gripsholm on the Mälar lake, were used to house the new battalions. What he did was for the sake of the State, which always came before his private interests. His temper, which rose quickly, led him into unreasonable actions, especially in the face of any opposition, and it is not hard to perceive why his opponents should regard him as a tyrant. On the other hand, his friendly intercourse with his subjects and his homely family life could not fail to endear him to the masses.

When he secured for his house the hereditary succession to the crown, it was a popular tribute to the national sovereign, though some of the nobles, whose wealth had been largely augmented by the growing prosperity, may well have been contemplating a return of their old privileges when he died. They could not hope to try conclusions with this king with any hope of success.

All accounts of him agree, however, in describing him as a man of immense energy and courage, with as great a mastery of detail as of men.

Able he undoubtedly was, and it is no reflection on his talent to describe him as an opportunist who had more than his share of good luck. In this he may be justly compared with the great Tudor sovereigns, Henry VIII and Queen Elizabeth. As previously mentioned, the Reformation is the central theme of his reign, and aided by his gifted servants, Olaus Petri and Laurentius Andreae, he so cleverly manipulated the intricacies of the movement that by 1544 he had already established three fundamental principles mainly through the agency of this national movement: (1) The crown was hereditary and so there could be no disputed succession. (2) The country was freed from Denmark and the Danish king recognised Sweden as a separate nation. (3) the separation from Rome was so complete that the Counter-Reformation found its strongest opponents in the very class which had resisted the early reformers.

It was partly by good fortune that Gustavus was able to turn the Reformation into a national policy.

At the very outset, the Pope, misinformed of the true situation, acted with inconceivable folly. He insisted on the restoration of Gustav Trolle as Archbishop of Uppsala. This prelate, in the minds of the people, stood for Danish misrule, and the clergy could not forgive him for the murder of the two bishops barely two years previously. A Papal legate, sent to extirpate the Lutheran heresies by Adrian VI, was flattered by the Swedish suggestion that he should become archbishop. He was duly elected by the Chapter and the news was sent to Rome, and the new Archbishop Johannes Magni was prepared to root out the heresies being taught by Olaus Petri and Laurentius Andreae. The Pope, however, utterly refused to confirm the appointment and ordered the immediate reinstatement of Trolle. Gustavus replied in hot anger that he would not consent. The Pope's answer was to appoint an Italian to the see of Skara. Gustavus refused him admittance into Sweden. While this dispute was going on, Olaus and the Lutherans had been gaining ground. He had been at Wittenberg under Luther in 1517 and was strongly influenced by Melanchthon. On his return to Sweden he had been appointed Chancellor to the Bishop of Strängnäs when he had completely convinced the old archdeacon Laurentius Andreae, and also his brother Laurentius Petri, of the need for an active campaign for reform. In 1523 to 1524 Olaus, or Master Olof as the people called him, and Andreae came to Stockholm, the former as Secretary and Chaplain of the city and the latter as King's Chancellor. It was thus at a crucial point in the history of the Reformation that Gustavus came into close contact with these Lutheran converts. He was impressed by their sermons, and still more by the fact that Luther had " clipped the wings of this antichrist, the Pope " and advocated a severance with Rome which would put the wealth of the Church into the hands of the State. The movement, however, met with opposition from two unexpected quarters. Bishop Brask, an ardent nationalist, insisted that the Pope must remain as head of things spiritual. The peasants rose in a body to protest against the sacrilege of the king and the pagan sermons of " these sons of Sodom and Gomorrah ". The king in 1526 openly sided with the reformers, stating that the Holy Scriptures were the only authorities by which new doctrines could be tested, and that the monasteries were corrupt and the priests lazy and ignorant. The wealth which came under the control of the State was used, so the king maintained, solely for the benefit of the people, so that a purified Church was to be established throughout the kingdom. Gifts were bestowed on Uppsala University, where there was a growing band of enthusiastic reformers and where future priests should be educated. In the same year, the New Testament was translated into Swedish so that all should read the word of God "purely and simply".

Master Olof himself superintended the translation which, like the Authorised Version in England, became the model of the national language.

Towards the end of the year, the struggle grew fiercer and disorders greater. Two-thirds of the tithes were applied to improve the national budget, while the good Bishop Brask was ordered to close his printing press and cease his anti-Lutheran pamphlets. The nobles scented danger. They might well be the next victims of the royal greed. Thus when the king summoned an assembly of the four estates at Västerås in 1527 there was a strange alliance of bishops, nobles and peasants in opposition to the king's ecclesiastical policy. The nobles, however, were so thoroughly alarmed by the social aspirations of the peasants that the king ordered them to come armed, yet there was considerable danger of the nobles attempting to regain their power and take the government into their own hands. They were particularly incensed with the favour shown to low-bred clerks in the civil service. Their attitude was that social disorder among the peasants must be suppressed, and the rising in Dalarna was a forcible argument for their contention. They demanded that the Chancellor, Andreae, should be dismissed, and that Brask should be recognised as the head of the Swedish Church (still Catholic) and appointed to the still vacant see of Uppsala. The burgesses, who had not suffered financially were, on the whole, in favour of a modified Reformation, but were not unlike the "unknown quantity of waverers" in a modern Parliamentary election. It is now known that the current belief was that the assembly was summoned to find means of securing order and suppressing unrest. The religious question would naturally come under review. The bishops and some of the clergy, fearing an attack on Rome, had held a secret meeting beforehand binding them to resist any resolutions against the Pope. The surprising proceedings prevented them from carrying out their design, and the written protest was not found till 1542, when it was dug up under the floor of the church where they had met.

During the whole of the last two years, Gustavus had been free from outside interference. Denmark had fallen to Frederick, while Christian II was still in the Netherlands unable to gain any active help from Charles V, who had begun to be suspicious of his leanings towards Luther's teachings. Rome was in no position to interfere, the Pope himself had been in danger, and the year of "The Recess of Västerås" saw the barbaric sack of Rome and the flight of the Pope. Thus Gustavus felt strong enough to declare his hand and this he did in his own fashion. The meeting was opened by the Chancellor, who recited the story of the king's personal sufferings and privations, his courage his patriotic devotion and his gallant leadership. Then followed the benefits which his people had received at his hands. Finally, he insisted that to maintain the State the increased revenues were a necessity. Bishop Brask replied for the opposition, stressed the freedom of the Church from lay jurisdiction and asserted that the only Head of the Church was the Pope, who was the supreme judge on spiritual matters and the Vicar-General of God. The King sprang to his feet with angry denunciations of his ungrateful people. "No longer will I be your king," he cried, burst into tears and rushed from the hall, leaving the delegates in consternation and dismay. He retired to his castle surrounded by his guards and admitting no one save Andreae and Master Olof. How far this was a premeditated move to win complete submission or whether he really felt the attitude of the people to be so deeply ungrateful that he suddenly decided to abdicate, will never be known. Certain it is that no other man or combination of men could take his place. After three days of negotiations he won a great victory, and the moderation with which he used the supreme powers over Church and State, conferred on him by the four estates, places him among the greatest of patriotic statesmen. It showed him to be no self-seeker, no tyrant, and his studied restraint commands respect and admiration. Only once did his temper get the better of his judgement. The opposition of Master Olof and Andreae to his financial policy in 1539 roused him to anger. They objected to the king's miserly hoarding in the State treasury of the wealth collected from the Church. They had supported the levies, but desired to see more spent on social services. Gustavus, influenced by Germans in his civil service, resented their criticism and, fearing that "new presbyter were but old priest writ large", brought both his faithful ministers to trial. Both were condemned to death, but the unfair sentence was revoked, and they were released after paying crushing fines. They were allowed to continue their religious work but were never in the royal service again. Gustavus sensed that public opinion was against him, and religious reforms went still more slowly.

The main provisions of the Recess of Västerås shaped the future course of Swedish history, and their acceptance assured national unity. No reference was made to theology and the liturgy except that "the Word of God should be taught plainly and purely". The dreaded break of the Apostolic succession was avoided by the consecration of new bishops by Peder Månsson, Bishop of Västerås, whose own consecration had taken place in Rome. The Ordinances of Västerås restored order in the church services, but it was not until the Council of Örebro in 1529 that any changes in doctrine were sanctioned.[1]

The Västerås Recess dealt with the relations of the Church with the State and of the Swedish Church with Rome.

(1) The king became supreme head of Church and State.

(2) Bishops-elect were not to be confirmed in Rome.

(3) Peter's Pence were to be paid to the crown.

(4) All the clergy were amenable to the civil courts in matters temporal.

(5) The bishops' castles, cathedral Chapters, revenues and monasteries should be transferred to the Crown, which supplied the necessary revenues for the maintenance of the clergy. The surplus, which was substantial, was to be used by the State.

(6) The nobles should receive back all the lands taken by the Church since 1454. This measure won over the nobles to the side of the king.

(7) The Word of God should be taught plainly and sermons expounding and explaining the Scriptures and the true faith should be delivered every Sunday.

Bishop Brask, faithful to his convictions, could not subscribe to these articles and went into exile at Danzig. He kept in touch with his old friends, however, and was in treasonable correspondence with Christian II when he invaded Norway and who, it was believed in Sweden, was contemplating an invasion of that country. The exposure of this supposed attempt to restore Catholicism strengthened the link between Nationalism and the Reformation. In many ways the medieval Church of Sweden was

---

[1] The accounts of the Swedish Reformation show considerable variance, especially as regards the Swedish Mass. The scholarly and convincing study of Brilioth (1934 edition) generally accepted as the best authority, has been followed where opinions show much divergence.

ripe for reform. The country people, though Catholic and extremely superstitious in many of their beliefs, had preserved considerable independence of thought and action.

They were strong supporters of the Mass and at one time so great was the number of private Masses for material needs that special dispensations were ordained to allow these at irregular times.[1] Masses were said for every conceivable object—good crops, a good journey, freedom from disease, and so forth. Fasts were not observed before Communion, in which emphasis was laid on the "Memorial Act". It should be noted that the laity had begun to confine their observance to the Easter Communion with Lenten penances. The rite had become associated with the payment of dues, as unless these were paid at Easter, Communion and burial in consecrated ground could be refused, and the delinquent became a social and religious outcast. On the other hand, the pageantry and ritual of feast days were popular, and the influence of the bishops and clergy was considerable. Gustavus and his advisers were careful not to enforce any doctrines which might clash with the ancient usages until the reasons for the innovations had been given time to carry conviction. The meeting at Örebro was attended by supporters of the old order and those who advocated a "middle way", and the innovators were in a minority. However, the assembly condemned the worship of saints, Transubstantiation and such ancient customs as holy water, while fasting and pilgrimages were discounted in value, but not forbidden.

On the thorny question of the Latin Mass there is some doubt, but recent research has made it clear that the Swedish Mass took the place of the Low Mass, and that the Latin Mass was permitted until 1593 at High Mass. The marriage of priests was encouraged, but not ordered as in Denmark. In this connexion it might be pointed out that Messenius's account of Master Olof's wedding, written a hundred years after the event, is almost certainly incorrect, as conclusively proved by Brilioth.

> " On Master Olof's wedding day
> Our Lutherdom had made such sway
> That Mass in Swedish first was sung
> So all men followed their own tongue
> For so had Master Olof seen
> How things at Wittenberg had been."

[1] Brilioth *Eucharistic Faith and Practice*, pages 228-275.

The marriage took place in 1525, but such an innovation at that date would have caused a storm of protest from Bishop Brask and his followers.

It was from 1529 onwards that the Church was slowly and peaceably evangelised. The Swedish Church had its national characteristics and did not slavishly follow the later pamphlets and writings of Luther. This explains the more ornate decorations of its churches and such customs as seen in the Communion service where each communicant kneels singly at the altar rails. It was also ordained that a sermon should be preached at each celebration. The doctrine of the real presence was not preserved in the words of administration, "The body of Christ given for thee, the blood of Christ shed for thee."

The first Swedish Church Order was published in 1540 and, though in 1539 the Latin Mass was not abolished, in the next year it is ordered that the Swedish Mass should be used. Thus with the retention of the Apostolic succession and the synods on the one hand and the introduction of evangelism, a happy compromise was reached which satisfied all parties except a small number of extremists. That this was a compromise which endured can be deduced from the revised edition of the Liturgy of 1602. This confirmed the rulings of the Uppsala assembly of 1593 which is recognised as the termination of the Reformation movement and the defeat of the Counter-Reformation. John III died in 1592 and his son Sigismund, King of Poland, a militant Catholic, was King of Sweden by right of hereditary succession. His claims were resisted on a combination of religious and nationalist grounds. His uncle, Duke Charles, an extreme Protestant, led the opposition, yet the assembly refused to be driven into an uncompromising form of Protestantism or bow down to the liturgical demands of the Catholics. Thus, the surplice, the bishop's cope, vestments, the Sign of the Cross, and other usages of the old order remained, but union with Rome was firmly resisted. Such results were the fruits of the wise and carefully organised movement beginning in 1529. It is impossible to over-stress its importance. It was the mainspring of the defensive movement against union with or domination by Poland and also of the offensive movement of Gustavus Adolphus in the Thirty Years War. It is possible to regard the great Swedish enterprise of 1630 as an heroic action to save Protestantism or as an action to defend Sweden from invasion and ultimate absorption, or as an attempt to secure for Sweden the dominion of the Baltic, or with greater truth as a combination of all three. In any case, the exploits of Gustavus and his Swedish Chancellor Oxenstierna could never have achieved such successes unless the political and religious unity of Sweden had been firmly established by his grandfather. It has been repeated too often that " the history of Sweden is the history of her kings ", but it is true that in the reign of Gustavus Vasa his biography is Sweden's history.

The troubles with the peasants ceased after 1531. They had been a disturbing element rather than a threat to the throne. When a Swedish " Perkin Warbeck " claimed to be Nils Sture, the direct descendant of the great Stures, the peasants were ready to support him. The rising was suppressed with the King's usual severity, but the Sture family remained loyal to the Crown. The " Dacke " war in 1542, led by a " robber chief, traitor and heretic ", as Gustavus dubbed him, who received arms and subsidies from exiles and foreign princes, was a more serious affair. Småland rose in support of Dacke. Nils Dacke was a magnificent leader in the guerilla warfare, for which that part of Sweden was eminently suitable. The law-abiding elements were alienated from Gustavus by an attempted collection of superfluous church plate. Nils cleverly worked on their superstitions and they joined his outlaws. The royal forces sent in small detachments from the garrison depots suffered several defeats and it was only by mobilising his whole army that victory was finally won. Gustavus increased his army by the creation of a Territorial reserve on lines almost identical to those adopted by Haldane in 1908.

Reference has already been made to the temporary union with Denmark to overthrow the naval power of Lübeck and also to the beginning of the struggle in Livonia.[1] The Baltic had always been the chief arena for Swedish activities, but the reign of Gustavus Vasa marks the entry of Sweden into European politics. In 1542 the first of many treaties between France and Sweden was signed. It had its origin in the mutual fear of Charles V, who was regarded as a potential danger to Sweden as long as his brother-in-law, Christian II, was alive. Though its military terms were never implemented, it may be regarded as a forerunner of the famous compact signed at Bärwalde between Richelieu and Gustavus Adolphus, and the beginning of the lasting interest of France in Swedish

[1] *Vide* Chapter VII, page 109

affairs. A commercial treaty with England was proposed to sub-
stitute Swedish for the growing Russian trade. This came to
nothing, as there was no reason for England to abandon her
profitable commercial interests in Archangel, even if she extended
her trade with Sweden. At this time her Scandinavian intercourse
was confined almost entirely to Denmark, which included Norway.
The most enterprising and romantic approach to England was
made by Eric, the hotheaded and extravagant son of Gustavus.
He made determined efforts to marry Queen Elizabeth. When his
ambassadors failed to win her hand he determined to go in person,
but his ship was stopped from sailing by his father. Then he sent
his younger brother, who prosecuted his case with "burning
ardour". The Queen's reply was courteous and, while stating that
she preferred the virgin state, it was sufficiently ambiguous for
Eric to try again when he became king in 1560. It is said that
he was prepared to assassinate Leicester, who was reported to be
his rival. However, he got no satisfaction from Queen Elizabeth
or Mary Stuart or three other princesses, so he married in the end
the servant of a musician, who kept a public house. Though this
first essay in diplomatic marriage politics did not bring much
glory to Sweden, it shows that Sweden had begun to be recognised as
a country at least as important as Denmark, and before long she
found herself drawn into the full swirl of the European struggle.

"Old King Gösta" himself did not aspire to do more than
restore the ancient kingdom of Sweden, which included Finland,
and for the last sixteen years of his reign, his country enjoyed a
much needed peace. He never lost his untiring energy and to the
last was worrying about the fate of his people, when he was no
longer there to look after them. He was anxious about the dangers
which the rashness of his hotheaded son Eric might bring upon
the land in spite of the careful education and training bestowed
on him. By the Union of Inheritance of 1554, the hereditary
succession had been vested in the House of Vasa, and shortly
before his death on Michaelmas Day 1560, the old king delivered
a touching farewell benediction and address to his beloved people.
At this assembly he declared his intention of leaving the crown
to Eric, the son of his first wife, and the three younger sons, two
of whom eventually succeeded their brother on the throne,
received huge dukedoms and were invested with almost regal
powers. The intention was apparently to provide suitably for the

royal princes and at the same time give them sufficient power to curb any wild schemes on which the king might be inclined to embark. Eric was his son by his first wife, a German princess, while John, Magnus and Charles were sons by a Swedish noble lady whom he had married as his second wife in 1536. To John fell Finland, to Magnus Ostergötland, and to Charles the large fiefs of Södermanland, Närke and Värmland. Their central cities of government, Abo, Vadstena and Nyköping, were places of no little strength and strategic importance. At the outset, it was clear that the new regime could not work smoothly unless the brothers acted in harmony to preserve the united Sweden which their father had left.

The very natures of the four brothers made this almost impossible. Each inherited some of the qualities of Gustavus, but none had his balance and realistic outlook. The passionate strain of the Vasa was accentuated in Eric and after eight years of rule he was at times not responsible for his actions, and in fits of passion committed horrible sadistic crimes and murders. In John, the strain appeared in acts inspired by hastiness and suspicion and jealousy. Magnus soon disappeared from the political stage as he became insane and had to be put under restraint before he was old enough to become a danger. Charles had fits of ungovernable ill-temper and was easily irritated into actions of which he repented later; yet, with the exception of Magnus, each had inherited a fair share of their father's ability. Eric was a fine soldier and ambitious to use the strength of Sweden in extending her territory and crushing Denmark for ever, so that Sweden should be the acknowledged leader in the Baltic. We have already recorded how he had begun to look far afield for a wife from Western Europe. He saw visions of greatness for his country and himself, but he realised that these grandiose plans could never be successful while his powers at home were liable to be undermined. He moved at once to crush his brothers through the help of a Riksdag at Arboga in 1561, and to lay the foundation of his new Baltic dominion by the acquisition of Reval. He shared with John a cultured taste for the fine arts and literature, and the degradation of the last two years of his reign must not rob him of the credit of introducing culture to Sweden. He brought the fruits of the European Renaissance to his country, and John carried on this side of his work.

John was not a soldier and, had he not been drawn into politics, he might have been one of the leading theologians of his day. He had real learning and threw himself into the religious controversies which the steady progress of the Counter-Reformation was bringing nearer to Sweden. His ideal was a restoration of a Catholic Church, which should bring a purified and glorious Christianity to the world. He dreamed of a beautiful colourful religion based on fundamental truths. He tried unsuccessfully to restore much that was lost of the old order by the Red Liturgy of 1572. His contemporaries could not follow his ideals, which, not unnaturally, they considered a return to Rome and a threat to independence. The Swedish Church of Master Olof stood firm, and John's religious endeavours form an interlude in the ordered march of the Reformation.

Charles was a contrast to his brothers: a thrifty economist, frowning on the extravagances of his brothers, and in religion leaning to the severe doctrines of Calvin. Being in the centre of Sweden, he could watch events more closely than could John in Finland, and he used his considerable powers of statesmanship with no little skill. Outside events, the Polish wars and the Danish invasion, were not of his making, though he exhibited a lack of tact as regards Denmark, and the Sweden which he left to his son Gustavus Adolphus seemed to have fallen from its high estate. The underlying strength based on the national unity was still there, and it was not long before the country entered on the most glorious period of its history.

The chief events of Eric's reign (1560 to 1568) have already been mentioned from the Danish angle. It is, however, important to remember that Eric's defeat of John had not only made an enemy of Poland but had strengthened John's conviction that the best policy for Sweden was friendship with Poland, and he was determined on his own accession to power to put his ideas in action. He considered that Russia was the real danger and that the differences between Sweden and Poland were on the surface. A union or strong alliance would be in the interests of both. Clouds soon began to gather round the once attractive, lively and handsome Eric. John and his Polish wife were kept in prison for some years, but Eric still feared Charles and was suspicious of the nobles who resented his aristocratic ways, and he lacked the easy good humour which had endeared the old king to the peasants.

He fell under the evil genius of a sinister minister called Göran Persson. His suspicions grew worse, he consulted the soothsayers, he saw blood in the crystals, conspiracies in his horoscope. Göran Persson persuaded him to strike at Nils Sture, whom he degraded by humiliating treatment in the streets of Stockholm. The nobles were shocked and alarmed. Göran Persson whispered into his ears that his stepbrothers, the dukes, were contemplating treachery, and were in league with the nobles. A system of spies caused further unrest. The culminating point was their outraged feelings when he married Karin, the serving maid, and made her queen in 1568. As his mistress she could have been tolerated. She was a lovable girl, who soothed him as the flashes of insanity grew more violent and more frequent. She read poetry to him and played the lute, but she was not the simple and pure girl from the country, as his followers tried to make out. It must not be supposed that he had no supporters. At his coronation he had created two new orders—counts and barons (friherrar)—which have continued to this day. They counter-balanced the older landed nobility. and were well aware of their dependence on their sovereign. These orders proved useful to Gustavus Adolphus in his struggle with the older nobility. Meanwhile the Danish war went badly. Alvsborg had fallen. Rantzau threatened to march on Stockholm. Eric summoned his nobles to a Riksdag at Uppsala. Some he imprisoned, accusing them of treason, among them Nils Sture and his father Svante Sture. In a frenzy, he rushed into their cell and committed murder with his own hands. Eric, with "hands dripping with blood", fled into the country from imaginary pursuers. Finally, in a state bordering on madness, he shut himself up in a castle. Suddenly he emerged, released his brother, John, and led an army against Rantzau. He was sufficiently successful to check the Danish advance, but his mental recovery was only temporary. No reliance could be placed on him. He was governed by his capricious moods. The end came when John and Charles united, and Eric was formally deposed by the Riksdag, and the crown was offered to John. Eric dragged out a miserable existence in one prison after another until his death in 1577. probably by poison. Owing to the exhaustion of Denmark, no advantage was taken of this civil war, and John was able to sign the peace of Stettin in 1570.[1] By this treaty, Alvsborg was restored

[1] *Vide* page 113

to Sweden, though Jämtland remained Danish, and the clauses by which Sweden gave up her conquests in Estonia and Livonia to the Emperor on payment of Swedish war debts were never carried out, and so they remained as useful outposts in both Russian and later Polish wars. John was not long in putting his Russo-Polish policy to the test. Success did not come immediately. It was largely due to the military ability of his general, de la Gardie, a Frenchman by birth, and to the Polish attacks on Russia. The Swedes were thus able to secure Narva in 1581, possession of which safeguarded Estonia from invasion. The Russo-Finnish boundary was settled for the first time, and Russia withdrew her claims to the Baltic. The first part of his plans had met with sufficient success to encourage John in an attempt to secure the election of his son, Sigmund, to the throne of Poland. In 1587 he was duly crowned, and Sweden can be said to have taken her place as one of the most important countries of Europe, and without question the most powerful in the north-east. Eric had looked from his windows on the great countries of the West. John had opened the door and had arrived.

Somewhat overawed by this diplomatic triumph, and afraid of what complications might ensue, he ordered his son, a devout Catholic be it said, to abdicate and return to Sweden. The Swedish Council refused to sanction his return, and so Sigismund remained King of Poland and heir-presumptive to the throne of Sweden. This attitude of opposition was warranted by John's religious policy at home and foreign policy abroad. He offered to make an alliance with Philip II of Spain, who was the active agent of the Counter-Reformation. He had been in constant communication with Rome, and no less a person than the Secretary General of the Jesuits had visited Stockholm and carried out negotiations. His attempt to introduce the Red Liturgy and the Catholic entourage of his wife and son would have been enough to throw suspicion on the king's designs. Politically, John hoped that by helping Philip II with ships against the rebellious Netherlands, and becoming his ally, he would protect Sweden from the full blast of the Counter-Reformation. His idea of a world Christian faith not administered from Rome was incomprehensible to his subjects, to whom an alliance with the greatest Catholic state seemed immoral and dangerous.

John pleased no party. The Pope was alienated, the nobles

and people definitely antagonistic. The Duke Charles became the centre of the Protestant opposition. The triumph of England had strengthened their case. The Counter-Reformation and Spain were not all-powerful. What was to be the fate of Sweden when Sigismund, King of Poland, succeeded his father? Could the oath taken before coronation be made binding? Did it include the preservation of the laws of the Church as well as the laws of the State? If not, civil war must ensue. The constitutionalists were strengthening their position as regards the crown. It was not forgotten that John III himself had become king through the deposition of his brother. Here was a useful precedent.

In 1592 these were questions in everyone's minds, and openly discussed in some quarters. The suppression of Calvinism in Saxony and the execution of Krell by its new king had not passed unnoticed. Would Sigismund use these methods against the non-Catholics in Sweden? No certain answers could be prophesied, and suddenly in the midst of this unrest came the news that the king was dead. The crisis had arrived.

Sigismund wavered as to what course to pursue, and consulted his Jesuit counsellor Malaspino and delayed his departure to Sweden.

Duke Charles acted quickly, and was present at the Convention (möte) of Uppsala, where the clergy drew up the Swedish charter of their Reformation. It was agreed that Sigismund should swear to respect this document ensuring the continuance of Protestantism as well as taking his coronation oath. Until a promise should be received that the new king would consent, no ships should be sent to bring him to Stockholm. In 1594, Sigismund came up through Finland, his father's old dukedom, and sailed from Åbo in Finnish ships. With him came a host of Catholic adherents and priests, including Malaspino. After much delay he swore to observe the charter and was duly crowned in Uppsala Cathedral on February 19th. His followers were angry at his betrayal of the Counter-Reformation movement, but he excused himself to Malaspino by saying that he had accepted the Uppsala charter and Confession of Augsburg under duress, and that he felt justified in breaking the oath as soon as a propitious moment arrived. After four months in Sweden, during which the Papal power began to reassert itself, and the Romish priests crept back to their churches and monasteries, Sigismund returned to Poland. No definite arrangements were made for the government of Sweden. Duke Charles was nominated at Protector, or Regent, but royal deputies were appointed in all the provinces and these were directly responsible to the King of Poland and Sweden. Two of these, Klas Fleming in Finland and Eric Brahe in Stockholm, were determined to secure the downfall of the Protestant Duke Charles. When this had been accomplished, they foretold the triumph of Catholicism and the complete restoration of Papal authority under the aegis of Sigismund. They had not recognised the strength of the people or the character of Charles. The orders of the king were openly defied. Charles, with the backing of the Riksdag but not the Council, ordered all Catholic priests to leave the country. Many nobles, who had supported Sigismund, fled to Poland, and assured the king that Sweden would rise to help him if he brought a strong force to defend those who hated Charles. There was some ground for this opinion. Much resentment was felt at Charles's high-handed actions to the nobility, and his persecution of the nuns and monks. His " visitors " had maltreated many innocent folk on slender excuses. The flogging of nuns, who clung to the old faith, had shocked public opinion. The expulsion of the revered Brigittines had wounded national pride, which regarded Vadstena Monastery as a heritage. What the malcontents failed to see was that, hated as Charles undoubtedly was by the adherents of the old order, the introduction of that very order would be more hateful to the people.

Catholicism and foreign domination were still bound together in men's minds. Sigismund's stay of four months had strengthened that belief. A recent treaty with Russia at Teusina had raised Charles's stock in the people's eyes. Charles represented security and national independence, which outweighed the sentimental repulsion at his methods of securing the unity expressed by the President of the Uppsala Convention, " Now Sweden is one man and all of us have one God ".

Sigismund planned a dual attack—one led by his deputy Fleming from Finland to strike at Lake Mälar district—the other led by himself to strike at Kalmar.

Charles struck first and secured Åbo in Finland before Sigismund was prepared. When the Catholic army arrived in South Sweden, it received an enthusiastic welcome. Kalmar opened its gates to Sigismund and victory seemed assured as nobles streamed down to meet him. The victory was short-lived. After two months, his army was annihilated at Stångebro in September 1598, and Sigismund fled to Poland. Charles was master of Sweden and was acclaimed king. He refused, however, to assume the title until Duke John, the stepbrother of Sigismund, had renounced his claim to the throne in 1604.

Charles struck down his opponents with his accustomed severity. The supporters of Klas Fleming in Finland were the first to suffer—they were hanged without trial from the nearest trees. The Swedish councillors and nobles who had shown any leanings towards his nephew were executed after a farcical trial at the Massacre of Linköping. Charles, in spite of many repellent characteristics, resembled his father in several ways. He had the gift of winning respect from the common people and making them believe that he was necessary to their salvation. He firmly pursued one clear line of policy and beat down all opposition. His hardiness and utter lack of humanity deprived him of any affection or love, but he had no desire to inspire such feelings in his subjects, whom he despised.

Yet Sweden had reason to be grateful for this unlovable sovereign. His economic policy bestowed considerable benefits to agriculture and the mining industry, and his reform of the coinage assisted commerce. He saw the need for Göteborg, and a regular trade grew up with countries across the North Sea, especially with the Netherlands. His great service, however, was that he saved from destruction the structure of Sweden, united in politics and religion. His methods may seem repulsive, but their good results cannot be denied.

The war had been won, the independence of Sweden was assured for ever, the freedom of the Swedish Church had been won, but a struggle had begun with Poland which was to last sixty years. War with Russia broke out once more, and it was only the enmity of Poland and Russia which allowed escape for harrassed Sweden in this triangle of enemies. Denmark seized the opportunity to declare war, using as excuses the fact that the fishing rights in the north of Norway had been granted by Charles to the inhabitants of Göteborg, and the somewhat belated protest that Charles had called himself "King of the Lapps" at his coronation. In 1611 the tide was setting in Denmark's favour—Kalmar had fallen and Alvsborg was on the point of falling, and

Charles was sick and weary of life—he, like all the Vasas, led a full life, his only joy was in his young son, Gustavus Adolphus: in him he saw the saviour of his country, "Ille faciet", he is reported to have said shortly before his death. The father was right—the boy, scarcely seventeen years of age, found himself king of a country beset by enemies, with the hated Danes on Swedish soil, yet he triumphed, not alone as his father would have tried, but by his reliance on every section of the Swedish people.

CHAPTER IX

THE BALTIC EMPIRE AND
GUSTAVUS ADOLPHUS

WHEN Gustavus Adophus came to the throne in 1611 he was but seventeen years of age and inherited the legacy of three wars, which threatened not only his crown but the very independence of Sweden. The unwarranted attack of Christian IV, resulting in the fall of Kalmar and Alvsborg,[1] seemed to be the most dangerous, and called for a supreme effort. The young king, who had already seen service under de la Gardie, struck hard and out-manoeuvred the pincer movement on Stockholm on land from the west and the south, and by sea from the east. This was his first triumph, but the peace of Knäred (1613) left him saddled with a huge indemnity for the return of Alvsborg, a stronghold abso-lutely necessary for Sweden's trade, guarding as it did her only outlet to the North Sea.

This peace, negotiated by James I of England, was not the unqualified triumph for Denmark which it might have appeared at the time. It demonstrated the innate weakness of Denmark, which had been unable to take advantage of Sweden's internal troubles due to the disputed succession, and also the strong power of Swedish resistance. The navy had been able to withstand all attacks on the east coast and maintain lines of communi-cation with the army operating on the southern shores of the Baltic.

The Polish war, sometimes called the Sixty Years War of Succession, lasted from 1600 to 1660 with only occasional cessations of hostilities. The first armistice was obtained by Gustavus in 1618, after this struggle had become merged in the Russian conflict in a similar manner as the second part of the Polish war soon afterwards became part of the great Thirty Years War.

The war with Russia marks the beginning of the Russian question, but whether its full import was recognised at the time

1 *Vide* page 118

it is difficult to say, as Russia was only just emerging from the "troublous times" following the autocratic rule of Ivan the Terrible. The question as it appeared to most contemporaries was whether Russia or Sweden or Poland should control the Eastern Baltic, although to Charles XII, to Peter the Great and to Polish kings and statesmen of a later date, it was something far deeper. Was the vast mass of Russia to find room for expansion eastwards or westwards or southwards? To Russians, who had already imbibed something of Western culture, the answer was west and south. From the Russian war, which was closed in 1617 at Stolbova, till the present day, the question has recurred at regular intervals and the threat has sometimes been pointed at Turkey and Persia, sometimes at Poland, sometimes at Finland and Sweden. Although Russian eyes were directed west and south, it did not mean that eastern ambitions were abandoned. Quiet expansion was destined to bring Russia into conflict with Japan and China, but this lies outside the scope of Scandinavian history.

It will be remembered that the first serious clash occurred in the reign of Eric XIV, when the Knights of the Sword lost their power and the grab for Estonia, Livonia and Courland began. Ivan the Terrible, by methods of unprecedented suppression and ferocity, had enforced a unity on the countless hordes which inhabited the extensive lands henceforth called Russia. On the death of his elder son Feodor in 1598, the throne was seized by a nobleman named Boris Godunov, who was supposed to have murdered the younger son, Dmitri. However, Sigismund, King of Poland and claimant to the throne of Sweden, produced a man who swore he was Dmitri and therefore the rightful Czar. It has never been established whether he was Dmitri or not, but it suited the Polish plan to support him and the king expected not merely to gain some profit from Russia, but with Russian aid to capture Finland and so defeat Charles IX and regain Sweden. A Swedish-Polish kingdom would make an effective barrier against Russia, ensure the hegemony of the Baltic, and restore Catholicism. The enterprise seemed full of promise when Moscow fell to Dmitri and his Polish allies. The Russian nobles, however, disliking Dmitri and his Catholic aliens even more than the defeated Boris, rose after a short interval and murdered the Czar. There were then two candidates for the throne: Vladislav, son of Sigismund, and Vassili Shuisky, who immediately enlisted the help of Charles IX. An agreement was made that in return for Kexholm on Lake Ladoga, a Swedish army should help Vassili against Sigismund and his son Vladislav. This suited Charles, as he secured the eastern boundary of Finland and helped an enemy of Sigismund. In the light of subsequent Russian history, it is interesting to note two powers trying to use Russia as an ally against each other and hoping after victory to be able to control the policy of the Czar. The able Swedish general, James de la Gardie, captured Moscow in 1610, but his mercenaries and Russian allies mutinied on the approach of Sigismund's troops. In a masterful retreat, he extricated his Swedes only to find that Kexholm had not been delivered as promised. In the late winter he captured Kexholm, and in 1611 Novgorod. This city suggested that one of Charles IX's sons should become its king. The offer was made while the citizens were still ignorant of the Swedish defeat at Kalmar, but nothing came of it owing to the death of Charles IX. De la Gardie tightened his grip on Novgorod and when finally a Russian revolution, or perhaps it should be better described as a nationalist movement, drove out the hated Poles, Michael Romanov signed the peace of Stolbova with Gustavus in 1617. Kexholm, Novgorod and Ingria were ceded to Sweden, which had gained a secure foothold on the Southern Baltic. It was a great stroke for Sweden. Russia was excluded from the Baltic and her ambitions were seemingly directed south or at the heart of Poland. Sigismund asked for peace in the next year and thus in six years Gustavus and his Chancellor Oxenstierna had made Sweden secure from her three most dangerous enemies, and continued the work of consolidating the resources of the land, so sorely in need of rest.

Charles IX, unattractive and forbidding as he may seem, had handed down to his son something besides unsuccessful wars. By his firm, but cruel, opposition to Catholics, he had created an undivided country. It was impossible at that period to dissociate religion and politics. Catholicism meant Polish aggression, and the rule of Sigismund. Intolerance alone could bring union. Dissident nobles joined Sigismund, if they could escape from the king, but it was better so, and Gustavus and Oxenstierna continued this policy. It cannot be called enlightened, but it was necessary, as the country was in deadly peril. The policy was relaxed as regards sects of Protestants other than Lutherans, greatly to the advantage of Swedish industry, which profited so extensively from the work of Louis de Geer, one of the ablest industrialists of all time. He was a Walloon, and his key men were Walloons, and that meant they were Calvinists.

Thus Gustavus was fortunate in being rid of possible disloyalty or even treachery due to religious conviction.

Secondly, he was fortunate in finding an efficient generation of educated and able Swedes on which he could draw to administer the affairs of State or command in the army.

Gustavus Vasa had been compelled to seek help from outside —his secretariat was German. The change was not sudden nor can credit be ascribed to Charles IX, except that in his autocratic rule he might well have attempted to suppress talent which did not support him. The group of constitutionalists under Sparre had sprung into prominence during his reign and the de la Gardie family had become naturalised Swedes. Foreigners became Swedes if they were to serve the State: they ceased to be foreign employees of the king.

The young generation of seventeenth-century Sweden forms one of the most brilliant circles in European history. It had the enterprise of the Elizabethan age and had not lost spirited action in its search for culture. In this particular it presents a sharp contrast to the highly civilised court of Gustavus III, which owed so much to French influence of a later date. First and foremost came the young Chancellor, Axel Oxenstierna, under thirty years of age when he became first minister of state. He supplied the qualities which were lacking in the young king. Cool, calculating, and endowed with an incisive and penetrating judgement, he guided the machine of State for over forty years. He was highly educated and combined a profound knowledge of theology and economics. On the king's death he was regent in all but name. Though charged with nepotism, he maintained his position and never lost the esteem of the nobles and the people. His younger brother, his son John and his cousin fulfilled their duties well and justified his choice.

Like other families, the Oxenstierna family added to their already substantial wealth. Axel's opinions were not unlike those of the aristocratic Whigs in eighteenth-century England. The landowners should be leaders of the people, and though they had privileges, they had duties and responsibilities. Service to the State came to be the hallmark of nobility. At the same time the wealth of the nobles increased. Gifts of land became the common reward, and the rapid transfer of crown lands to those noble servants grew rapidly under Christina. This century was the great building period, castles and public buildings sprang up under the influence of foreign architects. The brilliant band of nobles serving the State—de la Gardie, Wrangel, Bonde, Bielke, Horn, Brahe—can be identified by their many still existing castles, and the Riddarhus itself stands as a symbol of that circle. It must not be assumed, however, that noble birth alone qualified a man for service. Many of these families could trace their ancestry no further back than the reign of Gustavus Vasa. The first Brahe was one of his secretaries, and a lineal descendant held a post of distinction under Bernadotte, so firmly had the family established itself in the service of the State. Pontus de la Gardie was of French origin and became naturalised in the reign of Eric XIV. It was possible to rise in the social scale and be admitted into a new class of the nobility by sheer merit. An outstanding example is John Skytte, the tutor of Gustavus, who had already been utilised by Charles IX for a mission to England, and his wise counsel was of much service to Gustavus after his coronation. This remarkable man has not received his full mead of praise. In many respects he resembles Alcuin, the education minister of Charlemagne. He was a diplomatist and educationalist. He was behind the throne on many occasions and was responsible for most of Gustavus' educational ideas and reforms. A high degree of education was required in the sons of nobles, and special schools were established. These schools were not exclusive and, at two at least, boarding fees were granted to those unable to attend otherwise—an embryo scholarship and maintenance system. Generous endowments were made to Uppsala University. Such enlightened policy redounds to the credit of the king, who throughout his reign required money to pay off old debts, and when these were met, after thirteen years, more money was required for his military and naval commitments. The "many-sidedness" and exuberance of this age, coupled with the inevitable religious intolerance, produced some strange results. Uppsala University was the scene of a battle between two professors worthy of the Council of Trent or Oxford in the nineteenth century. Gustavus deposed both, but gave them other appointments as he was unwilling to lose their undoubted talents. Rudbeckius, however, as Bishop of Västerås, displayed Catholic leanings, and Messenius, according to all accounts the better scholar, as a civil servant went even further and got into communication with Sigismund as leader of the Catholic cause in North-east Europe. The latter was condemned to death, but his sentence was commuted to life imprisonment provided he pursued his historic studies. For a scholar this must have meant paradise, freedom from outside administrative distractions and peace in which to pursue his researches. The result was a History of Sweden ("illustrata") to which all Swedish historians owe a profound debt. Raleigh's *History of the World* springs to mind and the circumstances in which it was written, but in that book controversial topics could not have appeared, whereas Messenius' invaluable work bore directly on the history of Sweden preceding the reign of the king. It sheds an illuminating sidelight on this interesting age, intolerant on the one hand and thirsting for unbiased opinion on the other. It is impossible to describe the burst of literary and scholastic activity of this spacious age, but the picture would be sadly deficient without mention of the beginning of the Swedish Industrial Revolution, which preceded England's by a century. Although the mineral wealth of the country was well known, and the iron and copper mines had long been worked at times by Germans, it was not until the coming of Louis de Geer that the various industries were co-ordinated and developed. This "father of Swedish industry" had been in business in Amsterdam, where he had come from Liége on account of religious difficulties. He first became interested in Swedish affairs when Amsterdam bankers advanced a loan, with the proceeds of a tax as security, with which to pay the indemnity for the release of Alvsborg. Impressed with the possibilities of Swedish industries, he left Holland and in 1627 became a naturalised Swede. Gustavus Adolphus had realised the importance of encouraging native merchants and industrialists and had granted a monopoly to "The Swedish Trading Company". It had not been a success and was dissolved in 1628. De Geer began almost single-handed to reorganise existing mines and works, build new factories in suitable districts and sink new mine shafts. Walloons were imported, and in less than twelve years Sweden became an industrial power with a growing export trade. A map showing the extent of his concerns in 1640[1] reveals the

[1] *Bruk och domäner* (Almquist).

immense range of his activities. Norrköping, Jönköping, Fins-
pong, Nyköping with thousands of acres, freehold and leasehold,
formed the central block, but the largest tract was the comparatively unexploited area north of Lake Vänern. Copper, iron,
brass, steel, were the "heavies", utilising the unlimited water
power which was harnessed to their use. To ensure contact abroad,
a *huvudkontor* or head office was established in Amsterdam, as
well as the central headquarters in Norrköping. His ideas were
international, though it was the country of his adoption which
was the chief beneficiary of his wide outlook. In this expansion
of industry, agriculture was not forgotten. Owing to Gustavus
Vasa's personal interest in scientific farming it was ahead of many
European countries, and care was taken that industrialisation did
not harm agriculture. The land above the mines had to be cultivated
and to this day farm bailiffs are attached to mines, and the surface is not disfigured by the slag heaps which Englishmen associate
with the mining industry. The towns which grew round the
factories were well spaced and contain not a few worthy buildings.
It was fortunate that the industrial growth synchronised with the
increased interest in architecture. Sweden owes a debt to Holland
in both spheres. Some of the Swedish manufacturing towns recall
the Dutch, whilst the buildings of this period, notably the
Riddarhus in Stockholm, might well have been transplanted
from Holland. Louis de Geer's work was duly recognised, and
in 1641 he was raised to the peerage—the "First Knight of
Industry".

Alongside this industrial activity at home came the attempt to
encourage overseas trading companies like the English East India
Company. These never became serious rivals of England and
Holland, while "New Sweden", founded in Delaware in 1638, was
absorbed in the Dutch "New Netherlands" seventeen years later.
The object of the colony was not to provide room for emigrants
but to provide a trading depot for exporting American products.
The foundation of a Swedish trading company in America had
been propounded to Gustavus Adolphus in 1624 by Usselinx, but
Swedish resources were then inadequate. In 1637, the dispatch of
two ships under two Dutchmen, Blomaert and Minnit, the sus-
pended Governor of New Netherlands, differed from the original
scheme because the company, though partly financed from
Amsterdam, contemplated a settlement as well as a trading depot.

It met with initial trading success under the protection of its newly-built Fort Christina, but depended too much for supplies on the home country and immediately excited the jealousy of the Dutch, who were firmly established in America. After the bloodless conquest of the Swedish settlement, Stuyvesant, the Dutch Governor and Commander, showed great leniency to the Swedes, who retained their Lutheran ideals and the Swedish language is still heard in parts of Delaware. With the continued drain on men and material resources in the Thirty Years War, it is less remarkable that these colonies changed hands than that they could have been founded at all at such a time. Although " New Sweden " became Dutch, trade with Sweden expanded. These colonists showed the hereditary " adaptability " of their Viking forebears—a characteristic which was again in evidence when the steady stream of emigration began in the nineteenth century.

As was only fitting, the ruler, who saw the beginning of this " Golden Age of Sweden ", was himself bursting with vitality and energy. He was more than the mirror, he was the symbol of the age. It can be said with truth that he was both its father and child. To dissociate Gustavus from his contemporaries can only lead to a false judgement of his greatness because one of his most brilliant achievements was his accurate interpretation of his own people and the nation's enemies.

Gustavus was in some respects a true Vasa. He had their typical courage and strength of will and hot temper, but on the other hand, he learned self-control, and the hastiness which is sometimes ascribed to him showed itself only in small matters. His restraint in his early dealings with the nobility affords a strong contrast to the conduct of his father and grandfather. He displayed a balanced judgment, penetrating vision and a patience altogether his own. The outstanding example of this last virtue was his long-delayed entry into the Thirty Years War. In 1625 he refused the overtures which Christian IV accepted with such fatal results. His armies were not ready for such an enterprise, and clearly as he saw the menacing threat of the League, he wisely bided his time. His courage and love of danger laid him open to the charge of rash temerity, but it must be remembered that in those days, and especially in his own army, the personal nexus between the commander and his men demanded that the king should be seen during as well as before the battle.

Perhaps his generosity of nature and his capacity for making and keeping friends in all ranks of society were the chief factors in securing him the universal love, respect and unfailing devotion of his people. Unlike his royal predecessors, he appealed to all sections of the nation. He won over the nobles without losing the support of the peasants, and the constitution, which his faithful chancellor published two years after his death, was that of a balanced democracy showing no discrimination between various strata of society.

Some credit must be given to Charles IX for the careful education which he bestowed on his spirited young son. The influence of John Skytte has already been mentioned. Under his tuition he mastered seven languages and could speak four fluently, but his mind was trained to think and reason, and this part of his education served him better than his linguistic glibness. His military training was placed under the care of de la Gardie, and bitterly was he disappointed when his father forbade him to accompany the general on his Russian expedition in 1610. However, he had not to wait long before he received command of the force which successfully re-conquered the island of Öland on the east coast of Sweden. Thus he won his first military victory before his seventeenth birthday, which fell on December 9th of that same year. It was not long before he was to win more laurels in the peaceful recovery which he achieved for his country at home. So brilliant were the last two years of his life, when he stupefied Europe by his successes, that the solid patient work of the previous sixteen years has never received due recognition outside the country itself.

It in no way reflects on his military genius that he showed himself to be a profound statesman and a constitution builder, nor is it of more than academic interest to try and settle the question whether he was greater as a soldier or a statesman. As, however, his military career has until very recently entirely usurped the attention of historians, it is not out of place to quote a modern historical revision on this point.[1] " The seventeenth century is for Sweden pre-eminently the century of organisation. . . . The Sweden of Karl IX was weak, isolated and of no account

---

[1] *Historical Revision No. XCII* by Michael Roberts published in *History* 1940. Similar conclusions were given by the author of this book in a series of lectures delivered on behalf of the Red Cross before the above was published.

in Europe; the Sweden of Gustav Adolph grew to be a great power; behind the change lay the most remarkable of Gustav's achievements—the unification of Sweden for national ends, its administrative reorganisation, its firm impulse lay along paths of healthy constitutional progress." Based as is this review on recent Swedish researches, one is bound to concur with the truth of its content. Without the solid foundation, Gustavus could never have turned the whole course of the Thirty Years War. Evidence of its solidity is made abundantly clear by the successes and endurance of the Swedish armies after the king's death at Lützen in 1632. The Treaties of Westphalia in 1648 and Roskilde in 1658 bear witness to the fact that his work did not die with him. It was a triumph for the whole nation, of which he was the inspiration. His statesmanship must share the honours with his military genius. If he had lived to found the " Corpus Evangelicorum " under the leadership of Sweden, it is a matter of speculation whether such a union of Protestant states in Germany would have endured.

On the one hand, it may be remembered that Prussia was able to form the North German Confederation on somewhat similar lines, but on the other hand, it was clear that Richelieu, the Catholic cardinal, allied with him for political reasons, had already begun to be nervous of Sweden's predominance in Germany. The glittering court of the Swedish king at Mainz (1631–2) had been viewed with great suspicion, and had excited the jealousy of France. Without French support it is improbable that such a scheme could have been founded. In the face of French opposition it could never have lasted after the death of its founder.

Gustavus Adolphus did not ascend the throne until two months after his father's death in October 1611 because a Council of Regency under the Queen-Dowager had been previously appointed to function for the two years before he legally came of age. The Queen, however, urged members of the Råd and Riksdag to override this will immediately in view of her son's obvious suitability. At the same time, his cousin John, always treated with favour by Charles, renounced his claim to the throne for the second time. Gustavus was fortunate in being rid of the embarrassing circle of royal relatives which had been a menace to the sovereign ever since Gustavus Vasa had so richly endowed his three sons. John, who remained loyal and showed no signs of being in league with his stepbrother, Sigismund, died in 1618, and Charles Philip, younger brother of Gustavus Adolphus, died in 1622.

There is no doubt that the talents and ability of young Gustavus had already been recognised. He had regularly attended Council meetings and actually spoken at the early age of ten. He had received practical experience of administration, as well as instruction at the hands of John Skytte and de la Gardie. The people of this superstitious age were not long in marking him as a man of destiny, and an earth-born Messiah to save the cause of Protestantism. Had not the Danish astronomer Tyge Brahe discovered the new star in the constellation of Cassiopeia? In him they saw the new star of the North. Did not the anagram of his name spell "Augustus", the greatest of Roman emperors? Could this mean anything but that he would restore the Protestant charter of liberty—the Confession of Augsburg—in that very city, the city of Augustus?

The king himself, no doubt, did not put much faith in such prognostications for he was a man of piety, though no theologian like John III, and he was a sincere believer in God and God's Word, and paid but little attention to soothsayers. He was a logical realist. His followers, however, could make good use of such omens, and these served him better than did the globes and crystals of his rival Wallenstein in adding lustre to his reputation. His first act as king was to choose Axel Oxenstierna as his chancellor, a choice which he never regretted. It pleased the aristocracy because they thought that once more they would return to power, and this belief was strengthened when concessions were made to their demands for a monopoly of executive posts in the government. As time went on, they were to discover that this bargain did not altogether work out as they had anticipated.

In the confused period which had followed the death of Gustavus Vasa, there were three powers in the State—the king, the nobles and the people. The Church had been merged in the State, and the support of the nobles for the Reformation had been secured by granting them a share of the Church lands. The people had also become adherents of Lutheranism owing to the gradual educational methods adopted to ensure the proper understanding of its implications—both political and religious.

The two bodies representing the nobles and the people were

the Råd and the Riksdag.[1] The Råd was chosen by the king from the aristocracy and its functions were in essence both advisory and executive. It was often at loggerheads with the king and at times some of its members were in correspondence with his enemies—especially Danes and Poles. Its powers were vague and illusory, and the confusion had become aggravated by the bureaucratic use of a royal secretariat. Before the accession of Gustavus, Sparre and the constitutionalists had brought forward suggestions to regularise the situation and there is little doubt that Oxenstierna and the king subsequently made free use of them. The most striking example of the nebulous nature of the constitution was afforded by the important Uppsala Convention, at which only one member of the Råd was present.

The powers and functions of the Riksdag, of which the nobles formed one of the four estates, were even still more nebulous. It could be summoned at the king's pleasure, but there was no guarantee that it should ever meet. In these circumstances it had gradually become a tool in the hands of the king. The good sense of Gustavus Vasa had ensured that it assembled in matters which concerned the whole nation. Notable were the occasions when it voted for a national effort to expel the Danes, and later to carry through the Reformation. Eric XIV, however, employed it against the nobles, and Duke Charles to oppose the Counter-Reformation and finally to dethrone Sigismund, the rightful king. To such an extent and so often did Charles exercise his influence on the people to give countenance to his own arbitrary acts, that the nobles nicknamed them *jabröder*, which meant something more than mere "yes-men". The fourth estate was not content with this role and its members objected to the frequent and expensive journeys which ended in their giving assent to the policy of the king, who would have carried it through had that assent been withheld.

Thus it is impossible to agree with the view of an eminent English historian that "Charles by his wise administration had succeeded in uniting the king and his nobles and was able to hand on to his son the government of a united and prosperous nation". It was united in one respect only—opposition to the foreigner and

---

[1] It is convenient to call this body the Riksdag, though strict historicity would demand that on some occasions it should be called *herredag*. Not till the seventeenth century was this latter name dropped entirely in favour of Riksdag.

Catholicism. It was the tact, skill and generosity of mind shown by the young king which induced the many noble emigrés and relatives of those massacred by Charles at Linköping to return to their country, and gradually welded together the component parts of a poorly constructed machine.

It is not easy to apportion the due share of credit between the king and the chancellor. Neither would single-handed have been able to bring cosmos out of chaos and establish a systematised working government, served equally well by the three orders—king, nobles and people—who at the beginning of the reign were suspicious of each other and at the end were acting in complete harmony.

The measures by which this triumphant result was achieved were not passed in one year and cover the period from the passing of the charter in 1612 to the confirmation of the constitution in 1634. In 1612 the king assented to the abolition of the secretariat and granted that all the executive officers should be drawn from the nobility. This was regarded as a victory and a curtailment of the royal power. In practice, however, it harnessed the nobles to the service of the State, which soon was recognised as the acid test of nobility. The nobles ceased to be merely courtiers, and as civil servants it soon became necessary for their sons to be highly educated. Special schools were instituted and, not without some grumbling, the younger generation found that the better posts did not fall to their lot unless they fulfilled certain requirements. To ensure that men of ability were not lost to the State, a new class of nobility was instituted, into which commoners could rise on promotion to civil and military offices of state.

Later, on Oxenstierna's suggestion, the Riddarhus was built in Stockholm as a place for meetings of the nobility—social and political. Lines of political action would be discussed in the Riddarhus, but it had no law-making powers. As members of the Råd and Riksdag, the nobles could propound their suggestions in either quarter or put their ideas before the sovereign. Here all grades of the nobility met and it did much to cement the cleavage between the old and new aristocracy. Socially the difference between the old landed aristocracy and the new remained in evidence for many generations, and in some quarters is not yet dead. The influx of new titles subsequent to these measures accounts for the high percentage of Swedes with " a handle to their names ", and has caused a belief among foreign visitors that the country is a relic of the " ancien régime " instead of a balanced democracy. The creation was a democratic movement which forestalled Napoleon's principle of " La carrière ouverte aux talents ".

The nobility still were chosen to compose the Råd and it still remained as one of the four estates in the Riksdag. Its executive powers in administration were modified by the creation of " Colleges " or Boards. There were five main Colleges set up, though not all in the same year, and they were grouped round the old five highest officers of the State—the Chancellor, the Marshal, the Treasurer, the Lord High Steward and finally the Admiral. Each Board had its president appointed by the king, its councillors mostly members of the Råd, and its body of permanent civil servants. Its policy and efficiency were scrutinised by the king and the Råd. This nucleus of Boards has developed into the elaborate system of committees which is a notable feature of the constitution of to-day. Lastly came the Riksdag itself, organised in the old four estates by the Ordinances of 1617. Attendance was no longer voluntary for the nobles and it is an illuminating sidelight on the enhanced importance of the fourth estate and indeed of the Riksdag itself, that by 1632 the only complaints were that it was not summoned as much as members would have liked—a strange contrast to the complaints of the previous reign. This was a legislative body with the added right of endorsing a declaration of war after it had been proposed in the Råd. It is worthy of record that Gustavus did not decide on entering the Thirty Years War. It was his policy, but the decision was made by the Råd and endorsed by the whole Riksdag. The weakness of the Riksdag lay in the fact that it could not initiate legislation but only pass or veto suggested measures. In the early stages, however, it would not have had the legislative experience and the right was granted much later. Another weakness lay in the power of the king to legislate by proclamation. It is true that confirmation of the royal proclamation was usually sought, but the sole right of legislation was not acknowledged for two centuries. Again, though it possessed rights over taxation, it had no right of audit or control of appropriation, and as Roberts aptly writes, " it had no notion of using its tax-granting powers to blackmail the executive into a policy ".

This, in outline, was the constitution which was introduced

into Sweden at a time when Charles I of England had prorogued Parliament for eleven years, and Richelieu began the suspension of the States General, destined to remain in abeyance till 1789. The fundamental principle was democratic—all classes could record " yea " or " nay " in the Riksdag. The councillors were to be drawn from an aristocracy trained in a tradition of administration with a constant stream of new talent which would encourage progress. The ideal of a union of all classes was expounded by the king himself when he declared, " The King and estates higher and lower represent under God the high royal majesty". The system can be expressed broadly in diagrammatic form thus:

The King

Executive and Advisory	*Legislative*

The Råd   The Riksdag
(Nobility of both classes)   (Four Estates: Nobles,
                       Clergy, Burghers, Peasants)
The Colleges or Departmental Boards
{ President: a member of the Råd }
{ Councillors: majority members of the Råd }
{ Civil Service personnel }

From the above description it may be deduced that much depended on the good sense of king, the Råd, and the Riksdag to ensure the smooth working of this well-balanced fabric. Ordinances were published to define the functions and prevent overlapping, and special ordinances were published applying to the Riddarhus in case it assumed powers beyond the intention of the founder—Axel Oxenstierna. These, however, did not prevent a serious crisis during the minority of Christina. The five heads of the Colleges acted as a Council of Regency, and as three of them were of the Oxenstierna family, Axel, the Chancellor, was accused of nepotism and usurping royal power. John Skytte was one of the severest critics. Without a king, the balance was undoubtedly upset, and the Råd had some reason for complaint. The good sense of the Chancellor and his acknowledged integrity and patriotism averted the danger until the queen assumed her royal duties and reigned in person. The constitution lasted in its entirety with but few modifications for over two hundred years.

Perhaps its real fault is that it did not allow sufficient scope for development and changed conditions, but this criticism is to imply a maturity in constitution making far in advance of any country in Europe. It must not be forgotten that England did not find a constitution until the king had been beheaded and Cromwell had experimented with schemes distasteful to the nation. The Swedish experiment did not foresee political parties within the two main bodies, and if one may anticipate events of the eighteenth century, it was the formation of such parties that led to the disastrous and unedifying struggles of the Hats and Caps. On the death of Charles XII, Sweden endured a period of party government. Without a wise king to keep the balance, sectional interests predominated, the art of purely parliamentary government was in its adolescence. The growing pains grew worse and it needed a bloodless *coup d'état* by Gustavus III to restore the balance of the régime.

These important constitutional innovations were accompanied and in many cases preceded by changes in the judicial system. The procedure in the local and provincial courts was regularised. They were made dependent on a central higher court (the *Hovrätt*) in Stockholm, which not only acted as an appeal court, but also scrutinised and recorded the proceedings of the lower courts. Its work was subsequently decentralised by the institution of similar bodies in Åbo and Jönköping. Final appeal could be made to the king, or in his absence to the Råd acting in a capacity comparable to the Judicial Committee of the Privy Council or House of Lords. The new system was highly successful in promoting judicial uniformity and stamping out irregularities which had crept in during the troubled period of the three sons of Gustavus Vasa. These irregularities were uncommonly few on the whole, considering the huge distances and poor communications with the capital.

This digression on the reforms is necessary if the background of Gustavus Adolphus's success is to be seen in its right perspective.

Gustavus took his duties seriously from the outset and showed that he was determined to sacrifice personal inclinations to the service of the State. Having established peace by the treaties of Knäred and Stolbova, and an armistice with Poland, he proceeded to secure a Protestant alliance with Brandenburg by his marriage with Maria Eleonora, eldest daughter of the Elector. His mother was largely responsible for this match and in dissuading him from making the talented and beautiful Ebba Brahe his queen. Against his inclinations, he assented to this political wedding. An interesting sidelight is thrown on his early efforts in diplomacy after an incognito visit to Berlin to inspect his proposed bride. He proposed a Protestant alliance between England, Sweden and Brandenburg, to be cemented by two marriages—Prince Charles of England to marry the erratic and wayward blonde Maria Eleanora, while he should take her younger sister. James I, however, had other views and finally in 1620 Oxenstierna was sent to Berlin to escort the future queen to Stockholm. Gustavus proved a surprisingly patient husband and the marriage was not unsuccessful. The only child, Christina, was born in 1627, and her upbringing was left largely to her aunt Catharine and a tutor named John Matthew, owing to Gustavus' distrust of his wife's character. He did, however, show genuine affection for her as time went on and she accompanied him on his Pomeranian campaigns and reigned at his court at Mainz in 1631–1632. This alliance with the Elector was the beginning of Gustavus' Baltic policy which was to begin with the subjection of Poland and ultimately to lead to his participation in the Thirty Years War. The Russian question had been solved and it did not arise again until 1656, when the disintegration of Poland invited Charles X to attempt either a partition of that unhappy country or a united Swedo-Polish kingdom. Whichever was his aim, the jealousy of Russia was bound to be excited.

Gustavus then regarded his immediate problem to be two-fold —religious and political. To roll back the on-coming forces of the Counter-Reformation, the defence of Sweden on the south side of the Baltic must be strengthened. The first step must be the defeat of Sigismund, Catholic King of Poland, and still claimant to the Swedish throne. Gustavus perceived in him a political and religious danger. The Counter-Reformation leaders would find him to be a useful ally for their movement steadily advancing east and north, sheltered by the Imperial armies. The Swedish king and his chancellor realised that the preservation of Protestantism was absolutely essential for the existence of an independent Swedish nation.

They were not, however, prepared to play a purely defensive role, nor to share the hegemony of the Baltic with any other power. The Treaty of Knäred was never intended to be a final settlement, rather was it to be a temporary rest from the exhaustive wars which had preceded it. A Baltic empire was their ambition, though the exact form which this empire should take altered from time to time, as circumstances changed. The idea was not original nor did it die with the king. He clearly saw the foundations on which this empire must rest and, step by step, he patiently set about his task. The three primary essentials were a united home front, the elimination of Russia from the Baltic, and the destruction or absorption of Poland. With Finland and Riga in Swedish hands, he could, either by amicable arrangements or by force of arms, creep westwards through East Prussia and Pomerania towards Denmark itself. It has already been told how he accomplished the union of the home front and the elimination of the Russian power from the Baltic. The accomplishment of his third ambition became extremely hazardous as the religious and political factors became more and more tightly interlocked. They began to dominate his diplomacy and his military plans.

When Wallenstein appeared as the victorious leader of the Imperial forces and, in the eyes of contemporaries, as the champion of the Counter-Reformation, Swedish volunteers under the Scotch leader, Leslie, saved Stralsund and, by so doing, preserved Denmark from extinction. Denmark. a Protestant country, was no friend of Sweden, and the alliance was not cemented. Even when Wallenstein became " Lord of the Baltic ", Gustavus was not ready to take up the challenge. Poland was not entirely defeated, more Baltic ports must be occupied, and the Swedish army, with its many foreign elements, had not yet reached the high standard of efficiency which the king considered necessary.

Paradoxical as it appears to us now, Wallenstein was no advocate of religious persecution; in fact, he strongly advocated toleration, thus earning the suspicion of the Catholic League whilst his successes excited its jealousy. Richelieu was the first to exploit to his own advantage the interplay of religion and Imperial politics. It was his wily agent, Father Joseph, who breathed suspicion of Wallenstein into the Emperor's ears and so, with the support of Maximilian of Bavaria and other German princes, secured his dismissal. He also perceived the possibility of using this new Swedish adventurer for his own ends, but at the outset he never guessed that he was dealing with one of the greatest men of all time. Gustavus was convinced early in 1629 that war between Sweden and the Empire was inevitable. He had tried to secure an alliance with any countries hostile to the Emperor, including Turkey, but he had achieved nothing. Finally, he appealed to Richelieu, but it is significant that the actual declaration of war by his council was in the autumn of 1629, and the adventure began in June 1630 before anything was definitely settled. He established his bases without opposition and had cleared Pomerania by the following December. The whole line of ports including Danzig was in his hands, and Oxenstierna was acting as governor-general of the new Prussian acquisitions, some held on lease. It was in January 1631 that the Treaty of Bärwalde, to hold for five years, was ultimately concluded. The success of the king's bold action had turned the scales, and Richelieu considered that his aid would be of great value. In the same way, French financial help was a necessity for the furtherance of Gustavus' plans of action. A bargain was struck at Bärwalde. A French subsidy of 400,000 riksdaler[1] was to be paid annually for five years in return for a Swedish attack on North Germany. The French cardinal insisted that the Swedish king should respect the Catholic League. The pact admirably suited the ultimate objects of each party. Richelieu saw in it a way of weakening the power of the Hapsburgs, Gustavus a way of establishing a Swedish Baltic empire. Guizot tells us that " the Thirty Years War ended wars of religion "; more accurately it could be affirmed that the Treaty of Bärwalde marked the beginning of the end, and that the Battle of Breitenfeld was the end.

The real importance of Gustavus' victory over the Catholic armies of Tilly lies in the fact that Protestantism was saved. It proclaimed that both Catholics and Protestants had a right to their beliefs, and the doctrine of toleration was established. Hence it has come about that Gustavus has become justly famous as the saviour of Protestantism, but the brilliance of this achievement has deflected attention from his domestic reforms and the part he played in the drama of the Baltic empire. Taking a wide sweep of the history of north-eastern Europe enables one to understand the vast importance of this imperial ambition to Sweden and other countries.

In its most limited sense, the conception implied the command

---

[1] *Vide* Appendix III for explanation of Swedish currency.

of the "narrow straits"—the Öresund, the Kattegat and Skagerak. In its widest, as envisaged by Charles X, it meant Sweden, Finland, Poland, Pomerania, Denmark and Norway. In the mind of Gustavus, it took various forms. It is probably correct to say that Sweden, Finland, Livonia and along the coast to Pomerania, with the addition of Norway, was the original idea. Denmark would be a powerless satellite or a compliant ally. After the exclusion of Swedish delegates from the peace negotiations at Lübeck his attitude to Denmark hardened.[1] His second and more ambitious conception was that of a huge northern kingdom including Denmark and Brandenburg. He, or at any rate, Oxenstierna, quickly recognised the potentialities of the latter state under its new ruler, destined to go down to history as the Great Elector. Gustavus was ready to betroth his baby daughter, Christina, to him and the issue of that marriage would have inherited the huge kingdom which might have been won by Swedish arms. The final and best known scheme embraced the original ideas of the Scandinavian kingdom but to them were added the "Corpus Evangelicorum". It it quite wrong to separate the two ideas and though opinions vary considerably about the feasibility of establishing and maintaining such a confederation, it is quite certain that in the mind of the king, the corpus of German Protestant states was to be dependent on the support of the Swedish Baltic empire. Bismarck, under different circumstances, founded the North German Confederation, geographically not unlike the corpus, and this, with Prussia as its leading member, developed into the German Empire. If Gustavus had lived and carried out his matrimonial scheme, the history of Europe might have taken a different shape and Richelieu would have hesitated to pit France against such a formidable group. This, however, is an academic question for speculative historians. After the king's death at Lützen in 1632, the idea of the "Corpus Evangelicorum" was abandoned, but the Baltic empire lived on.

The prologue was over, and at Lützen the curtain had been lowered on the first scene of the first act of the Baltic drama. The programme tells us how the final curtain was rung down in the far-off wilds of Russia. Had Hardy decided to precede his *Dynasts* with an equally long historical tragedy on the seventeenth century, the layout might well have taken this shape.

[1] *Vide* page 119

DRAMA OF THE BALTIC EMPIRE

Prologue
1611–1629
Foundations and Preparations
Mise-en-scène—Sweden, Russia, Poland.

ACT I
European Adventure
1630–1660

SCENE I. 1630–1632. Gustavus Adolphus—triumph and death.
SCENE II. 1632–1648. Richelieu, Oxenstierna and the Swedish generals.
SCENE III. 1648–1660. Christina, Charles X—triumphs at Roskilde and Oliva.

ACT II
Sweden stays at home
1660–1697

SCENE I. The Regency.
SCENE II. Charles XI—building, banking and bullying.

ACT III
Swedish misadventure abroad
1697–1721

SCENE I. Charles XII at Pultava.
SCENE II. Baltic dream fades out at Nystad, 1721.

Epilogue

SCENE I. Political eclipse—scientific, industrial, cultural progress.
SCENE II. Russia or France? Bernadotte founded an independent Sweden and Norway which look *west*.

When the European Adventure began, neither the well-seasoned commander, Tilly, nor the Protestant princes estimated the victor of Poland at his true value as a general. That Gustavus was to revolutionise the art of war was hardly realised even after Breitenfeld. The changing opinion of Wallenstein is illuminating and of great assistance in any attempt to gauge the effect of the triumphant progress of Gustavus on contemporary opinion. At first Wallenstein wrote him off as a " King of Snow ", who would quickly melt in Europe. Then he regarded him with a lively interest, and lastly with a superstitious fear. The soothsayers were consulted, but the horoscope was not promising. The legend of an invincible " Lion of the North " grew apace.

The beginning of the campaign was discouraging. Tilly realised that the key position of Magdeburg was of vital importance and when the city declared itself in favour of the new Protestant leader, it was quickly invested. Gustavus saw the danger, but the Electors of Brandenburg and Saxony refused to allow his army to pass through their lands to the rescue of the beleaguered city. Neither recognised the strength of the new army which had arrived in Pomerania, and both dreaded the vengeance of the imperial commander. After a long delay the Elector of Brandenburg yielded to Gustavus' threats, but it was too late, and Magdeburg fell and suffered a fate at the hands of the victors worse than the sack of Rome. Between twenty and thirty thousand perished, and the city lay in ruins. The Catholics were jubilant and the blow killed the rising hopes of the Protestants. At this crisis Gustavus was not daunted, nor was it long before the craven John George of Saxony was begging for his help. The Swedish army began its historic march into Southern Germany, and piled victory upon victory, suffering no defeat until two years after the king's death. It is not proposed to follow these campaigns in any detail, but the methods and principles which Gustavus adopted changed the art of war and left an indelible mark on the history of Europe.

Happily, the records are complete, accurate and intimate, so that it is possible to probe the secret of the success and estimate the brilliance of this military genius. He was a pioneer and an innovator, and was recognised as such by military thinkers from Cromwell to Saxe, from Frederick the Great to Schlieffen. Cromwell, a peaceful landowner, studied his theories and read the *Swedish Soldier*. Leslie, Munro, and other officers had served under him and recorded his exploits and copied his principles. Frederick the Great developed the " oblique attack " which had contributed to, if it did not decide, the battle the Breitenfeld. Napoleon placed him among his " great captains " for his staff officers to study.[1] Schlieffen likens him to Hannibal, the model for all time, and from all available accounts, it is not extravagant to draw a parallel between Montgomery's famous " Eighth Army " and that seventeenth century creation of Gustavus, the first modern army.

What were the characteristics which justify such a title? Each might be found separately in this or that army, but the combination was unique and it is, indeed, hard to find a similar force until the battle of Alamein in the Second World War.

[1] Napoleon's notes on the art of war *Commentaires* VI, pages 171, 172 and 179, notes 24 and 41. Wallenstein is not included among the captains.

It was composed of fifty per cent Swedes and the rest Scots, Germans and mercenaries. Casualties were filled from captured soldiers willing to fight under any competent general who could feed and pay them. Thus, the first essential was a rigorous discipline, but never of the Prussian type. It was a reasoned discipline which was maintained by the Swedish generals and officers to the very end. Only the dashing and brilliant Banér allowed the looting which destroys discipline, and on his death Torstensson restored the old tradition.

Secondly, there was side by side with this discipline, a democratic *esprit de corps*—a certain personal camaraderie—which created a veritable " band of brothers ".

These characteristics were remarkable in a seventeenth century army, and still more remarkable was the insistence of an intelligent knowledge of objectives by staff and regimental officers and men.

Such, however, was of paramount importance to the development of initiative and to the understanding of the " new ideas ".

It took years of careful training and experiment in the Polish wars before the governing factors of mobility and surprise were perfected.

Mobility found its expression in the artillery, which was of a revolutionary nature. Instead of only siege guns and ships' guns which were dragged into fixed positions, there were light 4-pounders and 2-pounders which could be shifted by one horse or two men. These light guns were attached to each regiment, and proved disastrous to the enemy infantry armed only with muskets. They could be fired more quickly than the muskets, and the damage done was so great that even the finest infantry became unsteady in their presence.[1]

He introduced the cartridge as far as he could and these were, apparently, often made behind the field of battle and fitted into bandoliers.

The idea of combining infantry and artillery was developed further by using cavalry more closely with the infantry, and not

---

[1] On the first occasion they were met, the enemy considered that it was " not quite cricket ". A similar charge was made against Mohammed for using an offensive trench for the first time. The cartridge for muskets was an adaption of an earlier idea to solve the difficult problem of keeping the powder dry. Cromwell's order at Dunbar may be recalled " Trust in God and keep your powder dry." In 1560 " bagges of linen or paper " were used to protect the charges for cannons.

merely as a separate unit. Owing to the pike tactics of the Spaniards, cavalry had lost their old value. A charge against a bristling mass of pikes flanked with musketeers had little chance of success. The horsemen's functions had been reduced to foraging, pillaging, reconnoitring, and an occasional slow charge which ended before the pikes were reached. The riders discharged their pistols and retired. Gustavus changed all this. His cavalry was of two kinds—cuirassiers and dragoons. The former with the " tin helmet ", back and breast plates, were armed with sword and pistols, and charged at a gallop. The latter were, to all intents and purposes, mounted infantry, carrying a musket, sword and axe. Rupert and Cromwell both learned their tactics from the Swedish cavalry.[1] What, however, struck the Scotch officers[2] and Germans as the most extraordinary feature was the huge array of scientists, which comprised sappers, miners, mechanics, locksmiths, and armourers.

Not only did the Swedish tactics require this band of civilian soldiers, but the new arms required experts on the field.

Another innovation was the introduction of warm " uniform " clothing, but the names of brigades by colour did not refer to the wearing apparel, and it was not until some time later that all regiments wore distinctive uniforms. Gustavus's object was to promote an *esprit de corps* and also to ensure proper covering in cold weather. He was the first general to provide field ambulances and hospitals, and a staff of surgeons. After Tilly was wounded at the Battle of the Lech, a messenger was passed through the Swedish lines to Gustavus asking whether he would send his " chirurgeon " to try and save Tilly's life. To this request, he acceded in his characteristically chivalrous manner.

His novel equipment was designed to secure efficiency and quick movement. His tactics added surprise to mobility, and were by no means the same in each battle. The principles were the same, but their application differed according to the ground and the nature of the opponent. He, like Nelson, studied his opponent, and had

---

[1] As regards cavalry tactics, it may be noted that the Ironsides charged " at a round trot ", but Rupert used the " gallop ". It was not until Seydlitz, Frederick of Prussia's great cavalryman, that cavalry charged in formation at a *full* gallop. Gustavus kept control of his cavalry, so that they could reform after their first objective had been attained. Cromwell's superb handling of his cavalry owed much to Gustavus, but it is a point of interest to note that Rupert and he laid emphasis on different features, neither adopting his methods in their entirety.

[2] Munro.

an uncanny genius for knowing what he would do. A remarkable instance of the "Nelson touch" on land is to be found at the crossing of the Lech, April 4th, 1632. All the bridges were down and Tilly held a position ideal for defence. Realising that nobody would dream that he would be sufficiently foolhardy to attack, he waited for a gentle westerly breeze, started a long smoke screen (the first of its kind), and under cover of the smoke threw a pontoon over the river. An accurate and terrific bombardment followed (the king himself is reputed to have checked the sighting of sixty heavy pieces), and then the first modern army crossed in truly modern fashion. Curiously enough critics condemn his masterly move because of the casualties entailed, and contend that he should have marched south and made a wide detour. The loss was insignificant compared with the value of the object attained and probably actually saved lives in the long run. His usual disposition of the troops was quite new and original. Instead of the massed infantry flanked by cavalry, he adopted a more open order with small bodies of cavalry ready to assist any group of hard-pressed musketeers. The large groups of cavalry remained on the wings ready to charge or encircle as the circumstances required. His objects were to give a wider field of fire and to permit freer tactical movements. His regimental pieces allowed him to thin the infantry which was sufficiently trained and disciplined to enable it to hold its ground without mass formation. The freedom of movement attained in this manner triumphed at Breitenfeld, when the defection of the Saxons necessitated a sudden change of plan. New flanks were formed, an oblique attack was made, a sweeping surprise on the enemy's flank captured the Imperial artillery which was turned on to Tilly's own men, and an awkward situation was turned into one of the greatest victories of history—a victory for the preservation of the new faith of Protestantism and for the new tactics of Gustavus Adolphus.

Whether he should have made a direct attack on Vienna after his victory in the autumn of 1631 must remain a matter for debate. Actuated by humane motives, he marched from Erfurt through Thuringia to Würzburg, down the "Priests' Walk" (*Pfaffengasse*), as he nicknamed the line of Catholic states, liberating thousands of Protestants from oppression. Thence he turned west and entered the proudest city of the Rhine—Mainz. He had less than thirty thousand troops. Tilly, in the east, had, by November, mustered an army of forty thousand, and, by this movement to the west, the king had become embroiled with the Spanish forces of the Catholic League, some of whom formed the city's garrison. Richelieu's attitude was uncertain, and Gustavus showed that he was aware of his precarious position in a letter to the Council, admonishing them to look well to the defences of Göteborg. However, Richelieu did not desert him though viewing with manifest apprehension the brilliant court established for the winter on the Rhine itself. In the spring of 1632, Gustavus moved east again to settle conclusions with the Imperial forces. The great towns such as Nuremburg received him enthusiastically. Munich was entered exactly one year after the fall of Magdeburg. Was ever so much accomplished in so short a time?

The Emperor was alive to the impending danger, and recalled Wallenstein from his retirement. Maximilian of Bavaria, the most powerful of the Catholic princes, agreed, in spite of his suspicions, jealousy and hatred of that most popular of the Imperial generals. Wallenstein, a strategist rather than a tactician, built up a huge armed camp—*Alte Feste*—immortalised in Schiller's trilogy. Nothing would draw him from his chosen position, and at last the Swedes had to make the assault. For more than two months, the two great leaders had been jockeying for position like ocean racing yachts before the signal. The moment for the start was decided by the departure of Pappenheim with some troops on a special mission. On November 6th, 1632, the battle of Lützen brought the last victory in death to the Swedish hero. Cut off by a thick mist, he was shot by some Croats in the middle of the battle. As his riderless white horse brought the news down the ranks, the Swedes were blinded with fury, and surged forward to revenge the death of their beloved leader. For once, discipline went, and the old " berserk " spirit took its place. Panic seized the Imperialists, who fled in disorder. Pappenheim, returning at this juncture, was shot, and his men joined in the disordered flight. Fog, coupled with exhaustion, alone saved the immense army of Wallenstein from complete annihiliation. Victory went to Sweden once more, but they had lost their great king and the price paid was heavy indeed. The curtain fell on the first scene of the European Adventure, but sixteen years were to elapse before the end of the Thirty Years War.

CHAPTER X

THE BALTIC EMPIRE

(a) 1632–1660

THE king's death was a shattering blow to the Protestant forces and that there was not a complete collapse must be ascribed to the steadfast calmness of Axel Oxenstierna. Until 1632 his genius had been somewhat eclipsed by the brilliance of his master, but in the remaining sixteen years of war and political manoeuvre, he displayed such supreme qualities of statesmanship, that even Louis XIV afterwards described him as the greatest minister of the seventeenth century—a high compliment from the Grand Monarch, who owed so much of his power to Mazarin and his predecessor, Richelieu. The personal leadership and magnetism of the Swedish king had gone, but his spirit lived on among his generals and the Swedish nation. The immediate danger lay in the vacillation, hesitancy and selfishness of the Protestant princes. The astute chancellor perceived that his opponents were hardly better served by the Catholic princes. Both Catholics and Protestants, with few exceptions, preferred their independence, guaranteed by the prevailing anarchy, to a victory which might lead to a strong overlord. When Gustavus entered Frankfurt, the city in which the election of the emperor took place and the head of the Holy Roman Empire was crowned, the possibility of his filling this role had been mooted, but the conception of a strong overlord and a united empire was out of time, and would have been doomed to a premature death. Thus it was that Lützen preceded two years of inaction and in that time Oxenstierna built up the Heilbronn League of Princes to form an alliance with Sweden. Maximilian, however, was determined to force the Emperor Ferdinand II into action. Always suspicious of allowing the Spanish influence and the Catholic League to gain too much control, Ferdinand was finally persuaded to dismiss Wallenstein, whose huge, though inert, army made him more powerful than his master. Had

Wallenstein allied with the Swedes or even signed a pact of neutrality, the southern states would have been lost to Catholicism. Wallenstein's dismissal was followed by his murder, and the war flared up once more. The Swedes, under Horn and Bernhard of Saxe-Weimar, suffered their first defeat when they were utterly vanquished at Nördlingen in September 1634, and the end seemed at hand.

Oxenstierna who, besides being regent for Christina, barely eight years old, was Legate Plenipotentiary of the Holy Roman Empire, was hard put to it in keeping the Heilbronn League together; in fact, the situation could not have been more desperate. Added to the military and political perils in Germany itself, the financial and economic structure of Sweden was threatened. That country could not have withstood the strain so long, had it not been for the French subsidy and the valuable revenue derived from the Baltic ports such as Riga, Memel and Pillau under the truce concluded at Altmark in 1629. The sums derived from these port dues were alone greater than the whole revenue of Sweden herself. Oxenstierna found himself bereft of both at the same time. The last French payment under the Treaty of Bärwalde had been paid, and the Polish king, who refused to recognise Christina's right to the throne, took advantage of Sweden's plight to declare war. To avert this last danger, the Great Elector was bought over by the cession of the ports and East Prussia, and undertook to ward off the Poles in the event of an attack. Oxenstierna then paid a personal visit to Richelieu and Louis XIII which not only resulted in a renewal of the Bärwalde subsidy, but active French military operations in the west. Richelieu was convinced that the destruction or withdrawal of the only remaining Swedish army would be fatal to French interests. His object was to ensure a divided Germany over the Rhenish border, a curbing of the Hapsburg power and the actual annexation of Alsace. He looked to securing "les limites naturelles" for France and a chain of outposts running from north to south on the eastern frontier of Germany. Sweden was to form the northern link and Turkey the southern. Later, French policy included Poland. This plan became traditional, and the friendship of Sweden and France, cemented by the two greatest statesmen of the seventeenth century, was to influence European politics till Napoleon altered the whole map of Europe.

The immediate problem was to preserve the Swedish army and

her Continental bases until the French were ready. Banér won a brilliant victory at Wittstock and then, by one of the outstanding military feats of the whole war, he extricated his little army of fourteen thousand, surrounded by sixty thousand Imperialists, from Moravia and safely reached Pomerania. Here he remained for a year building up new armies and awaiting a further French advance. Already France had achieved her first objective by the acquisition of Alsace.

On the death of Banér, Torstensson was appointed commander-in-chief, and the story of Swedish victories began once more. Of all the generals, Torstensson was perhaps the most faithful disciple of Gustavus. Careful preparation followed by lightning action, led to his victory at the second battle of Breitenfeld in 1642. Under him, Charles X received his military training, and so the tradition was carried on in spite of the weary length of the operations which might well have seen the decay of the small Swedish forces which were called upon to do so much. Overtures for peace were in progress before Christina became of age in 1644, but the action of the Danish king had excited Oxenstierna's suspicions. Christian IV was profoundly jealous of Sweden's growth of power, and had tried to offer himself as the mediator. At the same time, he refused to grant exemption from dues to the ships from the newly acquired Swedish provinces. His contention was that the agreement referred only to Swedish ships from Sweden herself. In other ways he tried to obstruct Swedish trade. Oxenstierna's answer was in action. Torstensson was ordered to leave Moravia and invade Denmark. With astonishing speed, his veterans arrived at the border and had conquered the whole of Jutland in a few weeks. The gallant old king displayed immense energy but, in spite of his heroism, he had finally to sign the peace of Brömsebro in 1645. This was a great triumph for Oxenstierna. Sweden gained Jämtland, Härjedalen, and the islands of Gottland and Osel, while Halland was to be held in security for the exemption from Sound dues.

Christina created him a count and granted him large estates, but from that time she began to chafe at his control and be jealous of his power. Their policies for the final settlement caused a definite split. Oxenstierna considered that a further series of victories warranted stiffer terms, while Christina, aware of the weariness of her people, wished for a settlement which bore promise of permanent endurance.

It was not till October 1648 that the Treaty of Westphalia was simultaneously signed at Osnabrück by the Swedes and the Emperor, and at Münster by the Emperor and the French. French successes under Turenne forced Maximilian of Bavaria to give his consent to the end of hostilities, while the Great Elector of Brandenburg-Prussia and John George of Saxony had already dropped out of the war after signing treaties of neutrality with Sweden. Thus it was left for the Swedish and French emissaries to play the major parts in the lengthy and tortuous bargainings with the Hapsburg Emperor at Westphalia.

This treaty was the most important Pan-European settlement till Vienna in 1815 but, except for the Scandinavian clauses, only certain of the main issues need be discussed here. It closed the epoch of religious wars in a spirit of realism by acknowledging accomplished facts. Both Catholics and Protestants recognised that neither side could be exterminated. A test year (1624) was agreed upon, and all lands were to remain in the same hands as on that date; thus the southern bishoprics remained Catholic, and the secularised bishoprics of the North, such as Bremen, Verden and Magdeburg, remained Protestant. Only in the hereditary dominions of Austria in Bavaria and Bohemia could the Counter-Reformation claim any advance. These arrangements, corresponding to the actual majorities in each state, were the result of the victories of Breitenfeld on the one hand and of Nördlingen on the other, and could have been made some thirteen years earlier.

The territorial settlements overshadow the religious, and tend to emphasize the complete change of motive since the beginning of the Thirty Years War. As we have seen, before the end, Catholic country had been fighting against Catholic, Protestant against Protestant. France had obtained Alsace and Breisach, and the three bishoprics of Metz, Toul and Verdun—so important from a military standpoint.

Brandenburg, by the acquisition of Eastern Pomerania besides other territories within the empire, was firmly established on the Baltic, though a Polish corridor running between Eastern Pomerania and East Prussia to Danzig denied her all she desired.[1]

---

[1] In 1641 the Elector had been granted by the King of Poland the fiefdom of East Prussia, which included the important town of Königsberg. The Dukedom of Prussia gained complete independence at the treaty of Oliva, but it was not till 1701 that Prussia and Brandenburg together with Cleves, Mark and Ravensburg, acquired in 1648, were united as the Kingdom of Prussia and acknowledged as such by the Emperor.

Oxenstierna would have stood out for Eastern Pomerania as well as Western or Upper Pomerania. However, by gaining command of the mouth of the Oder, Stettin and the Isle of Rügen, Sweden had a firm hold of the coast due south of Sweden strong enough in fact to allow the cession of Bornholm to Denmark at a later date. On the west of Denmark, Sweden acquired the secularised bishoprics of Verden and Bremen (but *not* the free city of Bremen). Thus, although the new Swedish territories were smaller than Oxenstierna or Gustavus Adolphus had wished, they secured a stranglehold on Denmark, a strategic command of the three German rivers—the Oder, the Elbe and the Weser—and the right of being represented on the German Diet. In addition, Sweden received a cash payment of 5,000,000 riksdalers from the German states. The esteem in which Sweden was held was recognised in the fact that France and herself were nominated as guarantors of the Treaty. The unsatisfactory features which were destined to disturb the peace in the near future lay in the unsatisfied ambition of an unscrupulous Brandenburg-Prussia,[1] the re-iterated claim of the Polish king to the throne of Sweden, and the position of the unhappy Denmark. With Skåne still in Danish hands, it was inevitable that the Swedish territories east and west of her should be regarded as bases from which to attack Denmark, and so force her to cede Skåne and the adjoining province of Halland, finally ceded to Sweden in 1675 under the terms of the Brömsebro Treaty of 1645.

A renewal of war in the north-east was only a matter of time and, had it not been for the peaceful inclinations of Christina and her assumption of royal authority which curbed the power and lessened the influence of Oxenstierna, the uneasy truce would not have been maintained until the year after her abdication in 1654. This remarkable woman was crowned on her eighteenth birthday, in 1644, and her reign, her abdication, and her character are still unsolved puzzles of intense psychological interest. The delight of novelist and of film and play writers she will remain, but to the historian of Swedish power she is a profound disappointment. Endowed with brilliant qualities of mind, she became one of the most learned women in Europe, happy to discuss philosophy with Descartes and the learned scholars of all Europe. At the same time,

---

[1] The Elector had some grounds for dissatisfaction, as he was unable to enter his promised lands for some years. The last Swedish soldier did not leave East Pomerania till 1655.

she had a masculine love of outdoor exercises and sport, and set a fashion among Swedish girls for riding, skiing, swimming and plunging into snow baths in winter. Christina did not disdain the admiration of many men, and her relations with Count Tott and Magnus Gabriel de la Gardie caused many a rebuke from the old chancellor, but she was no feminine Charles II to be reprimanded for frivolity by a shocked Clarendon. She was intensely earnest, intensely religious, and her refusal to marry was part of the triumph of her intellectual ego over sensual inclinations, which she considered must be suppressed.

Christina was a masterful Vasa, but she wished to be as masterful over her own self as over others. A restless and almost hysterical trait she inherited from her mother, but it was not this which made her dissatisfied with her position as queen of a Protestant country which had saved the faith from extinction. When she felt that peace of mind could only be found in Catholicism, her intellectual honesty showed her that conversion meant abdication. Whether this was her only reason will never be known. Some believe that she sincerely felt that she was not fitted to be a queen. Some believe that, unhappy in her sex which debarred her from gallant and daring acts, she was induced to startle the world by one of the most dramatic acts in history. Much can be argued in support of these views, but she has taken her secret to the grave and, for all her learning and brilliance, only four aspects of her reign have any real importance in Scandinavian history:

1. She hastened the Treaty of Westphalia.

2. She encouraged learning and love of the arts in Sweden—unfortunately at vast expense.

3. Her generous gifts emptied the treasury and cut the revenue so that the country was faced by bankruptcy.

4. She left the crown to her warlike cousin Charles X, one of her many rejected suitors.

Her love of French culture and French ways undoubtedly strengthened the bonds between the two countries, but it is somewhat fanciful to ascribe to her the growth of French influence a century later. It is still more fanciful to connect the physical fitness movement of the early nineteenth century with her masculinity. It would be truer to say that the legends surrounding her romantic

personality were utilised by the ardent devotees of these two strangely different cults—French literature and physical fitness.

The Sweden which her successor inherited was in no position to maintain her high place in Europe unless the national economy was completely overhauled and the financial situation improved by drastic measures. Christina had never faced the danger created by the alienation of crown lands and consequent loss of revenue. Her reckless expenditure had been increasing that danger up to the very time of her abdication. The old chancellor, chagrined by the Queen's neglect and in despair at her abdication, had been succeeded by his son, Eric Oxenstierna.

Together, the new king and chancellor appealed for heavy sacrifices from all classes at the Riksdag in 1655, to restore the revenue, which had lost over 60,000 silver dalers through the alienations of crown lands and which in 1632 had already reached 280,000 dalers, and by 1655 had reached the staggering total of 734,000 dalers.

The king, as son of the Count Palatine of Zweibrucken, was by no means *persona grata* in spite of his mother being Vasa. The nobility, however, rallied round him in spite of their being the chief sufferers, and the only matter of dispute was the amount each class should contribute. The personality of the king towered over the Riksdag and finally it was decided that the crown should "resume" all estates required for military purposes, the maintenance of the court and home government and the mining industry. A capital levy of a quarter was imposed on the other estates. Such a result could never have been achieved without opposition and open revolt had not the constitution of 1634 been firmly established.

Having successfully steered these financial reforms through the Riksdag, the king summoned a secret committee to which he revealed his daring foreign policy. In three days he persuaded them that a war against Poland was necessary and, in July 1655, he sailed with fifty thousand men and fifty warships on the second European Adventure. His ostensible reason was that the Polish king must acknowledge him as the rightful sovereign of Sweden and renounce his own claim. His real reasons were that Poland was in a state of disintegration and most of it, including the south Baltic coast, would fall into the hands of Russia. The situation, as he saw it, was not unlike that which induced Eric XIV to attack Livonia a century earlier, but with two important differences.

Russia was stronger and more united, and Brandenburg-Prussia was a formidable and ambitious state which could not be trusted. The war was to maintain and strengthen Sweden's hard-won hegemony of the Baltic and to prevent Russia gaining a highway to the sea. Had Poland fallen into Russian hands, Livonia, Ingria and Estonia would have been in constant danger of attack. The Great Elector, though no friend of Sweden, played a waiting game, which ultimately brought considerable advantage to the rising Brandenburg-Prussian state, though it was marked by an unscrupulous Machiavellianism foreshadowing the policies of the Third Reich. He feared the predominance of Russia in Poland which would threaten East Prussia. He was almost equally afraid of a renewal of Swedish military ambitions under the masterful King Charles X, but by skilfully playing off these three nations, he saw a great opportunity of enhancing his own power at the expense of Poland and Sweden.

He began by observing friendly relations with Sweden and professing a benevolent neutrality as the last Swedes left East Pomerania. He hoped that Charles would be swamped in the vast spaces and marshes of Poland and emerge with only sufficient strength to act as a buffer against Russia. He, however, was shaken, in common with the rest of a Europe slowly recovering from the Thirty Years War, by the swift advance and astonishing victories of a new " Gustavus Adolphus ". In five weeks after the landing in July 1655, all Upper Poland, including Warsaw, had been conquered. By the end of November, Cracow, the royal city, had fallen in spite of a heroic defence, while the king, John Cassimir, was a fugitive in Silesia. Having gained these objectives, Charles found himself in possession of more land than he could administer. The national spirit was aroused, and guerrilla warfare broke out, threatening communications and cutting off foraging parties. The religious flames flared up once again and were fanned by reports of the miraculous defence of a monastery by seventy monks and a hundred and fifty soldiers. John Cassimir crept back, and an army of resistance under Czarniecki, the gallant defender of Cracow, began to take heavy toll of the dwindling Swedish forces. The Poles' re-organised army is said to have numbered nearly one hundred thousand men, though these were not as well armed or highly disciplined as the Swedes. They were, however, fighting in a friendly country and willing to make fanatical sacrifices. Charles

forced the Elector into an unwilling alliance, and secured the promise of troops and supplies. The supplies were slow in arriving and the prices asked excessive, but they helped to stave off defeat and possible annihilation. Charles wished to extricate himself from Poland with honour, as he was slowly beginning to realise that neither his military power nor political machinery were adequate to control this vast hostile land. He was a brilliant general, modelled as already stated on Torstensson, but he had no clear-sighted administrator like Axel Oxenstierna to advise and cool his ardour. Faithful admirer as was Eric Oxenstierna, he had not the same prestige, nor could be have said to his master, " If my coldness did not cool your heat, your majesty would be burned to death ". Charles gloried in war, but had no definite schemes for organising his conquered lands. With the help of the Brandenburg troops he retook Warsaw after a skilfully executed siege lasting three days, although the Polish troops outnumbered his by four to one. But even so, what hope for the future? The Russians poured over the borders of Livonia and the Elector was already wavering and could only be persuaded to continue the alliance by the granting of full sovereignty over East Prussia. Further trouble awaited Charles. The King of Denmark seized this moment to declare war on Sweden. In alliance with the Dutch, who thought this would be a propitious moment to strike at Swedish naval power, he made preparations for the invasion of Sweden. Without hesitation, Charles left garrisons in key positions and withdrew his small army. Then, by forced marches through Mecklenburg, he hastened to invade Jutland from the south, reaching Holstein, where he was warmly received by the Duke, his brother-in-law, before Denmark was fully prepared. Overtures were made to Cromwell who had a genuine admiration for the Swedes as the bulwark of Protestantism, and also was anxious to strike a further blow at the Dutch. It seemed that the Thirty Years War might start again, when the Emperor supported Denmark and the Elector, having secured full sovereignty over East Prussia, changed sides and proceeded to declare war on Sweden. Charles's tattered army, however, maintained its old traditions and in a short campaign—a replica of Torstensson's—stormed the fortress of Fredericia, captured more prisoners than it had soldiers, and overran Jutland. When the ice froze the Little Belt, Charles boldly led his men across to the peninsula of Inversnaes, and the whole of Fünen was

his. Still more daring was the crossing of the thirty kilometres to Sjaelland under the guidance of the confident scientific engineer Dahlberg. The Danes sued for peace, and a general war was averted. Cromwell acted as mediator at the preliminaries at Roskilde which, with the Treaties of Oliva and Copenhagen (1660) may be said to have completed the Treaty of Westphalia and tied up the loose ends in north-eastern Europe. It is convenient to consider the terms of the three treaties together, because the Peace of Roskilde was unjustifiably broken almost immediately by Charles X, and the terms, with two alterations, were repeated two years later.

After Roskilde, Charles was determined to settle accounts with the treacherous Elector of Brandenburg. Apparently, he repented of not having utterly destroyed Copenhagen and the Danish power, when he had the opportunity after his brilliant and hazardous march across the Great Belt. He urged Denmark to form an alliance, but his offer had been refused. Without a declaration of war he had swooped down on Sjaelland. Kronborg fell into his hands, but instead of taking Copenhagen by storm, contrary to his usual tactics, he proceeded to invest the city. This allowed the Brandenburgers to send help to the beleaguered garrison, and the Dutch Admiral de Witt, after a memorable victory over Wrangel's fleet, relieved the capital. It is by no means improbable that, had Copenhagen fallen immediately, a united Scandinavia would have been established and the history of the Baltic would have been far different. As it was, the French, having ended their war with Spain, were instrumental in bringing a general peace which Sweden was willing to accept in view of her isolation after the death of Cromwell. Thus in the year 1660 boundaries were defined which have lasted to the twentieth century and few of the provisions of the settlement were altered before Nystad in 1721.

By Roskilde, Sweden established her natural boundaries on the north side of the Sound—Halland,[1] Skåne, Blekinge and Bohuslän became hers and have remained in her possession ever since. By the Treaty of Copenhagen, Trondheim and Bornholm were ceded to Denmark-Norway. The Treaty of Oliva at last ended the struggle between Sweden and Poland, which renounced the claim to the Swedish throne. Livonia was guaranteed to Sweden, which made a

---

[1] In 1660 Denmark advanced the claim that Halland under the 1645 treaty was held by Sweden as a pledge for thirty years, but was not ceded in perpetuity. This was conceded at the time, but in 1675 it became Swedish and has remained so since.

separate peace with Russia at Kardis. The Elector of Brandenburg was granted full possession of East Prussia, thus freeing himself of both Poland and Sweden, and laying the foundation of the future kingdom of Prussia, but West Pomerania and the other Baltic conquests, together with Bremen and Verden, remained in Swedish hands.

Although Denmark received Bornholm and Trondheim (as part of Norway), she had to renounce her suzerainty over Holstein, whose connexions with South Jutland (Slesvig) were to bring un-ending troubles to the Danish kingdom. By comparing the maps of north-eastern Europe in 1618 and 1660, Sweden and Brandenburg will be seen as having profited most territorially by this long struggle. Brandenburg-Prussia was a sturdy growing child, but Sweden was recognised as a great European state, the dominant power of the Baltic, and an ally eagerly sought by other powers.

She had almost invariably struck at the right moment and stopped before antagonistic coalitions had become too strong. In glaring contrast, Denmark had chosen the wrong psychological moments and consequently sunk to her lowest state—so exhausted and disintegrated had her economy become, that she fell an easy prey to a long reign of absolutism which seemed her only hope. Russia remained cut off from the Baltic, although her power had extended south and south-west at the expense of Poland which had exposed her strength and her inherent weaknesses.

A period of uneasy peace followed for the Scandinavian countries. Denmark humiliated by her losses, Sweden almost bankrupt, whilst Norway, nominally under Denmark, used her virtual independence unobstrusively to increase her fish and timber trades under enterprising, though unknown, individuals. The encouragement which she received from Denmark was spasmodic, being almost entirely dependent on the attitude of the governor or viceroy. Self-interest was the underlying motive, whether of the State or its servant. Yet from this period may be traced the growth of the Norwegian mercantile marine. The merchants and the searfaring people must be given the credit for the success of their enterprise in trade. Bergen had become a thriving centre after the decline of the Hanseatic League. Trondheim and Christiania (Oslo) were developed under the influence of Gyldenlöve, a natural son of Frederic III, but in Christiania alone was the Danish influence in any sense predominant. Even Gyldenlöve

Map III. Scandinavia, 1660

was not above lining his own pocket, while Schested, his predecessor, shamelessly indulged in purloining a large portion of the taxes, though he undoubtedly was a benefactor to Norway in other ways. The timber, especially from the west coast, had as high a reputation as its vendors and, in 1666, it was Norwegian timber which was largely used in the rebuilding of London after the Great Fire. The position of Norway was peculiar. To both Sweden and Denmark she was an enviable prize. Neither country was strong enough to make her a real possession, but owing to the geographical features, she could never achieve sufficient unity to stand alone, nor did she produce any statesmen of sufficient ability to overcome the natural difficulties and weld together the isolated elements. Slowly and imperceptibly, a national spirit grew, but not until the twentieth century did she achieve sovereign power and become a separate state.

(b) 1660–1721

The years following the peace treaties were not spectacular but were of great importance in the domestic history of both Sweden and Denmark. In the latter country, a clean cut was made in the form of government, which shaped the course of things to come. The new rule of aboslutism lasted for two full centuries with but little alteration. Other striking features were the decline of the old land-owning nobles, but with little or no amelioration in the lot of the peasant and the rise in power of the burgesses, especially in the growing capital, Copenhagen. Most remarkable of all was the increase of the mercantile marine and, after an interval, the navy also in spite of the impoverished state of the country's finances. Under royal patronage, or at any rate with royal encouragement, there was a marked development in scientific studies and learning. The king's secretary was the librarian of the Royal Library, and the post was regarded as the first step to power.

With all the power centred in the king, the new " Colleges " or departmental boards of administration were staffed by a new type of business man, and a large number of Germans was to be found in these posts, though the Danish aristocracy was eligible and the ministers were Danish though rarely drawn from the old class.

In Sweden, the minority of the king necessitated a Regency whose extravagance has somewhat dimmed its other achievements. The Scanian Wars (1675–1680) in which Sweden found herself fighting against Brandenburg, Denmark and Holland, was succeeded by a short period of absolutism, unnatural to the genius of the Swedish people. This paved the way for the last of the Swedish Adventures ending in Charles XII's disaster at Pultava and the end of the Baltic Empire. With the Treaty of Nystad, Sweden and Denmark were seen in their modern orientations. It is the end of one epoch and the beginning of another.

The Russian bogey assumes definite shape, and Sweden was not the only country which had to fear the new Russia of Peter the Great. Poland, Prussia and Austria saw in her a dangerous aggressor or a potential ally against a rival. Even Denmark had her alarms and fears of invasion.

The position of Denmark and Sweden became precarious, but schemes for mutual protection were short-lived. Age-long antagonism died slowly.

In the eyes of other countries, Denmark's geographical command of the Sound, Sweden's natural wealth, and their combined marine strength rendered their independence a matter of supreme importance. Neither France, England, Russia, nor, at a later date, Prussia, could allow the balance of power to be upset by annexation, limitation of territory or curtailment of their independent action. The foreign policy of the Scandinavian countries was profoundly affected by this consideration and not unnaturally appeared to be unstable and wobbling. This was not new for Denmark, which had only been saved from being dragged into Louis XIV's wars by the skilful but tortuous diplomacy of Griffenfeld, who was accused of similar unreliability. Territorially as well as politically, Nystad forms a landmark—only two changes have occurred since that date, both at the expense of Denmark. In 1815 Russia acquired Finland in exchange for Norway, which was united with Sweden till 1905. Secondly, Slesvig, formally guaranteed to Denmark in 1721, was, by an iniquitous act of political immorality, annexed by Germany in 1864.

The Slesvig question was one of the first problems which confronted Frederick III on his accession to the throne in 1648. It was considered that the emperor's consent to an agreement reached by Duke Frederick III of Gottorp and King Frederick III in 1649, amended in 1667, had settled the knotty problem of South Jutland[1] and the Duchies, but unfortunately this was not so, and endless claims and counter-claims continued to occur. The whole question is fraught with danger at the present day and is now one of great importance to Denmark. At the risk of repetition, it has been treated as a whole in Chapter XIII, as in no other way could justice be done to it without dislocating the main story of Scandinavia.

Frederick was a learned, reserved and patient man—a striking contrast to his father, but he was acutely conscious of his royal dignity and chafed at the charter of royal capitulation which he had been forced to sign before his succession was confirmed by

---

[1] The term " South Jutland " is very loosely used by English writers. It has a political and geographical meaning and unfortunately it is the translation of two Danish words. (1) Sydjylland, which refers to the Southern part of Jutland, north of North Slesvig. (2) Sønderjylland, which since 1864 usually, and since 1920 universally, refers to North Slesvig (vide Chapter XII, Denmark and Slesvig-Holstein). Before Slesvig was formally declared Danish in 1721, " South Jutland " should be used in a geographical sense, but it will be found often to refer to North Slesvig and the region north of it. Strictly speaking, this is not correct.

election. The aristocracy, headed by the able Corfits Ulfeld, were determined to keep the whole of the executive power in their own hands, and although the king was emboldened by his initial personal success in Slesvig, he bided his time and did not strike at the fundamental status of the nobles for eleven years. He retained the services of Schested, a skilled financier and administrator who was no friend of Ulfeld, and this minister won the favour of Frederick's ambitious wife, Sophie Amalie of Brunswick. She was wildly jealous of Ulfeld's wife, the gifted and charming Leonora Christine, daughter of Christian IV. Round her centred the life of the capital and, though no evidence was forthcoming against her loyalty to the king, she was dangerously close to the royal line of succession, and accusations were made that she and her husband were plotting against the throne. Ulfeld, who had complete control of the foreign affairs, was absent on a mission to Holland where he had negotiated a treaty by which the Dutch, in return for a subsidy, were to receive the assistance of a substantial Danish naval force. The mission, lavishly conducted in royal fashion, cemented the Danish-Netherlands entente, but to the uninitiated Danes, appeared a waste of money and provocative to both England and Sweden.

Subsequent history proved that it was of greater value to Denmark than to Holland. It is true that when Cromwell became Protector, it did incline him to the Swedish orbit, and that Charles X was able to stress the danger to England of this alliance and even offer Jutland to England as a guarantee of security to the English trader in the Baltic, but England's hostility remained a threatening danger and active intervention never materialised. However, the treaty and the untrue story of the plot were sufficient to undermine the authority of the aristocratic leader who fled with his wife to Holland. This was the first step against the all-powerful aristocracy, and the king personally undertook the conduct of foreign affairs.

He was singularly unsuccessful. His was the sole responsibility for the attack on Charles X when he was embroiled in Poland. The fatal results of this action have already been recounted but their effect on domestic affairs was entirely unpredictable. The whole blame for the disasters up to and after Roskilde was thrown on the shoulders of the nobility. In the first place, Ulfeld, who had joined Charles X, brought unpalatable treaty terms to

Copenhagen. Not unnaturally he and the nobility were not immune from charges of treachery. On the second attack on Copenhagen the king behaved with great gallantry and was ably supported by Nansen, the burgomaster, and Hans Svane, Bishop of Sjaelland. The nobles were discredited, and after the signing of the peace, the king, burgesses and clergy were arrayed against the aristocracy when the first attempt was made to restore the financial chaos of the war. Lastly, the Brandenburgers, who had entered the city to help, stayed to loot and only with difficulty could be driven from the city. This grievance also tended to undermine the standing of the nobility still further when two years later it was discovered that the schemer Ulfeld had offered the Danish throne to the Elector of Brandenburg who, showing a touch of true Prussian diplomacy, sent his reply to the government at Copenhagen for all to read!

The Estates assembled in September 1660 and the king decided that the hour had arrived for which he had waited twelve years. The nobles were forced reluctantly to share the burden of the new taxation, which was admittedly unavoidable. The burgesses and clergy, encouraged by the king, were determined to go further and destroy the oligarchy for ever. Having assured themselves of the support of the citizen militia and small garrison forces in case of necessity, they proceeded to offer Denmark to the king and his heirs, male and female, as an hereditary monarchy, to rule "as should seem best to his majesty for general good". They then called on the nobles and council to concur. On their refusal, the armed militia turned out and the city gates were barred, and the king demanded an immediate answer. Five days after the submission of the nobles, October 18th, 1660, the king received the homage of all ranks in the square opposite the royal palace, and solemnly promised to give a constitution fair and just to all. The archives of the Council were removed to the palace, and an absolute monarchy had begun a reign of two centuries in the very year that Charles II signed the Declaration of Breda and ascended the throne as a constitutional monarch.

Since that day nothing has been seen or heard of the promised constitution. In 1661 a document was distributed throughout Denmark (but not Norway), and duly signed in every local assembly, granting absolute sovereignty to the king and his heirs, male and female, for all time. Thus nation and nobles abdicated and a king was appointed above the law of man, the only condition being that the sovereign must be a Protestant. The king's secretary, Peter Schumacher, better known by his later title of Griffenfeld, drew up to so-called *Lex Regia* or Constitution of the Monarchy in 1665, but it was not produced until the king's death five years later.

Events moved quickly. An undignified revenge was taken on Ulfeld, who was burned in effigy and the body quartered—a form of propaganda for the new régime's anti-aristocratic policy. The Queen wreaked vengeance on the devoted Leonora Christine, who had gone to collect a private debt from Charles II for her exiled husband. She was extradited from Dover and imprisoned for twenty-two years, and finally died in a cloister, unbroken in mind and spirit.

The administration was reorganised. Five Colleges or Departmental Boards were established, all directly under the king's two chief ministers—Hannibal Schested, the Treasurer, and Gersdorf, the High Steward. These in their turn were directly under the king, who began to rely more and more on his librarian and secretary, the gifted Schumacher. The Assembly of the Estates had met for the last time till the institution of parliamentary government in the nineteenth century. The sudden change in the régime had its repercussions in Norway, for theoretically she was on an equal footing, united under the same hereditary monarch but in no way subordinate to Denmark. It was in no small measure due to Hannibal Schested that the revolutionary change in Denmark did not rouse the latent urge for immediate independence. In spite of being convicted of peculation, he had been a good governor and popular, and happily for Denmark he had not lost his influence among the Norwegians when he became Frederick's treasurer, and for some years his adviser on foreign affairs. To draw a close parallel between the suppression of the States General by Richelieu and the Danish Assembly in 1660 is most misleading. The burgesses and clergy initiated the abdication though they little dreamed that they were not to be summoned under the new constitution which never materialised.

The Danish form of government has no exact parallel, but to students of political science it is of extreme interest. It bridges the gap between the ideal of the New Monarchy[1] and the Age of

[1] Vide Pollard *Factors of Modern History*, chapter III.

the Enlightened Despot of the eighteenth century. It borrows features from both, but cannot be classified as either.

After the death of Frederick III in 1670, it might well have become a benevolent despotism had not jealousy and impatience caused the fall of Griffenfeld; the benevolence died and the despotism lived on. It might, perhaps, be compared to a business concern—the king as chairman, with a confidential secretary, Schumacher—whilst the official general manager was Schested. It was a private company, and the shareholders had no votes. The balance sheet was straightened out by the sale of crown lands, and the revenue increased by granting monopolies and astonishingly wide powers to trading companies. The most notable were the Asiatic or East Indian and the West Indian, the king himself being a shareholder. Smaller companies, such as the fishing and trading company with a monopoly of Greenland's[1] commerce, all paid their tribute, and incidentally furnished a recruiting ground for sailors in case of war.

From a purely financial point of view, the policy might be termed long term, as time was required for the commercial projects to bring in sufficient revenue to balance the budget and replace capital. The mercantile projects began to bear fruit during the Anglo-French wars from 1692 onwards—the East Indian company secured much of the English and French trade, and the West Indian company extended its activities to China, and its zenith was reached when it could purchase S. Croix and participate in the molasses trade of the West Indies. For the success of the new régime there were two main essential requirements—peace for Denmark and an efficient personnel.

As long as Schested was Frederick's adviser, peace was maintained by a bewildering number of alliances with countries ranged against each other or actively at war. It is unnecessary to recapitulate all of these transitory treaties, but it is enough to recall a treaty with England in 1661 which endangered the Dutch alliance, another with France in 1663, although France and Sweden were still bound by their old agreements. Sweden formed an alliance with England in 1665, just as England declared war on Holland. When, however, a triple alliance was formed by England, Holland and Sweden, Denmark had to review her commitments, and successfully managed to come to an agreement

[1] Vide Appendix A.

with both France and England, thereby hoping to detach Sweden from both Louis XIV and Charles II. It was fortunate for Denmark that in the critical years 1669–1672 she possessed one of her greatest statesmen, Griffenfeld, who managed to steer clear of actual warfare by arranging alliances with the Emperor and the Elector of Brandenburg, and with the Netherlands which only involved her in war if France secured "another active ally". The unnamed ally was Sweden, whose active intervention in North Germany would probably mean war in any case. At the same time Denmark did not break with England, and secretly strengthened her pact with France. In the first four years of Christian V's reign, prosperity grew apace, the strength of the navy and mercantile marine actually doubled, Copenhagen began to rival the North Sea German and Dutch ports as a clearing house for European trade.

Thus the first essential for success had been satisfied, but the second—the efficiency of the administrative personnel, was not so satisfactory. The king began to sink into himself and became absorbed in mysticism and scientific pursuits. Alchemy became almost a cult under a notorious Italian who was installed in the palace. It is, however, true that encouragement was given to scientific research, and in this atmosphere Römer spent his youth and finally gained the highest place in the scientific world by the discovery of the velocity of light, and his invention of new instruments for astronomy and navigation. To try and improve the efficiency of government officials, many Germans were introduced, whilst others bought lands from the impoverished aristocracy. Except on the crown lands, the state of the peasants did not improve and it was in the towns alone that the increasing prosperity was enjoyed by the Danish people. It is true, however, that agricultural methods improved, though the conditions of the peasants deteriorated, especially in Sjaelland, where the Germans were most numerous. In an attempt to remedy some of these evils Griffenfeld, appointed as secretary of the new Privy Council, personally took the control of the five government departments. He was a virtual dictator, with his acts sanctioned by the royal assent and seal. In 1671 new ranks of counts and barons and the royal order of Dannebrog were instituted. In 1673 he received the order of the Elephant, hitherto reserved for royal persons.

His aim was still to preserve peace and enhance the prestige of his country, but his policy had excited opposition in three quarters. The old aristocracy hated the new orders bestowed on adherents of the minister for meritorious service to the State. The officers of the navy and army were chafing at their inactivity—they wished to retrieve the honour of the services and display their efficiency. Lastly, the vain and shallow-minded king was jealous of his minister and was listening to the voices which whispered that the lost provinces must be restored to their rightful owner—the King of Denmark.

To the chagrin of Griffenfeld, the Swedish attack on the Elector of Brandenburg forced his hand. The defeat of the Swedes at Ferhbellin, however, would have been sufficient to allow him to remain passively ready, as Brandenburg was in no danger. His peaceful policy could not be maintained in face of royal pressure, and so against his will Denmark entered the war. Still trying to keep on friendly terms with France, he planned to secure his southern frontier by attacking Christian Albrecht of Gottorp, who had promised help to Sweden. The victory of the Brandenburgers had prevented Swedish help coming to Christian Albrecht, who was easily defeated, and once more all sovereign rights over Slesvig were admitted to be Danish. Griffenfeld then determined to capture the Swedish provinces of Bremen and Verden, which he would only give back for the lost province of Skåne. Louis XIV was secretly notified of the scheme and promised Griffenfeld the friendship of France when the war ended. Unfortunately his answer was intercepted at Hamburg. Griffenfeld was arrested as a traitor and condemned to death, but the sentence was commuted and he lay in prison for twenty-two years until his death. So ended the greatest of Danish statesmen, broken by the absolutism which he had made effective, and condemned by virtue of the *Lex Curia*, which he had composed. There was not a shred of real evidence against him. The weak king had known of his French activities and had apparently agreed with his opinion that friendship with France was the true policy of Denmark. Subsequent events proved that he was right. Swept by a wave of national enthusiasm which expressed itself in anti-Swedish jingoism, the Danes invaded Skåne, led by Gyldenlöve and the king in person.

The finest Danish and Norwegian fleet seen in the Baltic for many centuries won the great victory of Köge Bay under Nils

Juel. Helsingborg had fallen, Landskrona had fallen, Göteborg was threatened. The Swedes rose in defence of their land and won a bloody victory on the hills near Lund; and though the Danish fleet before and after the Köge Bay victory swept the seas, the conquest of Sweden was no nearer. Christian V's army was defeated at a second battle near Lund in 1676. On the Continent Louis XIV was supreme, and at the peace of Nimwegen, Denmark was faced with the threat of losing her conquests and Wismar as well. In 1679 France forced a peace on Denmark and the far-sighted policy of Griffenfeld was vindicated. By the treaties of Fontainebleau with France and of Lund with Sweden, Denmark was compelled to surrender all her conquests. This year (1679) left her once more exhausted and her only gain was the strengthening of her southern frontier on the River Eider. Angry at her treatment by her allies and France, she turned to Sweden, and for a brief period the Scandinavian countries saw that they had common interests. To cement the friendship, Charles XI of Sweden married Princess Ulrica Eleonora. By a piece of dramatic irony, it was their son, Charles XII, who was to stir up the old rivalries, and once more bring the two countries into a conflict still more disastrous to their interests.

Peace was as necessary to Sweden as to Denmark, for the interval between the death of Charles X in 1660 and the outbreak of war had been one of social and economic changes, pregnant with dangers to the constitution established by Axel Oxenstierna in 1634.

Once again the sudden death of a warrior king left the throne in the hands of a regency. By the will of Charles X, the government was placed in the hands of the Queen Mother, his brother Adolphus John and the five leading Swedish heads of the departmental boards. It was immediately apparent, however, that the power would not rest with the Queen, who remained as a nominal member with the sole function of saying " yes " to all proposals. Adolphus John was excluded at the outset on the reasonable ground that he was not a Swedish national.

Three members of the cabal were outstanding in power, riches and ability, and all were heads of leading families of the aristocracy. Per Brahe had shown considerable administrative skill as governor of Finland, where he had ruled almost as an independent prince. There he acquired immense riches, but had brought considerable benefits to the Finns, and at the same time had strengthened the influence of the Swedes in that province. Magnus Gabriel de la Gardie, almost as wealthy as Per Brahe, had been the one-time favourite of Christina and had inherited her Francophil tendencies. He had a fertile imagination and dreamed of a Sweden becoming the "France of the North". He pictured a court rivalling Versailles, frequented by European artists, scientists and scholars, famous for the brilliance and wit of the aristocracy, while the presiding genius was to be himself, controlling the diplomacy of Europe—with the skill of the prosaic Oxenstierna and the magnificence of a Richelieu or a Mazarin.

The third of the trio was the honest military hero Wrangel, one of the greatest, if not the greatest, of generals in Europe at this time. He dwelt on the military glories of the past, and dreamed of further military glory to come. Together they formed an ambitious and expensive triumvirate—ill-suited for a Sweden needing peace and retrenchment and consolidation. As a makeweight against this powerful combination stood the Lord High Treasurer, Bonde, whose practical mind perceived that economy was essential to restore the impoverished treasury, and that a long period of settled peace was required to organise the new territorial acquisitions and convert them into profitable provinces with a Swedish outlook. The problems of Skåne, Livonia, Pomerania and Bremen and Verden, all differed in some degree, and the "grand manner" of the dominating de la Gardie was less adapted to solve them than a patient administrative civil service.

However, the successful "tidying up" of Charles X's wars ensured a promising start to the new régime, and the cession of Bornholm to Denmark was not regarded as of much importance in view of the other gains.

The first clash came in the Treasurer's insistence that the "Resumption of Estates" should be continued, but, as it was bound to arouse the hostility of the nobles, this was successfully opposed by Brahe and de la Gardie, who were the natural leaders of that party. Without money, the grandiose schemes could not be supported by a thinly-populated country like Sweden, and only two ways seemed open to maintain her position won by military genius and to some extent by the help of France. The first was by foreign loan, and the second by a substantial and speedy increase in Swedish commerce. This method, to the annoyance of the Francophil de la Gardie, was tried first, and a commercial treaty was signed with England in 1665, and by 1668 the triple alliance of England, Holland and Sweden seemed to have added some stability to this policy. This alliance was justifiably regarded as being aimed at France for the benefit of England, and when Louis XIV made his Treaty of Dover with Charles II in 1670,[1] the French party in Sweden seized the opportunity to approach their allies. To serve his Continental policy, the French king was anxious to have closer relations with the Swedes, and sent them concrete proposals in 1671. It was finally agreed that the Swedes should keep a standing force of 16,000 men ready to assist the French against the German princes if necessary, while they should receive an annual subsidy of Kr.400,000 in peacetime and Kr.600,000 in case of war. The Swedish cabal were jubilant at their success. The Resumption or *Reduktion* of 1655 was deemed unnecessary and could be laid aside. A standing army could be maintained at the expense of France, there need be no commercial break with England. It can now be seen that the arrangement was merely a temporary expedient and unsound at that. It made Sweden's economy entirely dependent on another nation. The French money caused a serious inflation in spite of the fact that the Swedes founded a state bank. Unfortunately, instead of regulating expenditure and enforcing proper audits, it was used for loans which were not properly covered. This policy was continued for many years and nearly ended in complete bankruptcy. However, the regency must have credit for being the first European government to put the idea into force, and ultimately it proved of great benefit. An even greater evil was that the French gold found its way into the pockets of the nobles, who were influenced in their opinions and their integrity was undermined. The subsidy was not used as it should have been, and the army and navy deteriorated in an alarming way. When the call came from France to implement the treaty, the military party rejoiced and gaily attacked Brandenburg. The result was disaster. The defeat of Ferhbellin was followed by the equally disastrous Scanian wars[2] and the regency was utterly discredited. The morose and saddened king had come to the throne in 1672 but had not yet begun to rule. At the end of the war he proceeded to wreak a terrible retribution on the regents, but reckless and extravagant as they

---

[1] The secret clauses were not disclosed at the time.   [2] *Vide* page 190

had been, their rule had not been wholly bad, nor could they be blamed for the European situation, which had affected Sweden as much as Denmark. Captivated by the glamour of the New Monarchy in France, they had not the " bigness " of Oxenstierna to gauge how far the Swedish interests coincided with the French. Their alliance smacked of subservience; Oxenstierna's was one of dignified equality. Their worst offences were reckless extravagance and class legislation to the benefit of the nobility.

On the credit side, however, was the encouragement of architecture, culture and science in many directions, and the wooing of the people of Skåne to Sweden. As a lasting monument of both there remains the foundation of Lund University, which has nobly fulfilled their highest intentions.

Charles XI was a singularly unattractive man and his uncouth manners, his taciturnity and his uncultured narrow-mindedness sooner or later would have brought him into conflict with the ministers and the court, had the misfortunes of the Scanian war not accentuated the differences and brought the crisis in 1680.

Embittered by his experiences in war and acutely conscious of the deficiencies of the army and the impoverishment of the treasury, he lost no time in summoning the Riksdag and striking at the ministers, whom all were denouncing as incompetent and even treacherous. The nobility made an abject surrender and the other estates wholeheartedly supported the king and his minister Gyllenstierna. Two Commissions were appointed—one was in effect a revival of the *Reduktion* or Resumption Commission, though invested with greater powers, and the other was to deal with the late regency.

Meanwhile, the foreign policy under Gyllenstierna was completely altered and an alliance with Denmark was signed and the French influence shaken off. The Commissions began their work immediately and the estates of the burgesses and peasants, delighted to see the fall of the nobles, were not long in placing all the power in the hands of the king. By 1682 absolutism had been established and the *ad hoc* measures laid the foundation of a despotism, foreign to the whole genre of Swedish history, which lasted to the end of Charles XII's reign.

Estates were confiscated and the regents were heavily punished. Nils Brahe, nephew of Per Brahe, and de la Gardie and their relatives were left destitute, the chief charges being peculation of public funds. Even the honest and respected general, Gustavus Wrangel, was fined 170,000 riksdaler. The king and his stewards worked solely to increase the revenue and put the administration on a sound basis. The condition of the peasant was undoubtedly improved by these confiscations, but the object of the king was not philanthropic. He sought to improve the land and see that the profits came to the exchequer. He formed a Territorial army in the true sense of the word. The soldier's pay, except for a highly-trained nucleus, was in the form of land, which was sufficient to support him, and at certain periods of the year he was called out for training. The navy was rebuilt, a regular naval base with royal dockyards was established at Karlskrona. All the time the king remained in his counting-house and his minions audited and checked every öre that came in and out. The financial despotism succeeded in its objects, drab though the life of Sweden had become. On his death, he left a solvent state to Charles XI, and a colourless sound administrative machine, but he had saved the land of Sweden from passing into the hands of nobles who had subscribed little by way of taxes into the exchequer.

So immersed was he in the nation's balance sheet and the suppression of the nobility that he left foreign politics in the hands of his ministers. On the early death of Gyllenstierna, the king entrusted this side to Bengt Oxenstierna, who faithfully tried to preserve peace while he executed another *volte-face*. He broke with Denmark and engineered an alliance with Holland and the Emperor, subsequently joined by Spain. This was obviously aimed at France and its new ally Denmark, but except for sending a few troops to the Netherlands in support of William of Orange, Sweden remained out of active warfare.

That Sweden had regained her prestige among the great powers by the end of his reign is seen in her being asked to mediate in the Peace of Ryswick in 1697, the same year as Charles XII ascended the throne.

At last peace reigned in Europe, and there was nothing to show that Sweden was about to enter on her Third European Adventure. The only ripple on the otherwise calm sea lay in the Holstein Duke Frederick, who had married a sister of Charles XII. This was a dangerous marriage, distasteful to Frederick IV of Denmark (1699–1730). Denmark had passed through an uneventful period after the end of the Scanian War, mainly concerned in keeping out of war and trying to build up her exhausted economy. As usual, the Danes showed astonishing resilience, and the mercantile marine had increased and trade flourished. The only matter of lasting importance was the publication of the *Laws of Christian V* in 1683, which long remained the standard code of Danish law. As a matter of fact, they were not new laws enacted by Christian V, but the consolidation of existing laws and the deletion of contradictory enactments. Its effect was to strengthen the absolute power of the king, who was the embodiment of the law and himself remained above it. The direction of foreign policy, as of all else, was in the hands of the sovereign.

Frederick IV was actuated by intense hatred of Sweden and was convinced that the Holstein-Swedish matrimonial alliance spelt danger on his southern frontier. There was good reason for this belief, and when Duke Frederick fell at Klissov in 1702, fighting for Charles XII against the Poles, the situation became at once more delicate and complicated, owing to the aspirations of the Gottorp-Holstein line for a Russian alliance as well. The only hope for Danish survival, in the opinion of Frederick IV, was to strike at the Gottorp-Holstein duke first and then win over the young ambitious Czar of Russia, who was destined to go down to history as Peter the Great. This background of Danish diplomacy and endeavour must be realised unless a completely erroneous, but all-too-popular, estimate of Charles XII is accepted. The young Swedish king inherited a dull but uninspired state, and it is easy to paint him as a knight errant, rattling his sword and thirsting for military glory. In whatever light his personal character and desires may be regarded, in whatever dazzling colours romantic narrators may paint his deeds of derring-do and his dashing campaigns, sober history points a different moral and adorns another tale. On no occasion did he declare war. He was on the defensive, but like all good soldiers he realised that the best defence was offence, and this maxim was drummed into his generals from the start.

In view of the danger of encirclement, Frederick IV opened the war by a swift attack on Holstein, having formed an alliance with Saxony and Russia largely through the offices of a discontented Livonian noble named Patkul. These countries were persuaded to enter into this compact on the understanding that

Poland should take Livonia while the other Swedish provinces on the Baltic should fall to Russia. It needed no little persuasion and diplomatic skill to bring Russia and Poland (whose elected king was Augustus, Elector of Saxony) together. The arrangement, however, suited the Danish king admirably, who saw in it the destruction of Swedish power in the Baltic and the removal of the menace on his southern frontier by the annexation of Holstein and the removal of the Swedes from Bremen and Verden. Charles XII, however, saw his danger just as clearly and his subsequent actions can only be explained in the light of the political situation as he weighed it up in 1700. As can now be clearly seen, Sweden and Denmark were in danger, but not from each other, if the old-time rivalry had been eliminated as Gyllenstierna had planned. The danger came from the East.

The attack of Frederick IV met with a swift reply by Charles XII, whose speedy descent on to Sjaelland, covered by English, Dutch and Swedish ships, forced Frederick to come to terms at Travental in August 1700. The terms were comparatively easy. The Danes had to promise to desist from any further act of war, break off their alliance with the Czar and the Saxon King of Poland and at the same time to allow the Duke of Gottorp-Holstein to build a chain of forts in Slesvig. This last clause was to act as a guarantee against any Danish action, because it threw open the whole of Southern Jutland to a would-be invader.

The Danish war was over and a treaty signed while the Russians were still leisurely investing Narva. In November 1700 Charles, against the advice of his generals, led 10,000 men to its relief. Forcing a pass held by over 6,000 men, he attacked a Russian army estimated at from 40,000 to 80,000 men. At 2.0 a.m., after a long night march over frozen bogs, he took the Russians utterly by surprise and by noon on November 21st, Charles had won his greatest victory and found himself in possession of prisoners three times more numerous than his own army. Europe was staggered once more by the Swedish arms led by a young Swedish king. The Spanish Succession War was just beginning and over-tures and specious promises were showered on Sweden by both sides. His ministers begged him to desist from further fighting in the East and turn his attention to the West, where glory and honour could be won. He firmly refused to listen and, so the story goes, when one old counsellor shook his head in disapproval, he made the only witty remark in his life: "No use to shake your head, you will find no ideas in it." His decision at this juncture is the surest clue to the purpose of his wars. It was no desire for military glory, but a firm determination to destroy the power of the three countries who, in his opinion, threatened the retention of what Sweden had gained in 1660. He had dealt with Denmark, finally as he thought. Russia had been beaten on to the defensive. Poland remained, and after he had conquered its Saxon king, he could turn on Russia and bring its barbarous Czar to his knees. It is difficult to find any other satisfactory explanation to accord with the facts, and unfortunately he left no written documents on which any theory can rest.

Thus after Narva he turned on Poland by way of Lithuania. The Poles, who were by no means happy under Augustus, did not readily support their king, who had to depend largely on his Saxon troops. Charles occupied Warsaw in triumph, won the brilliant victory at Klissov, where the Duke of Gottorp-Holstein was killed, and took Lemberg by storm. Again an indication of his purpose can be gleaned in that he made no attempt to annex Poland. He induced the Poles to elect Stanilaus Leszczenski as their king in place of Augustus, but by the aid of Russian help the Elector of Saxony was still able to keep the field. The contestants in the Spanish Succession War were anxious to know the intentions of this dangerous Swedish king. Afraid of injuring his Dutch and English allies, he had abstained from attacking Saxony itself as this might have caused a diversion of Imperial troops fighting on their side. After the victory of Blenheim, however, he considered that the Emperor would not interfere, so he invaded Saxony and forced a peace on Augustus at Altranstädt. Once more he received emissaries from Louis XIV and the Allies. He refused the blandishments of Louis XIV to cause a diversion in his favour and to the English plenipotentiary, no less a person than the Duke of Marlborough himself, he declared his policy of utterly subduing Russia. By this time he had been away from Sweden for five years and the army was feeling the strain, but Charles was determined to strike a crushing blow at the very nerve-centre of Russia—Moscow. Not for the first nor last time did the Russians use the scorched-earth policy and avoid a pitched battle. In 1708, after awaiting reinforcements which never came, Charles made an alliance with the crafty Cossack chief Mazeppa.

He turned southwards to the Ukraine with the intention of moving northwards again through Kiev after the Cossacks had risen. The march of the Swedish army during the terrible winter of 1708–1709, the hardest for three hundred years, was marked by sickness and many deaths from frostbite and privations. Lewenhaupt from the north brought no reinforcements, and the expected artillery train and supplies fell into Russian hands. The Cossack revolt never took place. The Russian army could not be drawn into a pitched battle but "scorched the earth" more thoroughly as it drew the army farther from any possible succour. In the summer of 1709 Charles decided to establish himself near Pultava and there await reinforcements from Poland, where they were being mustered afresh after Lewenhaupt's failure. First, he decided to invest the town and make it his headquarters. During the investment he was wounded in the foot. Suppuration and gangrene resulted and the king had to relinquish his command to Rehnsköld who, good general though he was, was not equal to the task set him. Peter advanced his army of some forty or fifty thousand men near the city, and on June 28th, 1709, the king from his hospital litter ordered Rehnsköld to the attack with his army now reduced to 17,000 men and not all of them in fighting condition.

The Swedes fought valiantly, but grave tactical errors were made and the inspiration and genius of the king were lacking. The Swedes broke and Rehnsköld was taken prisoner. The remnants were reorganised by Lewenhaupt, who had come south earlier in the year, and a general retreat to the Dnieper was begun. The king, carried in his litter surrounded by a bodyguard of 150 men, was the first to reach the river. At last persuaded to cross, he ordered his army to secure the river crossing and then follow him to Turkey, where he was scheming to stir the Sultan into action. He crossed, but the army refused to follow, and utterly worn out and dispirited, the men laid down their arms and were marched off into Siberia. Thus ended the Third European Adventure, but the final curtain had not yet been rung down.

When his enemies heard that Charles XII was an unwilling guest or honourable prisoner of the Sultan, the old alliance was revived. Denmark and Saxony renewed their hostilities, whilst Russia invaded the Baltic provinces and Finland, at the same time pressing the Sultan to deliver up the person of Charles and his two hundred Swedes. The story of the next few years can be recounted briefly. The Danes, who instantly invaded Skåne, were defeated at Helsingborg by an army of peasants commanded by Stenbock. The Russians were more successful and firmly established themselves in Finland by the capture of Viborg and overran Ingria and Estonia. A diversion was caused by the Turks declaring war on Russia, and gaining considerable advantage by the Treaty of Pruth in 1711, whereby the Turks were able to prevent further encroachments and pressure from Russia. Meanwhile, Augustus of Saxony had been restored to the throne of Poland and took up the Russian role of demanding the king's extradition. For two more years Charles remained at Bender trying to get help from the Sultan and other European countries, but the Spanish Succession War had ended and no major European country was anxious to get embroiled with the hopeless cause of Sweden. The Sultan no longer required Swedish aid against Russia, and before 1713 was trying to get rid of his expensive visitor. Charles also wanted to return to his country, which was in dire need of his presence. His way was completely blocked by enemies, as Hanover and Prussia were also ranging themselves on the side of Sweden's enemies. The former wanted Bremen and Verden, and Prussia wanted Swedish Pomerania. The able Stenbock, after his victory in Skåne, had conveyed an army across the Baltic to defend Stralsund and Swedish Pomerania. At last in 1714, the king, disguised as a horse dealer, and two followers crossed Europe—almost at a gallop—and managed after many escapades to enter Stralsund. The accomplishment of this journey, in itself an immense feat of endurance as they rode day and night with clothes and boots unchanged for the last sixteen days, raised the flagging spirits of the Swedes. But the coalition was too strong. Stralsund fell and Sweden was preparing to withstand another and greater invasion. The Czar, as Denmark's ally, arrived on Sjaelland with 30,000 men—only welcome guests if they did not stay too long. But stay they did, and no move was made to cross the narrow Sound into Skåne. Their presence excited the other great powers, including England, who had already quarrelled with Russia. At the same time, the whole coalition against Sweden was splitting up as each party had gained what it wanted at the expense of Sweden, and was suspicious that one of their allies should rob it of its prize. The English fleet manoeuvred in the Sound, and neither its purpose nor its use was very clear. It acted rather in the interests of George I, as Elector of Hanover, to procure Bremen and Verden, though ostensibly it was to safeguard English shipping in the Baltic. Charles XII, trying to take advantage of the dissensions, started to invade Norway. Whilst attacking Frederiksten he was killed by a stray bullet—possibly fired from the camp of his own brother-in-law, Frederick of Hesse—and Sweden, left with no direct heir to the throne, was stunned by the death of her king just as there appeared a glimmer of hope. The army, leaderless and disorganised, struggled back from Norway—the last journey finely depicted by one of Sweden's great artists, Cederström. Such was the tragic end of the great warrior-king who, silent and reserved, could command the devotion, respect, admiration and fear, but never the love of his soldiers and his country. Yet he deserves a better epitaph than Samuel Johnson wrote in his *Vanity of Human Wishes*, which takes note of the tragedy and not the purpose of his endeavour.

> His fall was destined to a barren strand,
> A petty fortress and a dubious hand;
> He left a name at which the world grew pale
> To point a moral and adorn a tale.

War did not end immediately, and peace was only attained gradually. Early in November 1718, the month of the king's death, Goertz had been secretly sounding the Czar, but the conditions were too severe and the Russian ships began to harrass the Swedish coast. Fearing the growth of Russian naval power England, in return for the cession of Bremen and Verden to Hanover, promised her support in November 1719. This was followed by peace with Prussia, who received the coveted Stettin and Eastern Pomerania. Sweden was left with Western Pomerania, which she held until 1814 when it was ceded to Denmark as part compensation for the loss of Norway. In June 1815 Denmark ceded it to Prussia in exchange for the Duchy of Lauenburg. Denmark, now thoroughly alarmed at being left isolated and becoming the tool of Russia, ceded all her acquisitions from Sweden in return for 600,000 riksdalers and a guarantee that Sweden would never again interfere in Holstein, and, most important of all, it was laid down that Slesvig should be part of Denmark and the boundary of the River Eider guaranteed by France and England—in other words, the Danish territory as laid down in the original treaty of A.D. 811 received the sanction of the great nations. Russia continued her naval raids until finally the Treaty of Nystad was signed in 1721 between Sweden and Russia, confirming again the Danish and Prussian treaties. By this, Russia received Ingria, Livonia, Estonia, part of Carelia and some boundary fortresses in Finland, which she promised to evacuate. Augustus of Saxony was recognised as King of Poland and thus retained Danzig and the corridor separating Prussia and East Prussia. The Swedish Empire of the Baltic had fallen and a new orientation of powers had arisen, which left Sweden and Denmark to play new roles in the history of Europe. The final verdict on Charles XII has not yet been given. He saw the danger of Russia to Europe as well as to Sweden. That danger, some would say, is not yet over, and may be that with better fortune he might have averted that danger, and Russian eyes would have turned to the vast undeveloped areas of the East. His dream of a Swedish Baltic Empire, and a reconstituted and independent Poland, if realised, might have founded a more peaceful and prosperous Eastern Europe, and rendered Russia less ambitious in the West. Whatever the verdict of the historians may be, it will never shake the belief of the Swedish people that Charles XII is the greatest Swede in all their history. If they do not fully realise the finer points of his genius, they see in him a hero who by his ascetic way of life fitted himself for his duties as a king. He is the model which parents place before their children, an example of self-abnegation and endurance. The first story they hear is how Charles ate mouldy bread with his soldiers—a story as familiar to them as Alfred and the Cakes is to us, and be it noted, with a sounder moral! History will never hurl the hero from his pedestal in the home.

CHAPTER XI

THE ERA OF FREEDOM—GUSTAVIAN PERIOD

THE Peace of Nystad in 1721 marks the end of an epoch more clearly defined in the history of Sweden than was the case in Denmark. For the former, the period of military greatness and European adventure was closed for ever. Unconsciously she was laying the foundations of a new Sweden, commercial, industrial, scientific and cultural. Her political development was arrested, but painfully and slowly she was learning the bitterness of faction and party struggles. The period of political adolescence lasted for more than a century and then at long last the true Sweden of Gustavus Adolphus and Axel Oxenstierna was to emerge once more. The pattern of the Constitution of 1634 was proved to be suited to the needs of the nation, and the dignified independent Sweden of to-day, with its healthy democratic spirit obliterating the class distinctions and party factions of the eighteenth century, stands out as an example of peaceful progress and points a path to the art of living.

Denmark, closely associated politically, geographically and culturally with the absolute rulers of North Germany, had a perilous journey under its long line of absolute monarchs and it was not till the middle of the nineteenth century that the modern Danish state found itself. Cruelly bereft of some of her rightful territory, she was unable till then to point a way in the two fields of popular and co-operative dairy farming. It was not, however, till the twentieth century that European nations began to appreciate the virtues of this peace-loving country. Norway trod a different path from either. Linked with Denmark till 1815 and with Sweden till 1905, she was never entirely dependent on either. The Norwegians remained sturdy individualists and were unaffected by the French influences in Sweden and the German in Denmark. Their timber and fish industries led to an expanding maritime trading fleet, which became the basis of their national economy when independence was finally achieved. So extensive indeed was the growth of their merchant fleet that it finally exceeded those of Denmark and Sweden.

After Nystad, Europe was left in peace so long as Walpole and Fleury dominated the foreign policies of their respective countries. When this peace was broken by the Polish Succession War in 1733, the influence of the peace-loving Arvid Horn was strong enough to restrain some of the warlike spirits in Sweden. He clearly perceived that the problem of the Baltic had undergone great changes since the days of Charles X and Charles XII. Two new powers had arisen, Russia and Prussia, and these had supplanted Sweden and Denmark, neither of whom could play an offensive role on land in North-Eastern Europe. Thanks to their navies, they should be able to defend their coastlines from the Russians, but there was a weak spot in both their defences— Finland and Slesvig. The Swedes were prepared to defend Finland and it was to be a Frenchman, Bernadotte, who was to perform the drastic surgical operation of cutting off Finland and stitching on Norway instead. In the new epoch, the development of Sweden and Denmark proceeded on different lines and only at rare intervals were they united in a common cause.

Their whole outlook was dissimilar and it is illuminating to compare the reaction of the two nations to the religious wave of Pietism which swept over the two countries at this time. The movement originated late in the seventeenth century to oppose the narrow and creed-ridden Lutheranism, which broadly speaking had been the work of Melanchthon. Possibly in Sweden more than in Denmark the direct appeal to the Bible, which was Luther's cardinal principle, had been lost in the formulae which had become dear to the pastors and university theologians. Their niceties appealed to the head and not the heart. The pastors had assumed an even more tyrannical sway than had the priests— "New presbyter was but old priest writ large". On the other hand, the Calvinists laid most stress on the Christian Life and this sect had increased before, during and after the Thirty Years War. The attacks on Lutheranism by Protestants had been fierce and sustained before the work of Spener, the founder of Pietism. "The font, pulpit, confessional and altar had become four dumb idols" proclaimed one tract. The aim, then, of the Pietists was to combine the original faith of Luther and his appeal to the Bible with the ideal of a Christian Life. In this shape, Pietism arrived in Denmark and Sweden from Germany. In Denmark it was forcibly imposed by the king; in Sweden it was sown among the people by missionary preachers and returned prisoners of war.

Christian VI had been sorely aggrieved by the wickedness of his father, Frederick IV, who had made two bigamous marriages and finally married his mistress. Educated under stern and pietistic German tutors, he proceeded to cleanse the Church and people. His bigotry was all the more remarkable because he was a patron of learning, founder of the Academy of Science and School of Arts. He rebuilt the University of Copenhagen, reformed the Latin Grammar Schools, built primary and secondary or middle-class schools throughout Denmark, greatly assisted by a brilliant scholar and educationalist, Hans Gram. Partly through the medium of the school, partly through the pastors, he enforced a new life. Dancing was forbidden, theatres shut down and non-attendance at church was severely punished. Absence from church was punished by fines, by exposure in the stocks, and in some places floggings were administered for breaches of his moral and religious ordinances. In other ways he was an able administrator, but the dull, drab " goodness " which was forced upon the court and people surpassed anything ever contemplated by the strictest Puritan. The Danes were aching for peace and contentment after their long struggles and in this form of " pietism " they found none. The Danes loved dancing, colour, and a joke, and this sudden cloud rendered them resentful, sullen and longing for deliverance.

When it came with the death of the king in 1746 it was followed by a burst of licence unknown in the history of Denmark. Led by the king, Frederick V, the court and nobles indulged in twenty years of debauchery and vice. Parties roamed the streets smashing windows, raping women and maltreating the more sober-minded citizens. The king, revolting from his narrow upbringing, was almost pagan. Adultery and fornication were no longer crimes. There were special hospitals for mothers bearing illegitimate children and nurseries for their offspring. The king founded the first hospital in Europe for venereal diseases. The better life movement had ended by introducing these social services and an educational system which was shorn of its bigotry during the reactionary period, but in its object it had failed completely.

In Sweden, the movement without royal patronage resembled in some respects the Wesleyan in England. The returned soldiers and war-weary people hoped to find in it some peace in this world and consolation in the next. Opposed by the pastors, whose work and ways they attacked, the Pietists became fanatical zealots. Forming themselves into groups, they appeared a danger to the Church and some of their practices, resembling penances and mortification of the flesh, smacked of Rome. This led to their suppression from above, but at the same time, as in Wesley's case, it led to a purification of the Swedish Lutheran Church, which became more human in its appeal. On the whole, the joyless creed of the New Life did not have a wide appeal. Many of its devotees emigrated to America and joined the many Swedes already there.

The movement was not followed by any wild reaction and it was submerged in the great intellectual and scientific advances which were then being made in the steadily expanding educated classes. A parliamentary system, based on the Estates and a unified House of Nobles, had a long life of fifty years after its inception in 1719 and 1721. The power of the crown was reduced to nothing, but as long as Arvid Horn retained his power opportunity was given for a vigorous national life to flourish. It was in the twenty years preceding the victory of the Hats in 1739 that a new Sweden was born with new ambitions and aspirations. History has been blinded to the importance of this period and to the debt which the country owed to its minister by the unedifying struggle which followed between the Caps and the Hats, subsidised and bribed by Russia and France respectively.

In these years many Swedes gained enduring European reputations, but one man stands out pre-eminent as the embodiment of the age. Swedenborg,[1] until the end of the nineteenth century, was chiefly famous in the Anglo-Saxon nations as a mystic and founder of the new church and the Theosophists, but now it is generally recognised that the work of the first fifty years of his life entitles him to be regarded as one of the greatest scientific thinkers of all time. Nor was he a thinker only. With

[1] His real name was Svedberg. The *en* was added, when he was raised to the peerage by Queen Ulrica.

a mind resembling, but superior to, that of Leonardo da Vinci, he attained the Greek ideal in leading "the life practical and theoretical ". His inventions were turned to practical uses, his discoveries and theories forestalled those of our own day and yet at the same time he was a sound administrator and a brilliant speaker in the House of Nobles. He reflected the many-sidedness of his age and his refusal to take the Chair of Mathematics at Uppsala University or to become a political chief was due to his strong conviction that he was able to be of greater service to his country if he remained unfettered to any narrowing loyalty or a special post. Swedenborg (1688–1772) was the son of a theological professor at Uppsala University, who was opposed to the dogmatism of the Lutherans and was almost a Pietist in mind, though he never supported such uncompromising fanaticism and so joyless an attitude to life. He advocated a closer communion with the Divine Being, and in this he may have sown the seeds of the " Swedenborg philosophy " which his son believed and taught for the last thirty years of his life to the exclusion of all else. After leaving the university, Swedenborg visited England, France and Germany, studying natural philosophy and writing Latin verses. From 1716 to 1718 he studied science, mathematics and mechanics. At first, when he was appointed Assessor of Mines by Charles XII, his knowledge was applied to the mining industry and the smelting of iron and copper. His inventive genius showed itself in every conceivable field, and the tale seems to belong rather to the nineteenth and twentieth centuries than to his own. He invented plans for submarines, tanks with artificial wind for testing model ships, landing-stages (forerunners of the " Mulberry " of 1944), aeroplanes heavier than air, ear trumpets, heating stoves, a " Davy Lamp " for miners, a pianola, a machine-gun, smokeless chimneys, and an air pump using mercury which gave Celsius the idea for his centigrade thermometer. It is interesting to observe that Swedenborg was one of the first, if not the first, to study the floor of the ocean, a subject of especial interest to Swedes and Norwegians. Observations were started from Göteborg which received but little attention and the prevailing belief was that the ocean bottom was flat except for gentle slopes near the coast. Only seventy-five years ago Huxley stated this as a fact. From Göteborg in 1947 started a scientific expedition on a well-equipped motor schooner of 1,400 tons to gain more details of the mountains of the sea. This, however, gives only some of Sweden-borg's extraordinary activities.

As a crystallogist and geologist he was of immense service to Swedish industry, of which mining was the most important with its growing export trade in pig-iron to England. His studies in physics and astronomy anticipated many modern theories by over a century. To mention only two—the nebular theory of the sun and planets, and of the cosmic atom—suffices to illustrate how far he was in advance of his day. In this field, as in others, his theories and discoveries were put to a practical use in his laws for naviga-tion, by which longitude and latitude could be determined at sea. No account, however brief, can ignore his work on the brain and ductless glands because, apart from its modernity, this research on anatomy turned him to study the relation of body and soul. Always a devout believer in the power of God, he was strengthened by his scientific studies in his belief, and desired to probe deeper into the mysteries of the infinite. In 1747 he went to London, where he spent many years of his life, though constantly visiting Sweden and Holland. In 1772 he died in London, where he was buried, though his remains were taken to Stockholm in 1908 and buried in Uppsala Cathedral.

It was a strange break in the life of a man actively engaged in industry, science and politics. Politically he had supported Arvid Horn, though when the militarist party under Gyllenborg denounced the government's policy as spineless and dubbed the supporters "Night Caps", he did not affix a party label to his name. His main speeches had been on the curtailment of the power of the crown, trade, and the liquor laws. Incidentally, it might be noted that he favoured a system, afterwards adopted in 1865 and known as the "Gothenburg system", by which the manufacture and sale of liquor were leased by the State to various companies which were in their turn subject to local veto. Before the fall of Horn in 1739, Swedenborg had begun to take more interest in philosophy. In 1734 he had published the first of three volumes entitled *Opera philosophica et mineralia*. This was called *Principia* and dealt with the universe, and was quickly followed by the less-known volumes on iron, brass, smelting—in short, mineralia, their nature and uses.

The useless and unjustifiable Russian wars ending in the Peace of Abo sickened him as much as did the bribery and corruption which followed it. This degrading political scene coincided with his divine revelations. Three instances of these " excursions into the unseen world " are recounted by his followers, and his servants reported hearing his conflicts with evil spirits, but he himself laid claim to nothing beyond a sweet communion with God. He became an apostle of philosophic and Christian mysticism. God was the highest conception of love and wisdom, infinite and uncreated, and was reflected in the natural world by man. By goodness revealed in the Bible and through prayer, man might finally be drawn into the spiritual world, enter into communion with God, learn His will and become part of the Divine Spiritual Being when rid of the materialism of the body. This creed was never intended to be outside the Christian Church, but to amplify and explain its meaning. It had little appeal in Sweden, but Swedenborgianism soon had an extensive following in England and America, where societies were formed and still exist. The influence of Swedenborg as a seer has commanded more notice than as a pioneer in science, for he numbered among his admirers and followers such men as Carlyle, Coleridge, Kant (though he denied the existence of the revelations), the Brownings, Coventry Patmore and William Blake. Though Swedenborg is pre-eminent, reflecting as he does the many facets of the time, he did not stand alone. He was " primus inter pares " in the distinguished circle of men who were contributing to this age of intellectual vigour, enterprise and endeavour. Uppsala and Lund Universities were attracting scholars from England, Scotland, France and Holland. It is perhaps falling into a false comparison to describe the ideals of the northern university as the Cambridge and the southern as the Oxford of the north, but in Uppsala was established a school of natural science noted throughout Europe under the famous Linnaeus, and in Lund the schools of philosophy and theology under Rydelius. Each university, however, had schools of every branch of learning—too numerous to describe. It is, however, of interest to historians that at Uppsala the critical study of sources was instituted " as a course ", and its methods spread to other schools besides the exact sciences. This particular course is said to be the first of its kind, though individuals had, of course, studied " sources " for some definite history. Swedish scholars and learning were contributing in no small measure to European culture—this was recognised by other countries, who honoured their leading men, perhaps more in England than elsewhere, where as a tangible proof of respect, the British Royal Society enrolled Linnaeus as one of its members. Englishmen in particular have reason to be grateful to Linnaeus, for the Zoological Society owed its formation to the society named after him, The theatre and arts were equally flourishing. At the beginning of the century Sweden was influenced by English models, but after the middle of the century the French influence grew stronger, especially in the theatre. With the advent of Gustavus III, Sweden could with some justification be called the France of the North. He himself was a lover of that country where he had spent so much of his youth. He became a patron of the arts and drama and built the charming private theatre at Drottningholm, where performances still take place. The model figures, programmes and costumes at this theatre testify to the popularity of the French classical style of that day.

It is extraordinary that this age of progress should have coincided with the existing political chaos and corruption, but still more remarkable was the commercial and industrial development. The " Hats " leaned on France; Tessin and Queen Louise Ulrica definitely imitated the court of Versailles. Her salon was a political hotbed of intrigue, but the habitués had to adopt French manners, French ways, and at any rate to aspire to some degree of French culture. This, in part, explains the blossoming of the arts, sciences, drama and literature but the commercial progress was, for the most part, native-born. In fact the true genius of Sweden was making its bow. The nice balance of intellectual and practical enterprise was given freedom of expression, because the commercial outlook had shifted from politics-ridden Stockholm to the town of private endeavour—Göteborg. Individuals looked west for prosperity politicians and militarists looked east and south for glory.

As Swedenborg was taken as the symbol of this golden age of the intellect, so might Göteborg's growth be taken as the symbol of the golden age of an enlightened industrial economy. What was borrowed from England, and learned from foreign settlers, was readily adapted and absorbed. The English and Scots, especially in Göteborg, became Swedish except in name. They gave of their knowledge, but themselves acquired the outlook of the land of their adoption.

The Göteborg of to-day is a history of Sweden's new ambitions. The maritime museum marks the East India Company's headquarters of the eighteenth century. The lines of docks are a reminder that in the twenties of the eighteenth century her ships rose thirty-three per cent in numbers and by fifty per cent in tonnage. Her parks in and around the old city tell of careful planning to preserve the amenities of life and to drive away the squalor which Englishmen associate with dockland areas. Founded by Gustavus Adolphus, inhabited by Swedes mingled with Walloons, English and Scots, this city with its Swedish aspect, yet strangely reminiscent of its Dutch settlers, possessed a Western horizon, and soon had an international reputation. The town of Göteborg was founded on its present site in 1621 by gathering together Swedes from the three villages, Nya Lödöse (now known as Gamla Staden), Göteborg and Alvsborg. Gustavus was determined to strengthen the narrow Swedish corridor, some fifteen miles wide, which was the only outlet to the North Sea. Constantly ravaged by Danes and Norwegians who came from the north and south on the Danes' Way (still preserved on the north side of the Göta river), it could never hope to withstand these attacks with three open villages separated by a marsh. Its only protection was the fort at Alvsborg—now preserved as Skansan Lejonet. Three forts and the draining of the marshland in between fulfilled his military scheme of defence. To promote its commercial growth special privileges were granted to people of selected lands. The Walloons were responsible for the network of canals and the old moat which still give the lower part of the town a Dutch flavour. The Scots, followed by the English, settled in some numbers and soon appeared the British Factory and Congregation with a population expanding steadily, till in 1741 it received a special charter from "Frederick, by the grace of God, King of Sweden, Göta and Wende" for its religious community. In no foreign ports can be traced such an extensive body of British merchants with a continuous history dating from such an early date. It is a living witness that Sweden under Gustavus, the founder of the Baltic Empire, was also looking West. In the history of Göteborg and its growing importance can be read the change of mind from the Baltic to Atlantic and the Far East. The Göta Canal connecting it with Stockholm marked a further step in its development, and every increase in commercial prosperity is reflected by a growth in its population, which has now reached 350,000.[1] Alström, the man who was largely responsible for its rapid growth, borrowed freely from England both ideas and personnel. He took the best features of our industries, but improved on them and avoided the haphazard way in which our towns grew without a plan. He began his work at Alingsås on Lake Mjörn, some thirty miles from the town—near enough for commerce and far enough away to be free from Danish incursion. Textile factories sprang up like mushrooms and became models for other centres. The work of this enlightened founder of Swedish crafts did not die with him. His ideas of efficiency in the factory included the care of the workpeople, who were never regarded as human machines. Housing and cleanliness were part of the organisation. With such a start, it is small wonder that the Swedish industrial centres of to-day afford such a marked contrast to the grim "Satanic mills" which have bred so much strife and class hatred elsewhere.

Until the Enclosure Acts of 1757 consolidated the smaller farms and drove many of the people to Stockholm, it seemed not unlikely that Göteborg would become the largest city in Sweden, and it may well be that with the outlying suburbs it will not be far behind the capital in population, though it can never surpass it in the beauty of its natural surroundings.

Though private enterprise was the mainspring of industry, the State was not entirely divorced from commerce. It had control in many directions. The East India Company numbered among its shareholders the king, who derived some of the royal revenue from that source in return for certain privileges and monopolies. Trade was governed by a modified form of the mercantile system which tended more and more towards free trade under the influence of Chrydenius. Trade returns had to be rendered and Sweden was the first European country to furnish accurate statistical accounts under government supervision. The efforts of the seventeenth century industrialists undoubtedly began to bear fruit in the peaceful era following the Peace of Nystad, and had it not been for the folly of the politicians in embarking on aimless wars, the economic policy of the first fifty years might not have collapsed and caused a severe setback at the end of the eighteenth century.

[1] *The English Congregation,* Robertson and Adams, and sundry works on Commercial Göteborg. (Prof. Olof Jonasson.)

The policy was typically Swedish in that it tried to give the individual free scope for enterprise and grant financial aid where necessary, provided that the nation and state were to benefit. The principle was not dissimilar to that adopted in the economic blizzard of 1930 to combat unemployment and the housing shortage. The iron and textile industries and the mercantile companies were those chiefly concerned. Loans were granted by the Estates, but this did not prevent the raising of private capital. Special boards were set up to regulate these loans, to pool new inventions and provide technical advice. Under the mercantile system in Sweden the export of raw materials required for home production was controlled, and tariffs laid on the goods manufactured in the home country. Unfortunately, the system, not unlike that advocated by that apostle of free trade, Adam Smith, for young industries in new countries, was not administered in a scrupulous manner. Bribery and corruption sapped its very roots. Undue influence secured privileges and favoured one branch of an industry at the expense of another, nor could redress and exposure be expected in the Riksdag, when the burghers were themselves the chief culprits and the nobles open to a bribe. The Press was not free and the censorship severe. News and criticism were not easily published. The chief organs were in the form of weekly or monthly pamphlets not unlike the *Spectator* and *Tatler* of Addison and Steele. The Hats had a party magazine *An upright Sweden (En ärlig Svensk)*, which devoted itself to abuse of the Caps and in so doing did something to reveal the methods of their antagonists. The more famous *Swedish Argus* was more "upright ", and took a more critical and independent line under the guidance of Dalin. It was not until the inflationary economic policy, initiated it is true, by Horn, but taken to extreme lengths by the military Hats, had brought the country to a state of utter bankruptcy, that the Press was declared free in 1766.

It is now easy to criticise the work of the Swedish National Bank, because the world has had experience of paper money and can see the danger of rolling off paper notes to give credit and encourage an industry without retaining currency and reserve to back a certain proportion. The assignats in France, when bereft of gold and silver backing, had to be cashed in land filched from the Church and nobility. England in 1823 was faced with a similar crisis owing to the bank notes issued by private banks. Sweden was making the experiment from which other countries could learn wisdom, but politicians in Great Britain of the twentieth century have not been able to resist the temptation to create wealth. In normal times, the inflation often passes unnoticed until the abnormal, in the shape of a war or world economic crisis, arrives and then the crash comes. So it was in the Sweden of the eighteenth century.

The National Bank, instituted in 1668, had been an early user of bank notes,[1] in fact, the earliest in Europe. Behind these notes lay a sufficient reserve to meet their exchange into cash. When, however, the industrial loans were made, more bank notes were issued. With the expansion of trade and a rise in the prosperity of the country, the demand for exchange was not sufficiently heavy to disclose the sinking reserve. At the end of the Russian War in 1743, more notes were rolled off, more subsidies received from either France or Russia. Arvid Horn had failed to see the danger. It was one thing for Gustavus Adolphus to receive his French subsidy for the specific purpose of the war, and an entirely different thing to receive a subsidy in times of peace to patch up an unbalanced budget.

The final exposure of the exhausted Treasury and the precarious state of the industrial finances did not come until the Press had gained its freedom, and prices had risen to an alarming extent. In the years 1767 to 1769 Swedish foreign trade was caught in the vicious circle. With its enhanced prices it could no longer compete with England. During the Seven Years War, the demand had been so great that it was possible to sell the goods, but the inevitable slump had arrived within two years of the Peace of Paris (1763). The crisis was the direct cause of the fall of the Hats, but the Caps in 1768 to 1769 were not successful in their attempts to cope with the situation. They withdrew a large proportion of bank notes and then tried to force up the face value of the remainder. People hoarded notes in the hope that they would be able to exchange them at a later date at the full rate. The confusion was desperate. The value of the notes fluctuated violently and consequently prices at home fluctuated so rapidly that trade came to a standstill. Meanwhile, the parties abused each other—not without good reason on either side—and it seemed more than likely that a class war would break

---

[1] Bank notes must be distinguished from fiduciary notes, letters of credit, and such like, issued to a particular person or for a particular deal.

out between the Hats, who had the support of the nobles, and the Caps, who controlled the two lower Estates through their Secret Committee. Such was the position which faced young Gustavus III in 1771 when he ascended the throne and succeeded to a royal power reduced to a "rubber stamp."[1] This young man of twenty-six was fully aware of the lamentable state of party faction into which the kingdom had fallen. He hastened from Paris, which had been his spiritual home, and was determined to end the rule by Estates which had lasted fifty years. By a daring and bloodless *coup d'état*, he seized the power in August 1772 and put an end to the so-called "Age of Freedom" or "Era of Liberty". The economic factor played a large part in the fall of the party rule. The parties had brought the country to the verge of ruin when the opportunity had been offered to them to place it in the forefront of European nations.

The commercial and industrial progress was checked, and the recovery was slow. Half a century and more was to elapse before the country could boast a real recovery. Happily, the merchant navy did not suffer so heavily from the financial crash as did others. The Navigation Laws of 1724–5, similar in many ways to the English, had caused a substantial increase in Swedish shipping. The rate of expansion between 1723 and 1726 had been phenomenal. In 1723 there were 228 ships registered, but in 1726 there were no fewer than 1,844, mostly of greater tonnage. This rate of increase could not be maintained but, in spite of the two wars, the merchant fleet was more than doubled. The trade had become oceanic, and Göteborg had become the great port of the West. After 1772, these ships did not always return to Sweden at the end of each trip, but traded between other ports. It was found to be more profitable while Swedish industries were under a cloud. This practice has continued to the present day, and the Swedish ships, like the Norwegian, are found in every part of the world, carrying freights between the ports of other countries.

Though the economic factors which preceded the Gustavian Revolution are the most fundamental, the depressing picture of the political aspects must not be ignored.

The party struggle began on the death of Charles XII, who had

---

[1] This is not a mere figure of speech. A stamp, though not of rubber, had been devised bearing the King's signature, and was used by the ministers without consulting the King.

left no heir to the throne, which was hereditary in the House of Vasa. There were two claimants, Charles Frederick of Holstein, grandson of Charles XI and Ulrica Eleonora, sister of Charles XII, who had married Frederick, Prince of Hesse. Charles Frederick was backed by Peter the Great, who had betrothed his daughter, Anne, to the young duke. Needless to say, his claim was strongly supported by the crafty Goertz, who had already been associated with a Jacobite plot in England, and was secretly negotiating with the Czar before Charles XII's death. He was the most powerful man in the government, and the late king's confidant. On the other hand, Frederick, Prince of Hesse, was fighting for Charles and, in fact, he was strongly suspected of compassing his death even if his hand did not actually direct the " fatal stray bullet ". Being on the spot, he was able to secure the support of Arvid Horn, and Ulrica Eleonora was elected after signing a Coronation Oath which virtually signed away all the royal prerogatives. When she abdicated in favour of her husband in 1720, and he had to swear the oath once more before he ascended the throne as Frederick I, Goertz was executed as a traitor in spite of an eloquent defence, but "the Holsteiners" formed a strong party in opposition to Horn.

There was much to be said for their view. Friendship with Holstein was the cornerstone of the anti-Danish policy. Russia was the menace. The Holsteiners argued with some justice that their candidate would have secured Sweden against Russia and have rendered Denmark vulnerable to attack from the south. Holstein would take the place of the lost Bremen and Verden. Furthermore, if the hereditary principle had any weight, Charles Frederick had a better right than Ulrica Eleonora, whose husband had none at all. Horn's anti-Holstein view was ostensibly that the coronation of a Holsteiner would lead to trouble with Denmark, excite suspicion in Germany, or at any rate involve Sweden in German wars, and finally lead to the reduction of Sweden to the position of a vassal state of Russia. Sweden needed peace, and only by the succession of Ulrica Eleonora could that be attained and a democratic government under the Riksdag be re-established. His arguments were sound though his motives are not above suspicion.

HOLSTEIN GOTTORP LINE
Illustrating its connexion with Russia, Denmark and Sweden

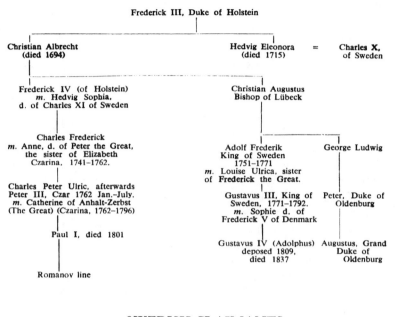

Frederick III, Duke of Holstein

Christian Albrecht (died 1694)

Hedvig Eleonora (died 1715) = Charles X, of Sweden

Frederick IV (of Holstein) *m*. Hedvig Sophia, d. of Charles XI of Sweden

Christian Augustus Bishop of Lübeck

Charles Frederick *m*. Anne, d. of Peter the Great, the sister of Elizabeth Czarina, 1741–1762.

Adolf Frederik King of Sweden 1751–1771 *m*. Louise Ulrica, sister of Frederick the Great.

George Ludwig

Charles Peter Ulric, afterwards Peter III, Czar 1762 Jan.–July. *m*. Catherine of Anhalt-Zerbst (The Great) (Czarina, 1762–1796)

Gustavus III, King of Sweden, 1771–1792. *m*. Sophie d. of Frederick V of Denmark

Peter, Duke of Oldenburg

Paul I, died 1801

Gustavus IV (Adolphus) deposed 1809, died 1837

Augustus, Grand Duke of Oldenburg

Romanov line

SWEDISH CLAIMANTS

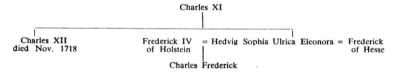

Charles XI

Charles XII died Nov. 1718

Frederick IV of Holstein = Hedvig Sophia Ulrica Eleonora = Frederick of Hesse

Charles Frederick

A glance at the genealogical table shows how Russia was becoming involved in Scandinavian history through Holstein. With the matrimonial alliance, a Russian sovereign could virtually control Holstein policy unless a palace revolution at Moscow suddenly caused a *volte face* in the Romanov alliances. When the other Holstein branch actually ascended the Swedish throne in the person of Adolf Frederick in 1751, the arrangement had been forced on that country by the Czarina Elizabeth as a condition of peace at Abo in 1743. The situation was delicate from the very outset, and credit must be given to the minister for keeping the peace. The tragedy lay in the way in which this object was attained. Subsidy after subsidy was obtained from France, and substantial bribes were received from French and Russian sources by members of both parties.

At first the only points of difference between the political parties lay in their foreign policies. Both supported the curtailment of the power of the Crown and the Constitutional Law of 1723. The Estates consisted of the original four—nobles, clergy, burghers and peasants—and the Council was constituted as before. The fundamental change was that the executive power passed from the crown and its ministers to a secret committee chosen from only the three upper orders. The President of the House of Nobility was president of this committee, which gradually gained almost complete power. Once chosen, its members could only be ousted by the committee itself, which proceeded to secure new members of its own party. Thus "the art of government lay in the ability to satisfy the expectations of the Estates. Against those who failed in this respect, sufficient cause for removing them from their office could always be found, while even grave mistakes were readily forgiven the obedient humble servants of the Estates." Thus, in practice, this experiment in a democratic constitution was far removed from the constitution of 1634. When the Holstein question had assumed a different aspect on the death of Peter the Great in 1725, Sweden was almost forced to show her hand by joining one of the two European combinations. Horn, President of the House of Nobility and Secret Committee, favoured England, France and Hanover led by the two peace ministers, Walpole and Fleury. The Holsteiners, influenced, it was alleged, by Russian gold, wished for closer relations with Russia, Austria and Spain. Horn's dominating position secured the acceptance of his policy and the expulsion of the "Holsteiners". This party receded into the background, but still had many adherents. The European situation changed and with it the principles of the Swedish parties. France began to show its old aggressive tendencies in the Polish Succession War of 1733, the Anglo-French *entente* was cooling down, and the succession of Anne to the Russian throne in 1730 appeared to have severed the Russo-Holstein connexion. The Duke of Holstein had sunk to the status of an uninfluential German princeling. With peace still the primary object of Horn's party, the natural tendency was therefore to swing away from France, and obtain an understanding with Russia, which preserved the neutrality so essential for the growing prosperity of Sweden. The French ambassador, Casteja, seized this opportunity of fomenting discontent against Horn, whose failure to help France in the Polish War had been considered by some cowardly and a lowering of the dignity and prestige of the country. French gold was freely poured into the hands of the opposition, and shamelessly accepted. The opposition, under the astute leadership of Gyllenborg, was vociferous in its denunciation of the sleepy "night caps", as he called the ruling party. "Glory for Sweden", "Revenge on Russia", "Recovery of the Baltic States"; these were the slogans of the party which assumed the title of Hats, as a symbol of greatness.[1]

In 1739 Horn was persuaded to resign, and the majority of the Caps left or were expelled from the Riksdag. The triumph of the Hats coincided with the diplomatic triumph of the French minister at the Treaty of Belgrade and the opening of the Austrian Succession War. Eagerly, the ministers and army officers, but less eagerly some of the burghers, received news of the French overtures to Sweden to join with them against Russia and Austria.

Very little effort was made to justify this war. At the outset, the Swedish army crossed the Finnish frontier in alliance with Elizabeth, daughter of Peter the Great, who had engineered a Moscow Revolution. Once on the throne, she demanded the withdrawal of the Swedish army, and dispatched a Russian army to enforce her demands. In vain, the Swedes asked for their reward for the assistance they had given her. The answer was a Russian attack on General Wrangel which resulted in his capture and the defeat of his army.

Far from gaining Livonia or Ingria, the Swedes lost part of Finland, and were only saved from further defeat and humiliation by agreeing to acknowledge Adolf Frederik as heir to the Swedish throne. The Treaty of Abo (1743) might have been more severe had not the Czarina Elizabeth's protegé from Holstein been accepted. The old danger from Russia and the disastrous war threatened the position of the Hats. They cleverly extricated themselves under the brilliant Charles Tessin, by throwing the blame on

---

[1] To wear a hat in the presence of royalty was in medieval times one of the highest privileges. It is preserved in England by the privilege accorded to the Seigneur of Sark to remain covered.

the generals who were publicly executed and by promoting a feeling of healthy patriotism, subtly directed against the Russians. Tessin, whose father and grandfather had been distinguished architects, was a cultured man whose sympathies and tastes were French, and he set himself to rebuild the shattered strength of the country and himself to be the central figure of a court modelled on Versailles. The old king, Frederick I, was a frivolous, weak nonentity, and the new régime found its spiritual home in the salon of Louise Ulrica, sister of Frederick the Great, wife of the newly-elected Crown Prince. Elizabeth's scheme was not having the intended result because the power had passed to the French party led by Tessin and the Princess who was an even greater admirer of France than was the minister. Thus, when Adolf Frederik became king in 1751 and signed an even more stringent oath renouncing royal authority, the Hats, having utterly defeated the Caps now in Russian pay, were firmly seated in authority and openly allied with France.

Louise Ulrica, on the other hand, had hoped to regain the royal power on becoming queen, and was bitterly disappointed. She tried to urge " a court party " to stage a revolution in favour of the crown. It was discovered, and Axel von Fersen, the young leader of the House of Nobles and Secret Committee, humbled the king and queen by forcing them to make abject apologies. It suited both the political parties not to expel them, as was contemplated, but to retain a " roi fainéant ", who was even deprived of the right of seeing the laws to which his seal was attached.

The rebels were condemned and executed in the traditional manner. The final insult came in 1756 after the Diplomatic Revolution engineered by the cunning Kaunitz, and Madame Pompadour had united France and Austria against Frederick the Great. Sweden was called upon to fight on behalf of France, and thus the queen saw her army landed in Pomerania in a war directed against her brother. No interest of Sweden was served by its entry into the Seven Years War on the side of France and Russia. Its trade and friendship with England were severed and, as previously recorded, the economic slump which followed the Peace of Paris caused the downfall of the Hats. The only unforeseen result was the introduction of the potato into Sweden by the soldiers on their return from Pomerania where it had been a welcome addition to their rations. It is still known in Sweden as the " Potato

War ".[1] The sudden abdication and death of Peter III in July 1762 had saved Frederick the Great, who lost no time in forming an alliance with his ambitious widow, Catherine II (the Great). The immense power of Russia had made itself felt in the closing stages of the war, and Frederick was the first sovereign to try and turn it to his own advantage. His policy was to try and divide any spoils with his neighbour, and in 1772 it led to that supreme act of political immorality, the first partition of Poland. It was subsequently discovered that another equally immoral act was contemplated in 1769, when a secret treaty was signed between Russia, Prussia and Denmark for the dismemberment of Sweden. Denmark little realised at the time that she herself would have been the next victim. Catherine realised that it was necessary to support the chaotic political situation in Sweden until the time was ripe for the planned attack. With this in view, the Russian ambassador was supplied with ample funds to bribe and corrupt the Caps and so enable them to retain the power which they won from the Hats in 1767.

At last, however, good fortune smiled on Sweden once more. Gustavus III's *coup d'état* was successfully carried out at the very time that Catherine was engaged in the rape of Poland, and she was too occupied with disputing over the spoils with Maria Theresa and Frederick the Great to take any action. Her attitude was bitterly hostile to the new régime, and by continuing her methods of bribery, she tried to stir up malcontents, not excepting Louise Ulrica, who was furious at Catherine obtaining a position which had been denied to herself. This undisguised hostility between Russia and Sweden continued in spite of Gustavus's friendly approaches, and was only broken when Russia, Denmark, and Sweden formed the Armed Neutrality to protect neutral shipping against England's principle of the " right of search " during the American War of Independence. The Swedish sympathies were with France and the American colonies, and many Swedes enlisted as volunteers in the French army and navy.

In the politics of the Baltic, this Armed Neutrality had an effect which has often been disregarded. Gustavus considered the attitude of Denmark unsatisfactory. He considered that she had not played her part, and was convinced that in time the Danes would join with

[1] In Scandinavian history, the Seven Years War means the war of 1563 to 1570. The war of 1756 to 1763 is referred to as the European Seven Years War.

Russia in attacking his country. Had he known of the Treaty of
1769, he would have had clear evidence of this intention, but probably in 1786 the Danes were not planning any act of aggression.
Only by exerting pressure did Catherine II prevent Gustavus from
declaring war on the Danes. She did not want war at that moment
for trouble was brewing on the Turkish frontier, and Vergennes,
the friend of Sweden, had signed a treaty with England. Russia
might have been confronted with a powerful combination of
enemies, while the death of Frederick the Great in 1786 might
have deprived her of help from her Prussian ally. Poland was beginning to show signs of revival, and she had earmarked the whole of
the remainder of that country for herself. In gaining this object,
Prussian and Austrian enmity would be aroused. Thus Catherine
wished to finish off the Turkish conquests before proceeding to
dismember Poland and Sweden, and so she declared war on
Turkey in 1787. Gustavus III, who had spent vast sums in enlarg-
ing the navy and improving its efficiency, determined to seize this
moment to declare war on Russia. His only justification was that
Russia had been interfering in Sweden itself, and had actually
incited rebellion in Finland through the machinations of Sprengt-
porten, the younger brother of the very man who had helped him
in 1772. According to the restored constitution, the king, as in
Gustavus Adolphus's time, could not declare war. This was the
right of the Riksdag. The navy had already attacked St. Petersburg without great effect. The king's many opponents tried to
summon a Riksdag in his absence, and the very throne was in
danger. A conspiracy among the officers in Finland, who entered
into treasonable correspondence with Catherine, was discovered,
but so desperate was the king's plight, that he could not punish
the traitors. The officers signed "the Anjala[1] agreement" by
which they assumed common responsibility for asking the Czarina
for an honourable armistice. Suddenly news was brought that
Denmark had attacked the homeland. Gustavus speeded home
from the Russian front, ignored Stockholm, the nobles and the
Riksdag, and, with a theatrical gesture, prompted no doubt by his
love of the dramatic, he assumed the garb of a peasant and
appealed in person to the people of Dalarna. In him they saw
another Gustavus Vasa, the saviour of the people. With wild
enthusiasm, they flocked to his army. He hastened to Göteborg

---

[1] Anjala was a village on the Finnish frontier.

on which the Danish and Norwegian armies were converging. The
Danes had anticipated an easy march across Sweden and a welcome from the king's opponents. Instead, they found a nation in
arms. The intervention of the English, through Elliott, and pressure from France and Prussia at home persuaded the Danes to
leave Sweden and sign a peace, rather than incur the enmity of
three nations already not too well disposed to any Russian ally.
Gustavus returned in triumph to Stockholm and summoned the
Riksdag. The capital was full of troops and, when the king
angrily accused the nobles of treachery and disloyalty, the nobility
capitulated, and the king, backed by the Commons, became for
the time being a more absolute monarch than even Gustavus Vasa.
The ringleaders of the "Anjala revolt" were punished, and the
war against Russia was resumed wholeheartedly. The nation
believed that their king had been right. After being trapped at
Viborg and nearly losing the whole fleet, the king managed to
escape with considerable losses. The Russians were now well-
equipped and able to bring up more and more troops and ships.
Gustavus saw that he must strike a decisive blow or be defeated.
On July 9th, 1790, the day that the Russians had decided to hold
the victory celebrations, and only six days after Viborg, Gustavus
brought his fleet into action at Svensksund and won the greatest
naval victory in Swedish history. Sydney Smith, who had
previously served under Rodney, was naval adviser to Gustavus III,
and served with distinction in this battle. He received his knight-
hood for his Swedish services. England was particularly anxious to
prevent Russia becoming mistress of the Baltic. One third of the
Russian fleet, numbering twice as many ships as their opponents',
was totally destroyed. A peace, honourable to both sides, was
signed at Varela on August 15th, and the war was at an end.

The war had once more shattered the financial position of
Sweden, and Gustavus could boast of no territorial acquisitions, but
it was not without benefits to Sweden. Her prestige was restored.
She had withstood the all-powerful Russia. The era of bribery and
corruption was over, and she had regained her self-respect and was
no longer the pawn of Russia and France. Her alliances in future
could be formed in her own interests, and she had freed herself
from the subservience of the last seventy years.

Meanwhile, the great drama of the French Revolution had
riveted the eyes of Europe on France. In Sweden, as in other

countries, there was a sharp division of opinion, and sympathies were divided between the Royalists and the Girondists. The Franco-Swedish alliance and the return of the volunteers who had been fighting with the French in America, gave these sympathies a more personal and intimate note than in any other country. Gustavus was on the most friendly, almost affectionate, terms with the royal family and he had commissioned a well-known Swedish artist, Wertmuller, to paint a picture of Marie Antoinette and her children. IIis lead was followed by many of the older aristocratic families, and Axel von Fersen, son of the old Hat leader, had fought in America and subsequently planned the unsuccessful flight of the royal family to Varennes. This sympathy and anxiety for the fate of the royal family were shared by Catherine the Great, who saw in the Revolution a threat to monarchy. In 1791 a strange dynastic bond was sealed by the two antagonists, and it was arranged that a Russo-Swedish expedition should be sent to France under the command of Gustavus. Events in Sweden and France moved too quickly and this bizarre, though not ill-conceived plan, was never carried out.

The other party in Sweden looked on the French Revolution, at any rate until the execution of the king and queen, as a noble struggle for liberty, and with the dismal record of Frederick I and Adolf Frederik fresh in their memories, their leaders began to design in secret a similar revolution in their own country. The autocratic powers assumed by Gustavus in the crisis of 1789 had been retained, much to the disgust of many of the younger members of the older aristocratic families. It was amongst these, that the plot was hatched, and a ready tool was found in the person of a desperate fanatic, Anckarström. The assassination of the king was planned for March 16th, 1792, when he was expected to attend a masked ball at the Opera House. In the previous month, the news of the Russian alliance and possible expedition for the summer had fanned the flames of the opposition. Gustavus was openly declared a tyrant, thus the plotters considered that as soon as the king's death was accomplished, the country would hail them as deliverers. They had no clear idea of what the new constitution would be, but plans had been secretly laid to frame something on the lines of the French model of 1791.

Everything seemed to work according to their design. Horn gave the pre-arranged signal, Anckarström fired the shot, their followers in black masks spread the confusion by shouting " Fire ". But the king was not dead. He lingered for thirteen days, and in that time, sympathy for the king, and indignation with the assassins destroyed the hopes of the aristocratic revolutionaries. They were seized, but the king refused to hear their names or order their execution. He named his brother, Duke Charles, as regent for his young son, aged thirteen, and the revolution was over, and its only victim the king.

With his death ended a period of dazzling brilliance. On few men have more divergent estimates been written. Patron of arts in all its forms, he was assured of many admirers capable of singing his praises. Besides Wertmuller mentioned above, other painters, such as Roslin, achieved fame outside Sweden, competing with the Paris artists, and even in their special field of miniatures. Dahl, who was well-known and lived in England, was before his day, but Breda studied under Joshua Reynolds, and on his return to Sweden became one of the first portrait painters of the day. Sergel, the sculptor, was responsible for the famous statue of Gustavus at Stockholm. In this century there has been a great revival of the Gustavian cult, which ranks him as one of the greatest Swedish kings. As founder of the Swedish Academy, lavish friend of the brilliant writers and poets[1] of the day, his claims to be considered the founder of Swedish culture cannot be disputed. He himself was a writer of plays and could discuss with critical and appreciative insight, literature of all kinds. On the other hand, it is argued that the Gustavian school was largely modelled on France and did not display the native genius of the nation. There is some truth in this charge, but the Academy, founded, it is true, on the lines of the French, was able to foster the talent of the country when it had grown out of the tutelage of its original masters.

Though he was himself keenly interested in architecture, which had already begun to assume a Swedish style, he was not personally attached to philosophy and the sciences. They did not appeal to his artistic and pleasure-loving nature. On the other hand, the universities found in him a benefactor. How then does the sober and less romantic historian estimate this highly gifted king? On the debit side must be placed his reckless expenditure when economy was essential. Money, however, was not wasted, and corruption was checked. The defences of the country were his chief

---

[1] Kellgren, Adlerbeth, Bellman and others.

concern, and these included the static defences—fortresses and naval bases—as well as navy and army. His expenditure on the arts was, perhaps, ill-timed but justifiable, but his extravagant court cannot be defended. Sweden could never support a Versailles. His foreign policy, which appeared at times inconsistent, displayed a shrewd insight in the difficult years at the beginning of the French upheaval. It would not be far wrong to rank him as a great politician showing "the highest ability to deal with phenomena as they arose", but lacking the deeper qualities of a great statesman. Gustavus III will remain after his death as he was in life, "hated and loved, despised and admired"—the hero of a historical romance, the first actor in a drama, and a great, but not the greatest, king in Swedish history.

Whatever may be the truest estimate of Gustavus, there can be no doubt that his death was a sad blow. There was no brain capable of directing the delicate diplomacy, no hand to direct the state machine. The regent, Duke Charles, was well-intentioned, but of a weak and vacillating nature, easily attracted to mushroom societies promoting this or that of the many cults advocating the theories spread by the French Revolutionaries. At one time or another he was an ardent disciple of Rousseau, a Continental Freemason and one of the Illuminati. He began by dismissing all the old Gustavian followers and handing over his authority to Reuterholm, who tried to win popular favour and disguise his policy, such as it was, by executing the assassin Anckarström after spending three days in the pillory and being whipped through the streets of Stockholm. The other regicides were allowed to leave the country. He flouted European opinion by recognising the French republic after the execution of Louis XVI. On discovering a plot to upset the régime, he alienated public opinion by brutal treatment of the ringleader's wife, whose chief crime was to reject the amorous overtures of Duke Charles. In 1796, Gustavus became king, and the pendulum swung the other way, the Press was strictly censored, references to the French Constitution and the United States were forbidden, and the king offered himself as suitor to Catherine's grand-daughter. However, the differences of religion and Catherine's death prevented the marriage. He had become a complete reactionary, and in 1800 joined the revived Armed Neutrality of the North. After the battle of Copenhagen in 1801, Sweden was saved from a British attack on Landskrona by the dilatoriness of Hyde Parker, Nelson's superior, and by the assassination of the Czar, which led to Russia signing a peace treaty. The king was incensed against Napoleon for his execution of the Duc d'Enghien, who had been taken in Baden, the home state of his wife, and further enraged by the insulting remarks in the *Moniteur* about his incapacity and cowardice. The description was not inaccurate and therefore all the more distasteful. Finally, without any adequate preparation Gustavus declared war on France, and massed some thirteen thousand troops in Pomerania. There they remained inactive while Napoleon won the battles of Austerlitz and Jena. The inevitable occurred, and the French swept over Swedish Pomerania though a gallant, and at first successful, defence of Stralsund delayed the final evacuation and armistice by which the army was allowed to be transported back to Sweden and receive full military honours. The Treaty of Tilsit, between Napoleon and the Czar, spelt ruin for Sweden. Dazzled by the personality of Napoleon and the prospects of dividing the world with the conqueror, the Czar agreed to enforce the Continental System. In the winter of 1807–1808, Sweden was ordered to close all her ports against England, and, without any declaration of war, Russian troops marched into Finland as a forcible reminder of what might happen if orders were not obeyed. Sveaborg fell, betrayed by Cronstedt who believed that Sweden's power had ceased to exist, and that Finland would be more prosperous under Russian rule. The Finns, however, thought that they might achieve some independence if they aided the remaining Swedish forces which had retired northwards.

A magnificent war of national resistance ensued and, opposed by heroic leaders such as Sandels, Döbeln and Adlercreutz, the Russians were not successful in subduing Finland until late in the winter of 1808. The struggle has been handed down as a national saga of Finland by the poet Runeberg—it is one of the greatest fights ever put up by untrained men against a trained army. It was not a guerrilla war, for the Swedo-Finns fought a series of pitched battles at Oravais in November 1808. Final defeat was not acknowledged before fourteen hours of continuous fighting had left hardly a man alive or unwounded.

On the other side of Sweden, England had sent a force of some ten thousand men under Sir John Moore to Göteborg, as a protection against a Dano-Norwegian attack. Denmark, after losing her fleet at Copenhagen in 1807, had been ordered by France and Russia to declare war on Sweden. Finally, against her will, she was persuaded to organise an attack on Göteborg by the promise of the restoration of Skåne and other provinces in South Sweden. The British fleet was of greater assistance than the army, because the silly pride of Gustavus wished the troops to be under his own command. After two months' idleness and argument, Sir John Moore sailed home again. Their presence had been of value, however, because the Danes made no move and a Swedish general, Adlersparre, had been able to enter into negotiations with the commander-in-chief, the Duke of Augustenburg. The latter agreed to march his army back again on being promised succession to the Swedish crown. Adlersparre would then take his own troops back to Stockholm. The king got wind of the agreement and prepared to leave the capital and join the other Swedish army stationed in Skåne. General Adlercreutz, hero of the Finnish war, prevented this by arresting the king, thus averting civil war. The old regent was persuaded to ascend the throne as Charles XIII, and the pitiful king and his family betook themselves to Switzerland. He, as Colonel Gustafsson, died in poverty in 1837, and his son, styled Prince of Vasa, lived on till 1877 and, with his death, ended the House of Vasa with its chequered history of two hundred and fifty years.

In 1809, the Peace of Fredrikshamn sealed the defeat of Sweden, who lost Finland and the Åland Islands, its eastern outposts and Swedish Lappland in the north. Next year, Pomerania was restored on the condition that Sweden joined the Continental System. This same year, 1810, another tragedy befell the State. The new crown prince, who had already begun to win popularity, died suddenly at a military review. Who now was to succeed the colourless Charles XIII whose election had been merely *faute de mieux*? Adlersparre pressed the claims of the new Duke of Augustenburg; others advocated the King of Denmark as being the only way to a united Scandinavia which was mooted in many quarters but the old jealousies and recent wars seemed to many, insurmountable barriers. It was deemed advisable to sound the all-powerful Napoleon. So a young lieutenant, Mörner, was despatched to Paris with a message to the Swedish ambassador. However, he fell in with Bernadotte on the way, and told him of his mission. The bright idea came to him that a French marshal would suit the bill better than any of the suggested candidates. Bernadotte cautiously replied that he would be willing to become heir to the throne, and subsequently king, provided the invitation came from Stockholm and Napoleon gave his consent. On his return to Stockholm, the Council was staggered at the proposal, and Mörner's presumption. He was placed under arrest for insubordination, but gradually opinion veered round to his suggestion.

Bernadotte was well known to many Swedish officers who had been defeated by him in Pomerania. Here he had shown magnanimity and given evidence of sympathy with the problems of Scandinavia. The offer was duly sent to Bernadotte, and Napoleon gave his consent. Accounts differ considerably as regards the part played by Napoleon. He was not on very good terms at that time with Bernadotte and certainly he would never have chosen him after having previously approved of the election of the Duke of Augustenburg. Probably he thought that Bernadotte's loyalty would be restored by the conferment of this honour, and that Bernadotte would be able to enforce the Continental System, and England would find another door for her goods more tightly closed. Bernadotte, who married Joseph Bonaparte's sister-in-law, and had on more than one occasion criticised the Emperor's political schemes, did not prove to be the loyal servant of France, but at once began to view Europe with Swedish eyes. He took command of the administration and foreign policy. As regards the Continental System, which was being ignored by his new subjects, he realised that trade between England and Sweden was essential, so, to satisfy Napoleon, he declared war on England and let it be understood that trade could continue, and not a shot was fired on either side. Bernadotte's relations with Napoleon began to be strained when, in 1812, French troops overran Swedish Pomerania, which had been restored to Sweden in 1810. Bernadotte, always a realist in politics, decided to make an alliance with Russia, which was on the point of being invaded by Napoleon's Grand Army. He clearly perceived that Finland would never be returned to Sweden, and so he bargained for the acquisition of Norway in return for the help of a Swedish army of thirty thousand men. Denmark, it must be remembered, was the last remaining ally of Napoleon. Alexander and Bernadotte planned the strategy which ended in the battle of Leipzig after Napoleon's retreat from Moscow, and Alexander promised him a Russian army corps for the conquest of Norway after the defeat of France. At the battle of Leipzig, Bernadotte cunningly kept the Swedes out of action,[1] and, after the victory, immediately marched north into Holstein and thence into Slesvig and South Jutland. Denmark was powerless to resist, and finally, at the Treaty of Kiel, agreed to the cession of Norway, but retained the old appendages of Norway, namely the Faroes, Iceland and Greenland, as well as Swedish Pomerania. Sweden's part in the war ended at the Treaty of Paris (1814), which Bernadotte signed, although he opposed the return of the Bourbons.

Such was the remarkable chain of events which resulted from the unpremeditated meeting of the young Lieutenant Mörner and Marshal Bernadotte, Prince of Ponte Corvo. A new dynasty for Sweden, the union of Sweden and Norway, and a hundred and fifty years of peace for the kingdom stabilised by Napoleon's greatest marshal, officially known as " Carolus XIV Johannes Rex ".

[1] A detailed study of this battle demonstrates how Bernadotte saved his own men without the possibility of incurring the odium of shirking the battle.

CHAPTER XII

DENMARK, 1721–1839

BEFORE discussing the profound changes in Scandinavia following the settlements at Paris in 1814 and at Vienna in 1815, it is necessary to outline the main events in Denmark during the eighteenth century after the Peace of Nystad. Reference has already been made to the Pietist régime of Christian VI, who ascended the throne in 1730. In spite of the scandalous private life of his father, Frederick IV, the previous reign had not been barren of good for the country. Frederick manfully struggled to repair the damages caused by a series of disasters which afflicted Denmark in the last twenty years of his reign. The plague in 1711 attacked the towns and the countryside alike; six years later, the sea swept over the west coasts of Slesvig and Holstein, and caused immense damage.[1] These calamities were followed by a series of fires in several of the towns, of which the worst occurred in Copenhagen. Two-thirds of the town were razed to the ground, including the university and a state office, and many of the unexplored documents of early Danish history were lost for ever. Under Frederick IV, the first proper system for popular education was inaugurated. Previously, primary education outside the towns had been conducted by itinerant teachers who wandered from village to village from spring to autumn giving what instruction they could in reading and writing. This was highly unsatisfactory, and the results almost negligible unless the parents happened to be able to continue the work during the winter. In a few places this apparently haphazard method of instruction worked better than might have been expected. It is, perhaps, worth noting that in Iceland this parental-cum-pedagogue system lasted until the beginning of the twentieth century, and an English traveller in 1894 reported that the ordinary people of Iceland were 100 per cent literate. All could read and write and had a fair knowledge of the elements of

---

[1] The exact causes of this tidal wave are obscure. A submarine earthquake was possibly the cause, but seismography was then an unknown science.

231

arithmetic. This was a better record than had Great Britain when the Balfour Act was passed in 1902. Frederick, himself suffering from a lack of education, was determined to better the lot of the agricultural classes. He began by building some two hundred and fifty schools on the crown lands, and installing resident teachers. Under Christian VI, the system was extended, and as recorded in the previous chapter, he improved the secondary or " Latin Schools " which existed, and built others. These, in a truly enlightened manner, he regarded as a means of bettering the moral and religious standard of the people. Owing to his arbitrary methods, the school system lost much of its immediate value, but the schoolchildren of their reigns became men and women who worked for, and eventually secured, the emancipation of the peasant.

In spite of the revolt against the ultra-Puritanism, the fruits of the greater enlightenment bestowed on the people by these two strangely opposite monarchs and the two Bernstoffs were garnered in the humanitarian period at the end of the century. The peasants were emancipated by decree in 1792, and in the same year, Denmark led the way in abolishing slavery in the West Indies, an example followed by England and France many years later. Denmark also was far in advance of Germany in the treatment of the Jews.

This emancipation of the peasant was long delayed because, at the very outset, it became closely bound to other problems which vitally concerned the country—agriculture and the army. As the government was unfortunately dependent on the caprice of the sovereign, reforms were as quickly abolished to meet any emergency, as they were introduced to ameliorate the condition of the serfs. By the *Vornedskab*, tenants were not allowed to leave the place of their birth, nor were they given any choice as regards their houses. They were completely under the domination of the landowner, except that they were freemen, provided they remained on the allotted farms and did not sell their corn, except to the landlords. The women, however, held a position above that prevailing in most " serf " organisations. They were not bound to work on the land or remain in the place of their birth. Frederick IV abolished the laws of *Vornskab* for all born after 1702. The new law, *Stavsbaand*, however, led to considerable unrest, peasants migrating to the towns and emigrating to America. The exodus was so pronounced in the decade 1720 to 1730 that agriculture which was the staple land industry of Denmark, suffered severely. The king preserved the *Stavsbaand*, which, indeed, remained till 1788, but by introducing a militia bill, rendered the condition of the peasants worse than it had ever been before. The landlord had to furnish a quota of recruits, who were inscribed on the military roll for six years. During this time, they could not leave the estate. The choice of recruits lay with the landowner, and his decision was final. The old tenants in many cases became labourers and villeins, and their hardships were extreme, especially under Germans and Holsteiners, who had managed to acquire many of the estates of the old nobility. Christian VI abolished the militia bill within a few months of his accession, but re-imposed it in 1733 with the added proviso that all should be inscribed on the roll who were between the ages of fourteen and thirty-six. Thus, the state of the peasants was worse than ever before, and so it remained for some fifty years, until ministers, backed by public opinion, once more championed their cause. The opposition of the nobles was more easily overcome, as they too had suffered from the tyranny of the crown; in fact, as an English ambassador aptly put it, " The only consolation of the peasant was that he saw his master in as miserable state as himself. " Bernstoff ordered an enquiry into the whole state of the peasant in 1784, and inaugurated an experiment in Sjaelland by giving no fewer than 3,800 farmers and small tenants their farms. Tithes were abolished, fixed rents were paid, options of purchase in so many years were guaranteed, and compulsory labour was abolished. This experiment was followed elsewhere, and, in 1792, the Column of Liberty was erected in Copenhagen to commemorate the abolition of the serf. It marks the beginning of Denmark's agricultural prosperity though the harvest was not garnered till after the Napoleonic Wars. As so often in Denmark's history, she entered the war at the wrong time and on the wrong side. At one time she stood as the sole ally of a defeated Napoleon. Many years of patient industry were required before she could reap the benefit of the advances of the eighteenth century.

This disastrous alliance also ended a period of growing commercial prosperity. The East India Company had been superseded by the Asiatic Company in 1732. Its headquarters were built on the new Copenhagen which arose on the ashes of the old. The capital became the clearing house for Baltic trade, and re-exported goods from all parts of the world. Its credit stood high and during the long period of peace, which the ministers maintained by no little ingenuity, extending over the Austrian Succession and European Seven Years Wars. Copenhagen was no mean rival to the old established Hamburg. The collapse was sudden. The old established private banks collapsed, credit was lost, the Asiatic Company went bankrupt. By 1807 the merchants became dependent on Hamburg, the Continental System brought matters to such a pass that Denmark became " dependent for her means of subsistence on privateers, smugglers and contraband." Previous to her decision in 1807 to throw in her lot with France, cheap wares from England had hit her home industries very hard. Many countries had undoubtedly benefited from Napoleon's conquests, but Denmark gained nothing, and lost everything from her faithful adherence to the alliance with the fallen master of Europe. Indeed, it was the traditional resilience and endurance of the "small men" of Denmark which brought about her ultimate recovery.

The political history of Denmark in the eighteenth century is not marked by any outstanding events, until its end. Governed by a series of absolute monarchs, Denmark presents many glaring contrasts and kaleidoscopic changes, but the royal will, except for a brief rule by Struensee (1770–1772), remained unshaken. At the same time as King Christian VI committed the first of his two bigamous marriages, missionaries were sent by him to the East Indies and Finmark, and Hans Egede made his famous journey to find the lost Danes of Greenland (see Appendix I), and ended by christianising the Eskimos. While Christian VI is making "his children good", he makes his people miserable and joyless. While his queen is recklessly spending the funds needed for re-building Copenhagen, he abolishes the National Theatre, as it was in his eyes a sinful waste.

While rebuilding the university, founding an Academy of Science and a School of Arts, he subjected all learning, even scientific, to the dogmatic censorship of his clergy. The works of Holberg, the most eminent historian and playwright of the day, were taboo.

The rising prosperity of commerce and shipping which he sponsored and encouraged, was checked by taxation to build absurdly big castles at Christiansborg and Hirsholm to please his wife. So Denmark experienced in full measure the blessings and evils of absolute monarchy. It was particularly unfortunate that when the possession of Slesvig was guaranteed by France and Britain (and later by Austria and Russia), it was stated to belong to the *Crown*, not the *State* of Denmark. This was indeed natural at the beginning of the eighteenth century, and it could not be foreseen that astute German jurists would, a century later, argue that it was a personal possession of the reigning king. The first phase of the complicated relations of Slesvig and Holstein may be said to begin after the treaty of 1721. That the solution could have been found for all time by Frederick IV is not improbable, but he was not a far-sighted statesman and cannot be held entirely responsible for the evil effects of his shortsightedness.

Another opportunity was offered by Catherine II (1767 to 1773), but the dangerous situation was believed to be over. In the eyes of eighteenth-century Danes, the danger on the southern frontier appeared to be due in no small measure to the connexion of Holstein with Russia and Sweden respectively. They never realised that the real danger lay in German infiltration and the domination of German officials in the higher posts. When Slesvig was formally acknowledged as Danish, Frederick IV seemed to take no further interest in its affairs. The old customs barrier was retained between South Jutland[1] and Slesvig. The German language was used in the law courts, in the administration, and in the churches, yet the language of the people was Danish, as indeed was their origin. When the Duchy was formally annexed, the people were absolved from owing allegiance to the Duke of Gottorp-Holstein, but the big landowners were mostly Holsteiners, the officials came from Kiel University, and the Court of Appeal was not Copenhagen, but still Gottorp. It should be pointed out, however, that the question of a united *constitution* for Slesvig and Holstein did not arise until 1806 on the dissolution of the Holy Roman Empire. The legalities of the question so vital to the Denmark of to-day will be treated in a separate chapter, but it is well to make it quite clear that Slesvig was, from 1721 to 1773, in relation to Denmark somewhat analogous to that of a crown colony.

The Russian danger lay in the fact that Charles Frederick, Duke of Holstein-Gottorp, married Anne, daughter of Peter the

---

[1] *Vide* page 184 for note on South Jutland.

become Czarina, and himself the Czar. Twice, however, he was disappointed as regards his Russian aspirations, and, as previously narrated, the "Holsteiners" were outwitted by Arvid Horn in their endeavours to secure the Swedish throne. These setbacks embittered the Holsteiners against the Danish kings who succeeded Frederick IV. The embers of hatred smouldered on and when the Duke of Holstein died in 1739, his influence in Slesvig had grown, largely through the indifference of the Danish Crown to the complaints of its Slesvig subjects. His weak-minded son, Charles Peter Ulric, had married an ambitious and able princess from the small German state of Anhalt. On the antipathy of this strong and masculine woman and her effeminate husband, was destined to hang the fate of Denmark. Charles Peter was obsessed with the idea of annexing Slesvig and wreaking vengeance on the Danes by whom he considered himself snubbed. Catherine looked at Moscow and dreamed of ruling a Russian Empire from the White Sea to the Black. By the third change of succession since the death of Peter the Great in 1727, the totally unsuitable Charles Peter Ulric of Holstein found himself Czar of Russia in January 1762. As a German prince, he professed an admiration for Frederick the Great, and by his sudden desertion of France and Austria, he saved the Prussian king from defeat. His wife, Catherine, was not averse to this *volte face*, for she had a personal grudge against Maria Theresa, but she was furious with her husband for marching his Russian army into Mecklenburg to make an unprovoked attack on Denmark. Catherine realised that such action would excite the enmity of many of the European countries which were now opening negotiations for peace to end the Seven Years War. Furthermore, she saw in Denmark's fleet and geographical position a useful aid to the attack on Sweden which might be necessary for the furtherance of her plans. She knew well the traditional weak spots in the Swedish armour, Skåne and Finland. Happily, Denmark was being virtually ruled by the elder Bernstoff and Moltke, while Frederick V (1746–1766) enjoyed the pleasures of the theatre, the tap house and the brothel.

The Danish fleet was ready and set out immediately to blockade the Baltic ports of Russia, and a Danish army of some forty thousand men, well trained by a French general, St. Germain, prepared to meet the Russians on the borders of Mecklenburg. The army could hardly have withstood the whole force of the

Russians, who could have mustered at least one hundred and twenty thousand tried soldiers, but the fleet would have held them off the two main islands of Fünen and Sjaelland. Catherine realised the folly of her irresponsible husband, and had him removed from the throne in July 1762, only six months after he had been crowned. She immediately made peace with Denmark, and the two armies, which had been in sight of each other, withdrew after the officers had "exchanged compliments". Four years later she renounced the claims of her infant son, Paul, to the Dukedom of Gottorp-Holstein, and ceded them to the Crown and State of Denmark in exchange for Oldenburg and Delmenhorst. This arrangement, which affected the Holy Roman Empire as well as Russia and Denmark, was ratified by Maria Theresa in 1773, a year after the first partition of Poland, and six years after the Russo-Danish agreement. It satisfied Russia, as Holstein was too far away to be consolidated in the Slav Empire and, to Denmark it appeared that her southern boundary was secured for all time. Taking a long view, one can see from after events that it would have been better for Denmark had her boundary remained the River Eider, the southern frontier of Slesvig. The incorporation of Holstein served to bind Slesvig and Holstein closer together. In Slesvig the official language remained German, and, as before, the highest offices were given to Germans from Kiel University, but the people remained Danish. So close did the connexion become between the two duchies that the Holstein nobles began to promulgate the theory that the two duchies had been united in law even before 1460—the year in which appeals from local courts were ordered to go to Gottorp.

Thus ended the first phase of the modern question of Slesvig and Holstein, with the removal of the Russian menace and the apparent increase of territory for Denmark, but the insidious growth of the German power through Holstein continued unchecked and unheeded by the unsuspecting court at Copenhagen.

The ministers Bernstoff and Moltke (A.G.) can hardly be blamed for not perceiving the dangers of the German hold over the duchies. They had welcomed foreigners, especially Germans, to promote interest in scientific, artistic and literary studies and undoubtedly such men as Niebuhr the archaeologist, Oder the botanist, Klopstock the writer, and Reverdil the scholar, were of great service in their respective spheres. To Bernstoff must be attributed the notable advances in commerce and navigation. Treaties were concluded with the centres of Mediterranean trade —Genoa, Naples, Tunis and Turkey. These opened the way for the private traders, of which they took full advantage, until in the decade following the death of Frederick V it was said that no flag was so often seen in the Mediterranean as the Danish-Norwegian. Of the state-sponsored companies only the Asiatic Company fulfilled its promise. Commercial expansion was due to the individual endeavour and the success of the private enterprises in the fifty years preceding the separation of Norway and Denmark had an especially important bearing on the fortunes of the former. It was not involved in the disasters which overcame Denmark, and the Norwegian shipping communities emerged from the Napoleonic Wars stronger than before. When the king died in 1766 from excessive drinking, probably cirrhosis of the liver, he was succeeded by a pathetic lad of seventeen, Christian VII. His good nature and good looks had been destroyed by the brutal Count Reventlow, who was originally given custody of the Crown Prince. Cruelly beaten and ill-treated, the young boy had been forced into deception and cunning. Depraved and vicious court pages had delighted in debauching the wretched youth. When the cultured Swiss Reverdil tried to rescue him it was too late. The future king was almost an imbecile, depraved in mind and body. For a short time after his succession it seemed that the responsibilities of kingship had saved him. He tried to better the lot of the peasant, and on the crown estates he succeeded. Suddenly he realised that he was all-powerful and responsible to no one. For days and nights he gave himself up to drunken orgies with the vicious friends of his youth and prostitutes. He dismissed all the old ministers except Bernstoff. In despair of the ruin which he foresaw impending from the king's conduct, Berntsoff arranged a marriage as the only hope of regenerating the all-powerful but capricious youth. Caroline Matilda, the sister of George III of England, was sacrificed to serve the political ends of two countries. At the age of fifteen she was married by proxy in spite of her brother's knowledge of Christian's evil reputation. The charming and innocent young girl arrived in Denmark, where this boy and girl marriage was consummated in November 1766. She was hailed by the Danish people with great enthusiasm; they saw in her another gracious Philippa,[1] and their affection and delight knew no bounds at the coronation in 1767. After a short honeymoon the king relapsed into a state of imbecile licentiousness during which he treated his sixteen-year-old wife with ignominy and even cruelty. His boon companion Count Holck was even more depraved, but his iron constitution was better able to withstand the evil effects of their ceaseless dissipation. After the birth of the Crown Prince, the future Frederick VI, matters reached such a state that medical advisers had to be in constant attendance on the king, whose lucid moments occurred at rare intervals. During these he showed signs of his early good nature, but his hatred of the queen was not diminished and she lived in almost solitary confinement, bullied by Holck and his reprobate friends. Finally, in 1768 the king, on his way to visit some of the German courts, fell in with a gifted society doctor at Altona named Johan Frederick Struensee. The history of Denmark for the next four years reads like a medieval romance in the setting of the pre-French Revolution period. Struensee was the son of a strict Pietist who had been superintendent general of Slesvig-Holstein. Revolting against this paternal régime, the son became a pronounced atheist and disciple of the Encyclopedists. Undoubtedly clever in his profession, he had a winning personality which appealed to the opposite sex, towards whom he had no scruples. In his sinister use of certain uncommon drugs he calls to mind Dr. Faustus; in his political standards he follows the precepts of Machiavelli, but in his mania for ruthless reforms he tried to put into practice the ideals of Rousseau. Such was the uncanny and contradictory composition of this ambitious provincial doctor who for eighteen months was the dictator of Denmark, holding more absolute power than any ruler of that country has ever done. To call him a charlatan is to disregard the very qualities which governed his actions after he had won ascendancy over the weak-mindedness of the king and overcome the dislike of the queen.

The first important stage in his career, dramatised by Lundegård in his trilogy *Struensee*, was reached when Bernstoff appointed him as court physician and he accompanied the king on a visit to Paris and London. Instead of scandalising the French and English courts, as had been feared, Christian proved a charm-

[1] Wife of Eric, 1396 to 1439.

ing, generous and amusing guest. Public opinion voted him as a much-maligned person. During the whole of the time Struensee had been at his side. By what strange drugs and hypnotic influence the cure had been effected will never be known.[1] The results were not obscure. He was reconciled to his queen, but his saviour, the handsome Struensee, must never leave his side and was installed in the palace. When still a doctor at Altona Struensee had dreamed of himself as a great statesman founding an ideal state. In 1769 he mooted the daring plan of trying the experiment on Denmark. What better subject could be found—a crazy king and a crazy form of government? His battle was partly won through his domination of the king who, thanks to his medical skill, was not quite sufficiently insane to be dethroned. He still signed the decrees, as directed. The obstacles to be overcome were the queen, the respected Bernstoff, the disreputable Holck, the nobility, and the fact that he had no official post in the administration. The queen's dislike had been overcome by her gratitude for his care of her husband. Struensee had earned her thanks by saving the life of the young crown prince by a "double inoculation", then considered a dangerous operation. He laid seige to her heart, and this unhappy girl of eighteen, infatuated with his elegance and apparent solicitude for her happiness, became his mistress. The king, fallen into a state of imbecile acquiescence, made no protest and at times seems to have regarded their love-making as an amusing joke. By the autumn of 1770 Struensee had made himself supreme. At his order, the king dismissed Bernstoff, who retired with dignity and went into voluntary exile. In May the queen had a baby daughter, Louise, whom the king had to recognise as his own. He refused for some time, backed by Count Holck, but after this attempt to show a will of his own, Struensee allowed him to sink into a worse state than ever. Holck, who earned the hatred of the queen, was banished, and a sinister friend of Struensee named Brandt was made the king's personal attendant and keeper. A " Te Deum " was ordered in every cathedral and church to celebrate the baptism of the new prin-

---

[1] A medical friend has advanced the interesting theory that Struensee administered doses of concentrated coca bean. This would have produced the symptoms of the ease, gaiety and wit for occasions, apparent cure, and then collapse, when the doses were stopped. The coca leaves were commonly used by Peruvians and had come to Europe via Spain. Its properties, those of cocaine, were becoming known to the medical profession in the last half of the eighteenth century. Struensee was just the man to experiment on a royal " guinea-pig ".

cess. This was the signal for the first revolt against the régime, as all the congregation walked out before the " Te Deum ". The relations of the queen and Struensee were no longer a secret, but with Christian still acting as king their position was secure as long as they remained friends.

The political experiment began in December 1770 with the suppression of the Council, and Struensee started to revise the machinery of state and found his new state on the ruins of the effete monarchy. At first he found favour with the middle classes and peasants. With a stroke of the pen he abolished the censorship over the Press, in spite of the protests of archbishops and university professors. Voltaire sent him his congratulations. Authors and their works should be subject to the ordinary laws of the land and, in fact, he achieved in an hour what England won after a struggle lasting many years—the Freedom of the Press. He then ordered a commision to inquire into the condition of the peasant. Struensee, in July 1771, was made " Geheime-Kabinetsminister " and created count. This gave him the right to issue royal orders, and any verbal orders of the king had to come through him. No petitions could be sent to the king direct. Everything had to go through the hands of the dictator's secretary. Meanwhile, the brutal and sadistic Brandt kept the king closely confined. Any attempt to free himself from this man led to further ill-treatment. Later, at Brandt's trial, evidence was given that the king was sometimes locked in his room and beaten by his keeper, and on one occasion bitten.

The king was, however, necessary to Struensee as he kept up the pretence of acting on his behalf.

His next acts were in the direction of getting orderly, efficient and exact management of the finance of the State. The staffs of public departments were dismissed *en bloc* without pensions, and new men responsible to himself were appointed. Each government department or *College* was directly responsible to him. The pace was too hot to last, and however good the enactments, sufficient time was not allowed for their fulfilment, nor were there men to carry them out. Struensee, who knew no Danish at all, trampled on traditions and customs of old standing, and in many cases shocked the public's sense of decency.

In sixteen months he passed one thousand and sixty-nine laws, and it is only possible to name a few which illustrate the magnitude of his work, which touched the life of the people at every point. They also give some idea of his fearlessness in attempting to enforce the will of the majority which had no means of expressing itself. As he was the sole judge of what that will should be, no few inconsistencies arose in his blend of dictator and Rousseau. While exercising control over the finance, punishing peculation, instituting audit of expenditure, and strict economy and thrift, he promoted state lotteries and gambling, and voted 60,000 riksdalers apiece to Brandt and himself. Salaries were reduced nearly to starvation point, but he dazzled foreigners and his friends by extravagant and unnecessarily lavish expenditure on the court. Torture for extracting evidence, and capital punishment were abolished. The law courts were purified and democratised, and a special court of appeal established. Public opinion was shocked at his theories of " free love " and the equal status of the legitimate and illegitimate child. A chapel was converted into a hospital for venereal diseases and other buildings requisitioned for foundlings. In the capital, he tried to grant the people more privileges and opportunities of entertainment. Recreation grounds were opened in the gardens of Rosenborg, and amusements such as dancing and concerts were permitted on Sundays. This offended Sabbatarians but, when it was decreed that brothels should be open to all and free from police supervision, the good feelings of all the better-class citizens were outraged. These measures were passed after he had reorganised the municipal council and ordained membership by election.

The newly-formed council was rendered more democratic, but many of its old powers were taken over by the State, even in purely local matters such as the time for closing the gates and the opening of theatres on Sundays. Discontent spread from the higher classes to the factory workers when prices rose, corn became scarce and wages were depressed to fit into Struensee's scheme of economy. Free distribution of grain only partially pacified the people of Copenhagen, where in the name of liberty they found their ways of life suddenly altered.

The fall came as suddenly as the rise. A secret plot was formed against him, backed by the king's stepmother, the Queen Dowager Juliane Marie, and her son Prince Frederick. On the political side it was joined by the reactionary Guldberg, on the military, by the commander of the guards. After a *bal masqué* the conspirators seized Struensee, the queen, Brandt and some others. The king burst into laughter as he signed the order for arrest—at last he would be free from his tormentor' Brandt!

Next day the imbecile king was driven round the capital and acclaimed the liberator of his country. After some hesitation the conspirators decided to prosecute Struensee as a traitor to his country, and Brandt for *lèse majesté* to the king's person. Struensee put up a magnificent defence, but privately admitted to his immoral relations with the queen. She had heroically denied the charge to try and save her lover, but on hearing of this confession she also admitted the charge. It was on the charge of conspiring against the king, and not on this charge, that Struensee was condemned with Brandt to a public and barbarous death. So died one of the strangest figures who has ever flitted across the European stage. His scientific mind delighted in experiments, but his last was with human beings as his subject, and a country cannot be isolated like a specimen under a microscope. Had he been given more time and had he not tried to crowd a life's work into eighteen months he might have succeeded. As it was, he leaves the historian guessing. Was he merely a charlatan seeking fame, riches and power by means of his natural gifts? Was he really wishing to benefit humanity? Was he trying to test the theoretical political economy of the day? If his enemies had not risen and used his own weapon, the king, against him, would he have founded a state in which the general will of the people could have found expression? There is little to give us ground for this supposition, except his abolition of press censorship, and his reform of the Municipal Borough of Copenhagen. The verdict must depend on the view that a democratic state can be founded by a dictator after he has purged the country of the poison of monarchic tyranny. There is nothing to prevent it except human nature, but this is a powerful factor in history, and has so far prevented such a sequence in the forms of government. Maybe he was genuinely interested in seeing how his ideals worked out in practice, but he can never be absolved from the guilt of his unscrupulous methods, his vanity, and his barbaric treatment of the king, whom he had partially cured.

Happily, he had left the foreign policy in the hands of the minister, Count Osten, and Denmark had not been embroiled with other countries. The attitude to be adopted towards the queen after her confession was one of extreme difficulty. George III of England was her brother, and refused to believe in her guilt. After a committee had ordered her divorce and imprisonment, she was rescued by an English warship and taken to Celle, in Hanover, where she remained a tragic figure till her death four years later at the age of twenty-four.[1]

Great were the rejoicings over the fall of the German doctor, but the triumvirate who assumed power was not effective in making any progress towards a democratic constitution. The twelve years which elapsed before the crown prince came of age in 1784 were marked by a resolve to restore a "status quo ante", in fact stagnation. The Queen Dowager Juliane Marie, Prince Frederick, her son, and Guldberg did their best to obliterate the whole of Struensee's work, and had not the inclination to discriminate between the good and the bad. They did, however, appoint A. P. Bernstoff, nephew of the former minister, as Foreign Minister. He it was who successfully prevented Denmark from becoming embroiled in troubles which might have resulted from the Armed Neutrality of the North. He is often depicted as anti-Russian, but he would be better described as pro-British. Through his influence the treaties with Catherine II and Maria Theresa were successfully negotiated as regards Holstein. When Denmark was forced to join the Armed Neutrality with Russia and Sweden in 1780, Bernstoff at the same time signed an agreement with England to protect the important Anglo-Danish trade. Not unnaturally, this provoked the anger of Gustavus III, who accused Denmark of failing to play her part in the agreement. As laid down by Catherine, who was not violently anti-British at this time,[2] this stated (1) that neutral ships could sail to ports of belligerents and that all goods except contraband should be exempt from seizure; (2) that only certain named goods should be deemed contraband (e.g. arms and ammunition); (3) that no blockade should be recognised unless it was effective. The issue turned on (2) and (3). What was contraband? When was a blockade effective? England refused

---

[1] There are many accounts of Caroline's life, some biased, some fanciful, but as her life at Celle had no influence on the history of Denmark or politics of Europe, abortive schemes for her restoration are omitted, as well as the stories of her charities at Celle.

[2] This view of the highly controversial dispute follows Hunt, *Political History of England*, Vol. X, pages 208, 209.

to recognise these rules which would have been more detrimental to her than to France, Spain and Holland. The Baltic was her chief source of supply for naval stores. Bernstoff openly allowed fish and meat to get to England, and with them went Norwegian timber and naval stores. Juliane Marie and Guldberg were violently anti-British, and the ablest Danish minister was peremptorily dismissed. The reason given was that the enmity of Russia was being incurred, but there are grounds for believing that the court was jealous of Bernstoff's influence and ability, and merely used this as a pretext.

Two other important events in these years had much bearing on the future history of Denmark. In 1780 Louise Augusta, the lovely daughter of Caroline Matilda and Struensee, was betrothed to Prince Frederick Christian of Augustenburg, and six years later the marriage was consummated. She had been declared the legitimate daughter of the king, and in the eyes of the law her child would be the heir to the thrones of Denmark and Norway provided that the crown prince, a sickly child, had no children. The issue of this marriage was destined to play an important part in the Holstein and Slesvig question in the twentieth century.

Of far greater immediate importance was the Ordinance of 1766, that foreigners, i.e. all except Danes, Norwegians and Holsteiners, were to be excluded from posts in the army, navy and state department. The Danish language was made compulsory in schools, churches, army and navy orders, and on the stage. Only in Holstein did this not apply. The significance and effect of this measure cannot be exaggerated. There was a burst of national feeling never before known in Denmark, which must be considered as having been the partial cause for the Golden Age of Literature which was to follow shortly. The only opposition came from Bernstoff, who supported the linguistic clauses but stoutly proclaimed his disapproval of a measure which was to deprive Denmark of her German officials and in his opinion would separate her from German cultural and political intercourse.

When the young crown prince assumed the powers of the regency in 1784, Guldberg and the queen dowager were astonished when a document announcing the king's consent to the dismissal of the Cabinet was presented to the Council. The reactionary régime of Guldberg came to an abrupt end, and Bernstoff was restored to power. The old king's signature had been used by the Cabinet in the same way as it had been used by Struensee, but now the crown prince, as regent, virtually superseded his father, who dragged out his unhappy existence until 1808, when the shock of seeing French soldiers marching past his residence brought a sudden end to his futile life.

A long period of peace was only broken by the short war with Sweden in 1788, when Catherine II insisted on Denmark carrying out the terms of the 1773 pact signed by Bernstoff himself during his first ministry. The English, however, managed to arrange a peaceful settlement after the Norwegian army had approached Göteborg.

For the great progress in every sphere of national life the chief credit must be given to Bernstoff, who guided the State until his death in 1797. On the other hand, the crown prince showed a strong sense of duty and an unflagging devotion to the strenuous work of the State. This came as a pleasant surprise to his ministers and the Council, who regarded him as a sickly and unintelligent child. His physical recovery was in no small measure due to the rigorous remedial exercises and "hardening" which had been imposed by Struensee during the first six years of his life. Prince Frederick, heir presumptive, disappointed of the succession which his mother, the queen dowager, had hoped would be his, retired from politics, and thus the regent and his minister had no opposition to their scheme of benevolent despotism.

The rise of commerce, the betterment of the peasants' condition, commemorated in the Column of Liebrty in 1792, have already been mentioned. Great encouragement was given to higher education in schools and universities. The curriculum was broadened, though the classics remained the foundation of learning as in other countries. The State granted money to institute new professorships in scientific subjects, and the royal library was thrown open to all. The regent, who became known as King Frederick VI in 1808, was little interested in literature, though his reign covered the Golden Age of Danish Literature, which reached its peak in the two decades 1810 to 1830. Beginning before the end of the century, the movement, if anything, received an impetus from the troubles of the Napoleonic Wars. To English readers the name of Hans Andersen of Odense is a household word, but other writers show more essentially Danish characteristics. *Hans Andersen's Fairy Tales* had a popularity in

England greater than in Denmark itself, where the first series had been only a moderate success. In 1847 he became a lion of London society, and Queen Victoria, "who read but little", was his great admirer. Dickens heralded him as one of the greatest writers of children's stories. No less than fourteen translators have made the *Tales*, which continued to appear for another quarter of a century, a classic for both adults and children, and Andersen now deservedly ranks as a writer of international repute.

Blicher's tales of the peasants rank high in expressing the realities of life. Ohlenschläger, in the opinion of some critics, the greatest of all in a romantic school, entirely national, and Baggesen, as a satirist, soon became well known outside their own country. The man who exerted the greatest influence as a writer, thinker and teacher was Grundtvig. Born in 1783, he belongs to a later age, and even in his twenties he had begun to attract the notice of those who knew him. On leaving Copenhagen University he became absorbed in Icelandic studies—its mythology and language (now usually known at Middle Norsk). This was followed by an exhaustive study of Shakespeare, Fichte and rationalism, which had spread from England to Denmark and was shaking the very foundations of Lutheranism. This sincere and honest thinker, after passing through various stages of development, emerged as a great spiritual and national leader who influenced nineteenth-century Denmark and its leaders more than any other writer or preacher-lecturer of his day. He stimulated national pride by his translation of the sagas and the histories of Saxo Grammaticus and Snorri. He pricked the conscience of the theologians and exploded the fallacies of the rationalists by his thesis on religion, after which he was forbidden to preach for seven years. He then led a revivalist movement against orthodox Lutheranism which was almost a replica of Wesley's. His songs and hymns, like those of Wesley in England, became incorporated in the Danish services. In two ways he is almost unique. The poet and preacher was also politician and educationist. Though a firm believer in democracy, he was convinced that an uneducated democracy was not fit to rule. It must be remembered that he was an admirer of the English institutions, and his visits to England coincided with the great Reform movements of the thirties. His honest mind was not convinced that manhood suffrage to an uneducated populace spelt liberty. There is nothing to show how far his observations of English life at that time influenced him, but we do know that he set himself to improve the religious and intellectual life of Denmark. To him must be attributed the future success of the famous Folk Schools which have at long last become the ideal of twentieth-century educationists.[1] This great spiritual leader died at the age of eighty-nine in 1872, and the very style of the Grundtvig Memorial Church suggests the modernity of his mind, which with such discerning insight could assimilate all the good and discard the evil from past ages.

The bright picture of the intellectual side of Danish life at the beginning of the nineteenth century affords a sharp contrast to her dismal though honourable history from 1800 to 1815. The old Armed Neutrality of the North was renewed in January 1801 with the addition of Prussia. Besides suffering from the Copenhagen disaster, Denmark lost her important trading station of Tranquebar. Founded in 1620, it had become a busy port and was the Danish link in her Eastern trade. It was restored in 1814, but finally sold to Great Britain in 1845. The town still retains many features of Danish occupation, including its Lutheran mission, but when Negapatam, some nineteen miles distant, became the terminus of the South Indian Railway, it lost much of its trade and now has a population of barely 14,000 inhabitants. This was all the more unfortunate because Denmark had been an unwilling signatory to the Alliance. Her ambassador had been expelled from Russia for his pro-British sympathies, but the full force of Britain's naval power fell on Denmark alone. Sir Hyde Parker, with Nelson the spearhead of the attack, bombarded Copenhagen and smashed the fleet and shore batteries. Nelson, in his historic letter " to the Brothers of Englishmen, the brave Danes ", offered an armistice hoping that it " might be the forerunner of a lasting and happy union between England and Denmark ". Nelson, just before Trafalgar, left on record his opinion that the Danes were the finest seamen in the world, excepting, of course, his men of the old *Agamemnon*. At the time, he recommended to the crown prince that Will Moes, aged eighteen, should be promoted to the rank of admiral for his handling of a gunboat against his own man-of-war. It is a small incident in itself, no doubt, but showed the chivalry of the day, and that the war between the

[1] Vide *Future of Education*, Livingstone (1944).

English and the Danes was essentially distasteful and the outcome of events beyond the control of either nation. If this was true in 1801, it was still truer in 1807, when the second bombardment of Copenhagen took place. After the Treaty of Tilsit, when the Czar and Napoleon decided to ruin Britain by the Continental System and divide the world between them, Canning received information which led him to believe that Denmark was to be occupied, and the Danish fleet used against Britain.[1]

Canning immediately dispatched an amphibious expedition —the navy under Gambier, the army under Cathcart and Wellington—to enforce either the surrender of the fleet or an alliance against Napoleon. It is now known that on August 3rd, Napoleon had sent a letter with instructions to his ambassador at Copenhagen demanding that Denmark should declare war on Britain. Unfortunately, the crown prince was in Holstein with an army guarding the vulnerable southern frontier and never received it.

With our knowledge of the Danish national spirit we can be assured that this demand would have been refused, but before the letter arrived, Wellington had landed with 30,000 troops and Gambier was blockading the capital. The blustering and high-handed British emissary placed the British demands before the crown prince at Kiel, who, in ignorance of Napoleon's demands, not unnaturally refused. The crown prince rushed to Copenhagen, ordered its defence, and himself returned to Kiel. Jackson tried to meet him in Copenhagen, but he had gone, and the tragedy of the bombardment took place. For three days Copenhagen suffered terribly, and capitulated on September 7th, and the whole of the Danish fleet, valued at £2,000,000, was towed to England for safe custody. This defeat embittered the Danes, who had no intention of attacking Britain, and they remained fettered to Napoleon till their ultimate surrender to Bernadotte in 1814. For five years Britain occupied a Danish island and were masters of the Baltic gates of the Skagerak and Öresund. One cannot but admire the honourable conduct of the Danes, who remained true to their alliance with Napoleon, even after his defeats at Moscow and Leipzig. Denmark in 1813 undertook to supply him with 13,000 troops, but standing alone as they did on Napoleon's return to France they proved no match for Bernadotte.

---

[1] How the news arrived is one of the most interesting unsolved mysteries of history. *Vide Four Mysteries of History*, Sir John Hall.

The king had to bow to the inevitable at the Treaty of Kiel in 1814, and Norway was ceded to Sweden.[1] Rügen and Pomerania, which came as part compensation to Denmark, were exchanged for Lauenburg in 1815. Frederick VI, who had lost much of his popularity by his support of Napoleon, regained the affection of his people by his efforts at the Congress of Vienna, but he succeeded in gaining little except the sympathy of the Great Powers. The heir to the throne, Prince Christian Frederick, in 1839 Christian VIII, tried to save Norway, where he had been extremely popular as the Viceroy. However, it was quite obvious that nothing could be done without the support of Frederick VI, who, with no navy, wisely ordered him to leave the country and abide by the Treaty of Kiel. Sadly the Viceroy obeyed orders, leaving as a monument of his rule the new University of Oslo (Christiania). With the close of the Napoleonic Wars, a new epoch started throughout the Scandinavian countries.

[1] *Vide* page 281

CHAPTER XIII

DENMARK AND THE SLESVIG-HOLSTEIN QUESTION

FEW Continental countries had so little direct interest in the Napoleonic Wars and yet suffered so much as Denmark. Apart from the indignities which she had endured from both sides, she had suffered the loss of Norway and the greater part of her fleet. Once more in her history the people showed their remarkable resilience, and the recovery in the nineteenth century, though necessarily slow, gave her in some respects a higher place than she had ever attained. Denmark no longer sought naval or military fame, but in peaceful enterprise she attained an enviable position. Her most outstanding achievements were the immense merchant fleet, which was found in every quarter of the globe, and her dairy products, which are so well known in the British Isles. In the realm of education she led the way to a free and universal education. Her folk high schools and the wide opportunities for adult education have become models for the educationists of the twentieth century. When in 1870 England had decided that "it was time to educate our masters", the Danish people had already perceived the fact that having won a democratic government after centuries of absolutism, the people who controlled that government must have a proper education. It was not enough to be able to read and write; it was not enough to have practical knowledge only. Education must be available to the farmer and his labourer, to the manager and the workman. All must feel that they are citizens, with their responsibilities as well as their privileges. These "folk schools", which were the outstanding feature of the nineteenth century after about 1850, were soon copied in Sweden, and in both countries the sensible, restrained and balanced forms of socialism which prevail may largely be attributed to their influence.

That such victories of peace were won during the nineteenth century is all the more notable because it began with a period of constitutional struggle and a disputed succession, and for a whole century Denmark has suffered from German aggression in varying degrees and under such guises as open attack, invasion, occupation or infiltration.

The two outstanding problems of the Constitution and the Duchies, though seemingly separate, became intimately connected and ultimately inseparable through waves of liberalism and nationalism which swept over the European continent in the twenty-five years preceding 1848—the " year of Revolutions " Many of the difficulties in the Slesvig question might have been avoided and many of the reforms might have been unnecessary in Denmark had she not been governed by an absolute monarchy in those crucial years of Slesvig and Holstein history—1721, 1773 and 1806. It will be remembered that in 1721 Slesvig was declared to belong to the Danish crown and in 1773 Catherine II renounced a claim to Slesvig and ceded Duke Paul's part of the Holstein duchy, while finally in 1806 came the dissolution of the Holy Roman Empire, of which Holstein (*but not Slesvig*) was a member.

The term "Slesvig-Holstein question" was not commonly used until Bismarck created the province in 1862–1864, when Denmark became the first victim of the series of German acts of aggression which culminated in the First and Second World Wars. This first act of aggrandisement is closely connected with the present day problem because in 1947 Germans were allowed to pour into the essentially Danish province of Slesvig from East Prussia, Pomerania and other parts of the Reich. They number between 350,000 and 400,000 and the inhabitants are in danger of being swamped by this alien influx. By the Allies this fact seems to have been ignored, but in Germany it is sufficiently recognised for an ex-army officer to remark that " though we have lost the war, we have won Slesvig ".

Because this question is complicated, it must not be ignored for the second time by Great Britain and France, the two guarantors. In 1864 the two countries were bluffed and out-manoeuvred by Bismarck, while Palmerston dismissed it with the historic, but cynical remark: " Only three people understood the Slesvig-Holstein question. The first was Albert, the Prince Consort and he is dead; the second is a German professor, and he is in an asylum; and the third was myself—and I have forgotten it." The Danes of South Slesvig have not forgotten that remark, but after the victory of 1945 they have continued to hope for the help which is their due.

The so-called " Slesvig-Holstein question " has caused confusion in many diplomatic quarters because it has on several occasions been treated as one single issue, whereas in fact there are three different problems involved, and though related they cannot be treated as one. These are bound up with the relation of Denmark with Slesvig, Denmark with Holstein, and Slesvig with Holstein. The last two may conveniently be termed personal (at any rate in origin) through the rights of the Dukes of Holstein, but the relationship of Denmark and Slesvig stands on an entirely different footing. It is linguistic, ethnological and religious, and the southern boundary of Denmark was definitely set at the River Eider in A.D. 811, a boundary which also marks the line between Slesvig and Holstein. As this has been repeatedly reasserted down the ages and confirmed twice by the German Federal Parliament between 1806 and 1850, it is necessary to summarise the main historical facts which have preceded the long drawn out disputes of the nineteenth and twentieth centuries.

In the earliest times the Danish kings separated the southern part of the kingdom down to the Eider for purposes of government, and placed it under a Danish South Jutland duke, owning the king as overlord. In 1375 the line became extinct and the duchy was given by the King of Denmark to a Holstein Count of Slesvig who became Landsmand (lord lieutenant). In 1459 this line also became extinct on the male side, whereupon as the Salic Law as regards property operated in Holstein a new duke had to be appointed. The "high and great" men of Holstein unanimously elected the King of Denmark as Duke of Holstein (originally as Count). Thus the kings of Denmark became both dukes of the Danish Slesvig and the German Holstein, and through the person of the king there resulted two unions—the union with Denmark and the union between the two duchies. These lasted for four hundred years, but complications were bound to arise because the boundary of the Danish state lay between the two duchies and it might arise that the Duke of Holstein was not the King of Denmark. This indeed was the case, as the succession to the crown and to the duchy were not governed by the same law. As Danish Slesvig (North and South) kept the

MAP IV. DENMARK AND THE SLESVIG-HOLSTEIN PROBLEM

Danish customs and laws and Holstein the German, it can now be seen what a grave error had been committed in 1721 by not incorporating Slesvig with the administration of Denmark. After the Reformation, German influence dominated South Slesvig, as has been previously narrated, and with the customs frontier remaining between Jutland and Slesvig, the Slesvigers not unnaturally began to regard themselves as part of the Holstein administration. On the dissolution of the Holy Roman Empire in 1806, Frederick VI again missed the chance of a permanent settlement, though his reasons are understandable. It would have meant the loss of his dukedom of Holstein. Instead, he entered the new German Diet as duke, but at the same time declared Holstein to be part of Denmark by a very disputable Act of State. Regarded alone, this act may seem foolish, but it must be remembered that his prestige had been lowered by the loss of Norway and the further diminution of his possessions would have been regarded as a sign of weakness. It is in no sense comparable with the abandonment of Hanover by England under the Salic Law. The immediate results of this arrangement were that the German Federal Parliament was given a say in the affairs of Holstein but not Slesvig, whilst the leading families of Holstein resented the assertion that they were under Denmark.

Ideas of new constitutions were permeating the European air, and the first sign of opposition made its appearance when Frederick VI turned down a request from the Holsteiners for a constitution for a united Slesvig-Holstein. They appealed to the Federal Government, which gave a definite refusal because it rightly declared that Slesvig was Danish and that consequently it had no jurisdiction.

Christian VIII, however, granted a common government for the Duchies, with its seat at Gottorp at the north-east end of the Danevirke, and with a common court of appeal at Kiel. This at once increased the power of the Holsteiners to spread German influence over North and South Slesvig. The Danes put up a sturdy resistance and the already-growing national spirit in Denmark was profoundly stirred.

While favouring the Holsteiners in the place of government—autocratic though it was—the king stirred up the enmity of their most powerful family—the Augustenburgs. The Duke and his brother, Prince of Nör were dangerous and relentless enemies, closely related to the royal family. They were grandsons of the king's sister, Louise Augusta, who had been declared legitimate although known to be the child of Struensee. They became the recognised heads of a separatist movement, although they were even more violently anti-democratic than the king himself. The struggle was further complicated by the waves of liberalism and nationalism which were sweeping over Italy, France and Germany and had begun to surge into Denmark and the Duchies. The first to raise his voice for a democratic constitution in the Duchies was Lornsen, but he was speedily suppressed and imprisoned with the approval of the king and the Augustenburgs. In Denmark, however, the temper of the National Liberals was rising and their party was growing in numbers and influence though it had no parliamentary means of expressing its views. In 1834, as a mild form of appeasement, the king set up four consultative chambers at Roskilde, Viborg, Slesvig and Itzehoe (situated some thirty miles north-west of Hamburg). These were able to air the opinions of the members, but executive power they had none, and they only became centres of discontent where protests against the absolutism of the government were loudly expressed to little purpose. In them, the National Liberals soon began to predominate, and amidst various projects of reform three main lines of policy emerged. First, at home, they demanded one democratic constitution displacing the futile assemblies. Secondly, abroad, they favoured " Scandinavismen " (not necessarily under one ruler), and thirdly, as an obvious corollary of these two, they proposed the " Eider policy ", i.e. the severance of Holstein, and the granting of a common constitution for Slesvig and Denmark.

These definite policies found more and more supporters under the influence of their able party leader, Orla Lehmann, and soon after the end of Frederick VI's long reign of fifty-five years in 1839, Christian VIII could no longer turn a deaf ear to the complaints of the Assemblies.

Christian VIII (1839–1848) presents a strange mixture of decisive action in favour of reforms and an obstinate refusal to face the main needs. Whilst establishing self-government in the towns, counties and parishes, and a representative council for Copenhagen, and re-establishing the Icelandic Althing, he flatly refused to grant a constitution for the whole country. He muzzled the Press and imprisoned Lehmann, but at the same time put in force some of the Liberal programme by publishing an annual budget and an audit of public finance. Nor was he openly averse to Scandinavismen. Sometimes he even appeared to adopt the Liberals' "United Scandinavia" slogan. So when war broke out in March 1848 after the death of Christian VIII, the Swedes were sufficiently favourable to the idea of mutual defence that a force was landed in Fünen to assist the Danes in case of the invasion of North Jutland. Under Christian, the army was reformed and a modest but efficient force showed its worth against heavy odds when tested in the first Slesvig War, 1848–1850. As regards the pressing questions of a democratic constitution and the status of Slesvig and Holstein he proved short-sighted, vacillating and obstinate. Hoping to solve the two inter-related but not fundamentally cognate problems, he appointed the autocratic and antagonistic Prince of Nör as Governor of the Duchies. His hopes were not realised and a better statesman would have foreseen that no permanent settlement could have been evolved from this false policy of appeasement. Nör used his power to oppress the Danish element, and flagrantly flaunted the king's authority. Trying still further to attach the Augustenburg family to the Danish crown, Christian VIII decreed in 1844 that the Danish language would be permitted in Slesvig only if a deputy could not speak German. An outburst of Danish patriotism was caused by the expulsion of Hjort Lorenzen for addressing the Slesvig Diet in his own tongue in defiance of the king's decree. In Copenhagen, Lehmann, released from prison, had been appointed by the burghers as Vice-President of Copenhagen, and was regarded by peasants, burghers and nationalists as the hero of freedom. In 1846 Christian VIII became aware of the critical position, rendered all the more menacing because his only son, afterwards Frederick VII, had no male or female heirs, although twice married and twice divorced. This being so, the Holstein separatists maintained the Augustenburgs were the rightful heirs to the Duchies through their grandmother, and more than hinted that they were heir-presumptives to the Danish throne. This brought the crisis to a head in 1846. Christian VIII was forced to act, but his "Open Letter" satisfied no party, and it is difficult to gain any clear indication of his ultimate intentions. He insisted that the same law of succession was valid for Denmark and Slesvig (which could not be gainsaid), but as regards some parts of Holstein there was a doubt. However, he promised to preserve the union of Holstein and clear up the doubtful points and establish a uniform order of succession. The Diet at Itzehoe was indignant and framed a threatening address to the king and also appealed to the German Confederation. For the second time the Holsteiners were informed that Slesvig was Danish and outside their jurisdiction.

Meanwhile, in Denmark itself the Liberals had gone from strength to strength till at last in 1847 the king planned a democratic constitution, based on universal suffrage, necessarily implying the abolition of the four assemblies of Roskilde, Viborg, Slesvig and Itzehoe. He had undoubtedly become "Liberal minded", and even sympathised with the "Society of Peasants" who, under J. A. Hansen, advocated the emancipation of the peasant class, internal free trade (based on Maassen's idea of the Zollverein, which had spread over North Germany), universal suffrage, conscription and land-ownership. Whether he was intending to impose the new constitution on Slesvig or whether he intended to preserve the anomalous Slesvig-Holstein government will never be known, as he died suddenly in January 1848. Everything leads to the belief that he would have adopted the Eider policy, for already the Prince of Nör had been relieved of his governorship and six Holsteiners had been dismissed.

It was no easy task that fell to the new king, Frederick VII (1848–1863). He was known to be an authentic supporter of a new constitution but at the same time his two divorces and his avowed intention of marrying a ballet girl, Louise Ramussen, created opponents from all parties. Only ten days after his accession he announced his intention of publishing the draft of the new constitution and marrying Louise.

The constitution, as drafted, complied with many of the Liberal principles but confounded the Nationalists. There was to be a Common Assembly, but in spite of the introduction of manhood suffrage the distribution of seats gave to the Duchies, with a population of 820,000, the same number of deputies as the rest of Denmark, with a population of 1,450,000. Furthermore, the Assembly was to meet alternately at Gottorp and Copenhagen; in short, it appeared to the National Liberals that the Duchies, though partly German, were being put on an equal footing with the whole of Denmark, and the impression was intensified by the fact that the king's minister, Carl Moltke, was a Holsteiner. He was, in fact, an honest and impartial politician and was not attempting to load the dice in favour of the land of his birth. His faulty judgement was due to ignorance of the Liberal movement in the previous twenty years. Violent protests came simultaneously from a meeting of Liberals at Copenhagen and of separatists at Rendsborg. The latter sent a deputation to Copenhagen demanding a separate constitution for the Duchies, while crowds demonstrated before the palace demanding the incorporation of Slesvig in a united constitution with Denmark. Before the royal reply had been received in Slesvig, the separatists had revolted and set up a provincial government at Kiel under the Prince of Nör, and the Duke of Augustenburg had left his residence in North Slesvig to enlist the help of the King of Prussia. In April 1848 the rebels, after taking Rendsborg, were badly defeated near Flensborg, but an army of 30,000 Prussian and Federal troops under Wrangel overran Slesvig and the Danes were pinned to Dybböl and the island of Als. Denmark appealed to France, England and Russia, who had guaranteed Slesvig's union with Denmark; her fleet blockaded the Baltic ports, played havoc with the Prussian merchant vessels, and 5,000 Swedish and Norwegian troops landed to defend Fünen. Russia, backed by England, sent a strong note to Berlin demanding the withdrawal of Prussian troops. Berlin climbed down and a seven months' armistice was signed, during which time a mixed commission was to supervise the government of Slesvig.

The Holsteiners, however, failed to keep the terms, and Danish peasants rose to defend themselves against their oppressors. In April 1849 war broke out again. Strong Federal forces overran Slesvig and part of Jutland and finally invested Fredericia. A masterly attack by General Rye took the Germans by surprise, and after a fierce battle they were totally defeated and all their artillery, together with 2,000 prisoners, was captured by the Danes. A second armistice was concluded on the insistence of Russia and England and a commission was set up for the government of Slesvig consisting of a Dane, a Prussian and an Englishman. Swedish troops were to keep the peace in North Slesvig, Prussian in the south, while Prussia and Denmark signed the Peace of Berlin on July 2nd, 1850. The joint administration of Slesvig and Holstein was abolished and the rights of Denmark were restored on a " status quo ante " footing.

Before the month was out the rebels, helped by Prussian and German volunteers, attacked the Danes and, although the rebel army numbered some 34,000 men and was commanded by a German general, it was heavily defeated at Isted and finally dispersed. This ended the First Slesvig War, and the German Confederation professed itself ready to carry out the Peace of Berlin. Holstein was to be temporarily governed by Prussian and Austrian commissioners, while Slesvig was separately governed by a minister and court of appeal stationed at Flensborg, and the customs frontier was moved to the old Danish boundary of the Eider, and loyal Danish officials displaced the nominations of the Nör régime. Tillisch, the appointed minister, acted with commendable impartiality, and his solution of the linguistic problem offered the only possible chance of success. The two Slesvigs were divided into three belts: in the Northern, Danish was used exclusively, and contained a Danish high school at Haderslev; in the Southern, where Low German was in common use, German was the official language, and the high school at Slesvig remained German. The problem presenting the greatest difficulty appeared in the middle belt where the two languages were placed on an equal footing and a bi-lingual college was established at Flensborg. Unjustly, the Germans made exaggerated complaints of the hardships endured by this equitable division, which affords a striking contrast to the Holsteiners' own rule before 1848 and after 1864.

Meanwhile, the delayed constitution was ready for execution in Copenhagen. It consisted of a lower house (*Folketing*) elected on a universal suffrage basis, and a higher (*Landsting*) consisting from 1866 to 1915 of two classes of deputies who were partly elected and partly crown nominations. All citizens were to be equal before the law. In January 1852 it was agreed by Denmark, Prussia and Austria that Denmark, Slesvig, Holstein and Lauenburg should have separate administrations, but for matters which concerned the whole state (such as war and foreign policy) they should be bound by a common constitution. Slesvig and Holstein were to be separate, but Slesvig should not be incorporated in the Danish administration. In 1856 a common constitution for the whole monarchy was planned, but Germany protested that Holstein and Lauenburg could not be brought into it, and so that part of the plan was dropped. The whole period from 1853 to

1863 contained an endless series of negotiations and disputes over the status of the Duchies, and certain events brought them to a head when the position of Denmark had grown weaker and the attitude of Prussia had become more aggressive and ambitious. Outwardly it would appear that Denmark was stronger than she had ever been. Her trade and commerce had doubled. Sweden had proved herself a faithful friend. These were deceptive guides, because an over-confidence born of the victorious outcome of the First Slesvig War had allowed the navy and army to deteriorate. In armament and numbers both had fallen or, at any rate, not progressed with the new age of iron and invention. All energy and enterprise had been devoted to the pursuits of peace; commendable in a golden age, but disastrous for a neighbour of Prussia. The Scandinavian movement had also lost its appeal. One of the causes, no doubt, was the attitude of Russia, who was not on good terms with Sweden. Had it not been for the Crimean War in 1854 to 1856 it is more than possible that there would have been a Russo-Swedish War. Be that as it may, Sweden was clearly given to understand that this Scandinavismen was not acceptable to Russia, while Denmark was reminded of Russian pressure in Berlin during the Slesvig War. Only a few Danes realised how the moral assistance of Russia had contributed to their success. The problem of the succession had apparently been settled at the Congress of London in 1853. As Frederick VII had no sons it was decided to accept Prince Christian of the Slesvig-Holstein-Sönderborg line as heir. The Duke of Augustenburg, who lineally was two degrees nearer the trunk of the royal genealogical tree, renounced his claims on the receipt of a handsome cash payment. Unfortunately, the arrangement, endorsed by the Great Powers, was not presented to the German Federal Parliament. The success of the constitution building and the Royal Succession Act were largely due to Bluhme, his successor Örsted, and to the influence of the Countess Danner, the ballet girl whom the king had morganatically married as his third wife. Their tasks had not been easy, as many vested interests had suffered, nor did their programmes entirely satisfy the Liberals or any other party.

When Hall, the Danish Liberal leader, became prime minister, he was determined to end the uncertainty of the Duchies and to provide an improved constitution which could be applied to Denmark and Slesvig. He was clear-sighted enough to see the root of a century of unrest lay in the union of Holstein with Denmark, and its close affinity to Slesvig. Two things he did not foresee—the attitude of Bismarck and the failure of the Powers guaranteeing Slesvig to carry out their obligations.

The Chambers passed the new constitution on November 13th, 1863, but the king died on November 15th before it had been signed by him.

It was indeed a tragic moment for the new king, Christian IX (1863–1906) to ascend the throne. The London protocol had agreed on him as heir " to preserve the integrity of the Danish monarchy " as necessary " for the maintenance of peace ". He was informed that Prussia would declare war if the constitution was to embrace Slesvig and so break the Peace of Berlin, 1852.

Hall and the Liberals pressed for his signature. The crowds surged in the palace yard and cries were heard of " Sign or abdicate ". The nation, unaware how the defences had been neglected, only thought of their victories at Bov and Fredericia. The poems of Öhlenschläger had already raised the pride of the people in themselves. The Danes were more than a match for the Germans. The effect of a golden age of national literature had borne fruit. On November 18th the king signed the "November Constitution ". The Duke of Augustenburg, who had received his payment for renouncing his claims to the throne, transferred his old rights to his son, whom he proclaimed Frederick VIII.

In December, German troops were in possession of Holstein. Bismarck persuaded Austria to join him in the rape of the Duchies, and meanwhile he gave Christian IX forty-eight hours to withdraw the constitution or else, he declared, Slesvig would be invaded. Bismarck's only fear was that the Danes *would not fight* and then he might be unable to annex the provinces. He therefore intimated that Palmerston was threatening to come to the aid of Denmark in the event of war. The actual words of Palmerston are variously recorded. The new prime minister, Monrad, believing in the sincerity of England and France and backed by the majority of the people, refused to accede to the demand and appealed to France and England for the expected armed intervention. At this point Palmerston certainly allowed it to be thought that England would intervene, and he approached

Napoleon III with the object of obtaining joint action. Having found him unwilling, Palmerston made a protest, but Bismarck "called his bluff", confident that England would not fight alone. He was right, though Palmerston's death prevents any definite opinion of what efforts he would have made to save the northern part of Slesvig. Two superb poker players had met, but Bismarck, with four aces, found Palmerston with not even the Queen of England in his hand. For Palmerston's reputation as a great foreign minister, his death was timely.

The Danes put up a magnificent display of bravery at Dybböl, but the overwhelming and well-trained Prussian army with its Austrian allies had won the war as soon as the Eider was crossed. Outflanked at the Danevirke, the Danes retreated and crossed to Als to reorganise, leaving a retaining force at the Dybböl bridge-head. England tried to procure an armistice, but the Prussians refused until two months later they had pulverised the entrenchments and annihilated the gallant defenders. An armistice was concluded on May 9th, but as no agreement could be reached at a London conference, the war was resumed on June 26th. At one time it appeared likely that a line, approximately that of 1920, would be accepted for the partition of Slesvig into Danish and German zones, but it is now known from Bismarck's *Memoirs* that he was determined to annex all Slesvig, Holstein and Lauenburg to Prussia. The second part of this war was even more disastrous than the first. The Prussians crossed to the island of Als and the Danes evacuated their army with severe losses to Fünen. Deserted by all her allies, Denmark had to beg for peace and submit to the loss of no less than a third of her people and two-fifths of her territory.[1] Bismarck proceeded to play a perfidious game with his own allies. First of all, he declared that the Duke of Augustenburg's line had no claim to the Duchies and that therefore they belonged to Prussia and Austria by right of conquest. Secondly, by a clever arrangement, he conciliated Austria by bestowing on her the German Holstein, while Prussia took over Slesvig. In less than a year he found a pretext for attacking Austria, and after six weeks of fighting, the victory at Sadowa enabled him to force Austria to cede all Holstein to

[1] Almost immediately after this devastating loss of agricultural land, the Danes began to reclaim bogs, marshes and land from the sea. By 1906, it is asserted that an area of reclaimed land as great as the whole of Fünen was under cultivation.

Prussia by the Treaty of Prague in 1866. In that treaty, however, was inserted the important clause, known as Paragraph V, by which the Northern Slesvigers were given the right to return to Denmark if a majority by plebiscite desired to do so. This was due to the influence of Napoleon III, who was beginning to realise the Bismarckian menace. Napoleon III had been impressed by the use of the plebiscite in Italy (1860–1861), and with good reason imagined that the result would restore his prestige in the eyes of Denmark and England. His ill-fated Mexican Adventure, hanging in the balance, prevented his taking a stronger line than diplomatic pressure. Bismarck apparently yielded, but in reality he was biding his time to crush one by one anyone who stood in his way. The war against Denmark gave him access to the North Sea; the war against Austria made him master of Germany; the Franco-Prussian War (1870–1871) won him the coveted provinces of Alsace and Lorraine, and made him master on the Continent. Consequently he not only refused to hold a plebiscite in North Slesvig, but in 1878 he actually agreed with Austria to cut Paragraph V out of the treaty. On that paragraph rested the hopes of the oppressed Danes in North Slesvig. They had to wait until 1920, but after fifty-six years of deportation, eviction and suppression there had been sufficient sturdy resistance to the German mailed fist for the voters to give their verdict for a return to Danish rule.

It had been an unhappy beginning for the new reign, and the troubles of the Duchies have caused the progressive and enlightened activities in other spheres of Danish life to pass almost unnoticed by other nations. The whole nation seemed to have acquired a new life and a broader outlook, and it is difficult to find a country in which "liberalism" had a more profound effect in so short a period.

Free trade was an axiom of their commercial system, and they applied it not only to Denmark itself, but to Iceland and the Faroes, and to the remission of the dues for passing through the Öresund. Foreigners were allowed equal rights. Fish and corn had been two of Denmark's main exports, but the loss of Norway and the capricious habits of the herring had hit the fish trade, and the repeal of the English Corn Laws in 1846 and cheap American supply had hit the grain export. True to the principles of free trade, the Danish farmer turned to the produce which his land was best fitted to supply. Gradually, farming became intensive, as Denmark, like England, could not compete with the cheap acreage of virgin soil in the soft and hard grain localities of America and Canada. With the loss of agricultural Slesvig, the need for intensive culture and more scienific farming became intensified and, unpalatable as the truth may be, the leading position of Denmark in dairy produce owes not a little to Prussia's act of gross political immorality. The growth of the merchant service has already been mentioned, and it is computed that in 1863 some three thousand merchantmen were flying the Danish flag. As might be expected in a land of islands and marine highways, railways were late in making their appearance. The Copenhagen railways on Sjaelland, and the district lines in Fünen and Jutland, date from the sixties. It was not till the twentieth century that railways spanned the Little Belt at Fredericia by a bridge which is the pride of the Danes. The seeming backwardness of railways is offset by the first-class ferry boats, many dating from the nineteenth century, which still bear witness to the fine engineering work of that time, plying as they do over the frozen water of the Great Belt. The newest boats, luxuriously equipped with restaurants, baths, and cabins, are infinitely more comfortable than the more widely advertised (pre-war) German service at Sassnitz.

The loss of Slesvig, the sorrows of the Danes living in that province and, in spite of all, the survival of the Danish language and culture, all help the ignorant foreigner to understand the value and influence of the Danish folk or high school to which reference has already been made. It was shortly after the first Slesvig war that the first of these institutions was founded by Kold. Realising the ignorance of many of the farmers, and the difficulty of persuading them of the value of anything but empiric and practical knowledge, he sought to bring education of a wider kind to their doors. Those acquainted with the good men of our East Yorkshire Wolds or the Dales will know full well what was the immensity of the task which he set himself to accomplish. The schools soon " caught on " in Jutland, where they were regarded as something more than merely " schools "—they were the centres of Danish culture, in no sense technical or vocational, and the more the Germans tried to suppress them, the greater became their influence and the more popular they became. Even the infamous governor, von Köller,[1] could not prevent the peasants from attending them, although any speaking the Danish language or expressing sympathy with the Danes were liable to expulsion on twenty-four hours' notice. These schools spread from Jutland to the rest of Denmark and, aided by the great spiritual leader, Grundtvig, they became the bedrock of Danish provincial education.

The cession of Slesvig necessitated a change in the November Constitution, and this caused considerable discord because the new constitution of 1866 altered the balance between the two Houses, and the Lower House found itself on equal terms with the Upper as regards taxation. Thus began a long and unedifying struggle for a constitutional government which it was believed had already been established in 1863. Before following the course of Denmark's history from this point, it is well to see the fate of Slesvig vainly waiting for the promised plebiscite. The first question to be settled was that of citizenship, and, by the Peace of Vienna in 1864, the Danes had to choose within six years whether they wished to remain Danish citizens, in which case they were to be considered Prussian immigrants, or whether they wished to become Prussian citizens. Many Danes "opted" for Danish citizenship, and crossed the frontier to await the promised plebiscite, but most remained to endure the scientific brutality of the Germans. When finally the abrogation of Paragraph V showed them that no hope remained of a plebiscite, they returned to their homes in Slesvig where they found themselves without any legal rights.

The Germans treated them as "outlaws", they had no rights of citizenship, they were not allowed to leave the country on a visit to relatives, they were expelled from their homes, and any form of resistance meant imprisonment or banishment. This desperate state of affairs lasted until 1907, when at last they were allowed to become Prussian citizens. It should be noted that the disabilities of parents passed on to their children. The agreement brought little relief, for this Danish element became the victims of forced sales of land, which passed into German hands. The main part of the Danish population in Slesvig, roughly 400,000, found themselves subject to a series of racial enactments designed to Germanise the whole province. At church, school and law court, the Danish language was forbidden. Instead, however,

---

[1] A few reports of his actions reached England, but as the South African War, 1899 to 1901, was in progress, they received no attention.

of lessening Danish patriotism, it made the hatred of the German more intense, and provoked sympathy among their fellow-countrymen across the border. The anti-German element in North Slesvig became very strong, but no active steps were possible to throw off the yoke of their oppressors. The people themselves kept alive Danish culture and habits. The Germans, always irritated at frustration and unable to understand any dislike of the Reich, gave a tighter turn of the screw—Danish songs, costumes, actors, and lecturers were forbidden, and finally, in the twentieth century, not a word of Danish could be uttered at any meeting or country revel. In fact, everything Danish was *verboten*. Yet the Danes did not lose their spirit and, at times, their sense of fun.[1] The educational and linguistic difficulties remained in South Slesvig, after the North had been retroceded in 1920, and it cannot be too strongly emphasised that language and national feeling do not coincide. Nearly all the inhabitants north of the line, Danevirke-Husum, are of Nordic-Danish race, excepting, of course, German officials. Gradually, the South Slesvigers adopted a Low German (*Platdeutsch*) containing many Danish words. Names of towns, agricultural implements and household implements, bear witness of this, and it is not German as we know it; but on each side of the 1920 border many Danes speak German but " feel " Danish, and many south of it speak Danish and " feel " German, and at the same time in both districts the opposite is the case.

The South Slesviger preserved his Danish customs and manners, and the countryside north of the Danevirke, with its low, long farms, presents a complete contrast to the broad, high gabled farm houses of the Holstein pattern. Two quotations[2] from observers, before and after the German occupation, are worth repeating as neither can be termed biased in favour of the Danes. Fallersleben, author of *Deutschland über alles*, wrote in 1845: " These Slesvigers have practically no interests in common with other Germans, except language; the Danish nature is engraved on them and shows itself at every opportunity." The English Secretary of the International Commission (1919-1920) wrote, in 1934 when the Nazi régime had begun to proselytise the Slesvigers, " There seems to be more sympathy between the people of North Slesvig

---

[1] A story went round that a young Dane reported his bird for trilling in a Danish manner, and wished the mayor to advise him what to do! Instructions were duly sent!

[2] Quoted by Claus Eskildsen in *The South Slesvig Question*.

(restored in 1920) and South Slesvig than between those of South Slesvig and Holstein. The Slesvig population is of the same descent and has the same culture. The difference in language does not separate as much as one often believes."

Here is an independent witness to the justice of the present claim that the portion of land from Slesvig to Flensborg should not remain in German hands. In spite of severe pressure for eighty years, the temperament of the people is Danish. In 1918 the defeat of the Germans once more brought the Slesvig question before the Powers and was assigned to a Danish-Belgian Committee who had to make its report. There were several schools of thought in Denmark. Scavenius, the Foreign Minister, primed by the great Slesviger hero, H. P. Hanssen, inclined to direct dealings with Berlin first, others wished to press for a plebiscite for North Slesvig only, others for plebiscites for North and Middle Slesvig, and others for a plebiscite covering all the country from Kongeaa to the Eider. H. P. Hanssen had done much for the Danes as an elected member of the Reichstag, and probably could have gained a more equitable method of finding out the wishes of the people. Be that as it may, in North Slesvig 75 per cent voted for a return to Denmark. This division was duly carried out, and the Danes have given full rights to the German minority. The Germans had to assent to the restoration of North Slesvig at Versailles, but they had no intention of abiding by that clause for ever. It is significant that the maps (German) issued to the British army on their entry into Slesvig in 1945 showed the boundary between Denmark and Germany as that of 1866 (Kongeaa) and not the Tönder line of the 1920 settlement—A little confusing for the average officer so regrettably ignorant of European history.

In the southern plebiscite (Zone 2) 12,000 Danes voted for a return, but the majority wished to remain German. Flensborg, an essentially Danish town with Danish schools, returned a Dane as deputy to the Reichstag (before 1933). Banks and other institutions remained with the conquered Germans. The moderation of the Danish claims were remarkable in 1920, as indeed they are in 1947. They firmly adhere to the principles of self-determination, and refuse to lay themselves open to the charge of aggression. At the Versailles Conference the director of the French Foreign Ministry opened with this statement. " In the Slesvig question . . . we are face to face with a government (the Danish) which asks for less than they have a right to demand." Such is the case to-day. A plebiscite of those who have resided in the zone between the Danevirke and Flensborg for twenty years would undoubtedly be in favour of a return to Denmark. Many joined the Nazi party, hoping for a relief from the tyranny of the German Government and deceived by promises and gifts.[1] They were sadly disillusioned, and it is the duty of the Allied Mission of Control to see that full opportunity is given to the Danish element to express their views. The German officials are still in their posts, but they must not be backed by the Allied ministers who represent the triumph of freedom over oppression. History in Slesvig is in the making, and this book deals with the past background from which one can see that peace and justice cannot be established if Danish Flensborg is dominated by German Kiel. A few examples of the mistaken attitude to the German and Danish populace may be cited as warnings. Two thousand Danish parents in Flensborg wished their children to be transferred to the Danish schools after the collapse of Germany in 1945. A general permission had not been given by March 1948. Danish political and cultural societies are not recognised except for fourteen days round about the time of elections. There are no restrictions on German societies, except, of course, the Nazis. One can only ask why and hope for a reasonable answer, but the only reply seems to be that the fairness of the Danish Government has been mistaken for indifference.[2]

The final verdict of history must be that the line should run from Danevirke almost due west to Husum on the North Sea. Historical geography would point to the Eider—*Romani terminus imperi*—but history is not static. The open-minded Danish Government would never press for the Eider because they, in 1947 as in 1920, ask for less than they could historically claim, and the lessons of the past have not been ignored. One other urgent problem which affects this " burning question " is the disposition of the

[1] These gifts took many forms, likely to appeal to a simple and not very happy folk. Children attending the German-controlled schools were presented with sweets, clothes and toys from " Uncle Hitler ", and the now familiar Nazi propaganda was dinned into their ears, till they were almost forced to believe that they, too, belonged to the " master race ".

[2] To realise the moderation of the Danish Government, it is necessary to read the démarche to the British Foreign Office, and the Danish " Hansard " on the subject. They afford an example to Europe. Self-determination is their principle and to this they have adhered " even though it were to their own hindrance "

three to four hundred thousand Germans from East Prussia and Pomerania. These upset the whole balance of Slesvig's economy. It is inconceivable that the British and French Governments (not to mention the Russian) who have guaranteed Slesvig to Denmark can tolerate this gross injustice which can only lead to war.[1]

The question of the promised plebiscite in North Slesvig was raised again and again until the crushing victory of Germany in the Franco-Prussian War of 1870–71 revealed the strength of Prussia and its determination to expand and keep its grip on the North Sea outlets. The scheme of the Kiel Canal, which utilised the Eider, revealed still more clearly the Germanising policy in the Duchies. Bismarck pretended till 1870 that he personally desired the plebiscite, but that the Kaiser was obstinately refusing to sanction it. The real reason for procrastination was to keep Denmark hoping, so that there would be no Franco-Danish alliance when the Prussian attack on France was delivered. At one time, there was more than a possibility of a blockade of German ports by a combined French and Danish fleet. The price for Danish help was to be the return of Slesvig. However, the Danes were not willing to give open aid until the French had shown their ability to resist the oncoming Prussians. This they never did, and the secret reports on the inefficiency of the French army, which had been received in Copenhagen proved correct. Thus the French fleet sailed alone, and the question did not arise again until 1918 and 1945.

Danish parliamentary history from 1866 to 1915 is concerned chiefly with three problems—the reform of the constitution, the defences, and the adoption of free trade or tariff reform. The two latter involved the finance of the country, and in the twentieth century on these rocks, ministry after ministry was shipwrecked. The "June" Constitution of 1849, which was finally passed in 1866, satisfied no party except the Conservatives, because the Upper House (*Landsting*) was not truly democratic, as half its members were nominated by the crown. Thus began the struggle of the two Houses, which was not finally settled until 1915. It was not unlike the struggle in England before the Reform Bill of 1832, but in Denmark there existed neither the will nor the way to enforce the wishes of the majority in the Lower House (*Folke-*

---

[1] The refugee question is dealt with in Appendix II, which contains a short account of present-day Danish opinion.

ting). Thus Estrup, a Conservative, ruled from 1875 to 1894 against the will of the majority, and was forced to use unconstitutional means to enforce his financial budgets, which were necessary to carry out his defence measures. The tempo of this conflict was heightened by the growth of the Socialist movement, which received encouragement and inspiration from the Parisian upheaval in 1871. Their paper, *The Socialist*, was edited by a Frenchman, Pio, but its demands do not appear extreme according to modern ideas. Free education and a free Press were prominently advocated and received support among men of all parties. Its demands for regular working hours and the abolition of child labour also had many supporters. Its demands for a single chamber and the separation of Church and State at once roused opposition, as they directly attacked vested interests. This opposition became stronger when the more intellectual student movement of the followers of George Brandes threatened the very foundations of traditionalism in matters moral and religious. The Socialists were not a parliamentary party in themselves, but their ideas affected various sections and helped to divide rather than to consolidate the members of the Folketing and Landsting. On one occasion, however, in 1920 it was a Socialist movement which attempted to bring direct pressure to bear on the Government. First, they declared in favour of a republic, and on the next day engineered a general strike. The elections which followed, ended in a Radical rout due to the indignation of peasants, burgesses and the professional classes at the use of "direct action". The nomenclature of the Danish parties is apt to be confusing to Englishmen accustomed to Conservative, Liberal, and Labour. There were three main divisions with sub-divisions: (1) Conservatives and "Free" Conservatives, usually, but not always, voting in concert, (2) Social Democrats and Radicals, often, but not always, in alliance, (3) Moderate Leftists and Leftists.

On the chief issues of the day, they did not find agreement even in their own parties, and the confusion became worse when the landowners and peasants also formed their own groups. The number of cross-sections prevented any single party having an absolute majority, and for a considerable time the seemingly "unnatural coalition" of Conservatives and Leftists opposed the Radicals and Social Democrats. The object of the Left during Estrup's long régime was to unite all "anti-right" elements under the leadership of Hörup and Berg. In the elections of 1879 to 1881, the Conservatives had a very small following in the Folketing, but a substantial majority in the Landsting. The differences between the Radicals and the Leftists proved too strong to take any united action, for the extreme Radical measures were repugnant to the Moderate Left. Estrup resigned in 1894 when the illegal methods of raising money by taxes not sanctioned by the Folketing or Riksdag as a whole, was threatening to bring about a revolution. Nothing is more repugnant to the Danish people, and a compromise was arranged that, provided Estrup resigned, no questions would be asked about the finances or the fortifications. Even then, the Conservatives managed to retain power until 1901, in spite of the increasing demand for a new constitution.

At last Christian IX appointed a Leftist, Deuntzer, to form a Cabinet representing the majority. Eager to balance the budget, the Cabinet proposed to reduce the defence forces and sell the Danish West Indies to the United States. This measure was narrowly rejected by the Landsting, and violent dissensions broke out between the Leftists and extreme Radicals. Deuntzer had to resign, and a Moderate Leftist, J. C. Christensen, became premier, with Radicals in opposition. This began the understanding between the Left and the Conservatives.

In 1906 Frederick VIII, aged sixty-three, ascended the throne, and first tried to secure a closer friendship among the three Scandinavian countries before dealing with the constitutional problem. He had married Louise, the only child of Charles XV of Sweden, and their son had become King of Norway (Haakon VII) on its separation from Sweden. This had caused no little irritation in that country, who saw the possible renewal of a strong Danish and Norwegian *entente*. A personal visit of Christian to Stockholm did much to restore confidence, and there was a revival of an All Scandinavian Alliance, which, however, did not come into being until 1914. The elections of 1906 had brought back the Radicals and Social Democrats in great force, and Christensen lost his absolute majority and had to rely still more on the Conservatives. He had to resign owing to the notorious " Alberti " scandal, who, as Minister of Justice, had robbed the State by fraud and embezzlement, and even forgery, of millions of Krone. He was imprisoned, and Berg and Christensen heavily fined. The country was shaken, and the cry for a responsible constitution became stronger. The

Left was prepared to carry through the reform and a new Electoral Law, but the Conservatives or the Radicals had to be won over to gain a majority. The Conservatives were opposed to them on the subject of free trade, for they still adhered to a tariff. The Radicals were opposed to them on expenditure on the forces. Finally, a compromise was made—there should be a tariff of 20 per cent on certain goods, and any members nominated to the Landsting should not be unseated for eight years. The Radicals offered their support, confident that a new Electoral Law and an elected Landsting would bring them into power.

It was not until the next reign under Christian X (1912–1947) that the Reform Bill was actually passed, and its execution was further delayed by the outbreak of the First World War. On June 5th, 1915,[1] the new constitution, one of the most democratic in Europe, came into force. The Folketing, consisting of a hundred and fifty-two, was to be elected by universal suffrage, except for nineteen members to be elected by the outgoing Landsting, so as to maintain some continuity. By an arrangement not unlike the Parliament Act (1911) in England, the Landsting can be dissolved if it rejects a bill already passed once or in some cases twice by the Folketing. This might lead to an election of the Landsting, while the Folketing was still deliberating, but, up to 1939 the impasse had not occurred. The successful conclusion of this long and wearisome struggle without violence or excessive bitterness was attributable to the good sense of the people, and the tact and "parliamentary-mindedness" of Frederick VIII and, still more, Christian X. This sovereign retained the affection and love of his people through the First World War and the German occupation in the Second.

His advice was followed in foreign affairs in those difficult times. Though many were disappointed that the Danish Government did not secure South Slesvig or, at any rate, Middle Slesvig, including Flensborg, the king's crossing the border on his famous white horse to free the Danes in the north, was marked by a tremendous outburst of popular feeling. Some 100,000 Danes assembled at Dybböl to greet their monarch. The events of the Second World War are too recent to allow any judgement to be passed, but two short stories reflect the courageous attitude of the

---

[1] June 5th also being the date of the 1849 Constitution is annually celebrated as a national holiday—the *Grundlovsdag*.

king and the affection of his people. When Hitler, through Renthe Fink, informed the king that he considered the " two sister countries of Denmark and Germany should be under one ruler," Christian replied, " You must talk to my son, I am too old to take over so many people." To the very end, he rode on his white horse in the parks unescorted. " Who is that man whom everybody is greeting so respectfully? " asked a German officer. " The King, our ruler and protector," answered a milk boy. " Where are his guards? " "We are his guards. Me, too." These stories are indications of how this constitutional monarchy has entered into the hearts of the people and helped to weld them together by the very institutions which the former sovereigns had suppressed for nearly three hundred years.

The First World War upset the balance of Danish life and economy although neutrality was maintained. In spite of the agreement of the three Scandinavian monarchs at Malmö, Denmark was pressed severely by both sides. The blockade and the unrestricted submarine warfare created a false economy. A few imports and exports were allowed to Germany, America and England by agreement and a system of assurance licences, later known as " navicerts ". This worked, but not well, and it was only the high prices of the goods which kept the Danish industries in a flourishing " boom " state. The sale of the West Indies, S. Croix, S. Thomas and S. Jean, to the U.S.A. in 1917, in exchange for the guaranteed possession of Greenland and a cash payment, brought only a temporary financial relief. In 1921 the inevitable crash came—prices fell and foreign goods were dumped. In 1922 there was a wild spell of speculation reminiscent of the South Sea Bubble and Law's Mississippi Scheme. This completely artificial recovery was followed by a worse catastrophe—the failure of the Landsmanbank and the fall of the rate of Krone. The Government had to come to the rescue, but it was not until 1926 that Danish trade began to continue the expansion which had been so gravely shattered. The chief features of her commerce were the co-operative and the smallholders movements which have placed Denmark in the front of dairy producing countries.

The skilful growth in technique, both of production and marketing, is attributed to the agricultural societies among the farmers themselves. Although there were pioneers in this or that direction, the movement was more universal and popular, and not under the lead of a Jethro Tull or "Turnip" Townshend. There were many "Turnip" Townshends. The folk schools, it will be remembered, were started for the farming community originally, and undoubtedly the intelligence and broad outlook of the average Danish farmer are very striking. Marketing boards were established at an early date, and throughout the twentieth century the closest supervision of the standard of exported butter, bacon, and eggs have prevented any inferior produce harming their reputation.

Other well-known exports found in every part of the world are the famous Tuborg and Carlsberg lager beers, which proved serious rivals to the German pilsener, and the exquisite Copenhagen porcelain, highly prized and fetching high prices all over the world.

In spite of the growth of these comparatively new industries, the sea still provides the main sources of Denmark's prosperity. The carrying trade, shipbuilding, salvage, towage, and the age-long fishing industry, occupy the greater part of the population. Although the State companies like the Asiatic Company had ceased to exist and Denmark has only Greenland as a national outpost after the sale of the West Indies, her carrying trade before the First World War, and in the decade before the Second, had encouraged the creation of the huge mercantile marine nearly as big as Norway's. The ships were largely chartered by other countries, though there were regular sailings to every part of the world. The Danish lines specialised in cargo liners—a comfortable and cheap form of travel, as well as a fast and profitable method of freightage—and it is interesting to note that not only are they continuing to do so, but this is being imitated in other countries. One example must suffice to illustrate this characteristic which also applies to Norway and, to a lesser extent, Sweden. One of the large Danish companies[1] has nineteen cargo liners varying in size from 10,000 tons (D.W.) to 1,500, with a total of just on 100,000 tons, four fruit refrigerator vessels totalling 13,000 tons, and only nine purely cargo ships with a tonnage of 18,000 tons. Services are run to North, South, and Central America, and, with less regularity, for passengers to France and England and the Mediterranean. The size of the ships is of interest, because it is characteristic of Scandinavian shipbuilding. Both naval and

[1] Lauritzen Lines. The proportion is similar in the fleet of the United Steamship Company, Denmark's largest trading company.

merchant ships are " small size ". The big battleship or the *Queen Elizabeth* was beyond the capacity of the Danish purse or their stocks. The whole mercantile policy of the Dane was distinctly shrewd, and displayed a remarkably clear and realistic appreciation of the competition which would be encountered in any attempt either to build or to run a large passenger liner. Hamburg and the North German Lloyd, with its *Bremen* and *Europa*, the Clyde and the Cunard, with its *Mauretania* and *Aquitania*, were suffici-ent deterrents, and the Danes became the specialists of a certain type. Even such vessels as the Swedish *Drottningholm* and *Grips-holm*, or even the Norwegian *Stavanger Fiord*, are the exception. Danish yards turn out the 3,000- to 10,000-ton ships to perfection, affording models of planning such as the familiar vessels running from Esbjerg to Harwich, and the popular " pocket liner " the *Venus* of 7,000 tons, built for the Bergenske Company's service from Newcastle to Bergen. The Danes do not try to compete with the " Queens " of the Cunard-White Star, but the finish and sea-worthiness of their ships of the smaller type need no advertise-ment. The seamen's quarters are usually far superior to those in English ships of the same tonnage, and the general welfare of the sailors is a matter of concern to managers and skippers. Again we notice the emphasis laid on the training of their sailors. Their nautical schools are first-rate, and it is the rule and not the excep-tion for all types of the ship's crew to have been educated at one of these " sea Folk Schools ".

It is too soon to say how the war has affected Denmark, but it can be stated that after their captivity, the sense of relief and freedom has permeated the whole nation. There is a vitality to be felt, they have not lost their resilience. Their own joys and pleasures have been restored—the theatre, music, the dance, and perhaps most characteristic of all, the bicycle, play their old parts. In a foreigner's mind, one doubt must occur. Is it in the best interests of a nation for one city to be so predominant as is Copenhagen?

In 1864, after the loss of Slesvig, the population of Denmark was 1,700,000; by 1914 it had risen to 2,800,000, of which Copen-hagen claimed no fewer than 600,000 inhabitants. It might well be that development should be planned on the west of Jutland to balance the oversized Copenhagen, and this could be done without ruining dairy land, through further reclamation. On the other hand we must remember that Denmark is a democratic free state, and that its co-operative tendencies are the outcome of individualism. Nothing would be more repugnant to the Danes than the enforced planning of a central office, and their speedy recovery bears witness to the endeavours of individuals working for the benefit of the State.

CHAPTER XIV

NORWAY AND SWEDEN FROM 1815

AFTER the Treaty of Kiel in 1814, the history of Sweden provides a sharp contrast with the past. In the long unbroken peace which that country has contrived to preserve to the present day, it may be said that movements have superseded personalities. This does not mean that great men did not exist, but they did not monopolise the stage. That Bernadotte or Charles XIV John, as he became, was a striking personality cannot be denied, nor indeed can the influence of Gustavus V, who began his reign in 1907, be considered negligible, but the interests and outlook of the nation seem no longer to depend so much on the royal leadership. They owe their inspiration to groups, following the lead of writers, statesmen and industrialists, or sometimes to associations bound together by mutual interests and aspirations. The movements are closely related, and acting and reacting on each other to such an extent that the democratic life, which is the feature of the Sweden of the twentieth century, seems to reflect the shades of opinion of all classes of society. From the very beginning of the nineteenth century, the new-born national literature becomes the parent of a liberal movement. This in its turn becomes parent to the Continental reformers and the educationists of the 'sixties. Together they are united in promoting a sense of the responsibility of citizenship, so essential for the administration of central and local government. The growth of industrialism, with the construction of the railways, synchronised with the development of educational and political ideas. The demand for Sweden's natural riches synchronised with the demand for knowledge and the progress of the arts and sciences. The people, owing to the educational enlightenment, developed a remarkably high standard of intelligence and thus the nation attained an unusual state of social advancement. Industry was not divorced from Art. As Lord Sempill aptly put it, " Sweden encouraged collaboration between Art and Industry with the most happy results. . . . A proper comparison could perhaps be made between the two countries (i.e. Britain and Sweden) by saying that, while in a colossal output Britain has good designs among a number of bad, Sweden on the other hand has less to show, but almost all are good." Employers and employees did not live on different planes, and there grew up a mutual sense of understanding without the degrading conditions which Disraeli described as the "Two Nations". In the twentieth century, Swedes of all classes are found anxious and willing to discuss such diverse subjects as education, steel, timber, art, science, and books. It must not be imagined that this national character was forged on one anvil at one period. It was a growth. Many of the characteristics can be traced far back into the history of the past, but they were not welded into one whole until Sweden was freed from the long series of wars which had been her fate for so many centuries.

Though Norway shared in the freedom from foreign war until 1940, it was a period of restless activity. Never happy in the union, she was engaged in a continuous political struggle till its dissolution in 1905. This was closely connected with the growth of the Liberal movement which ultimately under Sverdrup's leadership, found a peaceful solution of the disputes in complete separation of the two nations. The country had developed on totally different lines from Sweden. The Norwegians, always independently minded, built up a commercial fleet which by 1880 was second only to that of England. The trade of the country consisted almost entirely of timber and fish, and so great had the latter become that in the twentieth century its herring fleet was the biggest in the world. Sweden's industrial progress depended on her exports of manufactured, or partly manufactured goods and raw materials as well as timber, and her interests differed accordingly. The Norwegian mercantile fleet did not share in the Swedish carrying trade, nor were Norwegian products alone sufficient for their enterprising seamen, and soon Norwegian ships were found plying between foreign countries and sometimes not visiting their homeland for many years. This practice has continued to the present day, though the crews are usually able to return home at regular intervals. A present day example well known to Englishmen is the Fred Ohlson Line serving the Canary Islands and this country. Like the Danes, both Norwegians and Swedes specialise in the cargo liner type. This immense increase in the Norwegian mercantile fleets caused a demand for a separate consular service

in many lands. Norwegian interests and the Norwegian preponderance of tonnage, according to the Norwegian Radicals in the
Storthing, made this separation not only just but imperative for
the continued welfare of the country. The request was refused by
Oscar II, whereupon the ministers resigned and the question of
the consular service became one of the two principles on which
no agreement could be reached and ultimately led to the dissolution of the union.

It seems almost paradoxical that one of Europe's greatest
soldiers should have been the man to inaugurate this new era. It
would appear that Bernadotte was determined to keep Sweden free
from any entanglements which might lead to war at home or
abroad. Having forced the Treaty of Kiel on an unwilling
Denmark, he found Norway even more unwilling for the union
with Sweden. The Norwegians, always insistent on their equality
with Denmark, had been strongly influenced by the ideas of the
French Revolution and before the treaty had been agitating far
more independence. The Viceroy, Prince Christian, had shown
considerable understanding of their aspirations, and in 1811 had
been instrumental in founding the Norwegian University at
Christiania (Oslo). Here was a focal point where democratic and
national ideas could be discussed and the young men could air
Radical views and their Norwegian sentiments. Jarlsberg, the
leading statesman, was unable to stem the tide of national feeling.
He pointed out that, although the Danish king had freed the
Norwegians from their allegiance to him, Bernadotte had the
backing of Russia, Prussia, and England, and, having ceded
Finland on the understanding that Norway would be his, was not
likely to forego his demand. Undeterred, the National Party carried
the day. On May 17th, 1814, the Storthing passed "The Fundamental Law of Norway", based on the "1812 Constitution of
Spain "[1] and the French Constitution of 1791. They, furthermore,
elected Prince Christian King of Norway, and in spite of pressure
from the three powers they prepared to fight the Swedes. Bernadotte advanced slowly up through Bohuslän into Southern Norway.
The Norwegians fought bravely in the difficult country, but gradually fell back to Moss, where an armistice was arranged. Bernadotte acted with tact and moderation. He offered to accept the

---

[1] This "1812 Constitution" was the battle-cry of the Italian Revolutionaries
in 1820 and 1830.

Fundamental Law of Norway with such modifications as union with Sweden necessitated. Prince Christian laid down his crown, and was recalled to Denmark, and the Storthing accepted the union "under one king with Sweden", but Norway remained "free, indivisible and independent".

The king could appoint a viceroy in Norway when he was in Stockholm, but three Norwegians would be in attendance on the king to discuss their country's affairs. Foreign policy would be in the hands of the king, but the Norwegian navy could not be used except with the permission of the Storthing. By a curious clause, it was laid down that the Storthing should consist of one Chamber, but that this Chamber should elect one-fourth of its members as a Second Chamber. Any law which passed the Storthing three times could become law without the consent of the king. Whether this applied to a change in the Law of the Constitution or only to ordinary laws, was not specified. There was plenty of scope for trouble in this act of union, which resembled an alliance rather than a fusion of two governments.

Disputes arose immediately. Norway refused to pay her share of the Danish-Norwegian debt, as agreed by Sweden, nor would she acknowledge the retention of Iceland, the Faroes, and Greenland by Denmark under the Treaty of Kiel. On the latter question Norway's claims were ignored, and it was not until 1818 that the Storthing paid her contribution to the debt, and then only three-sevenths of the amount due. Charles XIV was personally popular with the Norwegians, but his ministers and viceroys were continually at loggerheads until in 1829 it was decided that no Swede should become a viceroy. However, the two countries were too divided in ideas and ways of life for the union to become closer. Each concession to Norwegian sentiment produced the wrong effect, and was regarded as a triumph for the separatists. When Oscar I (1844–1859) gave the Norwegians their own naval flag, the movement for full equality or separation began to take shape. Charles XV suggested the abolition of the post of viceroy, but his Swedish ministers refused their consent, maintaining that Norway was in a sense "the junior partner", who did not pay her full share of the expenses for defence. The Swedish ministers and people had from the very outset taken a misguided view of the union. Originally it had been considered a triumph of Swedish arms over a semi-revolutionary nation. They had failed to realise the co-operation which had existed between the very moderate Norwegian minister, Wedel Jarlsberg, and the first two Swedish viceroys. The significance of the abolition of the rank of "nobility" was entirely misunderstood. It was not aimed as they considered, at Swedish sympathisers. The harmless celebrations of May 17th, Independence Day, were interpreted as a separatist demonstration, until finally, acting on the advice of the honourable, but narrow-minded, minister Platen, the king decided to forbid the national festivities. Matters might well have reached a crisis earlier, had the Norwegian forces not been divided. On the one hand there arose a peasant party, whose leader Uland was a member of the Storthing for thirty years, until 1862. He aimed at complete reform of the finances and a social, though by no means ultra-socialistic, programme, within the union. This party had a more violently nationalistic section, led by a young poet, Wengeland, which styled itself the "Young Norway Party" in imitation of Mazzini's "Young Italians". In opposition to this growing Peasant Party, whose members actually comprised nearly half of the Storthing, another party was formed under an able writer named Welhaven to promote the cultural relations of the past with Denmark. As long as these parties worked in opposition to each other Sweden was able to hold the balance, and in spite of continued friction, the position of the Swedish king was not seriously threatened, and Norway as a whole was not strong enough to throw off the yoke, even if the people had tried to combine their forces. The middle of the century showed a great advance in the material prosperity of the country. Communications were improved by the construction of roads and a few railways, by a system of lighthouses which vastly increased the coastal trade, and the abolition of the Navigation Act in England in 1850 more than trebled the trade between the two countries in little over ten years. The educational reforms had begun to take effect, and rivalry between purely Norwegian parties had become less pronounced. There was a distinctly better feeling and more unanimity in their aims. The question of aiding Denmark in her struggle with Prussia in 1864 brought into prominence the problem of the constitution in its relation to the union. The king of Sweden wished to give active aid to the Danes, but the Storthing insisted with no little justice that a Western Power—England or France—must promise active assistance in order to ensure success. The result of this clash of opinion was the formation of a committee to revise the union. In 1869, the Storthing passed a law that it should sit annually instead of triennially, being justifiably alarmed that the government might make enactments without its assent. To pass this law, the two biggest Norwegian parties combined, and thence forward the government ministers found themselves confronted by a union of the Liberals and the Peasant Party under the two ablest Norwegians of that time, Johan Sverdrup and Sören Jaabok. This became the most powerful party in the Storthing, and supporters of the Conservative ministry under Stang were hopelessly outnumbered. Though known as "Leftists", the new alliance was in effect National Liberal, and Sverdrup was regarded as its head.

Oscar II (1872–1907) a man of understanding and culture, against the advice of his ministers, abolished the post of viceroy hoping thereby to appease the Norwegian Nationals and give that country a sense of equality. It was, however the system that was at fault. The members of the Cabinet were not necessarily members of the Storthing nor did they explain their measures in debate. The bill to enforce the attendance of ministers in the Storthing was passed in 1871, but Charles XV had died without giving his approval or using his veto. Sverdrup brought up a similar bill in 1874 as the policy of the Liberal party, but the ministers, alarmed at the growing power of the Storthing, took the view that this was a revision of the Constitution and could not be passed without the king's assent. This view was confirmed by the Faculty of Law at Christiania University. The struggle continued, and in 1880 the Storthing passed the bill for the third time and declared it to be law, without the king's sanction. The ministry refused to publish the bill. The crisis was reached in 1882. The king came in person to dissolve the Storthing, and delivered a speech from the throne on the veto. This raised the "Left" to a point of fury, and the national poet and playwright, Björnson[1] added the force of his popularity and his eloquence to the supporters of Sverdrup.

A free republic was openly discussed at the elections which followed, though never advocated by Sverdrup himself. The "'82 Elections" resulted in a clear majority for the Liberals[2], who gained eighty-three seats to the Conservatives' thirty-one. The

[1] For the literary work of Björnson and Ibsen, *vide* page 290
[2] The Alliance of 1870 had become one party—the Liberals.

Storthing proceeded to impeach the Cabinet; and its head, Selmer, who had succeeded Stang, and three others were fined and all deprived of office. The king did not quash the sentence, but asked Sverdrup to form a ministry. With this first Liberal ministry it may be said that parliamentary government was achieved. The ministry was responsible to the Storthing, and represented the majority, and it only remained to revise the Constitution so that the king should not appoint a minister unacceptable to the Storthing, and should not have more than a suspensory veto. Various joint commissions were set up, but agreement had not been reached when the question of the separate consular services arose. It involved the appointment of a minister for foreign affairs. The Commission suggested that the choice of a minister should lie with the king. He should be either Swedish or Norwegian and act for both countries. This was turned down, and the Norwegians demanded their own consular service. When this was refused, the Storthing claimed the right to appoint the service, and the Norwegian ministers resigned in a body.

Hagerhup, the Liberal leader, and his fellow ministers persistently refused to act and finally on June 7th, 1905, announced that "as King Oscar II has declared his inability to form a government, he has automatically ceased to reign". Swedish indignation rose high and war seemed imminent. Troops lined up on either side of the border. Happily, however, an agreement was reached, and the Treaty of Karlstad was signed. It declared the separation of the two kingdoms, defined the boundaries, and delineated a narrow neutral zone running from the Skagerak to latitude 61°. Another clause which has had unforeseen repercussions in the Second World War gave Sweden the important right of exporting iron ore to the port of Narvik. In a plebiscite it was determined by 260,000 votes to 70,000 to invite Prince Charles of Denmark to become king. Swedish irritation was once more aroused but finally allayed when it was clearly laid down that this did not imply a union between the two countries. Prince Charles duly ascended the throne·as Haakon VII and with his consort Queen Maud, daughter of Edward VII of England, was crowned in Trondheim Cathedral in 1906.

Since their accession, the country has advanced in every sphere of life. Freed from outside control, it has been able to display the independent spirit which has marked the Norwegian all down

the ages. In politics, the trend had been socialistic, though the
Liberal party was still strong before the German invasion of
1940. In 1907 Norway was the first sovereign state[1] to give a
parliamentary vote to women, though there were limitations on
unmarried women based on the amount of taxes paid. Compulsory education and a system of primary, secondary (middle)
and upper secondary (gymnasia) schools has been instituted, not
unlike the Swedish.

The most marked change has been in the use of electricity,
for production of which the waterpower was there ready to hand.
Every small cascade and mountain stream is harnessed to bring
light and power to the smallest hamlet. Forty regional power
stations supply light, heat and energy to the bigger towns and
modern factories. It was this rapid development which enabled
no fewer than two hundred and seventy factories to be established,
exporting in 1938 some 36,000 tons of goods, mostly fish, valued
at £2,210,000 and in 1937 paper and pulp (1,900,000 tons) valued
at £2,330,000. In 1937 Norway claimed to be one of the two most
electrified countries in the world. The power per inhabitant aver-
aged 3,189 kw. compared with 622 kw. in Great Britain. Her poor
land communications east and west hampered her trade, and it
was not until 1917 and 1930 respectively that the Bergen–Oslo
railway and the road on the south of the Hardanger Glacier were
completed. The chief means of transport still remains the coastal
steamers, which collect their cargoes at the small ports on the
deep indentations of the fiords or at the few large harbours on the
long seaboard stretching from Oslo to Narvik. These coastal
steamers and the huge fishing fleets are almost entirely in private
ownership or, in the case of drifters and trawlers, the ownership
is shared by the crews in proportion to their rank. The trend to
capitalisation and monopoly has been countered by state aid and
loans to the independent fishermen and other forms of legislation.
The only exception is in the whaling fleets, which belong to fifteen
companies employing some 10,000 sailors on their thirty-nine
whalers and twelve floating factories.[2] The total merchant fleet in
1939 was the fourth largest in the world, a truly astounding
achievement for a country whose total population in 1939 was only

[1] The vote had been given to women in Finland just previously but Finland
was at the time still part of Russia.
[2] These figures are for 1939. There have been some amalgamations since 1945
owing to war losses.

two and three-quarter millions.[1] The most interesting feature, however, is the extent of the international freight carried by Norwegian vessels. Only 10 per cent of Norwegian tonnage is employed on coastal trade and 20 per cent on trade between Norway and other countries, the remaining 70 per cent, without any government aid, in fact taxed somewhat heavily in its home country, is engaged between foreign ports. These statistics may appear dry and out of place, but they are quoted to illustrate the importance of Norway and the independent enterprise of the Norwegian of to-day. It is the same spirit which inspired Nansen in his Arctic explorations in the *Fram,* Amundsen in his North-West Passage expeditions and in his discovery of the South Pole in 1911. The Norwegians of the twentieth century seems to have retained many of the characteristics of their ancestors.

Happily, the relations between the three Scandinavian countries have been good since the dissolution and there is a tendency in some quarters to revive the "Scandinavismen" of the past, but this must be left to another chapter.

While Sweden and Norway were joined for ninety years in their uneasy union, the history of Sweden itself seemed quite unaffected by these continuous bickerings and disputes. It went its own way and that way was singularly dissimilar from its neighbours. Though Charles XIV was genuinely respected and his death in 1844 was deeply felt, he never understood the Swedish people, whose language he never learned to speak. He had lived through the French Revolution and the Napoleonic Wars and had seen the fall of many European dynasties. It is not difficult to understand why he feared the national movements and was suspicious of associations whose aims had to be explained to him by his ministers, who themselves were often swayed by prejudice. His actual coronation took place in 1818, for until the death of Charles XIII he had been acting as regent, but some years previously there had been a growing rebellion against the Gustavian pundits of enlightenment. The body of men who had founded the Swedish Academy had set up standards of literature which was shackled by French classicism. The Academy threatened to stifle native talent, unless it conformed to the principles somewhat

---

[1] In 1939 Norway's mercantile fleet had 4,800,000 tons of shipping, but in June 1945 she had only 2,700,000 tons owing to war losses. By January 1946 she had 1,400,000 tons on order in foreign yards, 300,000 tons in Norwegian yards and had bought 450,000 tons of second-hand ships.

rigidly propounded by such men as Kellgren, the able author of *Stockholmposten*. The first attack came from Atterbom and Almqhist who, besides displaying a strong romanticism in their writings, vigorously attacked the old school. The professor Atterbom soon fell into a strange and detached mysticism, while Almqhist passed from Liberalism to an extreme form of Radicalism. From their publication *Phosphoros,* they were known as " the Phosphorists ", producing their literature with a gospel not unlike that of Shelley and the Freedom School in England, but they soon became more and more revolutionary in theory and thought under the recognised leadership of Almqhist, who propounded Rousseau's picture of a primitive golden age. He, however, made no popular appeal to the man in the street who was not ready for such strong meat, and it remained for the well-known trio, Ling, Geijer and Tegnér to found a union which received support among all classes of Swedes. Ling is known throughout the world as " the father of gymnastics ". It is not so well known that he was also a poet, very popular at the time, whose works have no particular literary merit and even his own countrymen no longer read them, except out of curiosity or in an endeavour to discover the cause of their influence. His purpose was to stimulate the Swedes in mind and body by a free exercise of their natural gifts and by recalling to them the physical grandeur of their ancestors. It can be asserted without dispute that he endeavoured to fit them for a useful life of action and in this he achieved a success which has led to the adoption of his methods in Europe and America. The other two leaders of the " Gothic Union ", as it was named, were both poets, writers and professors, Geijer at Uppsala, Tegnér at Lund. Geijer produced the first consecutive and pragmatic histories of Sweden and its people. Great stress is laid on the deeds of the House of Vasa and to him may be ascribed the somewhat misleading view, which certainly still exists outside Sweden, that " her history is the history of her kings ". Both the *Annals* and the *History* are tinged with his purpose of making his readers conscious of their great past, though his work was not written with political bias. He has been called the Macaulay of Sweden, but with more justice can his brother-poet Tegnér be likened to Carlyle. In prose and poetry he extolled the past. His *Frithiof's Saga* was widely read, and by many his idealised account of ancient Scandinavia was taken as true history. He went still further, and many of his portraits of great men might well find a place in Carlyle's *Heroes and Hero Worship*. The Gothic Union and its writers had many sympathisers and readers who were not actually members of their association. It is not quite justifiable to liken this movement to Hitler's Youth and Strength through Joy movement. The aims of Ling and his friends were healthy and nationalist, but not directed against any race or class of society. It might indeed be said that they afforded an outlet for energy which might have been directed into aggressive military channels. The revolutionary movements in Europe had their repercussions in the Sweden of 1830, but they influenced thoughts, feelings and political beliefs, and did not lead to violent action. People were stirred and began to criticise their political environment, while a religious movement aimed against the formalism of the Lutheran Church caused a great awakening. It is comparable to the Salvation Army revival of a later date in that it appealed to the heart and threw a spotlight on conduct. The success of the Liberal movement in Sweden probably owes more to the religious sects than is usually allowed. In Germany, where the old narrow Lutheran faith retained its hold, it is worth noting that Liberalism died away after the " Year of Revolution " (1848). Both the Swedish movements were in their respective ways based on an awakening of the mind, and the Liberals at first found their supporters in the new broader-minded Lutheran congregations who had begun to gather strength a decade earlier.

A focal point for these separate tendencies was found in the foundation of a Liberal newspaper—*Aftonbladet*—to which both Geijer and Tegnér became contributors under the editor and founder, Hierta.

The full force of the Liberal movement was not felt till the death of Charles XIV, when the new king—Oscar I, a Swede in every sense, showed himself to be in full sympathy with its promoters. It was considered that the time was ripe for a change in the constitution which would quicken parliamentary procedure, hampered as it was by the four estates with their equal powers. Two factors, however, delayed the proposed reforms. In the first place, agreement could not be reached as to the form which the new constitution should take. If, as the majority wished, there should be two Houses, should they both be elective? If so, should the voters be required to have different qualifications for electing members of the two Houses? Should there be a certain proportion of royal nominees? While these and other questions were being debated in 1848, revolutionary movements broke out in nearly every European country. The king and the Conservative party were alarmed. Others also considered that it was not the time for a change which might arouse any kind of popular agitation. This *volte face* on the part of Oscar I and his ministers might well have incited the people to some form of demonstration or even revolution had the country not been entering a period of intense industrial activity and prosperity. It was not until the feverish burst had somewhat died down that the new constitution was introduced, in 1866, on Liberal lines. Charles XV was fortunate in having two exceptionally able ministers in Louis de Geer and Grippenstedt, who were competent to guide the State in its constitutional and industrial policy.

A cross-section of the Liberal party turned its enthusiasm into " Scandinavismen ", a revival of the old idea of a general union of the three kingdoms. Oscar I was himself a supporter of the movement and he dreamed of ruling Scandinavia, or at any rate of being the guiding force. Russia viewed the growing *entente* with extreme disfavour, and when France tried to enlist the aid of Sweden in attacking her at the outbreak of the Crimean War, the situation became delicate. In 1855, Napoleon III, supported by England, signed the " November Treaty " guaranteeing the integrity of Sweden and Norway in case of war with Russia. Its publication had two immediate effects. The Czar, thinking that now Sweden was about to declare war and attempt the recovery of Finland, which had been loosely governed by Russia since 1809, made overtures for peace, which led to the end of the Crimean War. On the other hand, Danish opinion was alarmed lest she should become involved in a Russian war if the Scandinavismen continued to influence Baltic politics. Russia, freed from her commitments in the Crimea by the Peace of Paris, intimated through her ambassador in Stockholm that she might regard some features of this revival as a hostile act, and it was allowed to die a slow death. For a short period the reading public turned to works with nationalistic themes. Runeberg, the Finnish writer, took his place as one of the greatest Swedish writers of all time. In Europe he was best known for his epic on the struggle of the Finns against the Russians in the 1809 war, but his poems dealing with Scandinavian mythology were very popular in Sweden. The break from this type of writing was sudden. It might almost be described as a revolt against the romantic idealism tinged with liberalism which had marked the cultured works of Rydberg and Snoilsky. The "eighties" yielded place to the "nineties" with a more abrupt transition than in England, though in neither country were the giants thrown off their pedestals. Lyrical poets and stark realists grew up around them. Engström, though not the most distinguished perhaps, hit the popular taste with his books on the life of the people as it was, not an idealised picture of what it might have been. But the Swede to hold sway inside and outside his own country was August Strindberg, who died in 1913. His novels and plays cover a wide field and are not all of the same merit. His first drama to bring him fame was produced as early as 1878. In this play his treatment of the national figure Olaus Petri displayed consummate ability, and at the same time appealed to the taste for national themes. Though a great favourite in Germany, *Father Olof* did not meet with much success in Anglo-Saxon countries. The theme did not appeal to countries singularly ignorant of Sweden, both medieval and modern. His bold novels, such as *The Red Room*, brought his work before a wider field and after he had adopted a form of individualistic mysticism he was recognised as an outstanding genius. By the twentieth century critics placed him as the foremost of playwrights, and he undoubtedly inspired the realist writers of other countries. Strindberg, however, had a style so individualistic that his followers of the Swedish realist school failed to achieve success outside their own country.

The Liberal movement in Norway claims to have had a completely separate existence from that across the border, a further piece of evidence of the spiritual separation of the countries of the union. Björnson, the most noted writer of his time, became immersed in politics, and his later works, which had such a strong appeal at the time, have not the literary merit to have endured in countries save his own. The same cannot be said of Henrik Ibsen (1829–1906). His life for fifty years was a hard struggle. His theatre at Bergen went bankrupt, though happily it was restored shortly before the First World War, and he did little better at Christiania. In early life, he and his family suffered from extreme poverty, which compelled him to work for seven years at an apothecary's shop. His bitter experiences coloured his first writings, which also showed the influence of the Danish poet Ohlenschläger. In his first purely Norwegian play, *The Warriors of Helgeland*, he followed a new and original line freed from Danish tradition. It was a complete failure and his genius was not recognised. In 1862 the Storthing refused a grant to save him from dire poverty. Disgusted, he left the country, and from Copenhagen, Berlin, Trieste and Rome he began to pour that famous stream of plays denouncing the political and social life of the day, and upsetting all traditional beliefs in the sanctity of married life. He was acclaimed on the Continent as one of the greatest dramatists of his time. He did not confine himself to drama, and *Peer Gynt* is still considered in some quarters the most finished of his works. In *The Doll's House* (1879), he upset the conventions of the stage, and its realism offended the taste of many critics. It was strong meat for those days, but its power was unquestioned. *Ghosts*, in 1881, raised a storm of protest in some quarters. A satirical comedy in the following year, *The Enemy of the People*, dealt in an amusing manner with the efforts of a doctor to better the sanitary arrangements of his village, and achieved as much popularity as *The Doll's House*; and, incidentally, a saying in Act IV became an English cliché in the form— " The minority is always right ". His dark and gloomy *Wild Duck* still finds a place in the modern repertory theatre. In the 'nineties, Ibsen was introduced to England, and by the end of the century he was honoured by his own land, where his statue was erected on his seventieth birthday at Christiania. His originality and his sincerity and his power are admitted by all, though some dramatic critics still refuse to rank him among the everlasting band of world writers.

In sculpture, art and architecture, the nature of the Swede has been able to express its true self. Its statuary has an appeal to the many and is not the perquisite of a rich aristocracy. It is venerated and admired by the people in a manner reminiscent of ancient Greece. Their squares contain a wealth of good art which has upheld the traditions of their master sculptor—Sergel (1740–1814). Besides his well-known statue of Gustavus III at Stockholm, he produced many portrait busts, notably Queen Sofia Magdalena. He was followed by Per Hasselberg, and in the twentieth century

Carl Milles has proved himself to be an imaginative and yet restrained sculptor, particularly esteemed in America. The high level of Swedish sculpture recalls the "vivantia marmora" of Athens, and one cannot help feeling that the same intangible impulse which springs from a cultivated democracy has inspired their work. Just as their architecture shows a wonderful blending of designer, craftsman and builder, so their statues seem to fit in with their surroundings, whether outside or inside their buildings. The Swedes possessed a tradition of careful architectural design dating from the seventeenth century, and modern Swedish architecture has not lost its national features in acquiring a freshness of style which has been so happily applied to public buildings and even the humble middle-class house. Their huge blocks of flats are less offensive than most and some display a pleasing combination of straight lines. One of the outstanding examples of modern Swedish architecture is the famous town hall at Stockholm, which is not only admirable in itself, but in spite of its daring contrast to its environment is so exactly right in its honesty of design, seeming to proclaim its purpose and disdaining to pretend to date from the days of Gustavus Vasa. The result is an achievement worthy of the Italian Renaissance, when the artist and the master builder seemed to co-operate in creating something worthy of their town . . . and their own Creator.

Space does not permit more than a cursory account of the large and varied band of Swedish artists. Carl Larsson (1853–1919), with his spacious canvases in pre-Raphaelite style, his landscapes and his portraits (especially the "alive" portraits of children), was one of their leading artists at the beginning of this century, and shows a strong difference from the work of the early Swedish school (*circa* 1800) of von Breda, Roslin, as also does Linnquist from Martin. The delicate landscapes of Prince Eugen are justly prized for their merit, not merely for their royal creator.

There is a modernist school and a realist school which are less essentially Swedish, and a certain cult for "conversation" pieces. These, like Cederström's *Charles XII's Last Journey (Likfärd)*, portray historical events and not merely domestic scenes. The Norwegian and Danish artists, apart from their impressionist work, excel in this form of art—such as Munch and Wehenshiold in Norway and J. F. Willumsen and Hammershöj in Denmark.

Sol och Ungdom (Willumsen) is a masterpiece of this type. However, to a visitor, the most remarkable feature is not the art itself
but the interest of the ordinary man in art. The workman, the
artisan, the woodman and the rest want a picture in their room.
They are not content with an advertisement print or photo of a
film star stuck up on their walls. Why is this? That question is
not easy to answer. It is not enough to say that artistic design
in textiles and glass[1] and in nearly every article of domestic
use must be good. It merely brings the inquirer one stage further
back. Whence arises this demand? Perhaps the answer can be
found in the history of the last seventy years. The expansion of
mind which demanded a fuller education was accompanied by
the expansion of political responsibility, and these began to thrive
in the same period of Swedish history, which witnessed the
greatest expansion of industry. The same generation experienced
the granting of the constitution, the growth of the primary, real
(middle) and high schools, the voluntary folk schools for adults,
the introduction of railways, the immense development of the
timber trade, and the revival of iron, steel and copper industries.
Education was largely responsible for the fact that the native
talent for the appreciation of beauty which, though unexpressed,
is inherent in the inhabitants of a beautiful country, and was not
divorced from industry. It was no doubt fortunate for Sweden that
their Second Industrial Revolution (if the period from 1870 to
1900 can be so called) came late in their history, and that the
demand for education began to be satisfied earlier. It was no
doubt fortunate that responsibility in parliamentary and local
government was bestowed at about the same date, but it must be
admitted that the nation seemed conscious of what was going
on around it and took full advantage of the opportunities
offered. The people, or at any rate their leaders, must have been
aware that political liberty and manhood suffrage for an uneducated people means chaos, and that lack of understanding between
employer and employee means strikes. There may be subsidiary
reasons for the high standard of social progress, but these considerations disclose the main factors why, to the foreigner, the
Swedes appear to have solved the art of living.

---

[1] The beautiful designs and good quality of Swedish glass and china—mass-
produced—afford perhaps the most striking evidence of this combination of art
and industry.

It has already been described how the European situation combined with a lack of unanimity at home led to the postponement of constitutional changes till 1866. When agreement was ultimately reached as to the form and mechanism for the new form of democratic government, a constitution was established which has proved efficient and remained basically the same, and experience has demanded but few alterations. The main changes are the introduction of universal suffrage instead of manhood suffrage in 1918,[1] and proportional representation for both chambers. By these means parliamentary government and local government, which plays an important part in Swedish economy, were placed on the same electoral footing.

The Second or Lower Chamber consists of two hundred and thirty members and has to be re-elected every four years. The constituencies represent regional areas based on a combination of population density and area. The First, or Upper Chamber contains a hundred and thirty members, of whom one-eighth retires each year. This system of partial annual election is designed to reflect popular opinion during the session of each government and acts, together with the annual municipal elections, as an excellent barometer of political feeling. In order to ensure the representation of ability as well as party opinions, the candidates for the First Chamber are not chosen on purely regional grounds, and several from one district may be elected at the same election. They are not considered as representing any particular district, and in practice they are chosen in the national interest on their personal qualifications. There are seven main standing committees dealing with such matters as the budget, the constitution, trade and foreign affairs, and these prepare the bills and reports for the two Houses. This system is a relic of the old constitution of 1634, but the choice of these committeemen is entrusted to the parties in proportion to their respective numbers in the Second Chamber. In the event of a dispute between the two Houses, the resultant deadlock is avoided by a mass vote if the suggested amendments to the bill are not accepted after further deliberations by the committee. In practice this has worked satisfactorily, and the clogs to administration which might have been expected from a house containing no less than four parties have not been experienced. These parties, Social Democrats, Liberals,

---

[1] Married women had been given the Municipal vote in 1862.

Conservatives, and Farmers, have co-operated in a surprisingly harmonious fashion. The rise of the Social Democrats under the able leadership of Hjalmar Branting was marked by moderation and good sense, in fact the more extreme " Leftists " have broken away and formed a small party of their own. This was not altogether unlooked for, because the Social Democrats contained a great number of the old Liberals, and the party somewhat unjustly has been accused of disregarding the aspirations of the working man. After the so-called democratic revolution, the Conservatives were the leaders of the opposition, and those who remained Liberal formed a centre party which could, until 1923, determine the form of government in spite of the solid Farmers' block. Only twice, 1923 to 1924 and 1928 to 1930, have the Conservatives been able to command a majority, and only twice have Conservative governments been in power, 1926 to 1928 and 1930 to 1932. On none of these occasions was there an absolute majority. The general rule has been coalitions, e.g. Liberals and Social Democrats 1917 to 1920, and Social Democrats and Farmers 1936 to 1938.

The figures of the 1938 elections give an idea of the state of the parties.

	First Chamber	Second Chamber
Social Democrats	69	115
Farmers	24	36
Conservatives	41	44
Liberals	15	27
Socialists	0	3
Communists	1	5
	150	230

In 1947 the Social Democrats had still 115 representatives, but there has been a swing away from the Conservatives towards Liberalism and, to judge from municipal elections, there is every likelihood of a still further consolidation of the Liberals. The Farmers' party does not ally with either the Conservative, Liberal or Social Democrat parties except on specific questions, and only once for a short period in 1936 could it form a government. It should be noted that a change of government does not necessarily mean an election, the usual practice being for an alliance to be reached between two or more parties. The tendency at present is for all to unite against the Social Democrats on all matters involving some fundamental principle. In face of a national crisis, remarkable good sense has been displayed by all parties, and theories have been discarded to gain unanimity in solving immediate problems. This happy state of affairs is due in no small measure to the initial leadership of the Socialist party being centred for so long a period in the farseeing Branting. He insisted that the only weapon to be used in the parliamentary struggle was the proper use of the franchise. This co-operation, not reached, be it said, without some bitter debates, successfully coped with the housing and unemployment problems which arose from the world slump of 1929 to 1931. The two were linked together by means of state and local loans. The Social Democrats did not wish the State to enter the building industry but, by means of loans, to work through private firms or through individuals themselves, who constructed their own houses. The cost of this private building had to be repaid in twenty years or less, when the tenant became the owner. Industry, especially agriculture and forestry, was stimulated by loans which enabled new lands and new forests to become productive, and the inhabitants afforded an increased home market. The " new deal " was neither socialist nor capitalist. It was merely realistic. For two years loans were granted for public enterprises; on the third year the grants were made out of revenue, and on the fourth the short-term loans were repaid and income tax was actually reduced. This does not imply that the loans of the State to the householder were repaid, but that the borrowings by the State to make the grants had been repaid to the lenders. The system of state grants for houses, for university training or vocational training is continuous, but of the total " crisis loans " to private enterprises (viz. 14,040,000 Kr.), no less than 6,645,500 Kr. had been repaid according to plan " by 1938.[1]

The State exercises considerable control over forests by insisting on afforestation and preventing over-felling in any particular area, but the timber trade is in the hands of companies. To encourage people to live near the forests and in forest clearings, rent of land is fixed on principles strictly in accordance with the economic margin of cultivation, so strictly in fact, that in 1937

[1] An excellent account of the " New Deal " is given by the Norwegian economist Braatoy in his *New Sweden*, from which these figures are taken.

and 1938 an acre could be rented in one forest district for one Krone, thus giving space for house and garden. The fixation of rent is also based on economic principles, though certain reductions are granted for families "rich in children", as the clause puts it. The existence in flats in the towns was considered to be discouraging to family life unless special measures, of which this is one, were definitely taken to ensure adequate care of children. Another striking example of realistic co-operation is furnished by the combined efforts employed to meet the disastrous collapse of the immense Swedish Match Company. This undertaking, under the personal management of Ivan Kreuger, was the first international enterprise of New Sweden. It had secured state monopolies for the manufacture of matches in Germany and Italy, and had ramifications in nearly every European country except England, and was extending its interests to the continent of America and the Far East. The Swedish nation was proud of the achievements of its wonderful organisation at Jönköping. Then the crash came. Kreuger disappeared from a 'plane. Chaos and bankruptcy followed, which involved the banks and the Swedish shareholders who had staked their savings in this modern "South Sea Bubble." The State Bank came to the rescue and the industry was saved, though individuals lost money, as did also the governments of Mussolini and Hitler. It was not a swindle, but its failure was due to overcapitalisation and paper assets of no value at the moment. Given five years' credit it would probably have succeeded. These recoveries from a world slump and a disaster of this magnitude could have been achieved only in a balanced democracy which relies on citizens of all classes for its support. The local government has more freedom of action in dealing with local affairs, and the proportion of regional taxation compared with central is higher than in most countries, being in the ratio of five to six and a half. This undoubtedly partly accounts for the number of citizens taking part in municipal and provincial councils and committees. It is reckoned that as many as 34 per cent of the adult population takes some share, while the number of wasted and unused votes in elections is lower than in any country in Europe.

What, then, is the position of the king, who by tacit agreement asks the leading member of the party controlling a majority to form a ministry? He is the only minister who never resigns and his advice, based on long experience, is undoubtedly sought by his ministers. It must also be remembered that with three or four parties, negotiations to bring two parties into alliance, to form the required majority, are sometimes only successful through royal tact. The veto is practically non-existent since the establishment of complete democracy through universal suffrage in 1918. The disturbances of 1917 are not likely to be repeated. The king represents the nation and has an influence on foreign policy which it is hard to gauge. It is no easier to assess the personal influence of Gustavus V than that of Edward VII at the time of the *Entente Cordiale*. It is usually admitted that he was the prime mover in the neutrality pact of the three Scandinavian nations in December 1914. In the very delicate negotiations over the Åland Islands, it is believed that he did much in supporting Branting, who was faced with the unpalatable duty of appearing to desert Swedish interests at the League of Nations. The prime minister himself stoutly espoused the cause of the Swedish inhabitants who had come under Finnish sovereignty after the Russian Revolution and desired to revert to Sweden. True to the binding clauses of the League of Nations, the prime minister in the name of the king yielded to the surprising report of the League's legal *rapporteurs* that the islands were part of Finland and that the Swedes, comprising no less than 94 per cent of the total inhabitants, had not the right of self-determination. It was undoubtedly a difficult case because the islands had been taken over by Russia a century earlier and were in 1856 acknowledged to be under her rule. Sweden's self-abnegation gained universal praise and royal visits established more cordial relations with Finland, while the Ålanders were allowed a generous freedom—almost amounting to independence—in their own government. Until more is disclosed of the attempt in 1939 to form an alliance similar to that of 1914, it is as impossible to form a just judgement on the failure as it is to understand why the followers of Quisling in Norway favoured the German invasion. All that can be said with any degree of accuracy is that a note was sent to Norway, Denmark and Finland inviting their representatives to discuss the project at Stockholm. Perhaps then, it may be said that the king has more direct and indirect influence than had Edward VII and less than Queen Victoria. The orderly change to constitutional monarchy reflects great credit on Oscar II (1872–1907), one of the most gifted of all the kings of Sweden. His predecessor and elder brother, Charles XV, had never been willing to accept the position, though actual conflict had been avoided through the tactful work of his minister, Louis de Geer.

Oscar, who devoted himself to his royal duties, was one of the leaders in the development of the new constitutional machine. He and his ministers overcame opposition to democratic measures by the Conservatives and to necessary expenditure on defence by the Farmers' party. It would almost appear that they had studied Disraeli's *Coningsby*, in which Taper said musingly, " Tory men and Whig measures ", and possibly had read his speech in the House of Commons on the Education Bill (1874)—" Upon the education of the people the fate of this country depends ".

Oscar II, owing to the failure of his attempts to weld Norway and Sweden into one nation, has never received his due mead of praise. It was in his reign that the political, industrial, intellectual and artistic life of his people made such progress, and in all he (often it is true, relying on the judgement of his minister Boström) gave much encouragement to these diverse activities. Great as these were, the most fundamental of all was the educational system which has rendered the Swedes the most educationally-minded people in Europe. Even the Danes, from whose Grundtvig the Swedes originally borrowed the idea of their adult schools, have not the same reverence for education. Besides the four grades of free child and adolescent education, the primary, the real (or middle), the high school and the gymnasium, they have a wealth of institutions for further education besides the university and technical college. These form the distinctive feature of Swedish education and mark the blend of democracy peculiar to that country. These schools are blessed by the State and inspected by the State, but are not run by the State. They are in a sense denominational, as their names and origin plainly show. The earliest were the Farmer's Folk Schools, which owed their inception to the Danish models. These were followed by others, founded by the great Temperance Societies, Christian bodies, and finally by the A.B.F. (Workers' Educational Association) in 1912. They provide the widest possible curriculum of subjects— art, music, languages, history, science, economics, and in some cases " refresher " courses in technical subjects. Their object is to provide a broad education which will fit the students for the art of living and the duties of citizenship. They are widely attended by men and women ranging in age from twenty to forty-five and even older. Besides these regional adult schools, there are many correspondence courses which give advice for reading and study. They are patronised by people of all ages in town and country, and one such establishment boasts over twenty thousand correspondents a year. So great is the thirst for knowledge that sailors spend their spare time studying " their courses " as their profession prevents attendance at the other schools. Englishmen have an innate prejudice against correspondence courses because they have been accustomed to associate them with examinations and not education. These Swedish courses are tutorial and advisory, and the term superficiality could not be used in their connexion.[1] The consequences of this diffusion of knowledge are noticeable in the number of provincial newspapers, which regularly contain articles of a high order on books, music, art, drama, and scientific subjects. This can only mean that articles of educational value and interest have a " box office " worth. In some cases they are on the front page with headline news. Another consequence attributed to the schools is the understanding of other people and economic and political issues. The number of strikes is remarkably low—the direct action strike in 1902 and that of 1909 did not meet with the approval of the trade union leaders, who since that date have drawn a line between politics and industrial conditions. These were the only big strikes until the miners' strike in the last war. In a country which became industrial in such a relatively short space of time, the absence of friction is unique and bears testimony to the efficiency of the Arbitration and Conciliation Boards and the good sense of employees and employer.

The transformation of Sweden from being an agricultural into an industrial, agricultural and mercantile country was swift, and the steps are more clearly cut than in most similar movements. It should be explained that the use of coal in the iron industry had handicapped Sweden so heavily that her exports by the middle of the nineteenth century had fallen to a negligible quantity. Her charcoal smelting could not compete with the coal

[1] As illustration, it is worth quoting a personal experience when becalmed in a fog in a canal boat on Lake Vättern. The skipper who spoke perfect English was reading one of the three " good " English books, which he purchased annually. Their names—Trevelyan *History of England*, *Anthony Adverse* and Huxley *Ends and Means*.

smelting of England or Germany. Thus she had reverted to agriculture. Happily for her, as the demand for iron ore declined, the demand for her timber rose. For this trade, the railways and canals were developed at precisely the right moment, and by the 'sixties the lumber was tumbling down the inland rivers to the ports or being borne from the lakes by rail. Electricity was introduced in place of charcoal and coal wherever possible, and with waterpower in every valley, the new white coal drove the looms for the textiles, the saw mills for the lumber; yet the wealth of the mines in Dalarna and farther north could not be exploited in face of the modern methods adopted in other countries with coal on their doorsteps. An enterprising Swede named Göranson heard of Bessemer's experiments in South Wales and went to investigate the results of the new discovery. He saw its apparent failure but diagnosed the cause, which lay not in the method but in the ore on which it was tried. On his return to Sweden, after two unsuccessful attempts, he solved the problem of applying the Bessemer method and in a few years Swedish steel was the most prized in the world. Bessemer acknowledged his debt to Göranson, who as a true scientist had communicated his ideas to Bessemer, the inventor. Then he in turn experimented in Cumberland with complete success and the Bessemer steel process, after further experiments, was adapted to ores varying in content and malleability. The history of the oldest company in the world, and now one of the largest—the Stora Kopperbergs Berlags—illustrates the stages of the changes in Sweden's industrial history. The "Stora", as it is usually called in England, Sweden and all the world over, dated from the fourteenth century and was concerned with the copper mines. By the twentieth century it had added timber and iron, and as the demand for timber increased, so did the acreage under its control. Electricity provided sawmills, and with the revival in the iron industry its factories, forests, mines and agricultural land (and its own port) cover no less than 650,000 acres. This huge growth of mining interests, extending into the land of the Lapps, explains the importance of the agreement in 1905 which ensured the outlet through the Norwegian port of Narvik. The increasing volume of trade, which quickly recovered from a temporary slump in the 'seventies—the years of emigration —necessitated a corresponding increase of tonnage. Göteborg became the great port of Sweden, "Little London" as it was called, and docks and shipyards sprang up like mushrooms. It is remarkable that all the nine biggest shipping companies of Sweden, with the exception of one, date from 1890 or after. The Swedish American Line with three large liners was not established until 1914, but purely passenger liners are unusual; in fact, except for those of the Svenska Lloyd, it can be said that the Swedes, like the Danes, specialise in cargo liners. These provide first-rate, though limited, passenger accommodation, and maintain constant services with every part of the world.

The Swedes are justly proud of their mercantile marine which marks for them a return to the pristine greatness which brought them into contact with the civilisation of other countries. This civilisation they have enriched in the last century by their example of peaceful industry and intelligent political and social progress. It has been erroneously implied and even stated that since the days of Napoleon, Sweden has led an isolated and uninspiring existence in a corner of Europe. She has staged no wars and no revolutions, she has founded no colonies, she has grabbed no territories. By these antiquated standards, her history may be reckoned dull. Her achievements have lain in other spheres. She has shown that a nation can combine culture with industry, can maintain her dignity without military aggression, can establish a true democracy in which all citizens play their part, and can take a justifiable pride in herself without trying to impose her ideology on nations whose social progress is less advanced.

CHAPTER XV

ICELAND AND FINLAND

ALLUSION has already been made to the changes which the events of the early part of the nineteenth century brought to the outposts of Scandinavia—Iceland and Finland. No countries in the North present sharper contrasts in their early history, and the only point of similarity during the last thousand years is that each has preserved its own unique national characteristics in spite of the fact that both have only achieved the status of a sovereign state within the last few years. Finland received her famous "July Independence Bill" from Russia in 1917, but it was not until the election of Ståhlberg as president in July 1919 that the new republic achieved real independence. On October 20th, by the Treaty of Dorpat (or Tartu as it is called in Estonia), Soviet Russia recognised the Finnish Republic while taking the province of East Carelia and allowing Finland a corridor to the Arctic Ocean with the port of Petsamo. Iceland, without bloodshed, declared herself independent of Denmark in 1944, relying on the old charter of her union with Norway dating from 1264.

While the origin of the Finns is wrapped in mystery, no country has so full and detailed an account of early times as the Icelanders. There is no break from 874 A.D., when Arnason, a Norwegian, first settled in the island. Who were the Finns? The question has been asked many times and there is no positive answer. They were not Slavs nor Teutons nor Mongols and do not form part of the Scandinavian people, but as their history is so closely connected with Sweden since they were conquered and christianised and then partially organised by Saint Eric, the Englishmen Nicholas Breakspeare and Bishop Henry, and Earl Birger, some account of their history is relevant and necessary. They probably migrated up from between the Urals and the Volga in the days of the "Wanderings", some branched into Hungary, some arrived in Estonia and thence in two streams they penetrated into Finland, part going by land round the Gulf and part crossing direct. In Estonia and Hungary, some words are allied to the Finnish, but it is possible that the Hungarian words were brought by the Heruls on their journey through Estonia at a later date.[1] In Iceland, the written word dispels any need for speculation. It is known that Irish monks had visited the island at the end of the eighth century and some were probably there when the first Vikings arrived. The settlers in 874 found their books and other remains and certain place-names lead us to suppose that all had not gone back to Ireland. For the next fifty years, new settlers continued to arrive from Norway, Scotland and Ireland. The Norsemen predominated and it is a matter of controversy how far the Celtic influence helped to shape the culture which in two centuries so far surpassed that of Scandinavia proper. In 930 the Althing, a central parliament, was established, and a thousand years later its millennial anniversary was held on the flat rocky plateau where it had been inaugurated. Representatives and visitors from many countries attended the celebrations. Some shrewd observers were impressed with the independence of the inhabitants and ventured the prophecy that sooner or later Iceland would be separated from Denmark and become independent, or suggest some kind of alliance or loose union with Norway.

The thirty-nine districts were under separate chieftains who acted as spiritual and temporal rulers in a community governed by popular vote. One official—whose duties resembled those of a lawman and a "Speaker" of the Althing—was paid a fixed salary and a percentage of any fines imposed. He recited the laws and the penalties and summoned the chiefs and the people to "parlamentum". Four district courts sat, each with its own lawman, but the Althing was the final court of appeal. Thus, centuries in advance of other countries, was founded, as was justly claimed in 1930, the real "Mother of Parliaments", the assembly acclaimed by the people as the fount of justice and legislation. It has already been told how Christianity, with certain reservations for the private worship of Thor and Odin, was adopted in A.D. 1000[2] at the instigation of Olaf Trygvasson the Swede, who became King of Norway. About a hundred and fifty years later there were no fewer than eleven monasteries, but the

---

[1] Vide page 40.   [2] Vide page 25.

Icelandic Church had a peculiar national character, although it was at the height of its power after the spread of the Hildebrandic doctrines. The monks wrote in Icelandic, now termed Middle Norsk, and recorded even the heathen traditions and history of the past. The local sentiment of priest and monk might well have produced a stultifying parochialism centred round the island saints, St. Thorlac and St. John, but in fact it did much to foster the age of cultured literature which for nearly a century rivalled, if it did not surpass, that of any country in Europe. Their troubadors were as famous in the courts of Europe as those of Provence. To their historian Snorri Sturluson, foully murdured by his son-in-law in A.D. 1241, we owe our knowledge of Norwegian history to about 1170, and his Edda furnishes the original sources for his Norse mythology loosely grouped under the term *Saga*. His nephew Sturla Sturluson carried on the poetic and historical traditions of his uncle with lives of two Norwegian kings, a history of the civil wars and poems of the heroes. The independent attitude of Icelanders which was so evident in both Church and State and the growth of the power of the bishops and chieftains excited the displeasure of both the King of Norway and the Pope. The clash came in the thirteenth century when the chieftains, by this time powerful feudal barons with armed retainers, refused to submit to the claims of the Archbishop of Norway. King Haakon seized the opportunity to make terms with some of them whom he promised to reward with the lands of their rivals. After internecine wars lasting for some years in which many chieftains lost their lives or were deported to Norway, the Althing agreed to an Act of Union, which was signed in 1264. Thorvaldsson, the murderer of Snorri, was appointed as the king's representative or liegeman, but on his death in 1268, the country was divided into districts each with its own officer—corresponding to an English sheriff of the twelfth century—and the government of the country was vested in the Storthing under its elected lawman. With this modification, i.e. the abolition of the earl as governor, the charter of 1264 remained unchanged in theory until King Christian IX's visit in 1874 on the thousandth anniversary of Arnason's settlement. The two millennial celebrations proved almost as important as the events they commemorated. The charter stated unequivocally that the inhabitants should retain their own laws and power of taxation, and over and above

that the people of Iceland should have the same rights as Norwegians in Norway, and furthermore, that "if this agreement is
deemed by the best men (i.e. those attending the Icelandic Althing)
to have been broken, then shall they (i.e. the Icelanders) be free
from all allegiance to the King of Norway". The difficulties
which arose from this charter when Norway came under Danish
rule are obvious, but the easy way was followed and the Icelanders
were left much to their own devices. Trouble came first over trade
disputes with the English fishermen and freebooters, and Icelanders
had to appeal to Copenhagen for Danish help. The Danes forbade
the English to fish in Icelandic waters. The English fishermen
appealed to their king, Henry VIII, who was busily engaged in
severing the English Church from Rome by means of the Reformation Parliament (1529–1536). Denmark was anxious to impose
the Lutheran Church on Iceland, but her subjects stoutly refused.
Henry VIII by 1535 had made his Protestant and national Church
secure and conceived the brilliant idea of offering to buy Iceland
from Denmark. By this means, the English could continue fishing there, Denmark, much in need of money, would get compensation for a possession which brought in no gain and was a source
of considerable trouble. This bargain was never completed and
the purchase was never seriously contemplated again. The change
might have proved a success and certainly would have saved
Iceland from a religious war, which occurred shortly afterwards.

The Catholics fought a losing battle with the Lutheran
reformers as the only means of communication were through
Scandinavia. The monopoly of trade, originally exercised by
Norway, passed into the hands of the Hanseatic League when it
controlled the port of Bergen, and on the decline of the League
passed in turn to Danish merchants of Copenhagen, Malmö and
Helsingors (Elsinore), who were granted special privileges by
Christian IV.

Almost untouched by the Renaissance, Iceland was affected
by the Reformation in a manner which finds no parallel elsewhere. The doctrinal changes led to certain changes of belief,
but also stimulated a revival of Icelandic literature. After the
printing of the Old and New Testaments on presses secretly
introduced into the island, Arngrim Jónsson rescued the
old Icelandic writings and besides writing a history of his country
translated many of them into Latin for the benefit of European

readers. This delving into the past did not cease with his death in 1648, and was continued by the somewhat extravagant historian Torfason and reached its zenith under Arni Magnusson, who brought the whole collection of manuscripts old and new to Copenhagen. Paradoxical as it appears, it is hardly an exaggeration to say that a knowledge of the old inhabitants with their pagan myths and sober history was preserved through the intellectual stirrings and upsets caused by the incursions of the Lutheran Church. Whether William Morris would have admitted this when he introduced the Sagas to English readers is a matter of opinion. The interest in Iceland and its history returned from Denmark to the Icelanders and lent some impetus to the national movement at the end of the eighteenth century. A variety of causes had led to its growth. Never in the history of the island had so many various troubles afflicted the inhabitants. Smallpox began the tale of woe in 1707. It is said that a third of the inhabitants died of the disease, while many began to suffer from malnutrition and actual starvation. Bad harvests, famine and a series of minor eruptions further reduced the population, until the great eruption of the volcano Hecla in 1783 threatened to extinguish it altogether.

Denmark made some effort to alleviate the situation, and by 1800 the position had greatly improved in material ways. The inhabitants, however, perceived an insidious attempt on the part of the absolute monarchy established in Copenhagen to destroy their freedom and semi-independence. Colour was given to their fears when the Althing—the age-long symbol of their national freedom—was abolished in 1800 and a Supreme Court of Justice was set up in Reykjavik to take its place. Tales of the emancipation of peoples and countries had already percolated to the Young Iceland party. At first there was no talk of separation, but when Denmark became involved in the Napoleonic Wars in 1801, and again in 1807, the question naturally arose whether this union with Denmark was of any benefit to them. A curious parallel is afforded by the events which led to the separation in 1944. The plight of the Icelanders became acute after Napoleon had imposed his Continental System on Denmark. England retaliated with her naval blockade, and supply ships of much needed corn were held up and the island was reduced to starvation pitch. The wholesale capture of the Danish fleet rendered any help impossible—there was not an armed frigate left to escort the supply vessels. England, herself in need of grain, has never received her due mead of praise for an act of magnanimity, springing from a true sense of humanity. An Order of Council was passed, which declared Iceland a non-combatant and allowed food supplies to enter. Considering English views on contraband and that her dispute with Denmark originated from the hostile Armed Neutrality of the North, this action is worthy of record. The effect on the national party was immediate and the separatist view gained more supporters. When, by the Treaty of Kiel in 1814, Iceland found herself alienated from Norway, the traditional home of her ancestors, angry protests were raised. In view, however, of the intention of the Great Powers to enforce that treaty and the natural disinclination of Denmark to suffer further territorial losses, submission proved to be the only possible course of action, except a hopeless rebellion. The movement for freedom was not dead, even if separation was denied. Success ultimately rewarded the patriots and before the Danish Constitution of 1849 had been published, the Althing had been restored in Iceland. With the 1849 Constitution, another complication arose. The Danes not unnaturally wished to apply it to Iceland, and so have a uniform kingdom. This did not suit the independent islanders, and they appealed to the old treaty of union with Norway in 1264. On the rejection of the appeal, a civil war was only just avoided, but the able statesman, Jón Sigurdsson, one of the national heroes of modern Iceland, managed to prevent a rebellion which could only have had one result. In 1874, the anniversary of Arnason's arrival, Christian IX visited the country and granted a new constitution. The Althing, divided into two houses, was granted full legislative powers, and the king was to appoint a resident governor who should lay the bills passed by the Althing before him for sanction. No contribution had to be made to the defence forces or civil list, and local taxation was in the hands of the Althing which, however, had no voice in foreign affairs and had also lost its power as a final court of appeal. This was considered to be a satisfactory arrangement, restoring freedom to the people, but before long it was realised that in reality the Althing had become little more than a county council. The Minister for Justice was the Danish official in Copenhagen, and the king on his and the governor's advice, vetoed bill after bill.

Various measures of compromise were passed, all tending to give more independence to Iceland. In 1913 a fresh impetus and encouragement were given to the national party by the adoption of a distinct flag with the assent of the Danish king. Neutrality in the First World War brought considerable prosperity to the fishing industry, and as is usual in such times, agitation gave way to the enjoyment of material benefits, and it was not until the second national millennial celebration, that the separatists began to talk of the glories of the past and the possibilities of the future. Denmark fully participated in the festivities, but the crowds of visitors and representatives who attended from other countries were impressed with the national spirit, and shrewd observers were inclined to think that the old " Mother of Parliaments " might wish to take sole care of her children if danger threatened. The Second World War brought Iceland into the very centre of naval warfare. She had become the key to the North Sea. If Denmark remained neutral as she wished, it was soon clear that no such policy was feasible in the case of Iceland. A decision had to be made. A protective Allied force was given permission to form a base on the island. In effect, she was more in the war than one of the members of the British Commonwealth—Eire. Her fishing trade again flourished exceedingly, but it was almost entirely with Great Britain. The prices rocketed, and strange scenes were witnessed in Liverpool as the Icelandic seamen bought the English goods they prized but had never been able to afford. Not the least remarkable was the run on top hats to be worn on Sundays and festivals on their return to near the Arctic Circle. The advent of the well-paid American army brought further wealth, and it cannot be denied that the people were having "a good war". When Denmark was overrun by the German army, it was obvious to all that the Danish interests and dangers, in fact the foreign relations as a whole, were basically different. It was rightly argued that Iceland had become attached to Denmark through no act of her own, that in the circumstances she must make her own decisions, and that, by historic right (under the Treaty of Union in 1264), she was free to seek independence if " the best men " considered it right. The background to the Declaration of Independence of 1944 must be considered and the impression must not be given that it was passed in any spirit of disloyalty or desire for material gain. The Danish Government, always a firm supporter of the principle of self-determination, willingly acquiesced after the collapse of Germany and Denmark's own liberation. What will be the future of Iceland it is difficult to predict. Her strategic importance on air and sea routes has been visibly demonstrated, and that importance will grow greater, not less. If her independence is to be preserved, it would appear that a strong defensive alliance is her only chance of salvation. With what country or countries should she ally? Her history of a thousand years, her respect for individual freedom of action, inherited from her Norwegian parentage, all point the way to the democracy of the West. She is now looking across the Atlantic Ocean, and is proud of her post-war achievement in starting a regular shipping service of her own to America.

The fate of the Finns has not been so happy, coloured or romantic, but they, too, ultimately won their independence in 1920 and retained their national characteristics in spite of eight hundred years of foreign rule. Unfortunately, the nation was split by the very force which rendered its independence possible—namely, the Russian Revolution of 1917. The Finns had no literature with which to enchant Europe, but their natural love of music, the product of long ages spent in the trackless forests and isolated homesteads, has presented to the world one of the greatest musical geniuses of all time—Sibelius. He borrowed freely from the folk melodies which had been handed down from medieval times, and his symphonies received the enthusiastic approval of a discriminating musical, and a less educated musical, public. The last decade of the nineteenth century acclaimed him to be the greatest composer since Beethoven, only rivalled by the Norwegian, Grieg. Both were individualistic composers and defied imitation in their own spheres except in so far that the inspiration of their themes might have canalised lesser musicians into a field from which they could not rise to similar heights. In the case of Grieg, however, a follower, or perhaps more correctly, a disciple, has achieved a fame which promises to endure. The Yorkshire-born Delius owed his musical development to Grieg, under whom he studied at Leipzig on abandoning orange growing in Florida. The twentieth-century musicians of Finland, such as Klanu, have broken from the Sibelius tradition, and have not been appreciated outside Finland in proportion to their merit. The people of Finland are as much patrons of the theatre as they are of music. The smallest towns have their own theatres presenting plays by great masters, just as they have their own orchestras. During the Russian occupation (1809–1919), the local shows, dramatic and musical, were immensely popular, and it is fair to say that love of drama and music provides a certain bond between Slav and Ugro-Finn. It is, however, in architecture that the Finns have risen to their highest cultural levels. It cannot, however, be claimed as inherently national. The low homestead, with its cramped interior and steam bath, may be serviceable and represents the old style of Finnish domestic building. It has little in common with the fine buildings of Helsinki and the other major towns. They owe their inspiration to the Swedes, whose architectural genius had been displayed for many centuries. The Finns inherited the Swedes' facile ability to blend new materials as they became available and to organise a harmonising team of architect, builder, and decorator, and, less commonly than in Sweden, a sculptor as well. Americans, who were well acquainted with Finns owing to the continued stream of emigrants in the nineteenth and early twentieth centuries, were quick to enlist the services of Saarinen in the beautifying of Chicago City.

The Northern European countries are noted for their spacious, well-planned railway stations; in fact, the termini are uniformly good and usually beautiful in the proportion of their exteriors and interiors, yet most travellers, not only those condemned to Liverpool Street or Fenchurch Street, but even those familiar with the Quai d'Orsay or Pennsylvania Railway Station, New York, give their vote to Helsinki.[1]

The architectural taste and skill are legacies from the Swedes who, as has been already described, conquered and converted the Finns. So, indeed, it appeared in the official records. But Finland is a vast country of " ten thousand lakes ". As the crow flies, it is five hundred and fifty miles from north to south, and a wayfarer would find that his pedometer registered over six hundred before his journey was ended. Christianity touched the fringe of the coasts where the Swedes settled. The Finns were Shamanistic in their religion, and their adoration of nature—their nearness to Mother Earth, as it has been called—is still one of the dominating characteristics of the people outside the towns who are for ever

[1] It has been pointed out that the volume of traffic at Helsinki is considerably less than at the others. Does that really affect the question? The numbers attending York Cathedral and a city church should not influence architectural judgement.

battling against the rigours of nature, as well as the acquisitive-ness of man. The Swedish governing class, until the time of Gustavus Vasa and the Reformation, did not interfere much with the habits and customs and beliefs of the Finns. In the islands and on the coast from Åbo (now Turku) to Viborg (now Vipuru), they settled among them, intermarried, and started a new race of Swedo-Finns. If Finnish families objected to the intruders, they could migrate a hundred miles east or north, as had the Lapps before them.

The Reformation brought a change. Finns were sent, some to Germany, mostly to Wittenberg, and some to Sweden, to hear of the new faith. They were educated in their youth at the Cathedral School at Åbo and on their return they acted as missionaries and teachers of their own people. Michael Agricola, a disciple of Melanchthon as well as Luther, realised that until the Finns could learn to read and write, they would never become true followers of Christ and His religion as dispensed by Luther and Melanchthon. In the years between 1530 and 1548 he rendered the Finnish tongue into writing. He set down an alphabet book, a reading book, and finally produced a Finnish prayer book, a doctrinal guide (or catechism) and a New Testament. As his purpose in fixing a written language was to spread the gospel and educate a primi-tive people, he undoubtedly helped to defeat his own object by perpetuating no fewer than fifteen cases in the declension of nouns and founding the most difficult tongue in Europe. Had Gustavus Vasa insisted on the teaching of Swedish in the new schools, along-side the spoken Finnish if necessary, the political absorption of Finland might have been slower, but it would have been surer. The Swedish rule, which regarded Finland as one of its duchies subsequently privileged to have a vote in the election of the king, brought many advantages, but one grave disadvantage which the king could not remove was inherent in the Finns' geographical position lying between two rival states. The Swedes brought a greater degree of civilisation to this " silent introverted people ", the direct antithesis to themselves, but " there is no way of measuring the effects of the intercourse between the two races."[1] That is indis-putable. Probably the Duke of Finland, a Swede more often of royal blood, saved the Finns from an evil form of late feudalism and pre-served the local administration of law by the Finns themselves; nor

[1] J. Hampden Jackson, *Finland*, page 30 (revised edition.)

was it till the nineteenth century that racial feeling was stirred up. The cause was not so much due to internal squabbles as to the ancient rivalry between Russia and Sweden. This was the real misfortune of Finland. As a buffer country, she became the battleground of her neighbours. The Carelian borders were the key to Finland in the south-eastern corner; even if they were held, the long frontier to the north was still vulnerable and a possible route for an invader in spite of the long distance to the important ports on the Gulfs of Bothnia and Finland. Whatever the benefits bestowed by the fundamental laws of a separate constitution as granted by Gustavus III with his enlightened ideas, the geographical conditions made defence by a Swedo-Finnish army almost impossible against a determined attack by the overwhelming numbers of the Russians. The Finns fought magnificently in the war in 1789 after the exposure of the Anjala League plot which was the work of Swedo-Finnish nobles, but it is highly doubtful whether they could have withstood the full force of Catherine's power. After the Swedish naval victory over the Russians at Viborg, the mutual fear of the French revolutionary movements becoming a threat to all monarchies, drew Catherine and Gustavus III together, and Russian revenge was postponed till 1808.

In that year, the Russians crossed the border without any declaration of war, ostensibly as the allies of Napoleon who had declared war on Sweden. As already described, the Swedish fortress of Sveaborg surrendered without a struggle, but the Finns continued alone. It was this glorious fight against the Russians, lasting for fifteen months with ever-increasing ferocity, which consolidated the Finnish nation. Their commanders, three hitherto unknown officers, were matched against one of the greatest Russian generals—Barclay de Tolly—whose army was more than four times the size of the Finnish. During this second stage of the war, the Finns had been regarding Swedish aid as their only hope, for, in spite of victories in pitched battles and guerilla warfare, it was obvious that alone they could not hold out for ever.

One of the "glorious three", Döbeln, had gallantly held the Åland Islands which guarded the line of communication between Stockholm and the Finnish coast. When these fell to the Russians, and their Cossack horsemen were crossing the frozen sea to pillage Swedish territory itself, further resistance was useless. The final blow came when Sweden was forced to abandon her Finnish subjects and ceded Finland and the Åland Islands to Russia, at the Treaty of Fredrikshamn in September 1809. Thus abruptly ended the political connexion of Finland with the Scandinavian countries. To the joy of the Finns, Alexander I granted them a full measure of independence and in his manifesto of 1810 he guaranteed to them the full liberties and rights of their constitution. He stressed the point that he, as Grand Duke, came as a liberator, not a conqueror, and that the representatives of Finland had given the oath of fealty to him, whilst he faithfully promised to support the political existence of the Finnish nation. His manifesto was taken to mean that the union was to fulfil the spontaneous wishes of the people. It is difficult to know how far the Czar was sincere, how far under the influence of one of his philanthropic and mystical moods, and how far influenced by his two Swedish advisers, Armfelt and Sprengporten (the officer who had turned to Russia for help in the days of the Anjala League). Alexander remains as insoluble an enigma in his dealings with Finland as he was with Napoleon at Tilsit. However, he did appoint Sprengporten and Armfelt as governor and secretary, to the great satisfaction of the duchy. The Diet was re-established and a Senate appointed. Thus, apparently, it was through the influence of the Swedes who had deserted the Stockholm government, that Finland was to " find herself " and assert her own nationality. The seat of government was transferred to Helsingfors (Helsinki) in 1816, and the University followed in 1827. Finland had her own code of laws, her own courts, and her own schools, and yet all was not as it appeared on the surface. The Senate did not represent the people, and the Diet was never convoked until 1863. Finnish history lies outside the scope of this book except in so far as it concerns Scandinavia, but to understand the present situation it is necessary briefly to review the events which have made Finland once more the outpost of defence which she had been for so many centuries. The growth of the Finnish nation under the Russian rule and the realisation of its own entity were bound sooner or later to lead to a clash of wills. An outlet for the expression of Finnish aspirations was found when the Diet once more assembled and in the speech from the throne, Alexander II repeated the assurances of Alexander I. The audience of 1863 was vastly different from that of 1810. The population was doubled, it was educated, it had groups of Finnish writers and thinkers who had brought about what is sometimes termed the Finnish Renaissance. They saw in the Senate a minority of Swedes or Swedo-Finns who relied on Russia to secure their own wealth and power and who failed to respond to the aspirations of the true Finns. It was not unlike the days of the first assembly of the States General in 1789. No one quite knew what they wanted, except that they were not satisfied with things as they were. In Finland the issue was complicated by the national split over the linguistic question. The grievances were not so much material as spiritual. The domination of the Senate and the Czar's representative was resented on more grounds than one. The people were denied the voice in the government they had been promised, and the form of government, in theory fair enough, had in practice resulted in Swedes and Swedo-Finns retaining their positions as a ruling class. In the 'sixties there had begun a regular system of elementary schools, and a bitter struggle ensued between the Fennomans (Finland-for-the-Finns party) and the Suecomans who supported Swedish culture and the use of the Swedish language. With the spread of secondary education, the dispute became even more acrimonious because the Fennomans had appealed to the Czar who had issued a ukase to the effect that both languages should be on an equal footing. Which should be used in which school and court was to depend on the prevailing language in that commune. Each party then built secondary schools in which Swedish or Finnish was used according to the founders' wishes. The Fennomans accused the Suecomans of appealing to the Czar on a purely domestic matter and so breaking the constitution. It was the Russian government's actions which finally caused the formation of a united Finland. Firstly, they tried to force the Finns to fight in the Russian army in the wars against Turkey. In the end it was agreed that they would enter the conflict provided the Finnish regiments were commanded by Finnish officers and that Finns were not conscripted into the Russian regiments. The Finns fought splendidly in that war, but this was only the thin end of the wedge. In 1890 the Panslavists, who aimed at the complete absorption of Finland into the Russian orbit, began to win their way. Coinage and customs, and finally the postal service, came under the direct control of St. Petersburg (Leningrad). These moves aroused the anger of all Finland. For the last twenty years of the nineteenth century, the discontent grew and the pace of emigration to America grew accordingly and continued without cessation till the First World War. Even after the liberation in Finland, the stream continued, and the emigrants continued to be welcomed as they proved good workmen and were pleased with the wages received.[1] Open opposition broke out when Bobrikoff, notorious oppressor of the Baltic provinces, was appointed governor in 1899. His brutal methods united the Fennomans and Suecomans in a common anti-Russian union. By a manifesto early in the year, the Constitution of Finland was annulled. The Diet petitioned the Czar to no purpose, the Finns began a campaign of passive resistance. Bobrikoff, infuriated by the opposition of all classes, inaugurated a reign of terror. The Finnish army was disbanded, and Russian troops were sent over in their stead. Provincial governors, headmasters, judges, mayors, and other officials were dismissed. Resistance meant Siberia; mere expostulation, exile or a fine. The troops were followed by an army of police whose sudden domiciliary visits drove the helpless inhabitants to the hamlets, the forests, and the trackless wastes. The Russian spies and agents, often Carelians disguised as chapmen selling wares, followed them to the smallest towns and villages—nobody was safe. The Senate was weeded out and filled with sycophants, the administrative posts were filled by Russians or by Finns of low character who were their paid tools. Such was the desperate position of Finland at the beginning of the twentieth century—a Finland which had achieved a national character, language, and a national conscience and pride.

Its heroism had inspired Runeberg to write his patriotic poems, and Löuropp, a pure Finn, to compose a national epic in the Homeric style.[2] Whatever its purely literary merits, its influence a quarter of a century after its publication was immense, and the Finns, like many small nations surrounded by lakes, forests and mountains, have a strong unifying bond in the old song poems and folk stories. The imposition of the Russian language was a shattering blow. Swedish sympathy was aroused, but the Swedish government,

---

[1] One of the large American motor manufacturers had to post notices in Finnish as well as American, German, and Italian.

[2] It is not meant to imply that it had the lasting qualities of the *Iliad*, but according to Hampden Jackson (*Finland*, page 57), *Kalevala* is considered one of the great folk poems of the world. It is in the metre of *Hiawatha*—i.e., the metre of sing-song talk and its merits must lie in the themes. We await a Chapman or Messrs. Butcher and Lang to give a version, on which to pronounce a verdict.

itself immersed in the Norwegian trouble, could take no effective official action even had it wished to do so. Voluntary assistance was given to those wishing to emigrate, and Finns took advantage of this Swedo-Finn organisation in the "Bobrikoff terror" and again, to an even greater extent in the second period of oppression under the Stolypin and Seyn régime before the First World War. Numbers of educated but penniless bourgeois made America their home without losing interest in their mother country. A bond of friendly relationship was established between the two countries, not unlike that of Poland and the American Poles, who were largely responsible for the choice of Paderewski as the first president. Finland was not "news" to the majority of European newspapers, but the murder of Bobrikoff by a young patriot got into the headlines and the Liberals in many nations began to nurse anti-czarist ideas, when the provocation and persecution driving him to this deed became more generally known. However, it was not external pressure which brought a change in Russian policy to Finland. The Czar and his ministers were thoroughly shaken by the defeat in the Japanese War, by the outbreak of revolutionary movements and the speeches of delegates in the First and Second Dumas. The unrest found a ready response in Finland, where a general strike was called and paralysed trade of every kind. Such a movement would have had no chance of success twenty years earlier, but in 1905 parts of Finland had become industrialised, and the towns had shown rapid expansion through the exodus of the people from the country districts. Trade unions had begun to organise labour, and their leaders formed the nucleus of a Social Democratic party, which had been in communication with Russian revolutionaries. The strike was a complete triumph for this party, but confusion ensued when the police and minor government officials ceased work in sympathy. White guards were formed by the bourgeois, Red guards by the Social Democrats, and, had it not been for the unexpected surrender of the Czar's ministers, a class war might have ensued. As it was, a new and more democratic constitution was granted, and the Diet was restored. The principle of proportional representation and woman suffrage were introduced, thus went to a duchy of despotic czardom the honour of being the first country in Europe to recognise the equality of men and women. This is not so strange as it appears on the surface, as women had shared men's work and received men's wages. The new Diet included no fewer than twenty-five women. The Social Democrats returned 80 members, the Young Finns 25, Old Finns 58, Swedes 25, and Agrarians 9. Finland was soon to be the victim of further Russian persecution. The Russian press began a campaign against Finland as a whole, and the Social Democrats in particular. It was pointed out that the Social Democrats had been in communication with the Russian Revolutionaries and that they might easily command an absolute majority in the Diet, which would imperil the Russian power. Finland was painted as a dangerous hotbed where Nihilist plots were nurtured.

In 1908, Stolypin began the second period of persecution, heralded by the appointment of Seyn, the right-hand man of the murdered Bobrikoff. In 1910 the Finnish constitution was abolished and Russian tyranny was even more drastically enforced. Even the Old Finns and Swedish parties, who had believed that the new constitution under Russian patronage was best for Finland, were forced into the opposite view. The outbreak of war in 1914 changed the complexion of affairs. Trade flourished as never before, and no Finns were conscripted to fight Russian battles. This sudden wave of prosperity temporarily lessened the call for resistance against the Russians and the break did not come till the Russian Revolution of 1917. Thousands of Russian soldiers and workmen were in Finland, which was heavily fortified as a bulwark against Germany. Finns also were employed in great numbers and fairly well paid at first by their Russian masters. With the end of the Russian war, a sudden slump set in. Prices had rocketed and wages had not responded in the same ratio, the capitalists alone had reaped a great harvest. These inflammable economic conditions were bad enough in themselves, but when the revolution spread to Finland and Russian soldiers murdered their officers and roamed the streets to plunder and to rape, the situation became desperate. The old Red and White guards appeared once more. The Social Democrats temporarily made terms with the Bolshevists but it is probably true that they had no intention of surrendering to them the independence of Finland.[1] However that may be, the White guards and bourgeoisie saw in the Bolshevist triumphs the

[1] The accounts are so confused and contradictory that the exact purpose of the Democrats is obscure. Up against such big facts as the rise and fall of Kerensky, the " October Revolution " and victory of the Bolshevists, it is probable that the Social Democrats had no clear ideas themselves. The question is discussed on pages 89, 90 and 97, *Finland* (Hampden Jackson).

future subjugation of their land and the destruction of their own class. A resistance force was organised by General Mannerheim, a Swedo-Finn officer who had served in the Czar's army. He was joined by the peasant class and made his headquarters at the Bothnian port of Vasa. While training his irregulars, he appealed to Sweden and Russia for help. The former decided to maintain its neutrality, but volunteers and some much-needed help found their way across the Gulf. The Germans, though much in need of their own forces in the early part of 1918, first sent a party of Finns who, during the first three years of the war had volunteered to fight for Germany against Russia. They had been well trained in a Jaeger battalion. In March 1918 General von der Goltz arrived with his disciplined troops, and the end of the so-called War of Independence was a foregone conclusion. It is outside the scope of a survey of Scandinavian history to recount the hopeless and fanatical struggle of unorganised enthusiasm against rigid discipline. By May, a remnant of the Diet was summoned. It contained one Social Democrat, and proceeded to elect a regent who became a dictator under German protection.[1] From Sveaborg, his soldiers were sent to enslave the Finnish proletariat. Over seventy thousand are known to have suffered. The regent, Svinhound, believing in the summer of 1918 that Germany was going to win the war, decided to wreak vengeance on the enemies of his class. The latter part of the savage civil war had been fought by town and factory workers, helped by Russian Bolshevists against the educated classes, bourgeoisie and peasants helped by Germans. If the World War had not ended in November 1918, the future of Finland might have been dark indeed. With the general peace, the statesmen of Versailles could get a truer picture of Finland, while the Finns could see the world from which they had been so long cut off. To Mannerheim, much credit is due. His German associates were dismissed, the regent fell. His call for recruits to assist the White Russians proved that the Bolshevist connexion had been finally severed. The Social Democrats won an astonishing number of seats at the 1919 election, but they, too, purged themselves of the Communists which formed a small party of their own. Finally, under the wise guidance of the first president, Ståhlberg, who

[1] No true account of this strange and ghastly interlude can be written until documents are available. It is known that a request was sent to the Kaiser, asking that his son might accept the throne of Finland. Why? No answer in written accounts is satisfying. We must wait.

received more votes than did Mannerheim, an independent Finland re-entered the orbit of Scandinavian politics. The restrained action of Sweden over the Åland Islands was justly appreciated by the new republic. A great reception was given later to the royal Swedish visitors, and, since 1922, the relations between Sweden, Finland, Denmark and, usually, Norway, have been more cordial than ever before. Sweden, actuated by reasons of humanity, gave active though unofficial aid to Finland in her last struggle against Russia, and in this Norway followed her example. Behind this help there lurked a fear, whispered at many a street corner, that the danger which threatened the independence of Finland was also a menace to Sweden. Events since 1945 have intensified this sense of apprehension. The imprisonment of the ex-president, Ryti, the forced resignation of the honoured president and marshal of Finland, Mannerheim, the provocative insult to the memorial of Sandels, one of the three heroes of 1808–9, are driving starving Finland to despair and bringing home to all three Scandinavian powers the urgency of having a united policy, if not a defensive alliance. Though no longer a duchy attached to Sweden, she is just as necessary as a bulwark against the Communist forces whose creed is so repugnant to the Scandinavian nature. Finland's position is not enviable. She has been obliged to make a heavy contribution to Russia towards the cost of a war not of her making. It seems indeed hard that independent and freedom-loving Finland had to pay in 1919, and again in 1946, for wars which nearly ruined her land, while she was fighting for the very principles which were ostensibly those of the victors.[1]

[1] The above was written before the events of 1948, which confirm rather than impair the truth of any statements contained in the second part of this chapter

CHAPTER XVI

EPILOGUE

THE story of Scandinavia began far back, even before the days of written history. It has been partially unfolded and the curtain partially raised by the patient research of the historians and archeologists of many nations. This book has tried to bring the story as near to the present as even the most adventurous writer would dare. Many may believe that by so close an approach the true perspective has been lost. The defence must be that so many of the characteristics of the earliest Scandinavians have been preserved right down the ages, and some sketch of the countries as they are in our own time serves to show a continuity which might otherwise have been lost in their many struggles with other nations and between themselves.

Outstanding among those characteristics which have endured since the days of the Vikings, are the spirit of enterprise, the love of independence, and the power of adaptability. They may be, and often are, displayed in new ways, but in spite of their modern dress, they are plainly recognisable.

The spirit of enterprise still appears in their daring on the sea and the passion for discovery, but to this has been added an enterprise of the mind, a development of civilisation. The love of independence, so nearly crushed even in our times, has survived to be the basic motive of the lives of all three peoples. Their power of adaptability has grown stronger. They have shown themselves able to adapt themselves to new circumstances as well as to strange peoples. It is this gift which has led them to settle in other countries, rise to great heights, and yet not found colonies of their own in spite of emigrations relatively high to their populations. In this they share the characteristics which in Great Britain's history have so often distinguished the Scots.

Those three features are shared in common by the Scandinavian countries, but each country has an individuality of its own and displays it in different degrees.

Norway, which has been a sovereign state for less than fifty years, is marked by the strongest sense of individual independence. In the centuries during which it was attached to Denmark, it never lost that sense. The geographical factors may have been the chief cause of its preservation, but remain it did. The Nor-wegian people may have accepted, but never admitted, the position of "junior partner" and, when transferred to Sweden without being consulted, the rights of individuals to manage their own affairs was stoutly maintained. Their most important "affairs" were their shipping interests and, as already narrated, it was the determined efforts to secure freedom to exercise their independence in this national industry which ultimately led to separation.

Denmark, which has experienced the most troubled history of all, has weathered the many storms by individual rather than governmental endeavour. It was the resilience and determination of the inhabitants which time and time again helped the country's recovery. Their adaptability to circumstances was exemplified in the quick realisation of the agriculturalists that a change must be made from corn to cows. Rarely, if ever, has the farming fraternity of any country made such a drastic revolt from age-long customs as did the Danes in the nineteenth century.

In Sweden, the spirit of enterprise, so gloriously rewarded by the rise to power in the seventeenth century, did not die with the dramatic fall. It was diverted into other channels and has shown that it is very much alive in the scientific side of industry. With the strong sense of realism which so vividly marks the genius of the Swedish people, they experimented in new fields of political and social economy and from the success achieved they can claim to have progressed further along the path of true democratic self-government than any other country in the world.

Such are the sober generalisations which emerge from a singularly colourful pageant of history. How colourful that pageant is, may be gleaned by gazing at that glorious company of Scandinavians who played the parts. Just such a company as this might have inspired the writer of Ecclesiasticus,[1] when he called on his readers to "praise famous men". "Such as did bear rule in their kingdom and men renowned for their power . . . leaders of the people by their counsels . . . such as sought out musical tunes" and then comes the great paeon of praise for the people who left "no memorial" but "the peoples will declare their wisdom." This is a true picture of the Scandinavian pageant—shining personalities against a background of the people. Let us suppose that Canute, founder of the Scandinavian tradition, were set as Pageant Master

[1] *Ecclesiasticus*, Chapter 44.

watching the cavalcade marching in procession across the arena and brooding over his own ideal of a united empire. He would see no Rurik the Russ or Rollo the Ganger, as they had departed east and west to found new kingdoms. Perhaps the first to stand out from the warrior bands enveloped in the mists of war would be the figure of Absalon, the soldier Archbishop of Lund, renowned for his learning and military exploits, calling to mind another arch-bishop of Danish origin, Thurstan of York. Next would come Magnus Barnlocks, defender of the peasants' right and upholder of a people's law in Sweden. Following the three Valdemars, the great Margaret brought back the hope of a united Scandinavia to Canute. Would the great patriot and statesman, Engelbrekt, show Eric the folly of his ways and restore ideals of law, order and justice to the great Scandinavian Union? Alas, no! The dream fades out again, drenched in the "blood bath" of Stockholm. Had Christianity failed? Were the worst features of the Vikings' cruel, relentless nature to be perpetuated for ever? Such would have been the musings of Canute as he watched the procession before him. With the passing of the Union, the shining stars become brighter, and he could see that the virtues of the past heroes had not died with them, though the new aims were not his aims. Fine "old King Gösta", reminiscent of the sturdy people which made Europe tremble, founded a line of kings to herald a new age of greatness. Nor was he to be alone in restoring the sullied reputation of the old founders' race. Christian IV sent his seamen over the world. He tried to unite two of the old countries by founding a capital in Norway called after him, as a memorial of his work. The old man died fighting for his land. He is followed by another figure to shed lustre on the race—not by military prowess as of old—the first of the line of Scandinavian scientists, Tyge Brahe, the founder of modern astronomy. The list of famous men is growing apace as the greatest of all appears as a defender of his land and his beliefs, Gustavus Adolphus. His victories are heralded by a host of suffering Germans—a strange contrast to the welcome accorded to the Viking raiders. The Scandinavian conquering hero is acclaimed a friend and a deliverer. Will he succeed where Canute himself failed? Will he found an enduring Baltic Empire? Fate decreed it otherwise. The very people who achieved their first measure of unity and order, under Rurik the Swede, were deter-mined to see that this should never be accomplished. With the end of the Baltic Empire passes the last of great "rulers renowned for their power", Charles XII. The procession crossing the pageant's arena becomes less colourful, but the names of the actors must not be buried with them. The old spirit is still there—the missionary Egede is exploring the Arctic, as Swedenborg explored the mysteries of nature. The sinister Struensee is denied entrance despite his pleading that he followed the teaching of Rousseau and worked for the good of the people. A band of writers is escorted by the old Icelander, Snorri, whose works had been recovered from oblivion to hand down the tales of the heroes. Hans Andersen tells his stories for the children of the world, and the teacher and writer Grundtvig sees to it that the people shall be educated and so understand the glories of the past. Perhaps he would not approve what flowed from the pens of Ibsen and Strindberg, but he would have gloried in those who " sought out musical tunes " led by Grieg and Sibelius, translating into melody the very soul of their lands, and in Jenny Lind who delighted all Europe by her singing. Canute would gaze in wonder at the creations of the architects, the sculptors and the painters, but their appeal to him would be that they worked not for their own age alone. Sergel and Milles, Roslin and Carl Larssen and the fine old Willumsen from his own land have left a legacy to the world. One of the last to cross the arena would be Nobel, bearing in his left hand, explosives, and with his right bestowing prizes for peacemakers and discoverers in the arts and sciences. So the cavalcade could go on, with workers in glass and in steel, and seamen voyaging on every sea, but it would be fitting to end with those two great explorers, Nansen and Amundsen, embodying as they did all that was best in their forefathers—exhibiting the spirit of enterprise, endurance and daring not for glory or conquest, but in the pursuit of knowledge.

What, then, is to be the future of Scandinavia, which has played so distinguished a part in shaping the civilised world? In return for gifts bestowed, Civilisation must guarantee its preservation. How can this be effected? Can it be that Canute will see his dream come true? Who would not welcome a strong federation of the three countries, united as they are by common dangers, common interests and a common heritage? On such a federation, supported by freedom-loving nations, seems to rest the salvation of Scandinavia and Western Civilisation.

APPENDICES

APPENDIX I

GREENLAND

THE huge island of Greenland has flitted in and out of European history for nearly a thousand years. In the First World War it was of some importance as a meteorological station. In 1917 America confirmed Danish rights, which dated from 1721, when new settlers arrived in the wake of Hans Egede, who later became missionary to the Eskimos. With the development of air travel and transport, it has assumed a new and growing importance which may shortly place it on one of the short cuts across the North Pole. The first colonists came from Iceland in A.D. 985–6 under a hot-headed farmer called Eric the Red, and by the fourteenth century there was a colony of some five thousand souls. Then occurred a mystery which remained unsolved till the twentieth century when the Danish archaeologist, Poul Nörlund, found the complete answer as a result of his investigations, begun in 1920. From 1410, when the last ship left Hvalseyfjord, to that date, nothing was known of the fate of the settlers, and for nearly a hundred and fifty years Greenland itself was lost. Nobody tried to find it as the value of its trade had sunk to nothing, and there were no other inducements for mariners to visit a country which by a climatic change had ceased to be a " green " land, and had been converted into a treeless, bleak waste, whose coast had become blocked with pack ice. The full story of the life of the colony and its tragedy has been told by the master hand of Poul Nörlund in his *Viking Settlers in Greenland*, and in the foreword by Ellis R. Minns, it is summed up thus: "These men made a planned attempt to live the life of Europe, Christian, ordered and civilised beyond the limits that nature had set to such life. Yet nature seemed at first to promise a bounty of green pastures, and it was her failure to keep her promise that made the tragedy." That was the main cause, but there were others.

The Norwegian king, who claimed in the thirteenth century, the monopoly of the trade, failed to send the ship with supplies of certain goods necessary to the existence of the colony. The visits became fewer, and in 1410 ceased altogether, and the Greenlanders had no materials to make sea-going ships, and so the communications ceased. The exports of the islanders had been walrus ivory, furs, hides, and skins, but the demand ceased owing to the cheaper and better African ivory, the Russian furs which came from the North and Baltic, and the English and Dutch cloths, which superseded skins in the more temperate lands.

The final link might have been the Church. The Greenlanders had been converted by Lief, the son of Erik. He had been blown off his course to Norway and arrived amidst the Christians of the Hebrides. On arriving in Norway he was baptised, and returned to Greenland with a priest and other clergy. Erik's wife built the first church and finally Erik himself was persuaded to be tolerant if never a believer. The Church became a firm link with Europe. The Thor worship died out, and tithes were continued in place of the taxes paid to the god-house. Twelve parishes were demarcated in the east and four in the west, and by 1112 there was established under the Archbishop of Lund, an episcopal seat at Gardar, with its cathedral of St. Nicholas, the patron saint of fishermen. It was from the Vatican that came the last news of the settlers.

In 1890, a letter was discovered bearing the date 1492. This created Matthias Knudson bishop of Gardar "on condition he went there." That sentence is pregnant with meaning. His duty was to lead the settlers back to Christianity, as for the last eighty years the only consolation they had had "was the adoration of a corporale over which the Body of Christ had been consecrated a hundred years before." There was no wine and no meal for baking the Host. So for eighty years the islanders had venerated this relic, hoping against hope that relief would come.

From a chapter on Greenland in a book published in 1225, called *The King's Mirror*, the life and history of the settlers can be gleaned through the dialogue of a father and an enquiring son —not unlike the *Dialogus de Scaccario* or " Mrs. Markham " of a later date. Lief on one of his voyages found a fertile spot in America which he called "Vinland the Good", but subsequent expeditions failed to locate it, and succeeded only in establishing a route to Labrador. The natives (*Scraellings*) were hostile, and the colonisation which had been contemplated did not take place. However, communications were continued with land to the west until 1347, when the supply of sea-going vessels failed and new ships did not arrive from Norway. The excavations of the twentieth century have disclosed the whole life of the people and proved the answers of the wise father in *The King's Mirror* to be correct. Clothes dating from 1400 have been found in perfect condition preserved by the rise of the ground ice. The material is coarse, and the fashions are similar for men and women. The only difference between the costumes as they are now and as they were five hundred years ago is that the colours have faded. They are the everyday clothes of the peasant, farmer and fisherman and form a unique contribution to our knowledge of medieval dress. From the skeletons and bones it is clear that malnutrition was the cause of the decay of the colony and the powers of reproduction were reduced. These hardy farmers found their hayfields and their pastures destroyed by a change of climate. The pack ice deprived them of their seals and their walrus, but there was no means of supplementing this decline in their food supply as was done when a similar though slighter catastrophe occurred in the twentieth century. The ground ice rose and slowly destroyed the people but covered and preserved their civilisation which, with their homsteads, their simple amusements such as chess and draughts, with their churches, their school and their monastery, had tried to live a European life on a land which could not support it unless the intercourse was constant with its mother country. With a reversion of the climate to that of five hundred years ago and the regular visits of American and Danish ships and 'planes, there is a likelihood of Greenland—except in the hinterland—becoming a country of increasing interest to the world.

Note. It is worth recording that Davis, searching for the North West Passage, hit Greenland by accident but was unaware of the fact. In 1540 the east coast was re-discovered by Jon Greenlander, but no further attempts at colonisation were made. In 1700 the Darien Company contemplated a trading station but abandoned the idea.

From 1721 after Egede's missionary tour, when he passed over the old buried settlements, Greenland was again regarded as a possible station for Danish fishermen, but the old farmhouses, with their bathrooms, the churches and the cathedral, were not found till after the First World War,

THE SOUTH SLESVIG QUESTION AFTER THE SECOND WORLD WAR

The Editor of the *Lauritzen News* (Copenhagen) has kindly given his permission for the reprint of this article in English giving the Danish standpoint.

A

After the 1920 agreement, there remained in North Slesvig and in South Slesvig minorities of Germans and Danes respectively. In 1939, just before the war, the German minority in North Slesvig numbered about 30,000, and the Danish minority in South Slesvig about 20,000. It goes without saying that the Danish minority hope some time to be re-united with Denmark.

But now the population of South Slesvig also wishes for association with Denmark, pleading that the people of South Slevsig are of Danish origin and that they have been convinced by the events of recent years that they are more akin to Danish culture and mentality than to German. Naturally, it is not possible to say anything definite about the strength and endurance of this conviction.

A Note of September 9th, 1946, from the British Government to the Government of Denmark states:

"His Majesty's Government are prepared to consider any proposal either for an exchange of populations or a plebiscite followed by a frontier rectification or a simple frontier rectification without plebiscite."

It may be said that Denmark has a "historic right" to South Slesvig, since this territory belonged to Denmark right up to 1864, and large parts of the present population are descended from old Slesvig families. It is generally held in Denmark, however, that in matters of this kind the decisive factor is not "historic right" but the wishes of the present population.

Practically all sections of the population therefore agree that the question can be solved only through a plebiscite, and that such a plebiscite should not be held until after the lapse of several years, since Denmark would not be able to determine her attitude to any expressed desire for association with Denmark until later, when we can feel reasonably certain that this desire is not dictated by a momentary urge to get away from Germany and German affairs but by a yearning to merge with the Danish people. The Danish people must decide, quite independent of a plebiscite, whether it wishes to absorb new territory and new elements of population.

In accordance with these views the Danish Government, with the concurrence of the Danish Parliament, stated in its reply to to the above British Note:

" Since the German collapse in 1945 there has been growing ferment and national unrest in South Slesvig. The desire to get away from German rule and the wish to become attached to Denmark . . . have lately become very widespread and have found considerable support. However, the position is not yet clarified, and only time can show whether the change of mentality which has taken place in the minds of many South Slesvigers is of a permanent nature.

"In these circumstances the Danish Government does not intend to propose any alteration in the status of national allegiance of South Slesvig.

"Whether the population of South Slesvig desires to raise the question of obtaining access to exercising their natural right of self-determination must be for themselves to decide."

Though practically unanimous agreement prevails on the above points, opinions in Denmark differ widely about the extent and form of the support which should be granted to the Danish movement in South Slesvig.

The Danish movement is South Slesvig wishes South Slesvig to be severed from Germany as soon as possible, partly so as to secure for the population of South Slesvig the possibilities of free cultural development without German pressure, partly to provide better conditions for Danish cultural work, and partly that those who always declared their sympathy for Denmark may live free from fear of persecution on account of their pro-Danish attitude.

Further, it is desired that the German refugees now in South Slesvig and numbering about 300,000—the same as the native population—should be moved from South Slesvig territory. Not only is an increase of this extent a heavy burden from a materialist point of view, but bitterness is aroused when the refugees oust natives of South Slesvig from leading posts and important offices. Moreover, this large population reduces the possibility of a majority in favour of attachment to Denmark at a later plebiscite, while it is out of the question that Denmark should accept 300,000 pure Germans within her borders. (*Lauritzen News*, August 1947.)

B

The restrained attitude of the Danes and their strict adherence to the principle of self-determination make it imperative that justice should be done in the period which must elapse before the plebiscite be taken.

There should be a separate administration at Flensborg, a city which is essentially Danish and has declared itself in favour of a return to Denmark by the majority of candidates of the South Slesvig Association, who have been elected to the provincial council (May 1947). At present, Middle Slesvig is administered from Kiel and the Over-President, admittedly an anti-Nazi and a fair-minded man, was chief of Falkenhorst's staff in Norway. Not unnaturally, his administration has a strong German bias and Danish political associations are forbidden. The rapidly reviving Danish sentiment must be allowed to express itself and not be hampered by the presence of the German refugees and the German government at Kiel, which has been allowed to dominate Slesvig for too long.

The following statistics taken from *Sprogforeningens Aars-beretning* (Language Association Year Book), September 1947, speak for themselves. In reading the statistics it must be remembered that all South Slesvig, i.e. Flensborg and the district south of it, has been under German rule for the last eighty years, and every effort made to stamp out the Danish language, Danish culture, Danish sympathies and the Danish people.

Danish Schools in South Slesvig

	In operation	Planned	Total
August 1946	33	69	102
June 1947	49	107	156

Election for Provincial Council,
May 1947

	Percentage of votes used	Votes for German Candidates	Votes for South Slesvig Association Candidates	Percentage for South Slesvig Association
Flensborg West	84	11.384	17.922	61.2
Flensborg East	94	12.657	16.699	56.9

The day after this Appendix and Chapter XIII were completed the Danish Government resigned on this question (October 1947).

APPENDIX III

NOTE ON CURRENCY

Prior to 1776 the standard coin was the silver Daler. As the silver content was originally equal to its face value, this was in common use for the payment of indemnities, foreign trade and so forth. The separate Scandinavian countries had small coins for home use, e.g. Skillings, which were equal to one-eighth of a daler. In 1776 the depreciation of the daler introduced the Riksdaler, which in Sweden equalled six dalers. After the Napoleonic Wars the daler depreciated still further and the Riksdaler Banco had to be introduced for use with the daler, a system not unlike that of the German marks and reichmarks after the First World War. Consequently, there was considerable difficulty in the matter of exchange until the decimal system was introduced, when the Riksdaler Riksmint was divided into a hundred öre. In 1873 the present system was introduced in Sweden and Norway and shortly afterwards in Denmark. The Krone was taken as equal to 100 öre, but a large silver coin, known as the Riksdaler Specie, was minted to set a constant standard of silver content. Its value was four Krone, but it never was in common use. Payments in all Scandinavian countries are reckoned in Krone, but their exchange value among the three countries and, of course, with other countries, is variable. By reckoning four Krone to the daler throughout it is possible to get a rough comparison of the fluctuating dalers at different periods. It is believed by some that the American use of the word " dollar " instead of " thaler ", which was the coin originally brought to America, was due to the Scandinavian settlers.

BIBLIOGRAPHY

SOME BOOKS IN ENGLISH ON SCANDINAVIAN HISTORY

History of Denmark. Allen (C.F.).
Denmark in History. Birch.
Short History of Denmark. Danstrup [mainly 1789–1945].
Story of Denmark. Sedgwick (C.S.).
History of Sweden. Hallendorff and Schück.
Short History of Sweden. Vanström and Palmierstierna.
History of the Vikings. Kendrick.
Democratic Sweden. Edited by Cole and Smith for the Fabian Society.
New Sweden. Braatoy.
Gustavus Adolphus. Fletcher.
History of Finland. Hampden Jackson.
Scandinavians in America. Jansen.
Viking Settlers in Greenland. Nörland (published in Copenhagen).
Edda and Saga. Bertha Phillpotts.
Revisions of History in the journal *History*:
    (a) The Vikings (July 1924). Mawer.
    (b) Gustavus Adolphus (March 1940). Roberts.
School for Life. Mary Forster. [On Swedish Education.]

FOR GENERAL REFERENCE

Cambridge Medieval History, Vol I.
Cambridge Modern History (passim).
History of Europe. Fisher.
History of Europe (to 1521). Pirenne.
History of Russia. Pares.
History of England, Chapters III–VII. Trevelyan.

SYNCHRONISTIC TABLE OF EVENTS

A.D.	Sweden	Denmark	General
800	Vikings raid on Aquitaine		Charlemagne Emperor.
811		R. Eider to be Southern Boundary of Denmark, at Treaty between the Emperor and Heming, King of Denmark.	
826		Ansgar introduces Christianity.	
830	Ansgar starts a Christian mission without success.		
840–850		Vikings sack Rouen, Toulouse, Paris and other French towns.	Division of Empire into three parts.
855		Beginning of Danish settlements in England.	
860	Rurik in Russia.		
878		Peace of Wedmore, Danelaw boundary.	
911		By Treaty of S. Clair-sur-Epte, Charles the Simple grants Normandy to Rollo.	
940–986	Sweden and Norway remain pagan.	Harold Bluetooth, first Christian king of all Denmark.	
980		Norwegians and Danes invade England.	Ethelred II, King of England.
994		Olaf Trygvasson and Sweyn Forkbeard attack London.	
1008	Olaf baptised.		
1016		Norsemen established in Sicily and Apulia.	
1018–1035		Canute, King of England, Denmark, Norway and Iceland.	
1066	End of Civil War. Stenkil victorious.	Sweyn, King of Denmark. Olaf the Quiet, King of Norway.	William I, King of England.
1073			Hildebrand elected Pope as Gregory VII.
1104		Archbishopric at Lund.	
1130	Benedictines try to convert Sweden.	Civil Wars.	
1157	Crusade to Finland.		Henry II and Becket.
1168		Conquest of Rügen.	
1187	Stockholm founded.		Saladin conquers Jerusalem.
1202		Valdemar conquers Holstein.	Philip Augustus attacks Normandy.
1223	Sverker Dynasty extinct.	Valdemar the Victorious, prisoner.	Death of Philip Augustus.
1250	The Folkung Age. (1250–1371)	Struggle between Church and State.	Death of the Emperor Frederick II.
1276	Magnus Barnlocks.	Eric Klipping.	

A.D.	Sweden	Denmark	General
1319	Norway united to Sweden till 1371.		
1340		Valdemar Atterdag, King till 1375.	
1350	The Black Death.	The Black Death.	The Black Death.
1364	Albrecht of Mecklenburg, king till 1389.		
1371	Haakon VI, King of Norway.	Margaret, daughter of Valdemar, wife of Haakon, gives birth to Olaf.	
1376		Margaret, Regent of Denmark.	Wycliffe. Death of Black Prince.
1380		Margaret, also Regent of Norway	
1389	Margaret, Regent of Sweden, till 1412.	Denmark, Norway and	Peace between France and England.
1397	The Kalmar Union. Eric crowned king of the three kingdoms.		
1398	Gottland captured by the Teutonic Knights.		
1410–35		Wars with Holstein and the Hanseatic League.	
1415			Agincourt.
1434–35	Engelbrekt's reforms in Sweden.		
1470	The Sture family powerful.		Wars of the Roses. Warwick powerful. Turks threaten Venice.
1477	Uppsala University founded.		
1479		Copenhagen University founded.	
1495–97	Swedish war with Russia.	Danish troubles in Slesvig and Holstein.	
1517	Gustav Trolle deposed.		Luther at Wittenberg.
1520	Christian II's Invasion of Sweden. The Stockholm " Blood-Bath ".		Henry VIII and Francis I at Field of the Cloth of Gold.
1521	Triumph of Gustavus Vasa.		Diet of Worms. Luther declared a heretic.
1523	Gustavus Vasa King.	Frederick I King.	
1525			Capture of Francis I at Pavia.
1527	Recess of Västerås.		Sack of Rome.
1536		Reformation.	English Reformation Parliament ends.
1544	Hereditary succession of Vasa line.	Division of the Duchies.	Henry VIII of England and Charles V invade France

A.D. Sweden	Denmark	General
1560 Eric XIV.	Ditmarsken subdued (1559–60).	Death of Francis II.
1568 John III.		Revolt in the Netherlands.
1588 Sigismund, King of Poland.	Christian IV (died 1648).	Armada.
1593 Uppsala Convention.	Tycho Brahe *flor.*	Henry IV becomes Catholic.
1599 Charles IX repelled Counter-Reformation.		Philip III of Spain married Margaret of Austria.
1600 60 years War with Poland.		English East India Company.
1609 Russian War.		
1611 Accession of Gustavus Adolphus.	Christian began Kalmar War.	
1613 Peace of Knäred ends Kalmar War.		Elisabeth, daughter of James I, married Frederick of the Palatinate.
1617 Peace of Stolbova with Russia.		
1618 Armistice with Poland.		Thirty Years War.
1624	Christiania founded as Capital of Norway.	Richelieu, First Minister.
1626	Battle of Lutter: Holstein overrun.	Wallenstein.
1629 Truce of Altmark.	Peace of Lübeck.	Richelieu after fall of La Rochelle, begins active interference in Thirty Years War.
1631 Treaty of Bärwalde with France. Victory of Breitenfeld.		Sack of Magdeburg.
1632 Victory of Lützen; Death of Gustavus. Oxentierna Regent for Christina.		
1640 Armistice with Brandenburg.		Accession of the Great Elector.
1643–5 Tortensson's defeat of Christian IV.	Jutland overrun.	Death of Louis XIII, Mazarin Minister.
1645 Peace of Brömsebro.		Execution of Laud.
1648 Victories of Wrangel and Königsmark.		Victories of Turenne and Condé. Treaty of Westphalia.
1654 Resignation of Christina		Coronation of Louis XIV. War between Russia and Poland.
1655 Charles X defeats Poland.		Cromwell's alliance with Mazarin.
1658	Treaty of Roskilde.	Death of Oliver Cromwell.
1660 Accession of Charles XI brings peace in the North. Treaty of Copenhagen.	" Instrument of hereditary rights " established absolutism in Denmark and Norway.	Treaty of Oliva, between Poland, Brandenburg, and Sweden. Peace of Kardis between Russia and Sweden.

A.D.	Sweden	Denmark	General
1675	Swedes expelled from Eastern Pomerania after Fehrbellin.	Scanian War.	Great Elector powerful.
1676	Battle of Lund.		Louis XIV extends French territory.
1680	Diet of Stockholm established absolutism.		French and Dutch rivalry in India and Siam.
1683		Code of Christian V.	Sobieski the Pole saved Vienna from the Turks.
1697	Accession of Charles XII.		Peace of Ryswick.
1702	Charles XII in Poland and Saxony.	Abolition of laws of *Vornskab* (serfdom).	Spanish Succession War.
1709	Battle of Pultava.	War declared on Sweden.	Malplaquet.
1710	Russia captures Baltic States.	Defeat at Helsingborg.	Peter the Great aggressive.
1721	Peace of Nystad.	Slesvig incorporated in Denmark.	Marriage alliances between France and Spain.
1727	The beginning of the party struggles. ' Hats ' and ' Caps ' and commercial enterprise.		
1757–62	Pommeranian War.	Peter III threatens war.	Rousseau's *Contrat Social*. Preliminaries for Peace of Paris ending Seven Years War.
1772	*Coup d'état* of Gustavus III, supported by France.	Execution of Struensee.	First Partition of Poland.
1788	War with Russia and Denmark.	Peasants freed from Serfdom.	French States General are summoned to meet in following year.
1789	Act of Security.		Revolution in France and Netherlands.
1801		Bombardment of Copenhagen.	Death of Paul I of Russia.
1807		Seizure of Danish fleet.	Napoleon and Alexander at Tilsit.
1809	Finland ceded to Russia		Metternich chancellor.
1810	Bernadotte, Crown Prince.		Napoleon annexes North Germany.
1811	Sweden opposes Continental System.	Foundation of Christiana University.	Wellington frees Portugal from French.
1812	Bernadotte's secret treaty with Alexander. Promise of Norway in exchange for Finland.		Napoleon invades Russia.
1815	Sweden and Norway united.	Denmark receives Lauenberg.	Russia gets Finland. Prussia gets Swedish Pomerania.

(N.B.—The Peace of Kiel, 1814, between England, Sweden and Denmark, by which Sweden got Norway and Denmark Swedish Pomerania and Rügen, was altered at the Congress of Vienna. Iceland, however, remained Danish until 1944.)

A.D. Sweden	Denmark	General
1818–44 Bernadotte crowned as Charles XIV.	Golden Age of Danish Literature.	Prussia starts the Customs Union. (*Zollverein*).
1842	Danish language intro-duced in Slesvig Estates.	Chartists in England.
1848	The Free Constitution (signed 1849).	" The Year of Revolu-tions " in most European countries.
1849 Swedish help for Denmark.	Danish victory in the first Slesvig War.	Russia supports Denmark against Prussia.
1855–56 Tension with Russia.		The Åland servitude.
1859 Charles XV, Liberal movement.	" Eider Policy " fails to ease tension in Slesvig-Holstein question.	National movement in Italy.
1864	Peace of Vienna ends second Slesvig War.	Prussia and Austria take Slesvig, Holstein, and Lauenberg.
1865–66 Parliamentary Reforms. Notable maritime expansion in Norway.	Prussia defeats Austria and takes all the Duchies on promise of restoring North Slesvig to Den-mark.	
1875 Rise of Liberals in Norway, under Sverdrup and Björnson.	Estrup Prime Minister for nineteen years.	
1895.	Beginning of Democratic rule.	
1905 Separation of Norway from Sweden under Haakon VII.	New Liberal constitution granted to Iceland in 1903 operates success-fully.	Murder of Bobrikof in Finland led to greater freedom of Finnish Parliament.
1914 Neutrality preserved in first World War. Meeting of the three Kings at Malmö		
1917 Swedish Match Co. founded.	Sale of Danish West Indies to U.S.A. Greenland acknowledged Danish.	Unrestricted U-Boat Warfare.
1919		Finland regains her independence.
1920	Slesvig settlement.	
1921 Sweden accepts the Ruling of League of Nations about Åland Islands.		
1939 Neutrality of Sweden, Norway, and Denmark in Second World War		Russia invades Finland.
1940 German invasion of Norway.	German Invasion of Den-mark.	

(1944 Iceland declared Independent.)

INDEX